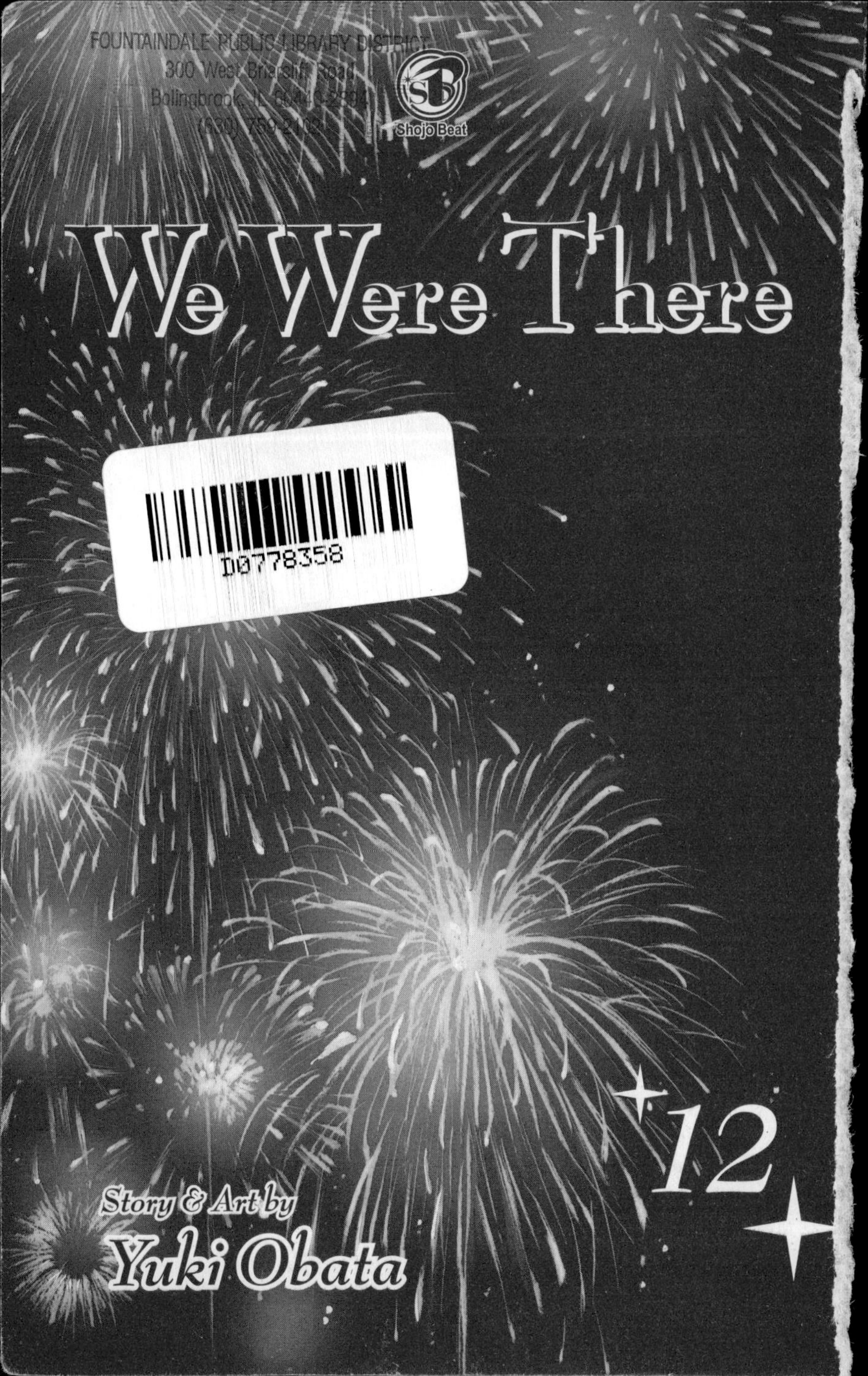
Shojo Beat
We Were There
12
Story & Art by
Yuki Obata

Contents

Characters

Akiko Sengenji
She was Yano's high school classmate in Tokyo. She works at the same company as Nanami.

Nanami Takahashi
Nanami works in Tokyo. She's in a relationship with Takeuchi, but...

Motoharu Yano
Nanami's ex-boyfriend. He's currently missing.

Story

Yano disappeared right after his mother committed suicide. Several years have passed, and Nanami is still unable to forget him. Takeuchi has been watching over Nanami and makes plans to ask her to marry him. Sengenji comes across a business card through her work and sees the name "Motoharu" on it...

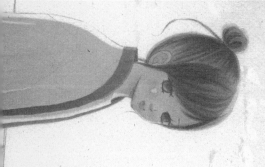

Chapter
45

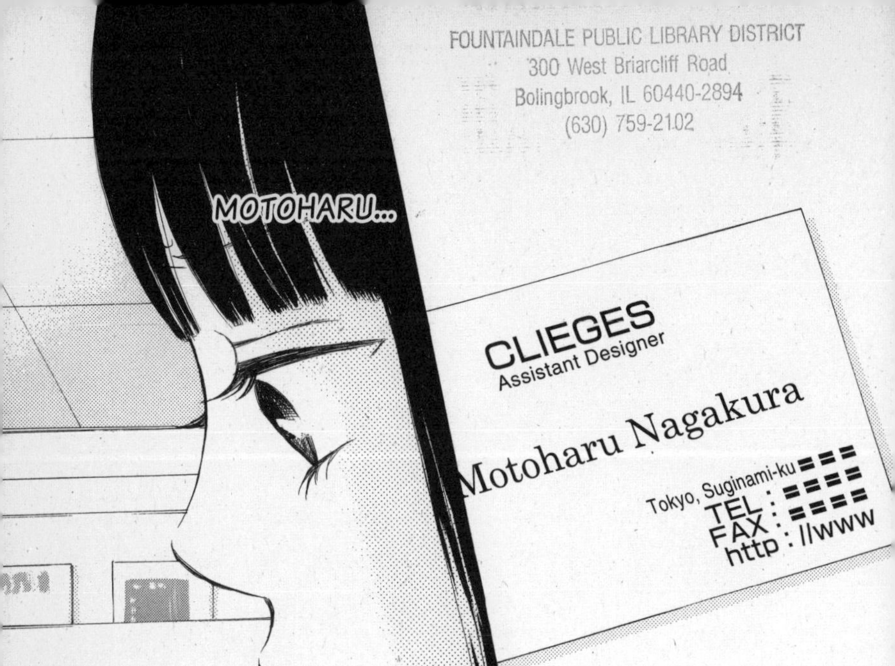
MOTOHARU...
CLIEGES
Assistant Designer
Motoharu Nagakura
Tokyo, Suginami-ku
TEL :
FAX :
http : //www
...NAGAKURA.

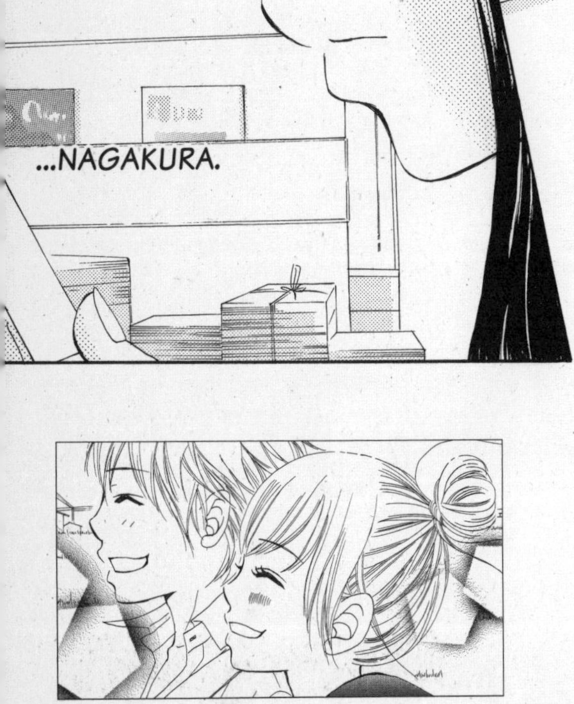

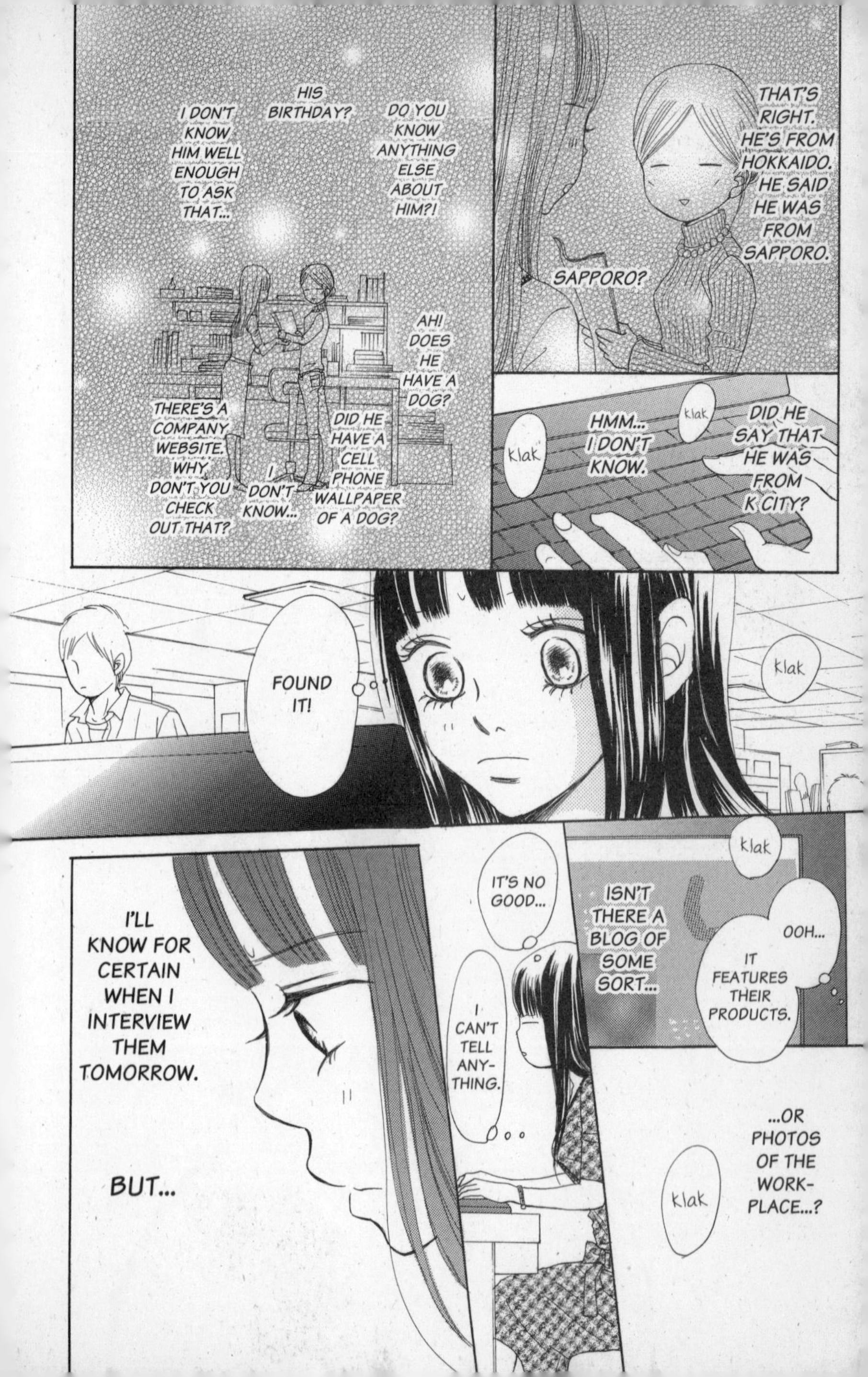
THAT'S RIGHT. HE'S FROM HOKKAIDO. HE SAID HE WAS FROM SAPPORO.
SAPPORO?
DID HE SAY THAT HE WAS FROM K CITY?
klak
HMM... I DON'T KNOW.
klak
DO YOU KNOW ANYTHING ELSE ABOUT HIM?!
HIS BIRTHDAY?
I DON'T KNOW HIM WELL ENOUGH TO ASK THAT...
AH! DOES HE HAVE A DOG?
DID HE HAVE A CELL PHONE WALLPAPER OF A DOG?
I DON'T KNOW...
THERE'S A COMPANY WEBSITE. WHY DON'T YOU CHECK OUT THAT?
klak
FOUND IT!
klak
OOH... IT FEATURES THEIR PRODUCTS.
ISN'T THERE A BLOG OF SOME SORT...
IT'S NO GOOD...
I CAN'T TELL ANY-THING.
...OR PHOTOS OF THE WORK-PLACE...?
klak
I'LL KNOW FOR CERTAIN WHEN I INTERVIEW THEM TOMORROW.
BUT...

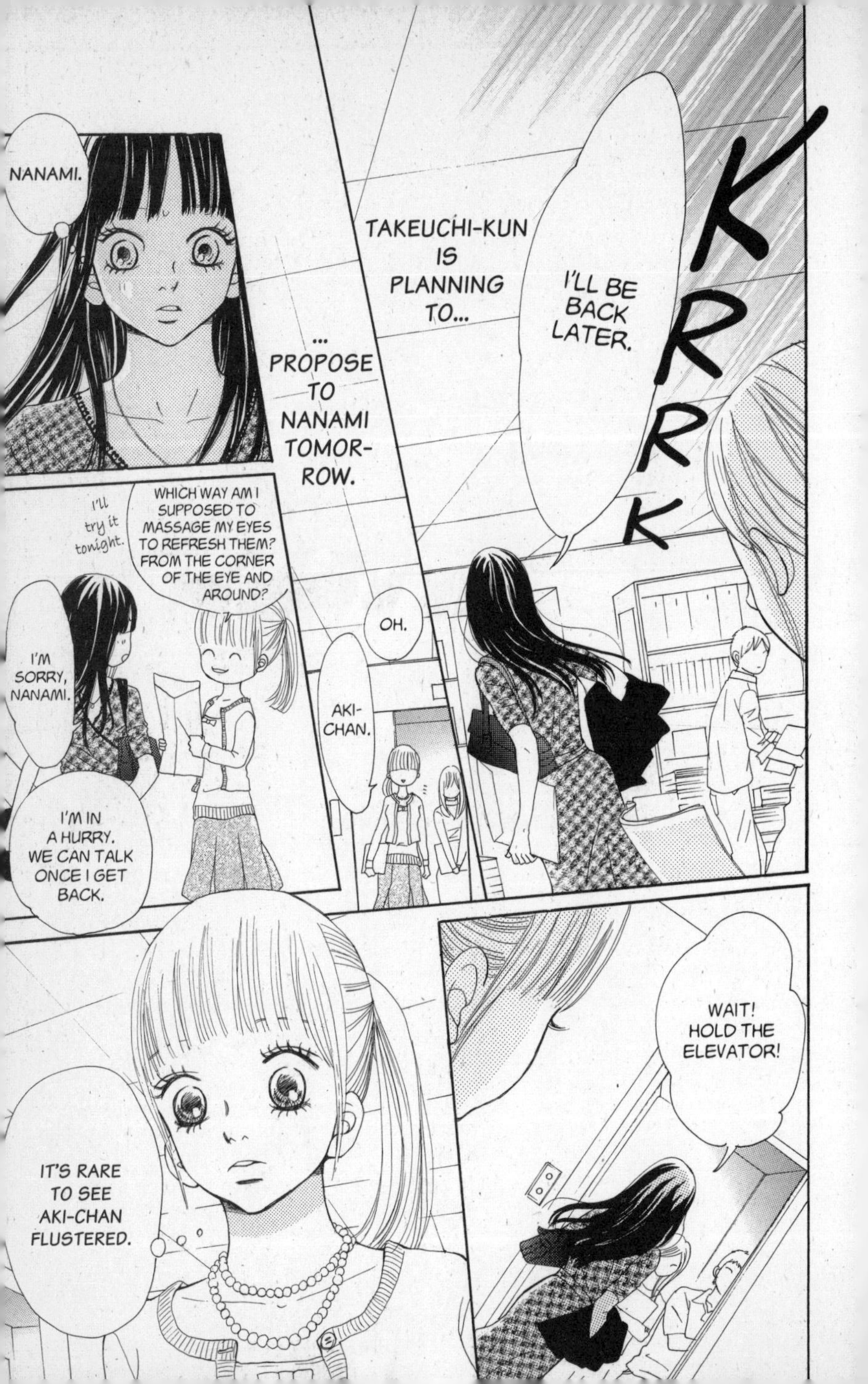
I'LL BE BACK LATER.
KRRRK
TAKEUCHI-KUN IS PLANNING TO...
... PROPOSE TO NANAMI TOMORROW.
OH.
AKI-CHAN.
NANAMI.
WHICH WAY AM I SUPPOSED TO MASSAGE MY EYES TO REFRESH THEM? FROM THE CORNER OF THE EYE AND AROUND?
I'll try it tonight.
I'M SORRY, NANAMI.
I'M IN A HURRY. WE CAN TALK ONCE I GET BACK.
WAIT! HOLD THE ELEVATOR!
IT'S RARE TO SEE AKI-CHAN FLUSTERED.

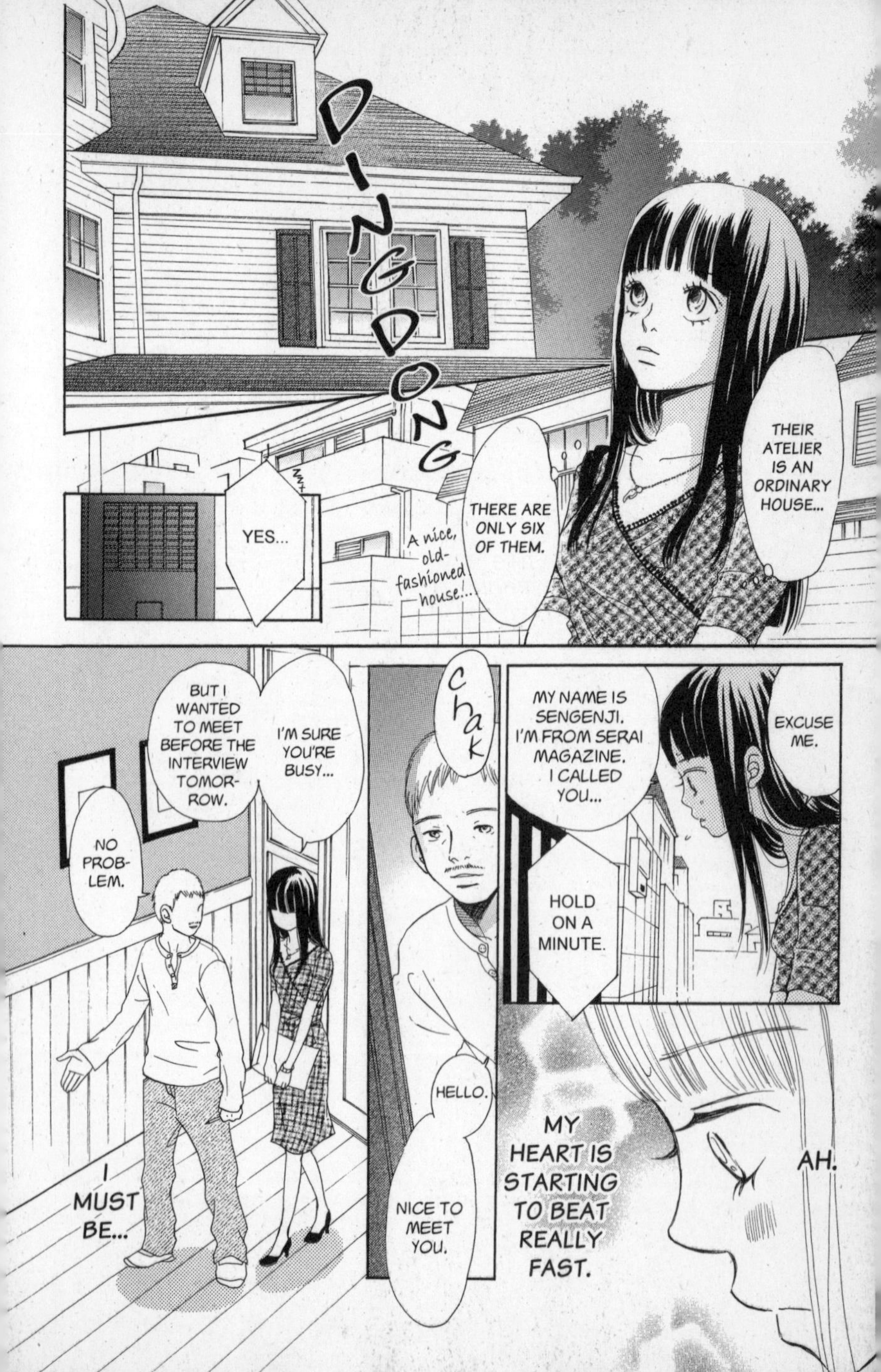
THEIR ATELIER IS AN ORDINARY HOUSE...
THERE ARE ONLY SIX OF THEM.
DING DONG
A nice, old-fashioned house!...
YES...
EXCUSE ME.
MY NAME IS SENGENJI. I'M FROM SERAI MAGAZINE. I CALLED YOU...
HOLD ON A MINUTE.
AH.
MY HEART IS STARTING TO BEAT REALLY FAST.
Chak
HELLO.
NICE TO MEET YOU.
I'M SURE YOU'RE BUSY...
BUT I WANTED TO MEET BEFORE THE INTERVIEW TOMORROW.
NO PROBLEM.
I MUST BE...

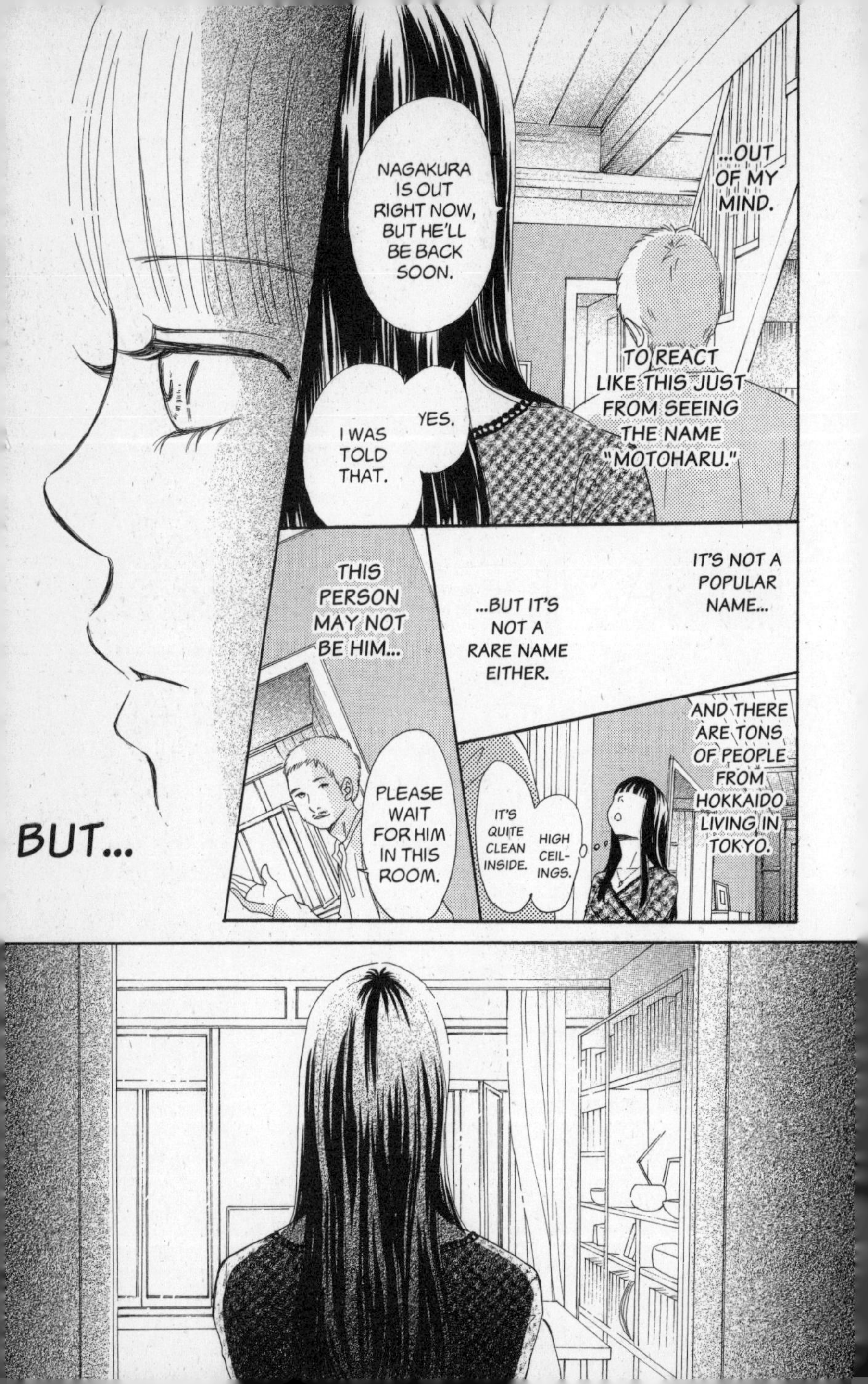

...OUT OF MY MIND.
NAGAKURA IS OUT RIGHT NOW, BUT HE'LL BE BACK SOON.
TO REACT LIKE THIS JUST FROM SEEING THE NAME "MOTOHARU."
YES. I WAS TOLD THAT.
IT'S NOT A POPULAR NAME...
...BUT IT'S NOT A RARE NAME EITHER.
AND THERE ARE TONS OF PEOPLE FROM HOKKAIDO LIVING IN TOKYO.
HIGH CEILINGS.
IT'S QUITE CLEAN INSIDE.
THIS PERSON MAY NOT BE HIM...
PLEASE WAIT FOR HIM IN THIS ROOM.
BUT...

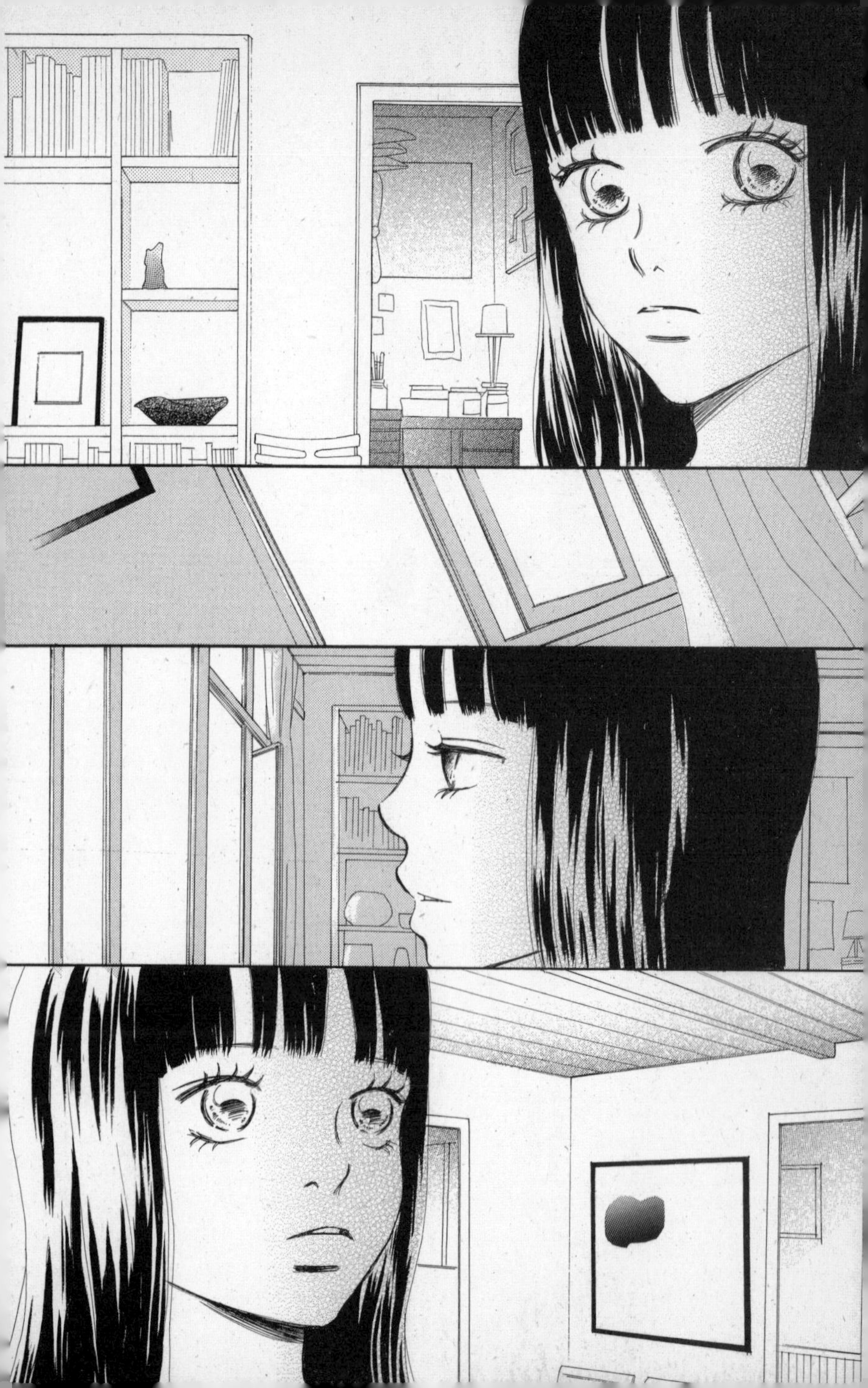

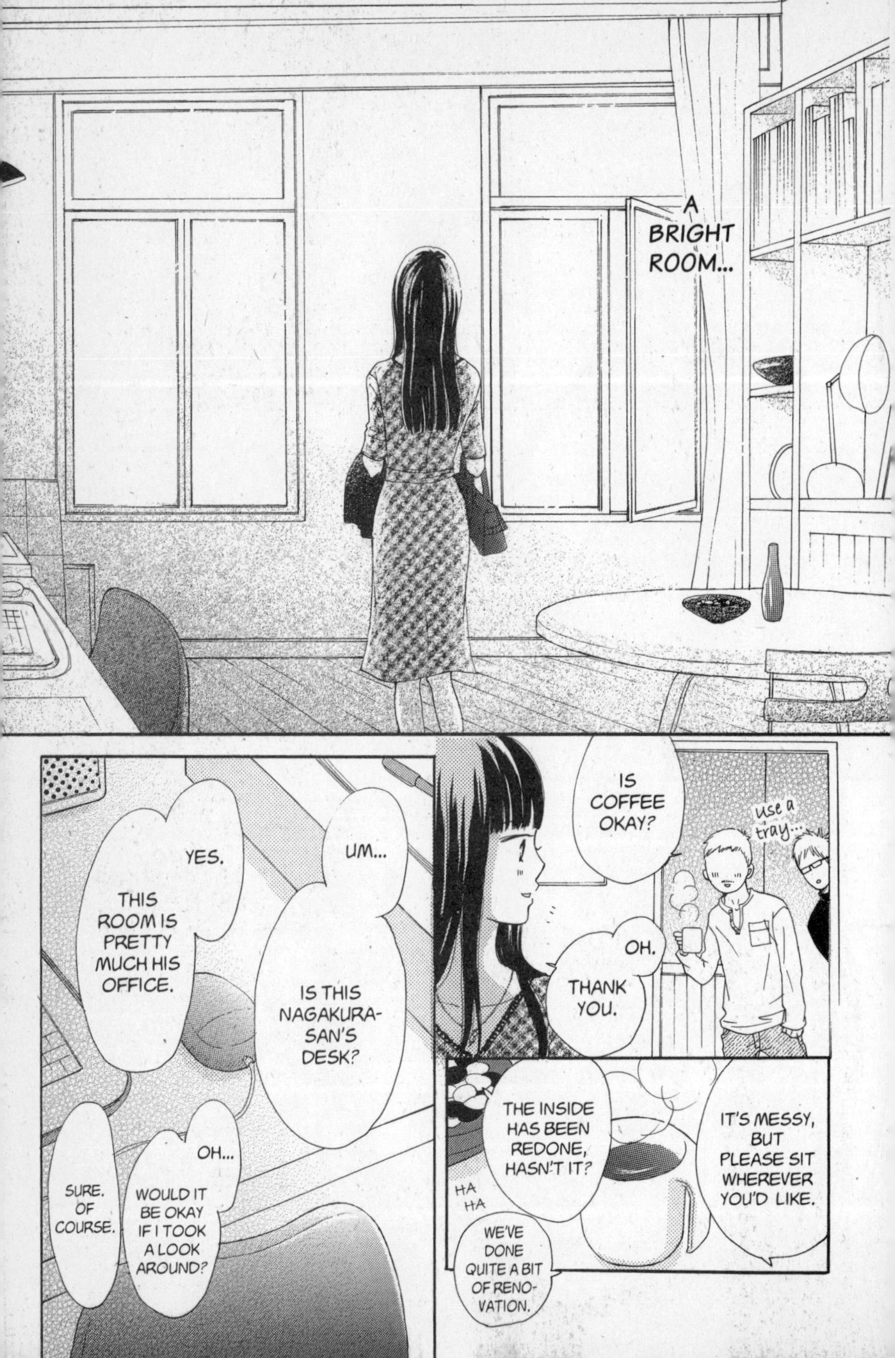
A BRIGHT ROOM...
IS COFFEE OKAY?
use a tray...
OH.
THANK YOU.
IT'S MESSY, BUT PLEASE SIT WHEREVER YOU'D LIKE.
THE INSIDE HAS BEEN REDONE, HASN'T IT?
HA HA
WE'VE DONE QUITE A BIT OF RENO-VATION.
UM...
IS THIS NAGAKURA-SAN'S DESK?
YES.
THIS ROOM IS PRETTY MUCH HIS OFFICE.
OH...
WOULD IT BE OKAY IF I TOOK A LOOK AROUND?
SURE. OF COURSE.

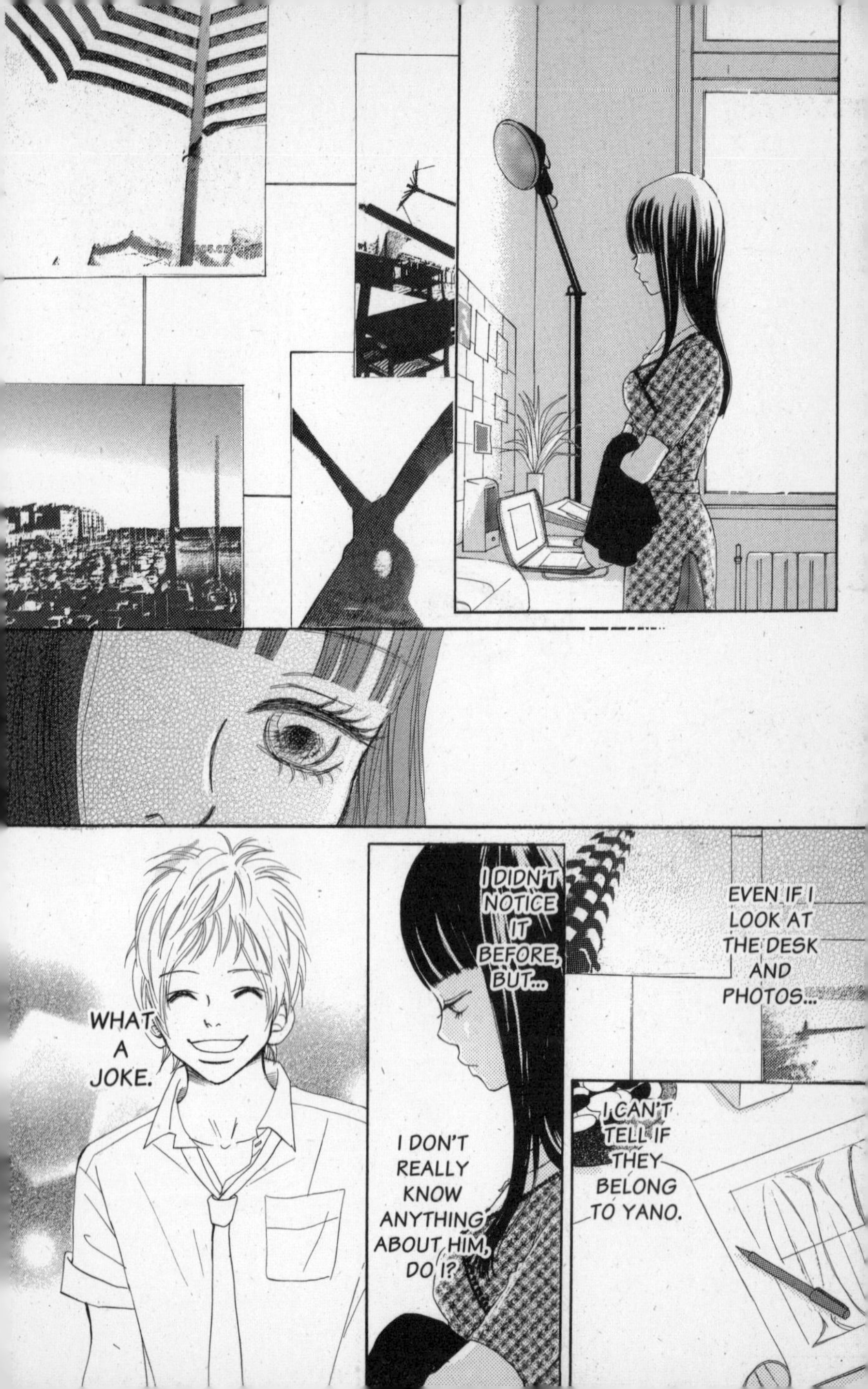
EVEN IF I LOOK AT THE DESK AND PHOTOS...
I CAN'T TELL IF THEY BELONG TO YANO.
I DIDN'T NOTICE IT BEFORE, BUT...
I DON'T REALLY KNOW ANYTHING ABOUT HIM, DO I?
WHAT A JOKE.

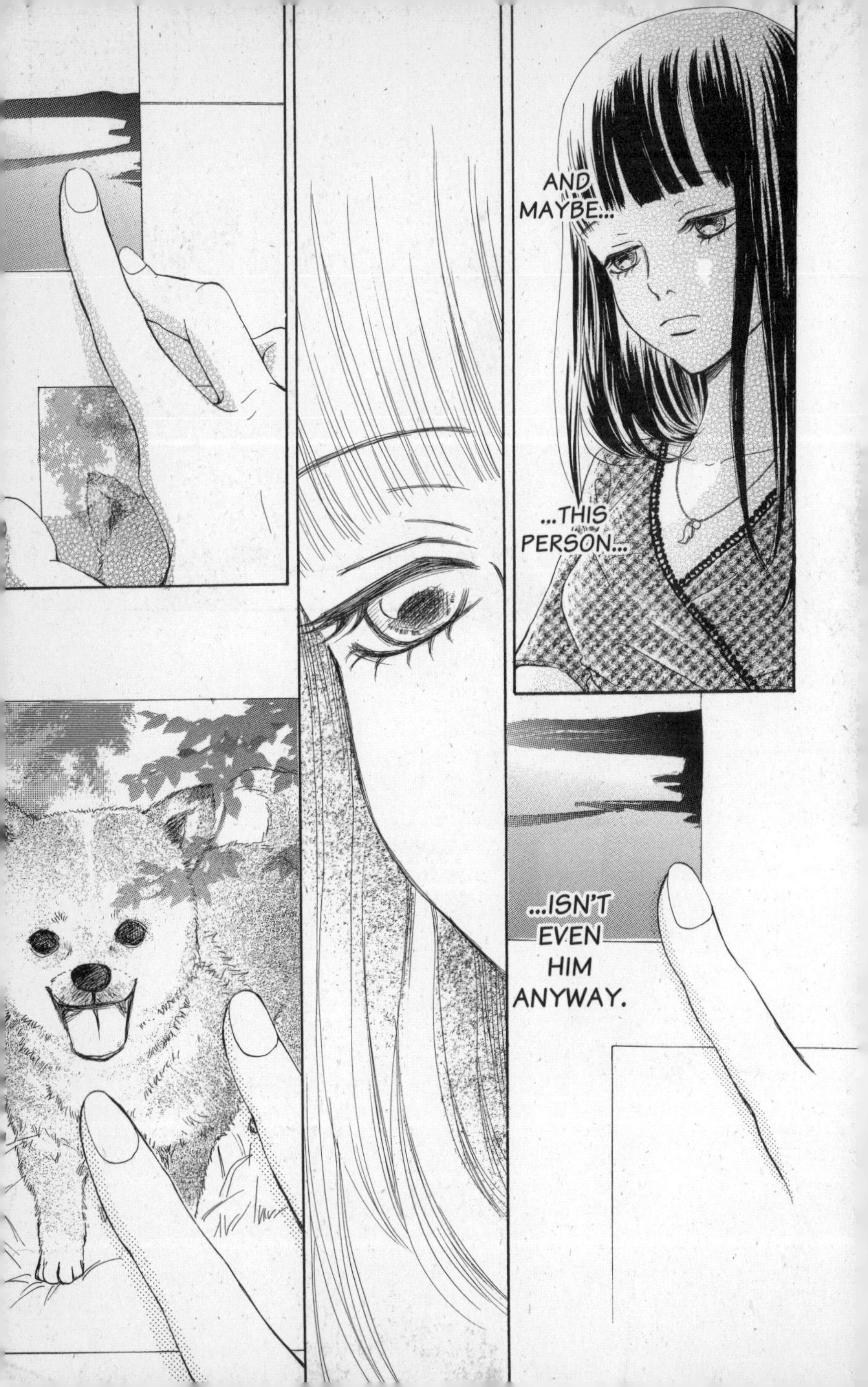
AND MAYBE...
...THIS PERSON...
...ISN'T EVEN HIM ANYWAY.

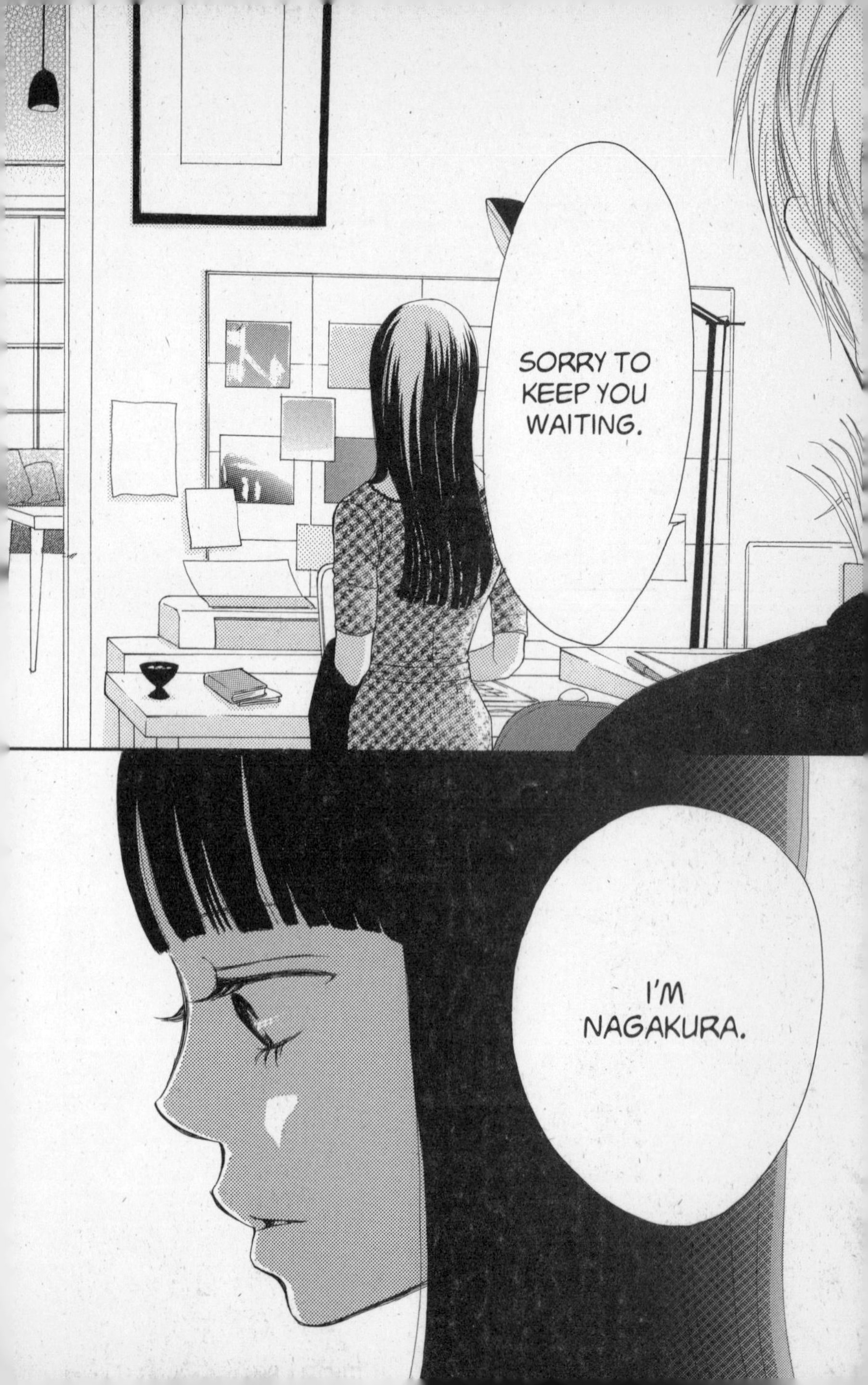
SORRY TO KEEP YOU WAITING.
I'M NAGAKURA.

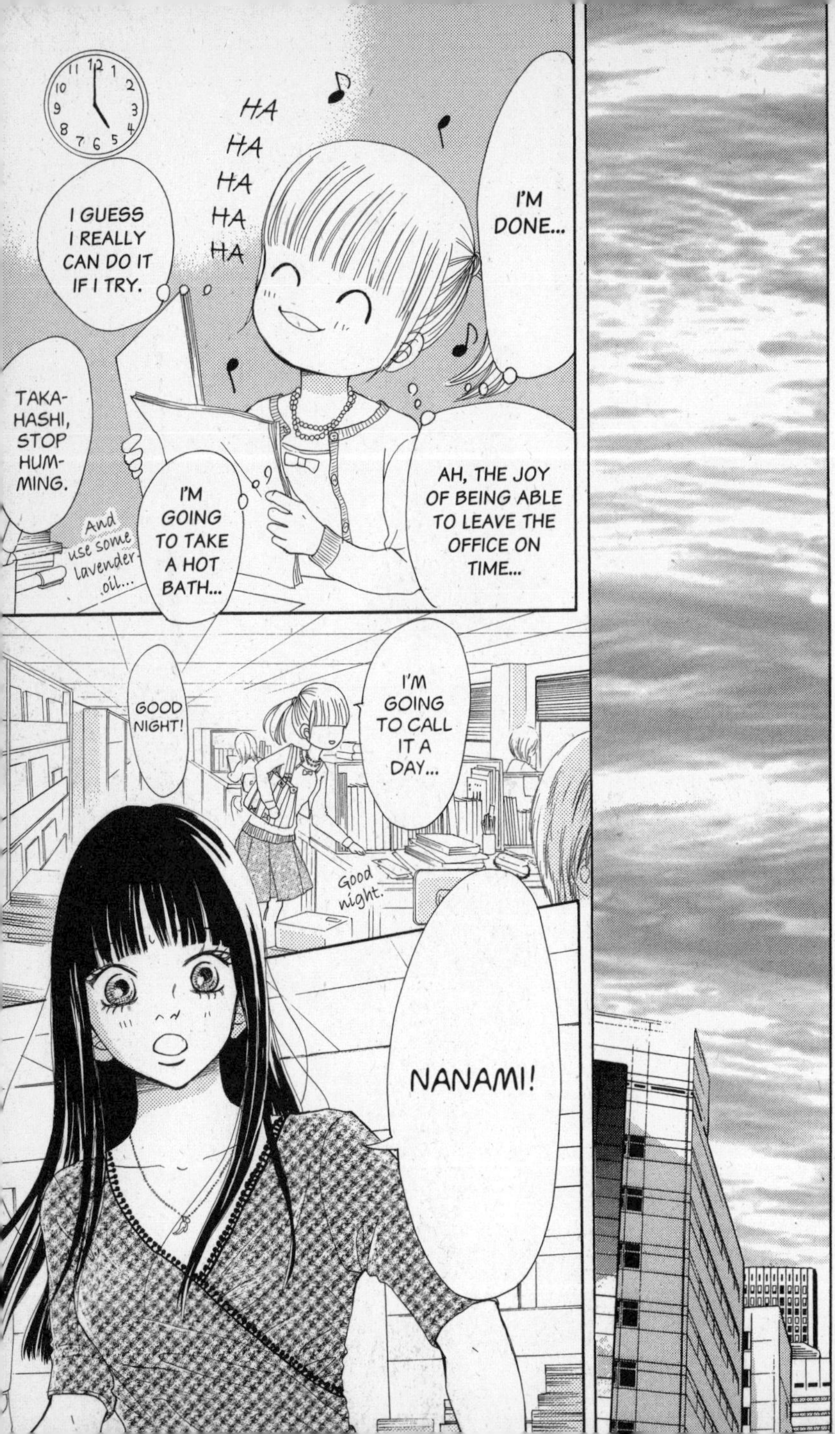
I'M DONE...
HA HA HA HA HA
I GUESS I REALLY CAN DO IT IF I TRY.
AH, THE JOY OF BEING ABLE TO LEAVE THE OFFICE ON TIME...
I'M GOING TO TAKE A HOT BATH...
And use some lavender oil...
TAKAHASHI, STOP HUMMING.
I'M GOING TO CALL IT A DAY...
GOOD NIGHT!
Good night.
NANAMI!

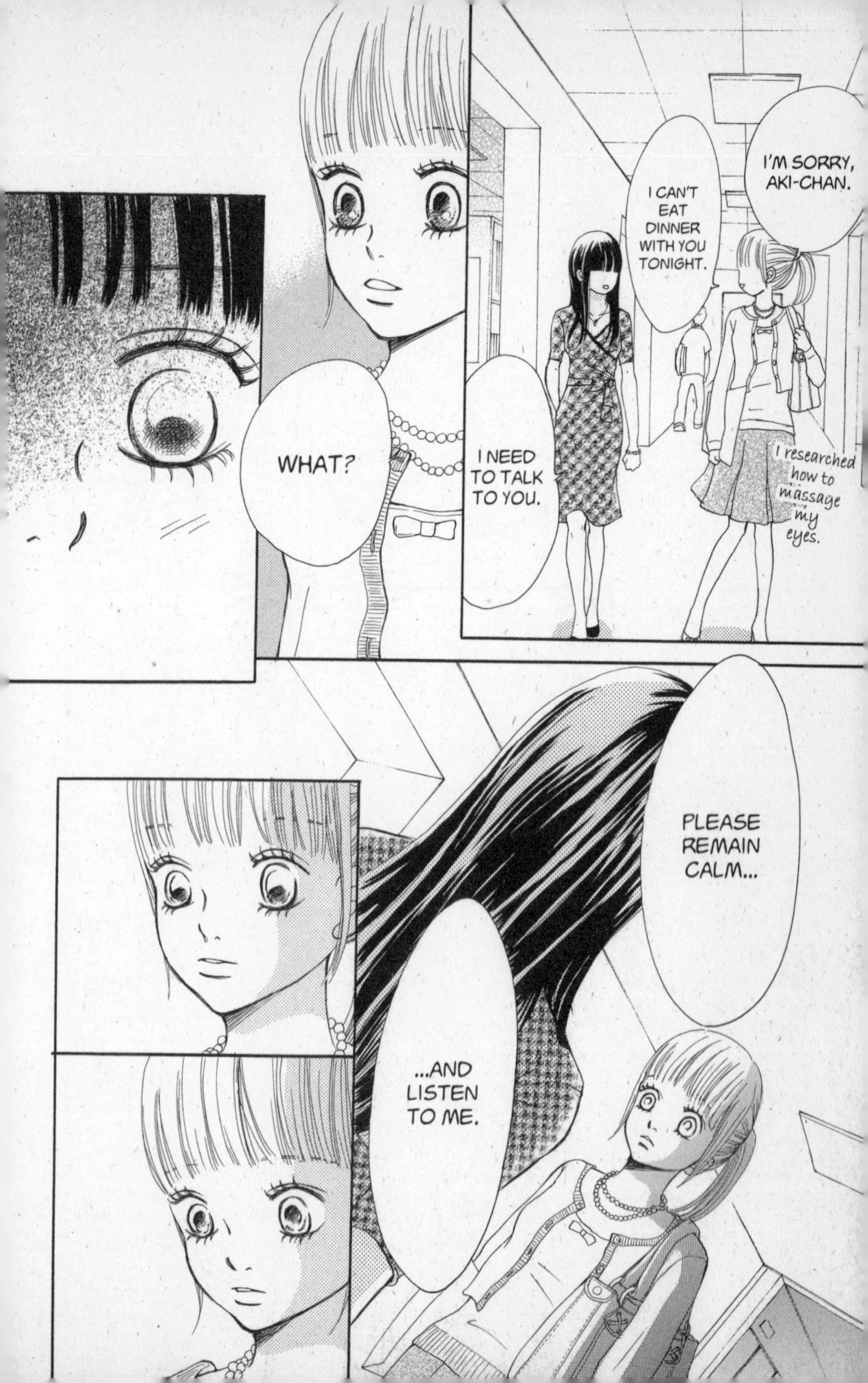
I'M SORRY, AKI-CHAN.
I CAN'T EAT DINNER WITH YOU TONIGHT.
I researched how to massage my eyes.
I NEED TO TALK TO YOU.
WHAT?
PLEASE REMAIN CALM...
...AND LISTEN TO ME.

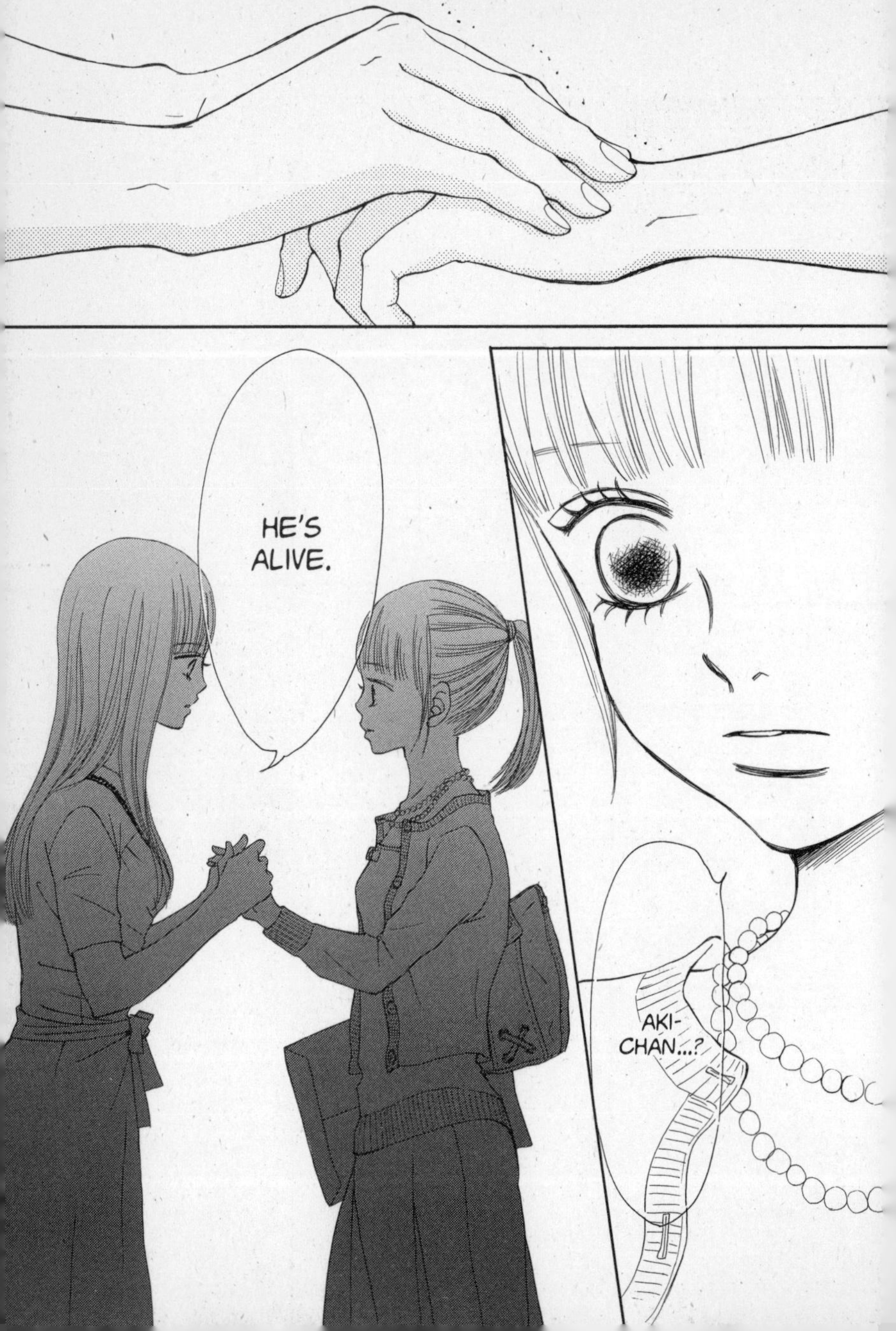
AKI-CHAN...?
HE'S ALIVE.

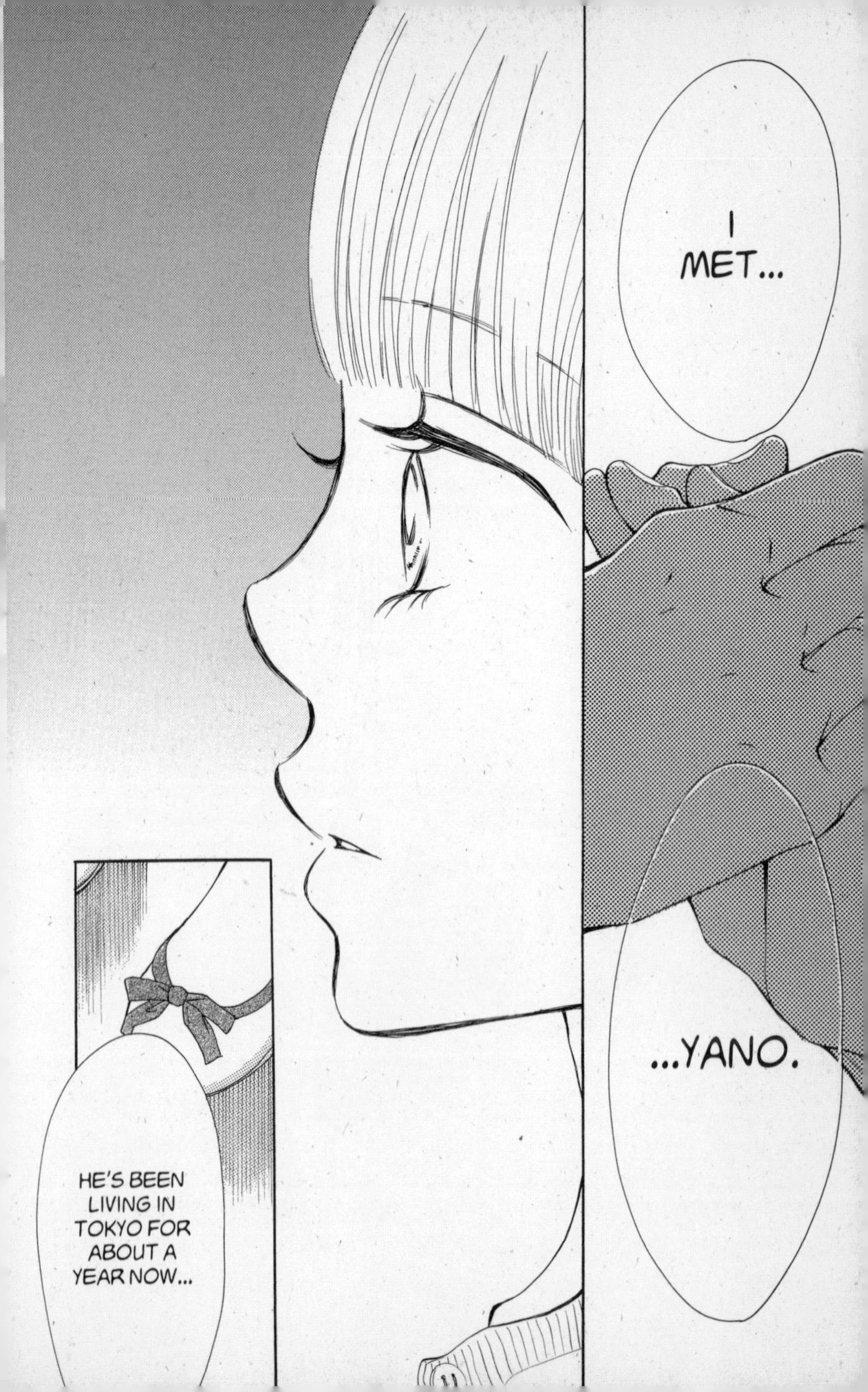
I MET...
...YANO.
HE'S BEEN LIVING IN TOKYO FOR ABOUT A YEAR NOW...

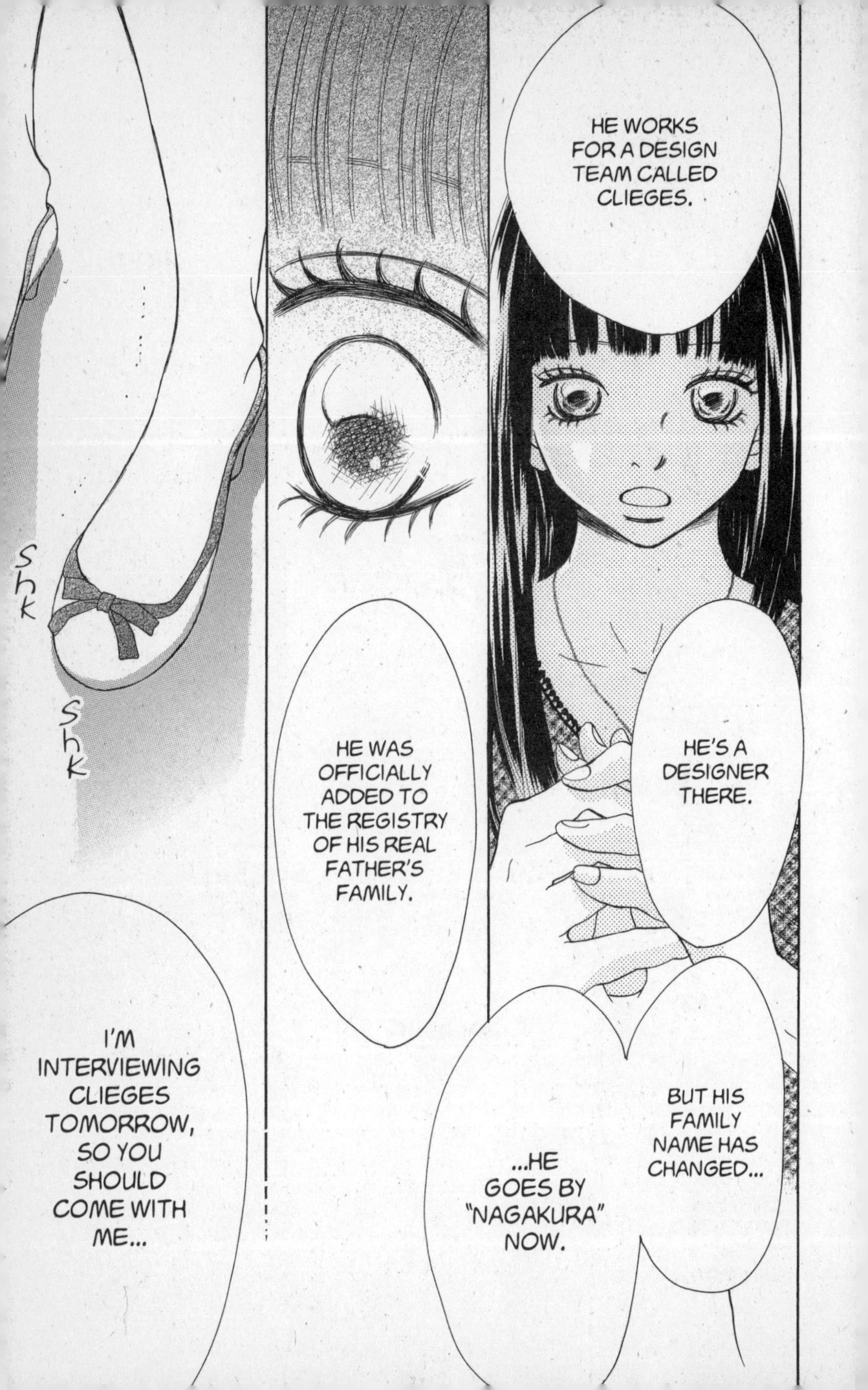
HE WORKS FOR A DESIGN TEAM CALLED CLIEGES.
HE'S A DESIGNER THERE.
BUT HIS FAMILY NAME HAS CHANGED...
...HE GOES BY "NAGAKURA" NOW.
HE WAS OFFICIALLY ADDED TO THE REGISTRY OF HIS REAL FATHER'S FAMILY.
SHK
SHK
I'M INTERVIEWING CLIEGES TOMORROW, SO YOU SHOULD COME WITH ME...

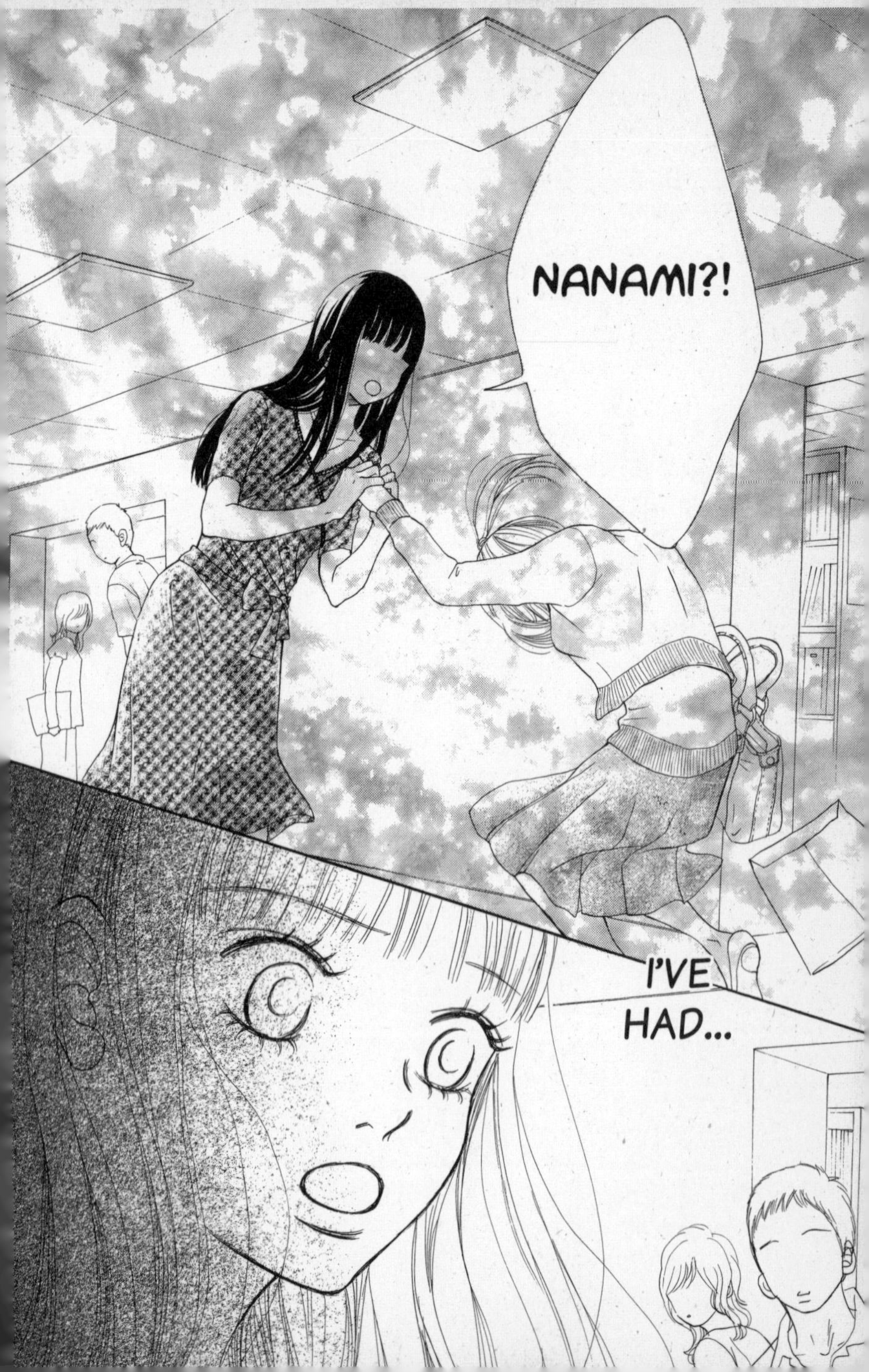
NANAMI?!
I'VE HAD...

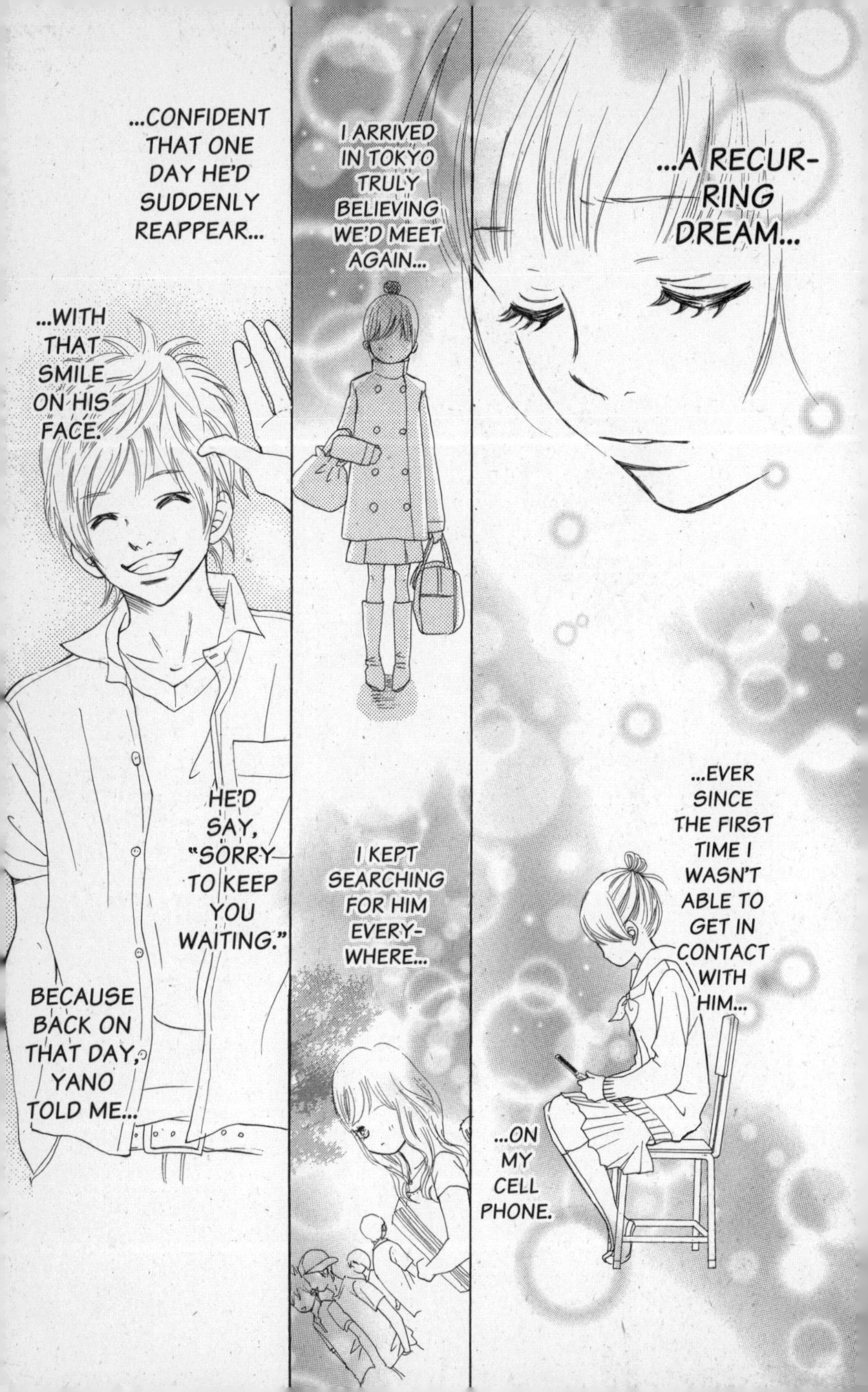
...A RECUR-RING DREAM...
...EVER SINCE THE FIRST TIME I WASN'T ABLE TO GET IN CONTACT WITH HIM...
...ON MY CELL PHONE.
I ARRIVED IN TOKYO TRULY BELIEVING WE'D MEET AGAIN...
I KEPT SEARCHING FOR HIM EVERY-WHERE...
...CONFIDENT THAT ONE DAY HE'D SUDDENLY REAPPEAR...
...WITH THAT SMILE ON HIS FACE.
HE'D SAY, "SORRY TO KEEP YOU WAITING."
BECAUSE BACK ON THAT DAY, YANO TOLD ME...

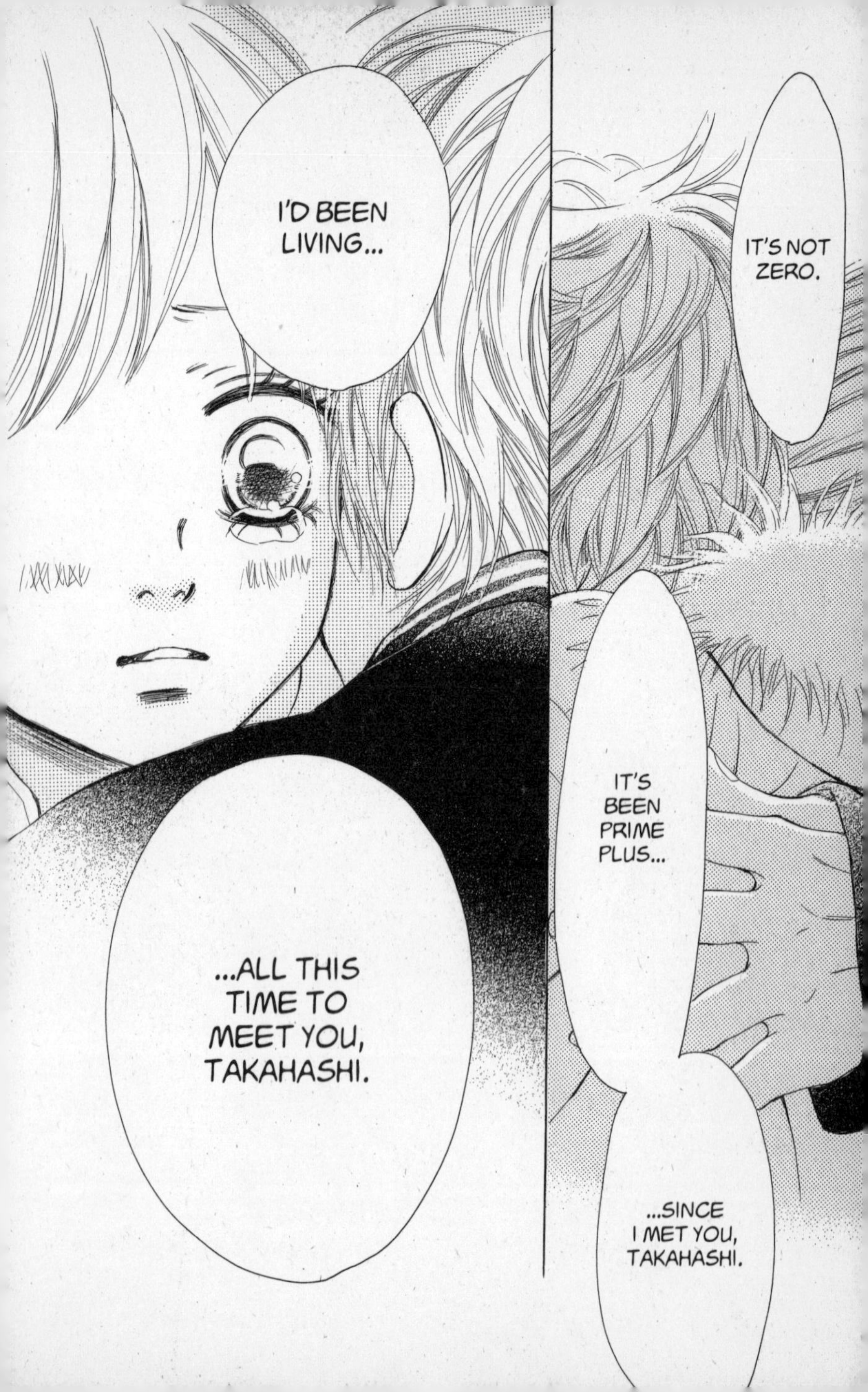
IT'S NOT ZERO.
IT'S BEEN PRIME PLUS...
...SINCE I MET YOU, TAKAHASHI.
I'D BEEN LIVING...
...ALL THIS TIME TO MEET YOU, TAKAHASHI.

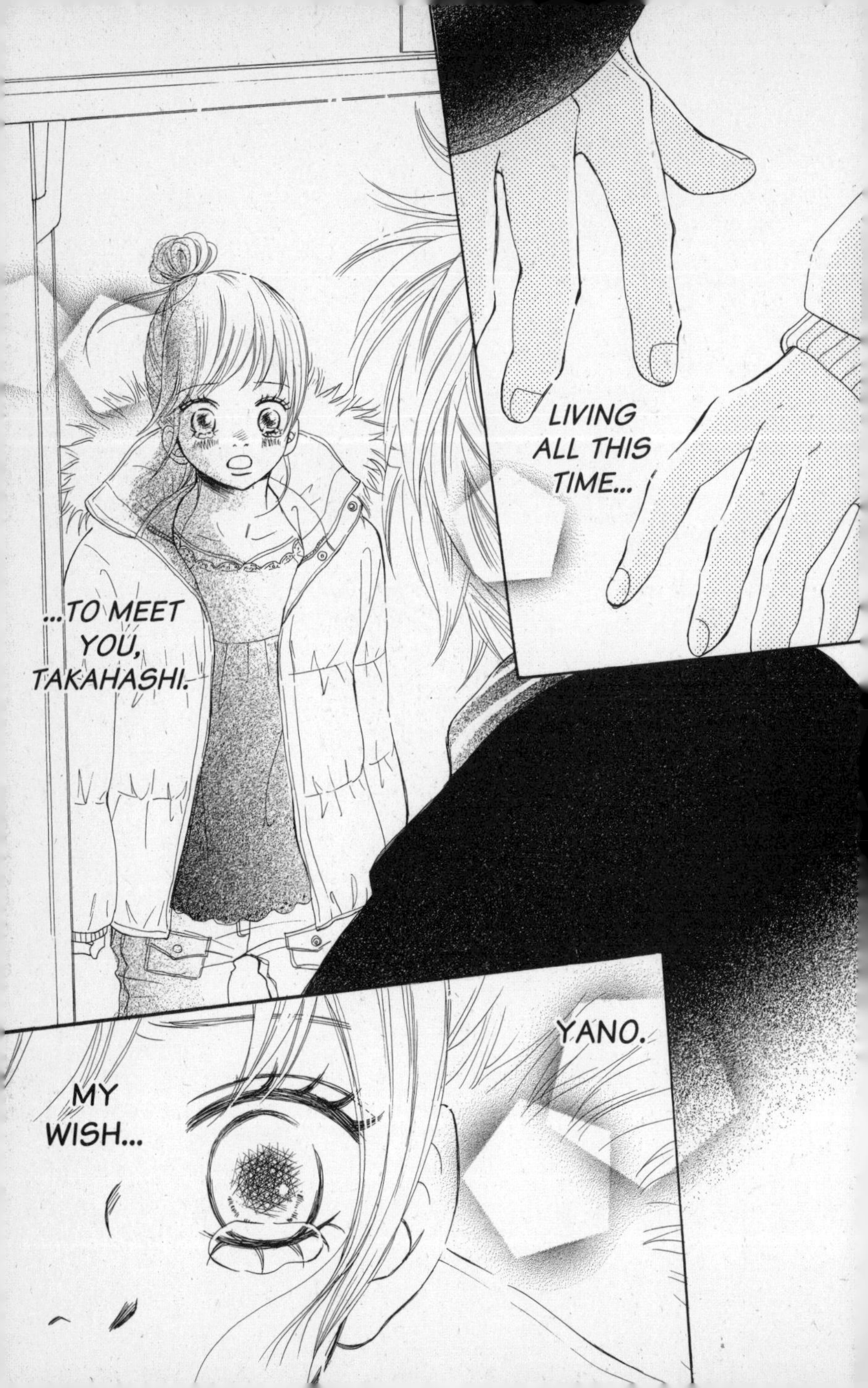
LIVING ALL THIS TIME...
...TO MEET YOU, TAKAHASHI.
YANO.
MY WISH...

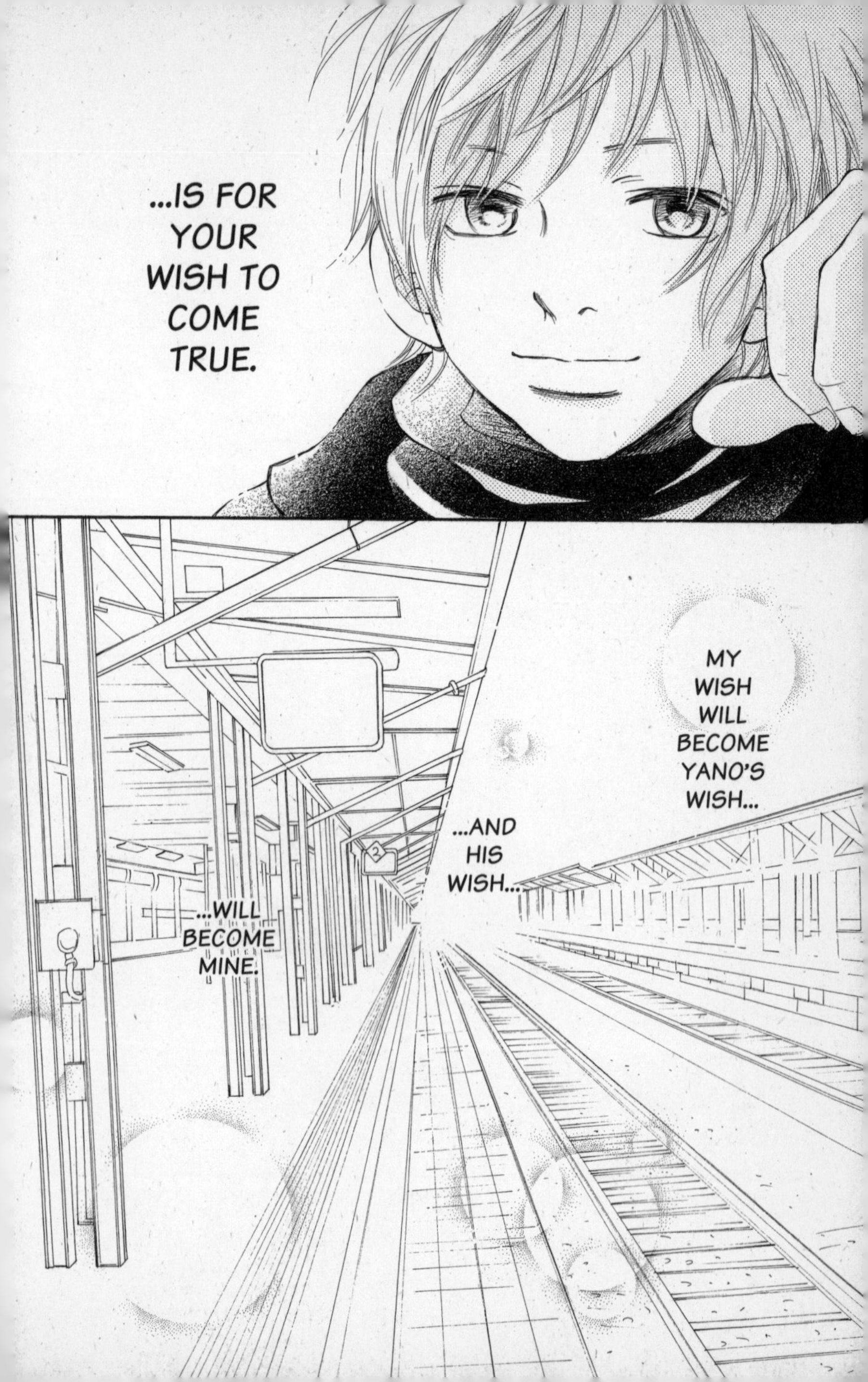
...IS FOR YOUR WISH TO COME TRUE.
MY WISH WILL BECOME YANO'S WISH...
...AND HIS WISH...
...WILL BECOME MINE.

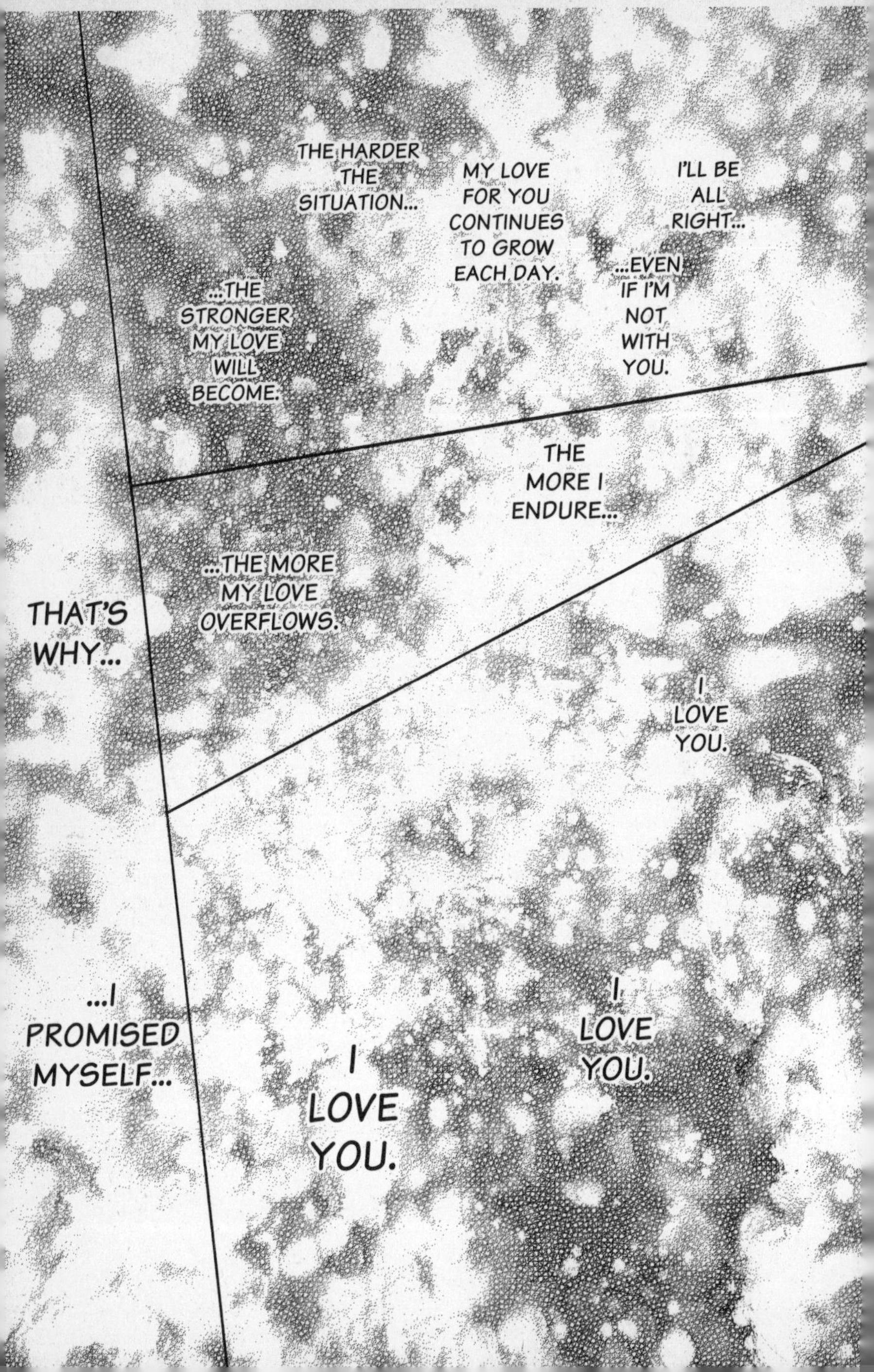
I'LL BE ALL RIGHT...
...EVEN IF I'M NOT WITH YOU.
MY LOVE FOR YOU CONTINUES TO GROW EACH DAY.
THE HARDER THE SITUATION...
...THE STRONGER MY LOVE WILL BECOME.
THE MORE I ENDURE...
...THE MORE MY LOVE OVERFLOWS.
I LOVE YOU.
I LOVE YOU.
I LOVE YOU.
THAT'S WHY...
...I PROMISED MYSELF...

...THE
NEXT
TIME
WE
MEET...

...I'LL
NEVER
LET YOU
GO.

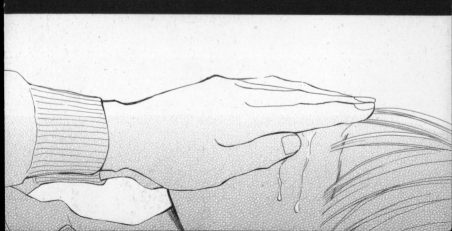

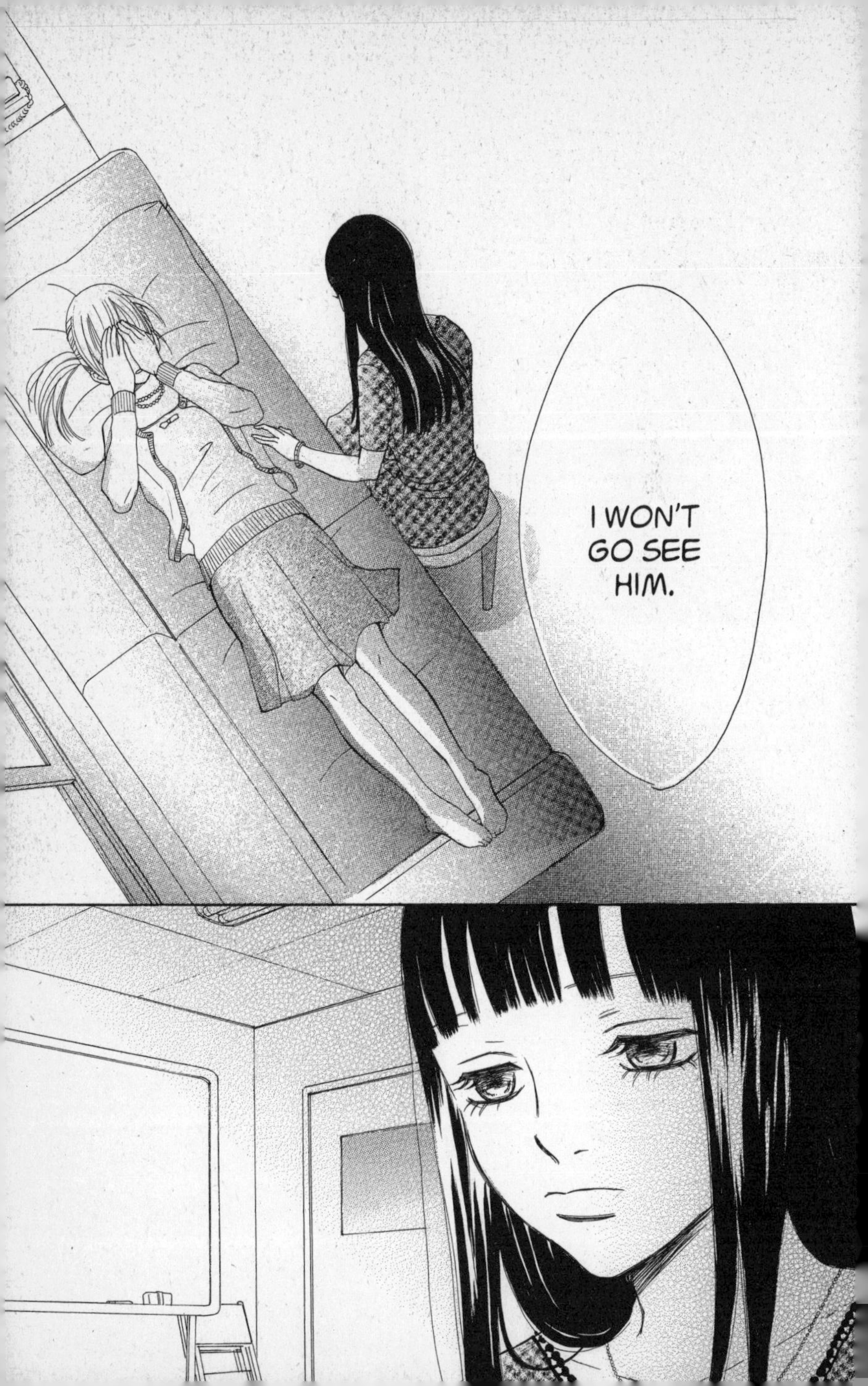
I WON'T GO SEE HIM.

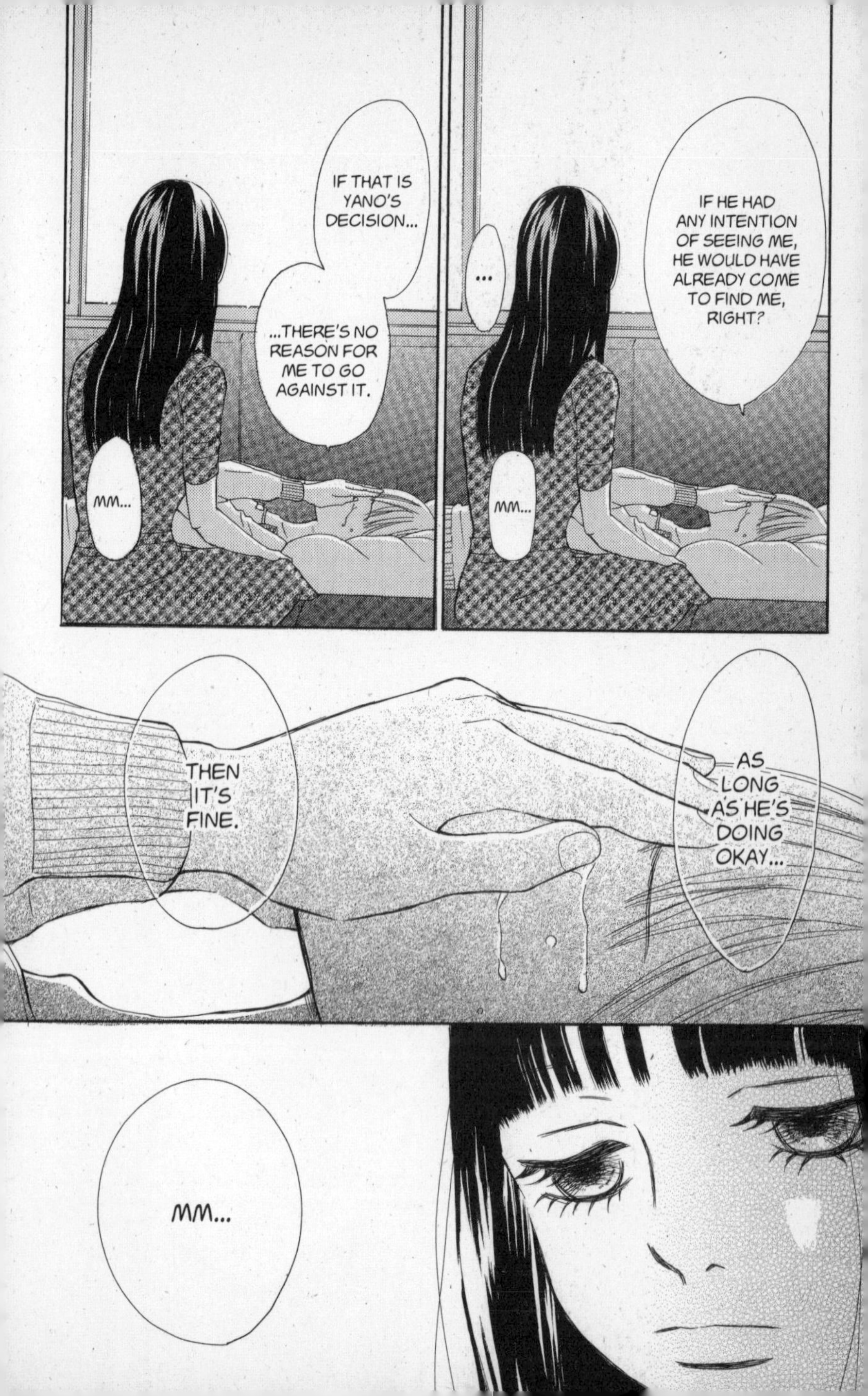
IF HE HAD ANY INTENTION OF SEEING ME, HE WOULD HAVE ALREADY COME TO FIND ME, RIGHT?
...
MM...
IF THAT IS YANO'S DECISION...
...THERE'S NO REASON FOR ME TO GO AGAINST IT.
MM...
AS LONG AS HE'S DOING OKAY...
THEN IT'S FINE.
MM...

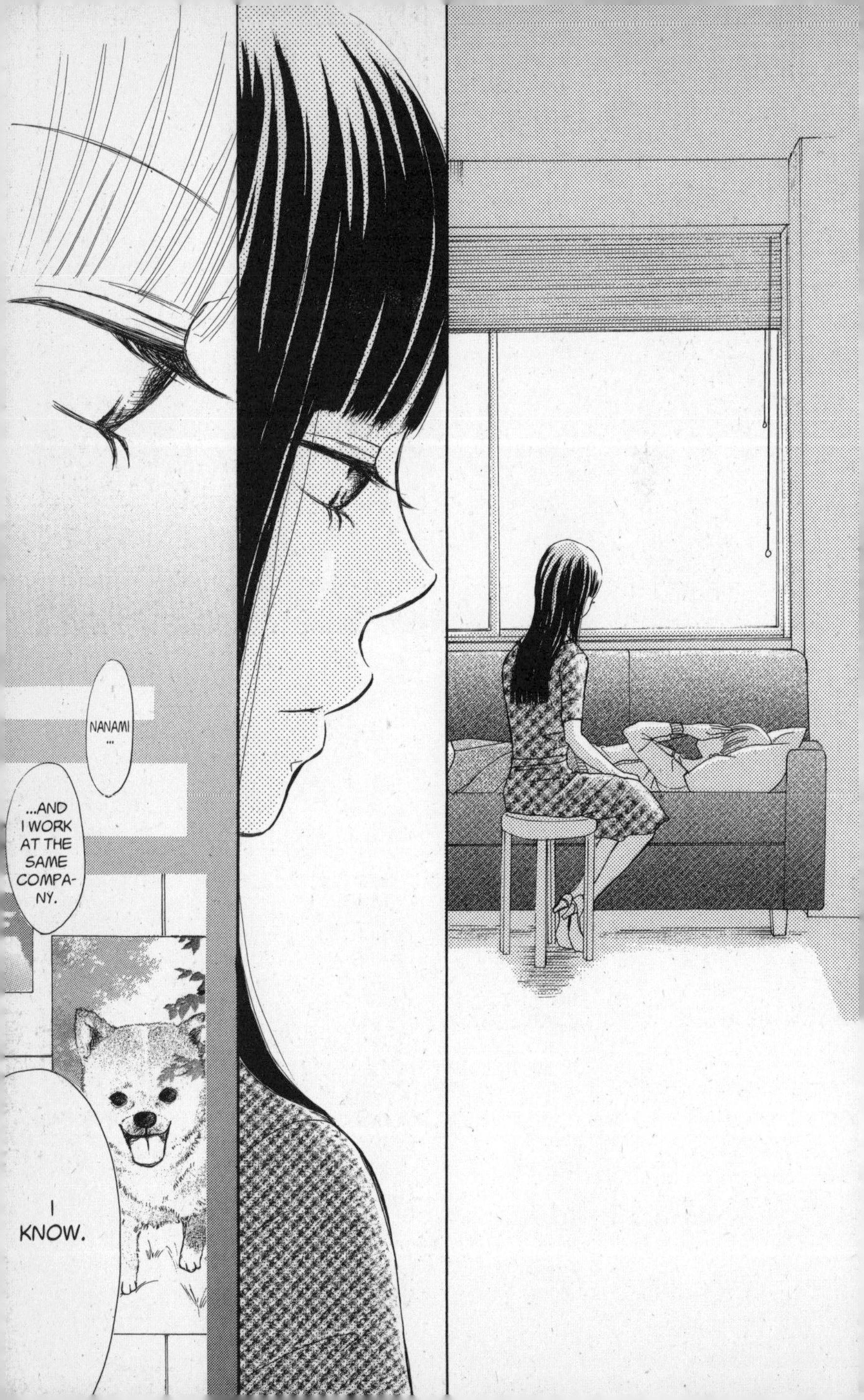
NANAMI ...
...AND I WORK AT THE SAME COMPANY.
I KNOW.

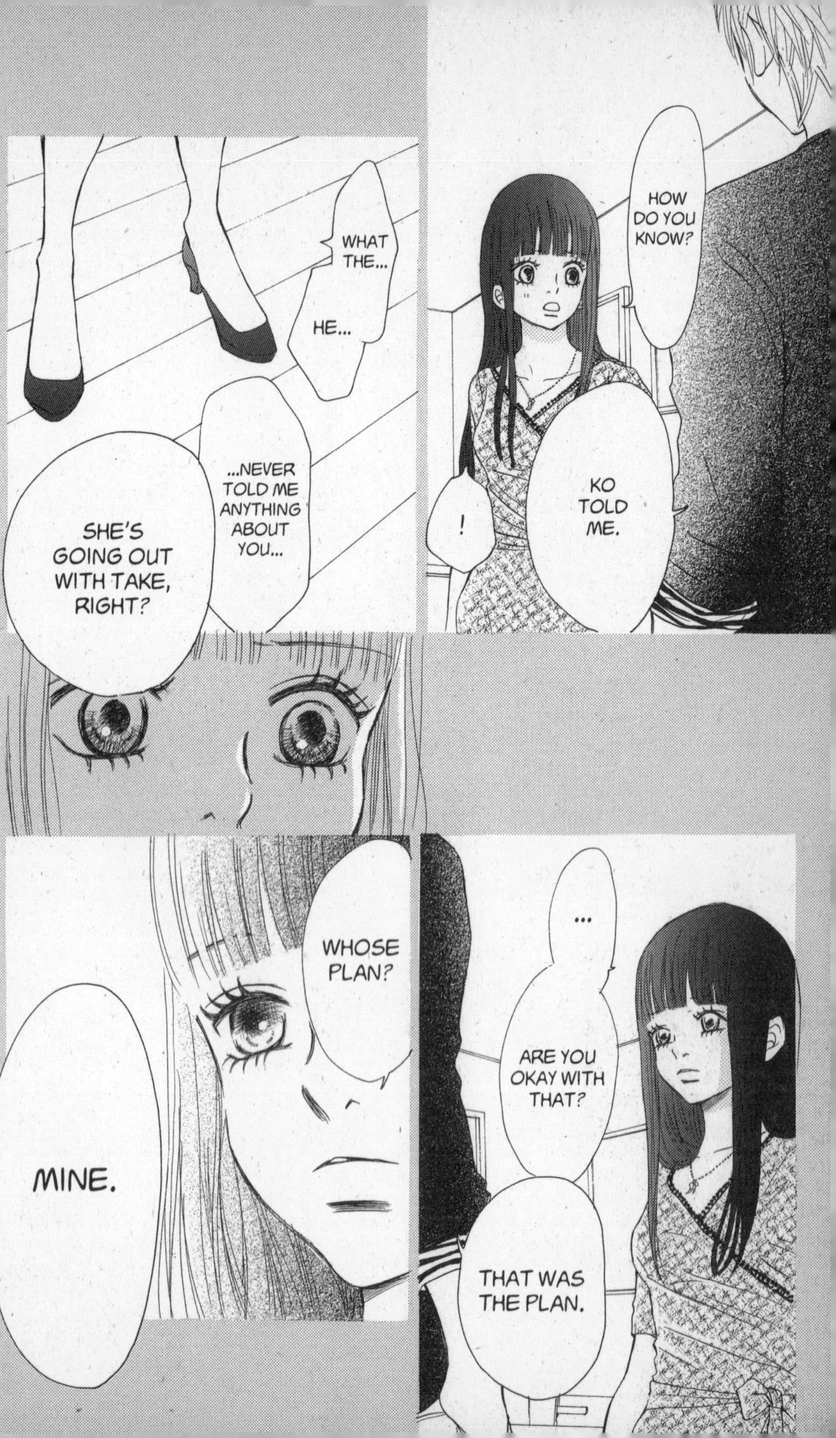
HOW DO YOU KNOW?
KO TOLD ME.
!
WHAT THE... HE...
...NEVER TOLD ME ANYTHING ABOUT YOU...
SHE'S GOING OUT WITH TAKE, RIGHT?
...
ARE YOU OKAY WITH THAT?
THAT WAS THE PLAN.
WHOSE PLAN?
MINE.

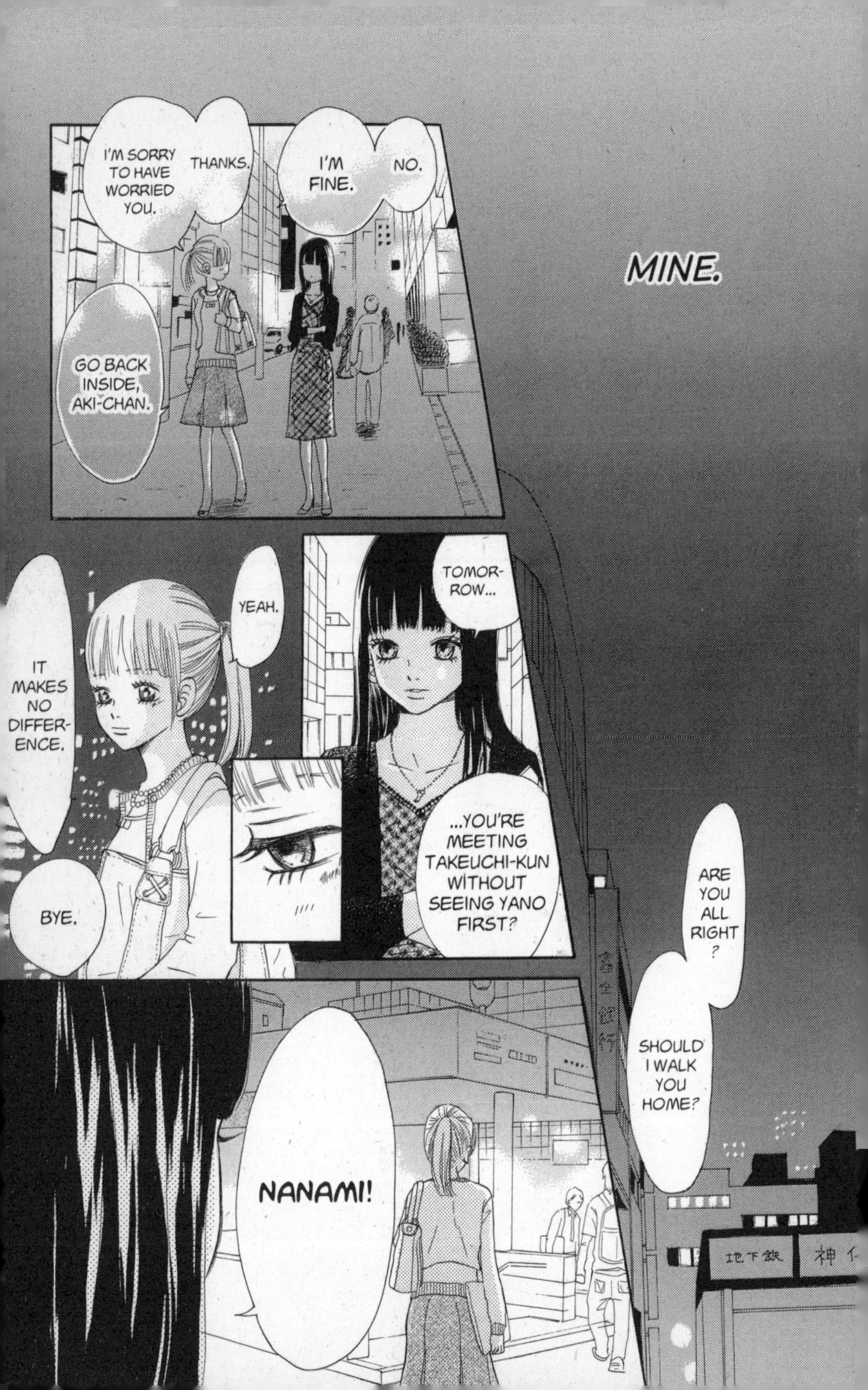
MINE.
NO.
I'M FINE.
THANKS.
I'M SORRY TO HAVE WORRIED YOU.
GO BACK INSIDE, AKI-CHAN.
TOMORROW...
...YOU'RE MEETING TAKEUCHI-KUN WITHOUT SEEING YANO FIRST?
YEAH.
IT MAKES NO DIFFERENCE.
BYE.
ARE YOU ALL RIGHT?
SHOULD I WALK YOU HOME?
NANAMI!

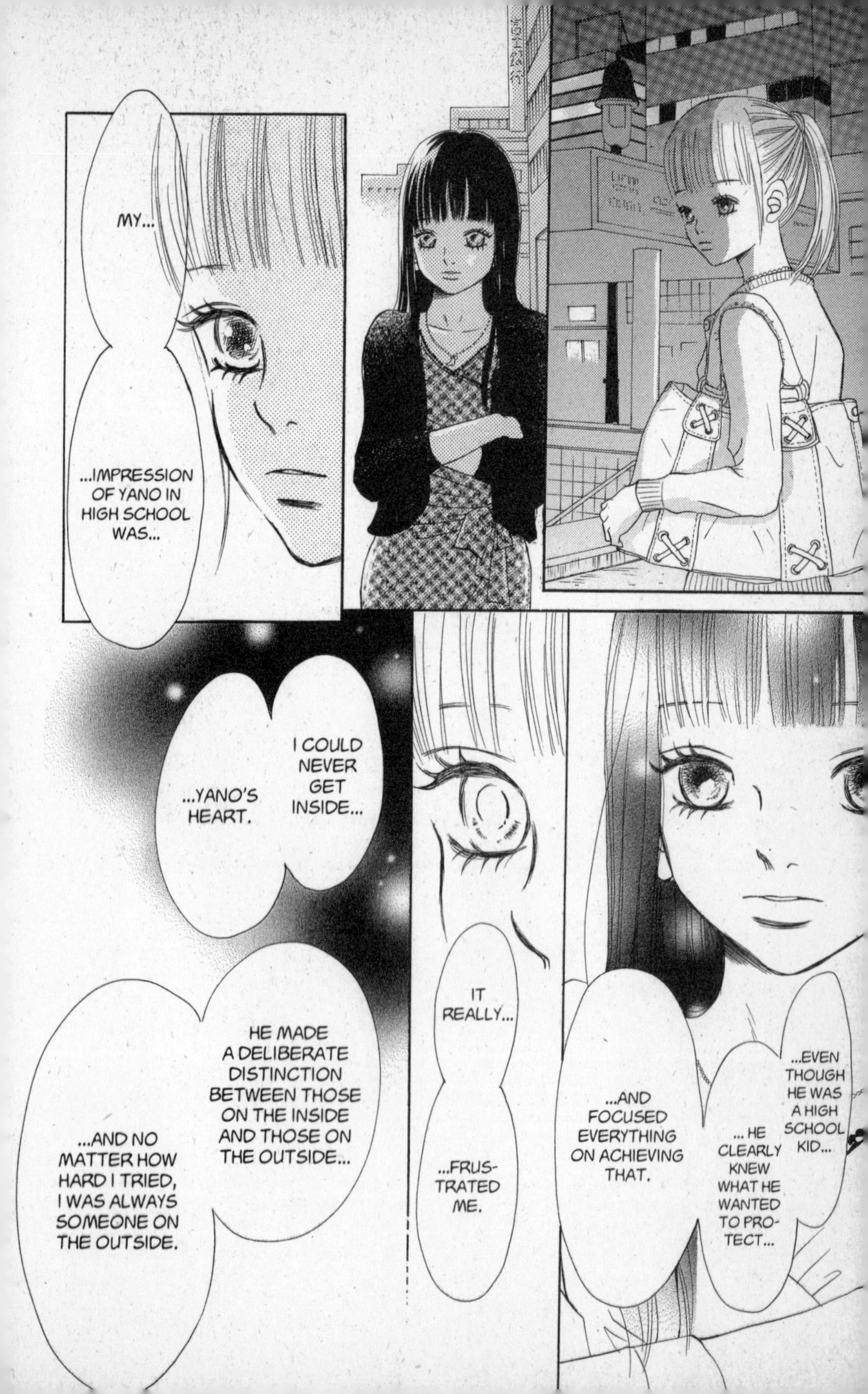
MY...
...IMPRESSION OF YANO IN HIGH SCHOOL WAS...
...EVEN THOUGH HE WAS A HIGH SCHOOL KID...
... HE CLEARLY KNEW WHAT HE WANTED TO PROTECT...
...AND FOCUSED EVERYTHING ON ACHIEVING THAT.
IT REALLY...
...FRUSTRATED ME.
I COULD NEVER GET INSIDE...
...YANO'S HEART.
HE MADE A DELIBERATE DISTINCTION BETWEEN THOSE ON THE INSIDE AND THOSE ON THE OUTSIDE...
...AND NO MATTER HOW HARD I TRIED, I WAS ALWAYS SOMEONE ON THE OUTSIDE.

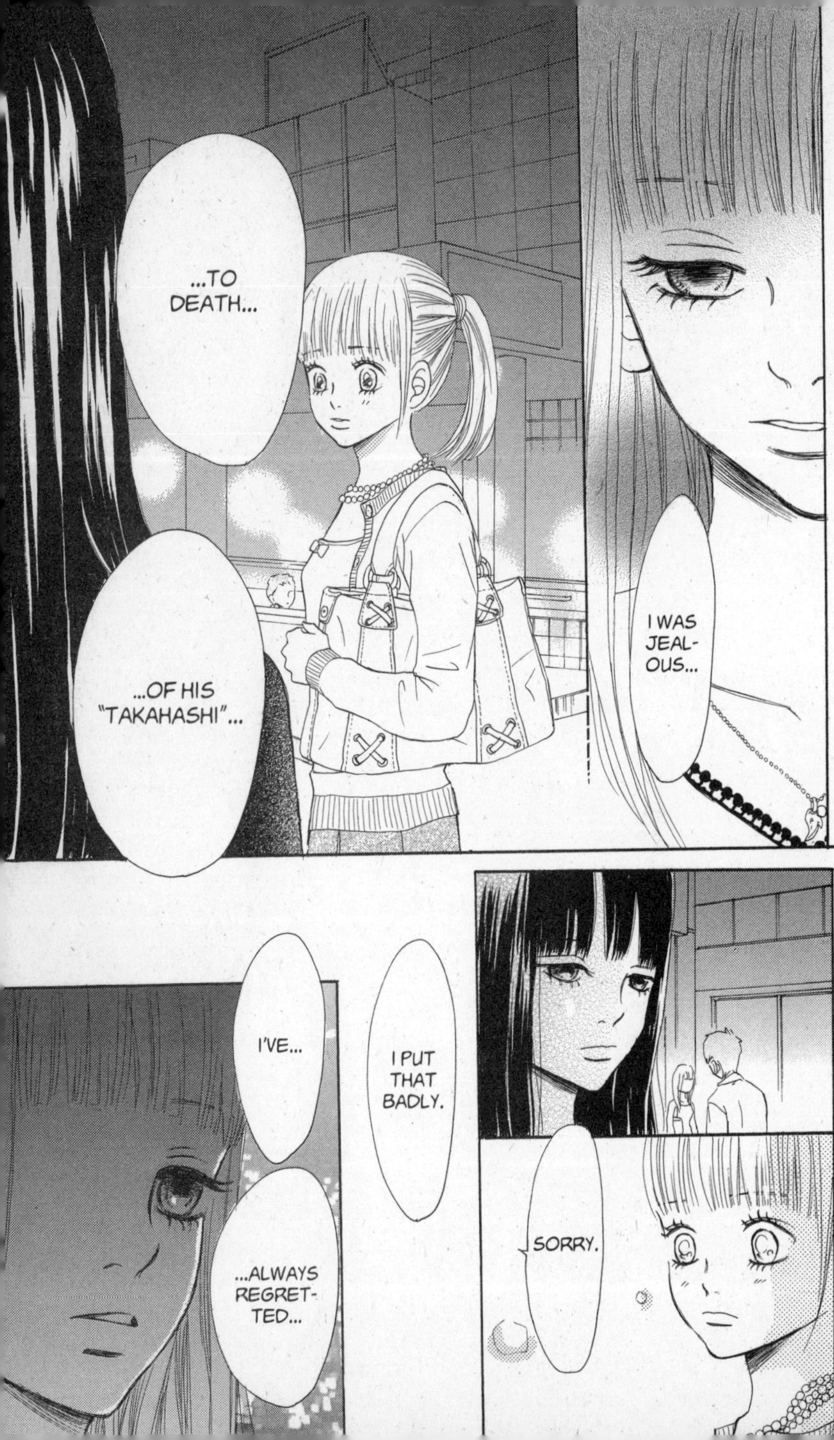
I WAS JEAL-
OUS...
...TO DEATH...
...OF HIS "TAKAHASHI"...
SORRY.
I PUT THAT BADLY.
I'VE...
...ALWAYS REGRET-
TED...

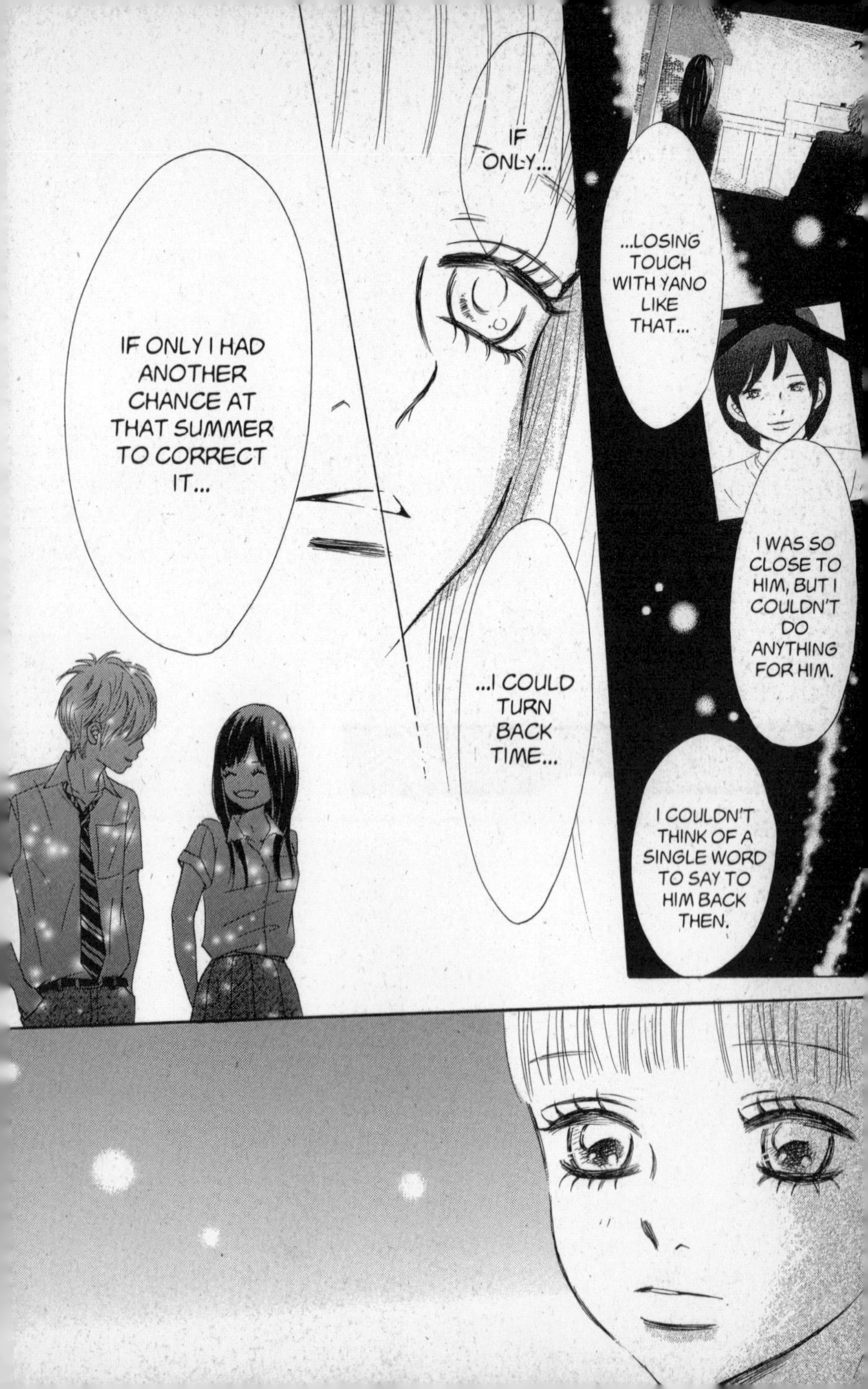
...LOSING TOUCH WITH YANO LIKE THAT...
I WAS SO CLOSE TO HIM, BUT I COULDN'T DO ANYTHING FOR HIM.
I COULDN'T THINK OF A SINGLE WORD TO SAY TO HIM BACK THEN.
IF ONLY...
...I COULD TURN BACK TIME...
IF ONLY I HAD ANOTHER CHANCE AT THAT SUMMER TO CORRECT IT...

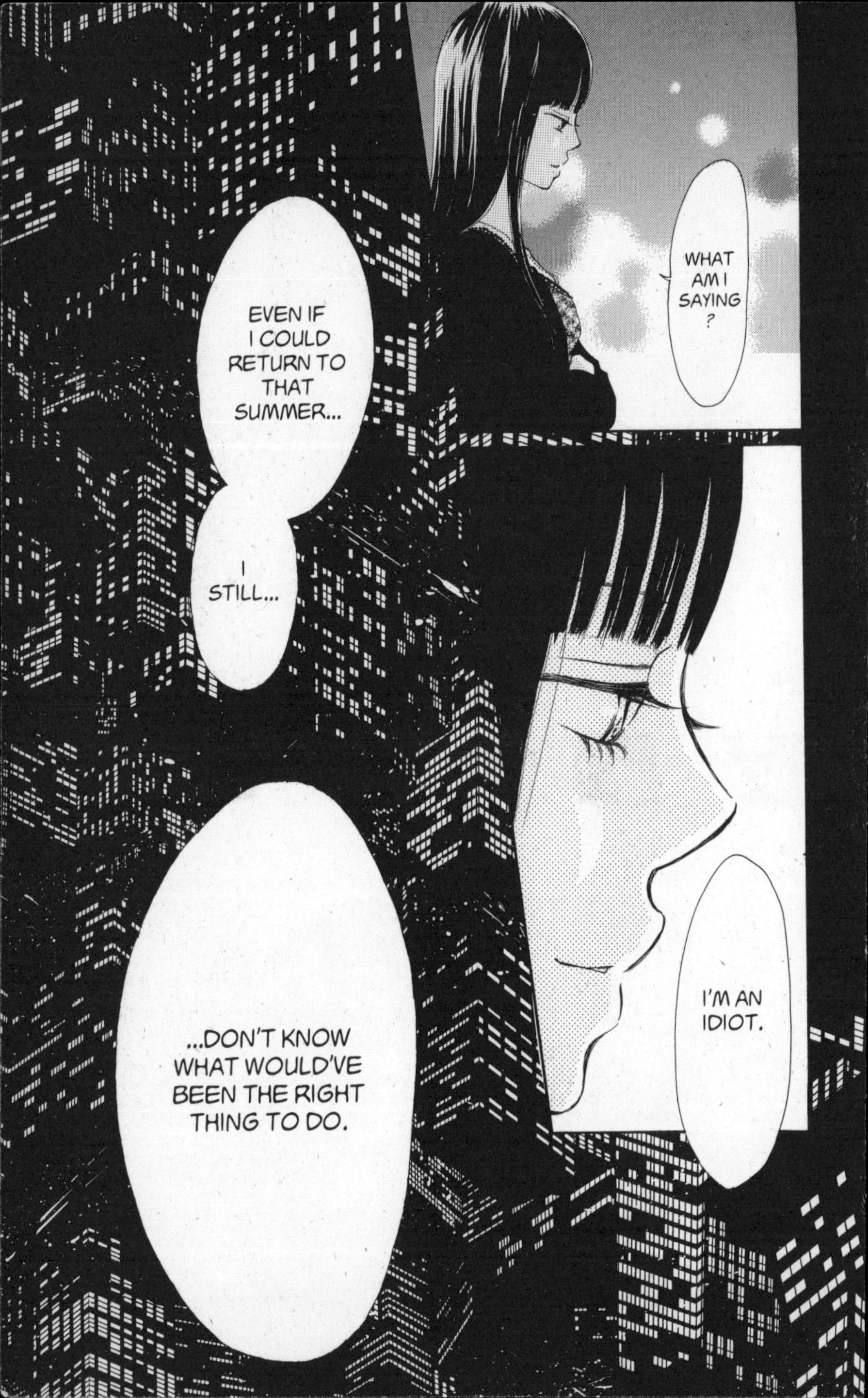
WHAT AM I SAYING?
I'M AN IDIOT.
EVEN IF I COULD RETURN TO THAT SUMMER...
I STILL...
...DON'T KNOW WHAT WOULD'VE BEEN THE RIGHT THING TO DO.

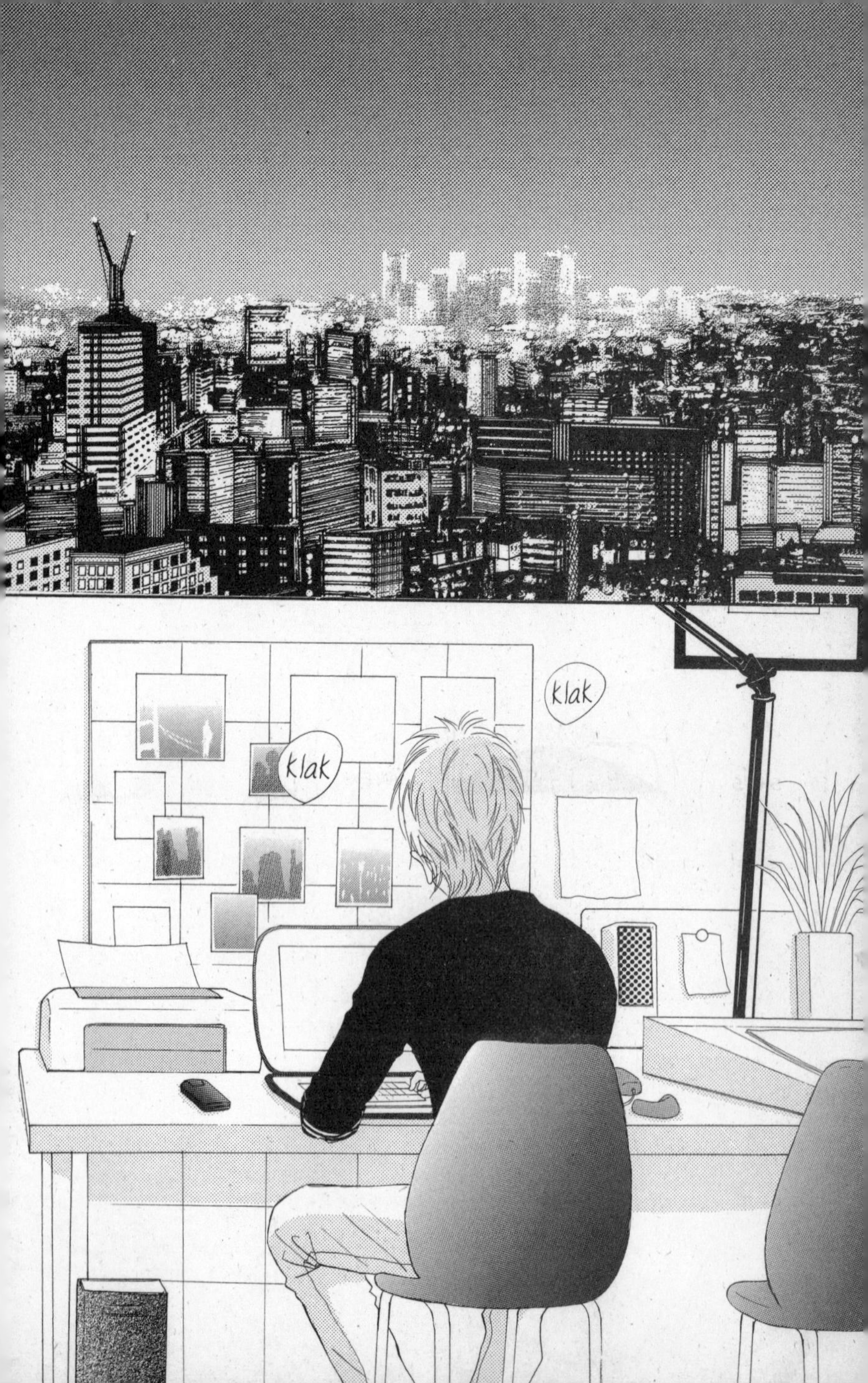
klak
klak

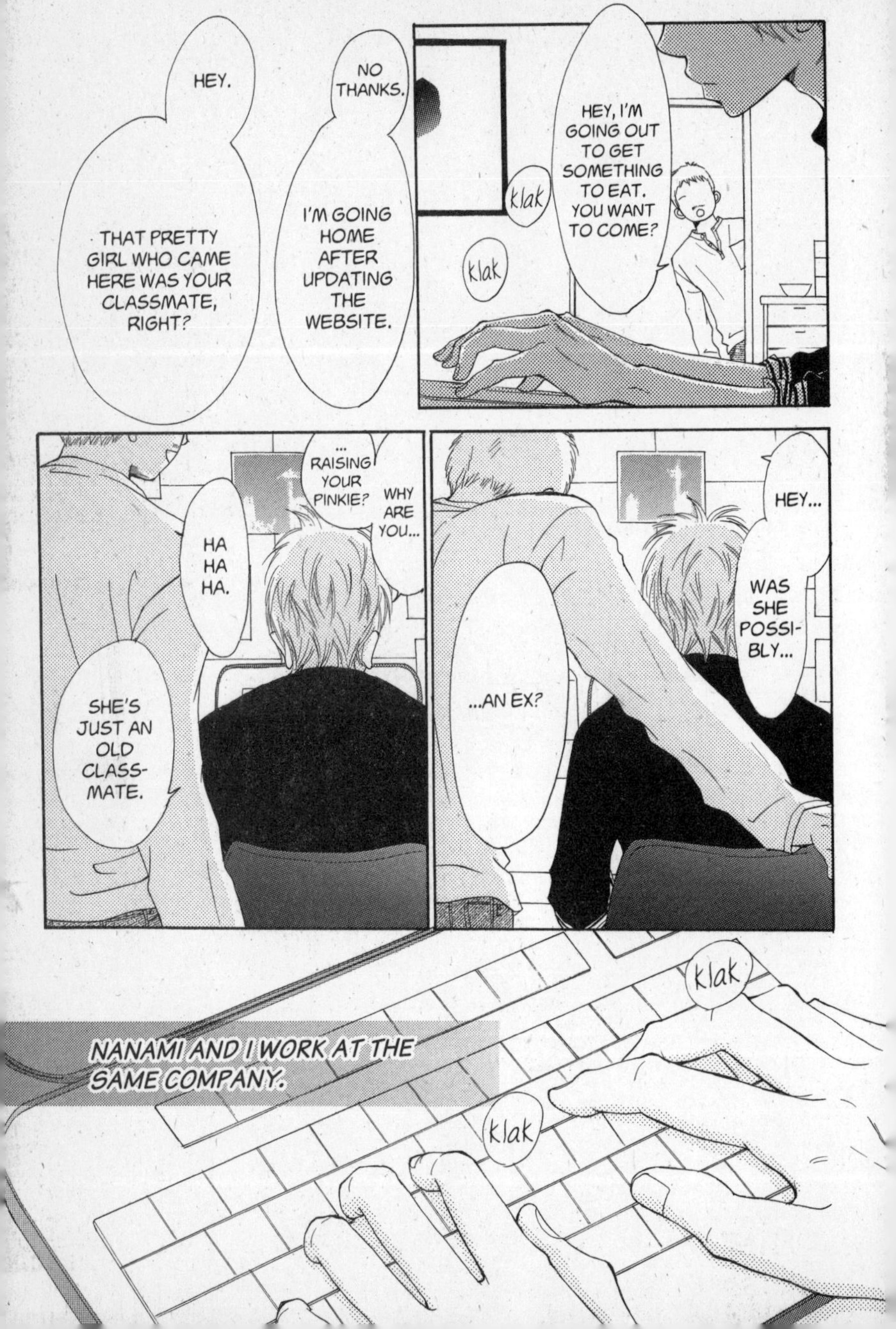
HEY, I'M GOING OUT TO GET SOMETHING TO EAT. YOU WANT TO COME?
klak
klak
NO THANKS.
I'M GOING HOME AFTER UPDATING THE WEBSITE.
HEY.
THAT PRETTY GIRL WHO CAME HERE WAS YOUR CLASSMATE, RIGHT?
HEY...
WAS SHE POSSI-BLY...
...AN EX?
WHY ARE YOU...
...RAISING YOUR PINKIE?
HA HA HA.
SHE'S JUST AN OLD CLASS-MATE.
klak
klak
NANAMI AND I WORK AT THE SAME COMPANY.

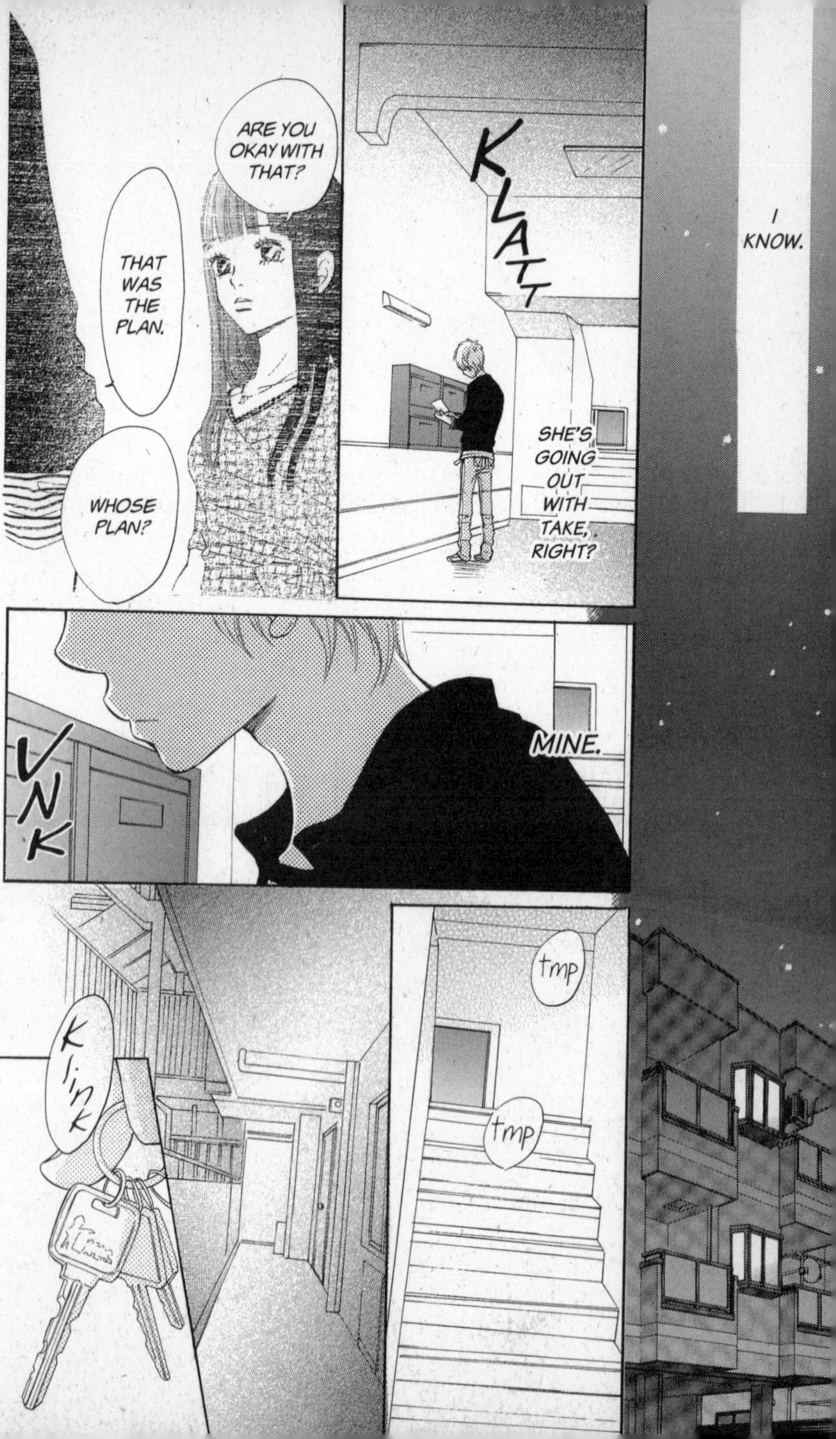
I KNOW.
KLATT
SHE'S GOING OUT WITH TAKE, RIGHT?
ARE YOU OKAY WITH THAT?
THAT WAS THE PLAN.
WHOSE PLAN?
MINE.
VNK
tmp
tmp
Klink

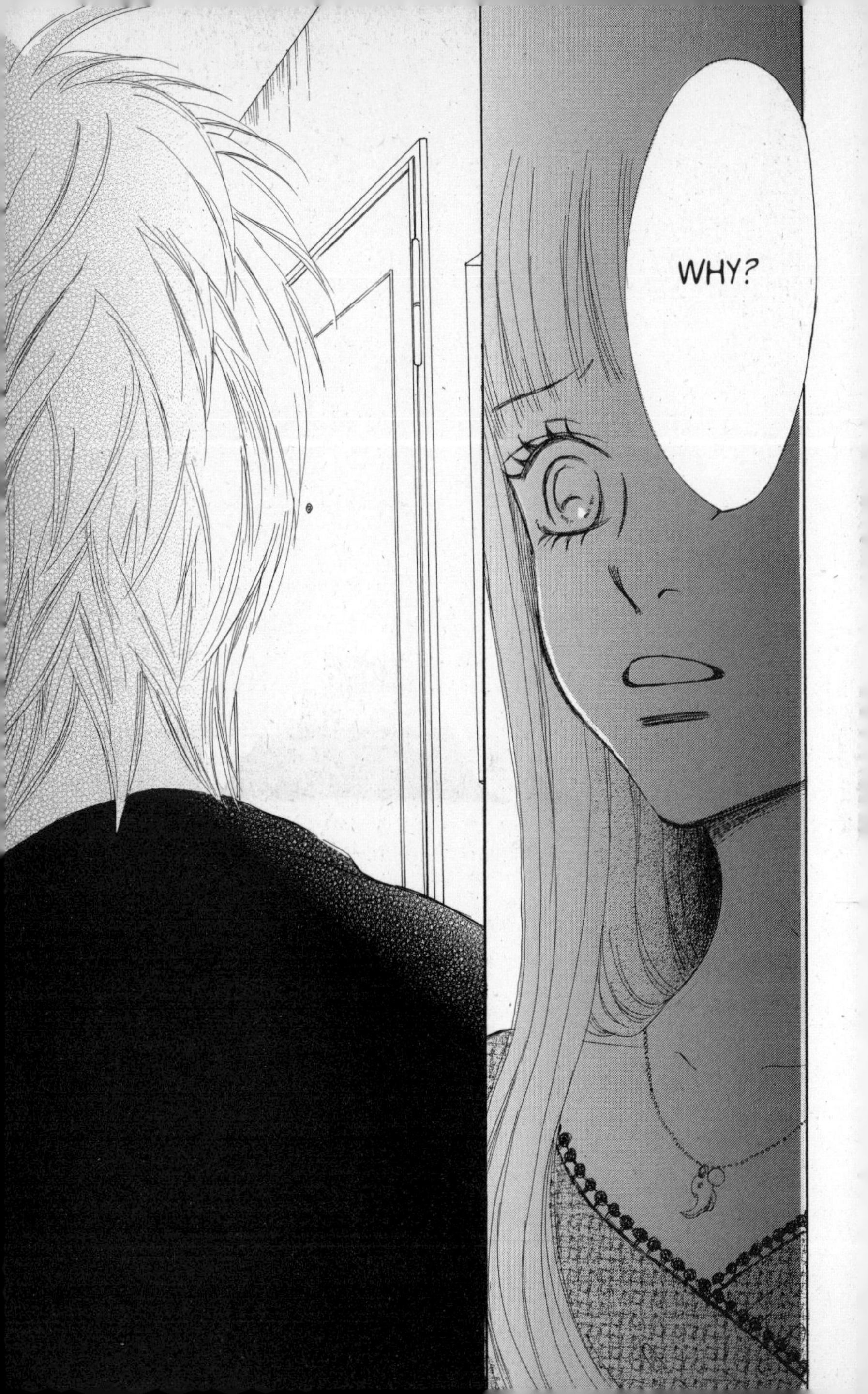
WHY?

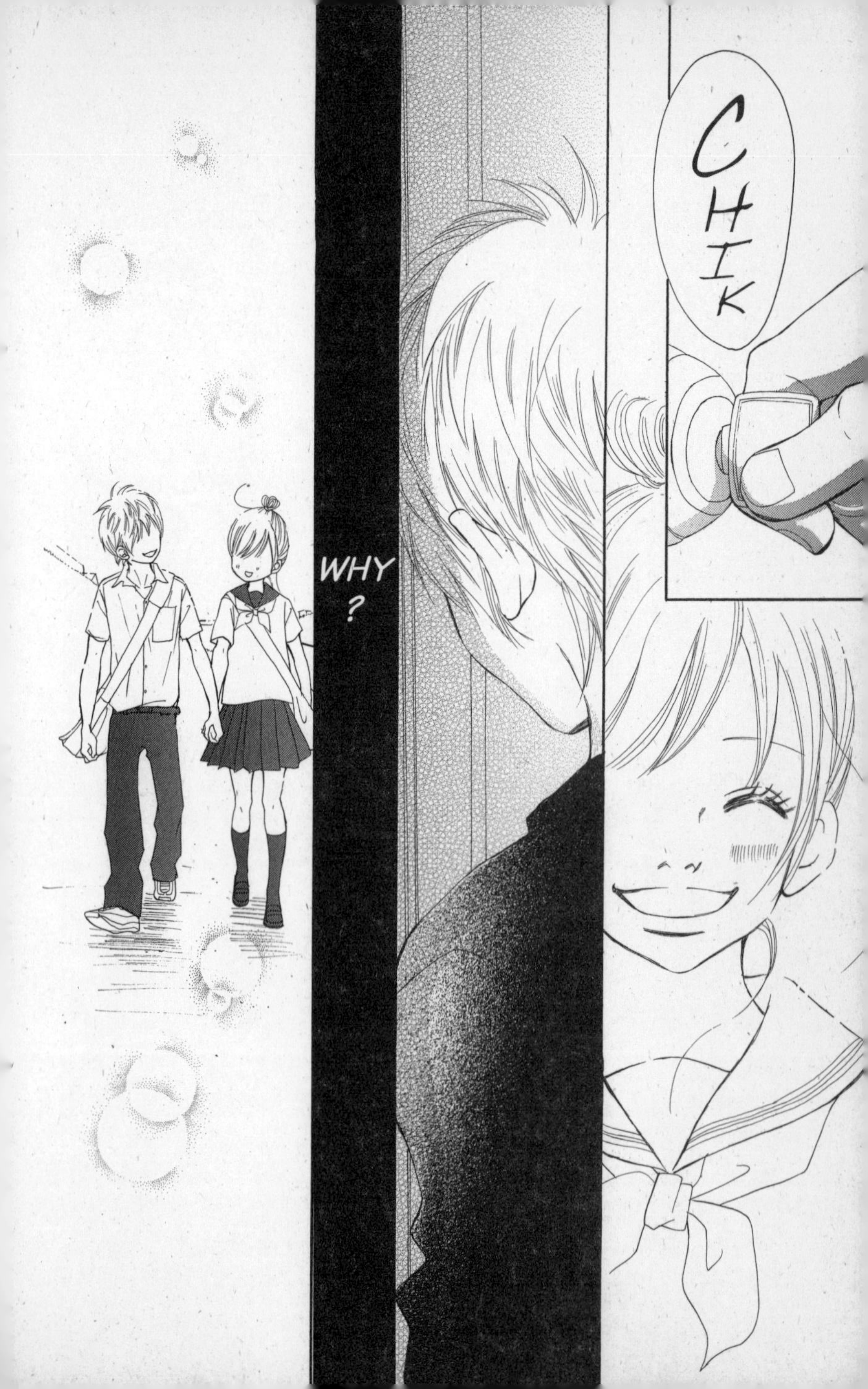
CHIK
WHY?

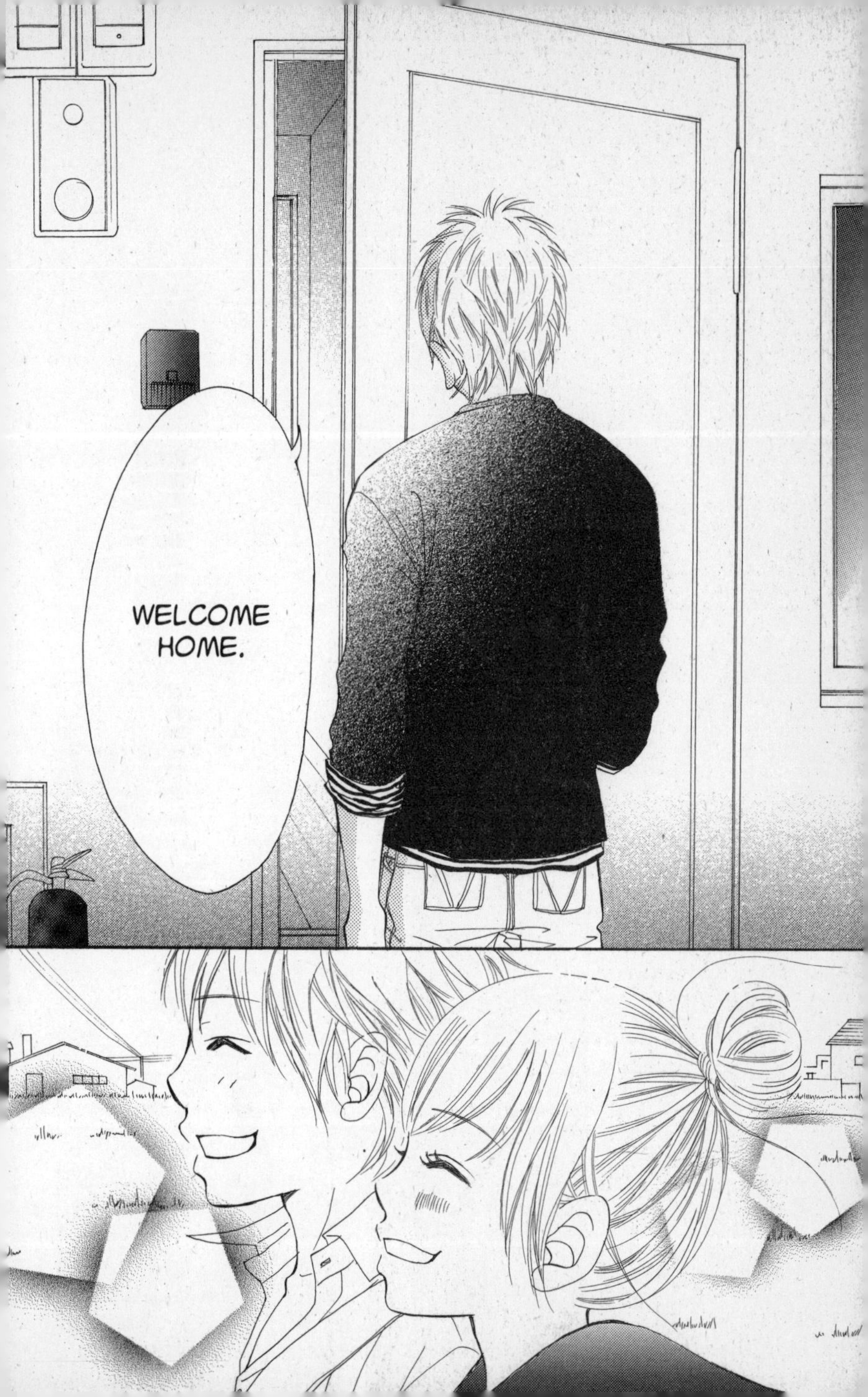
WELCOME HOME.

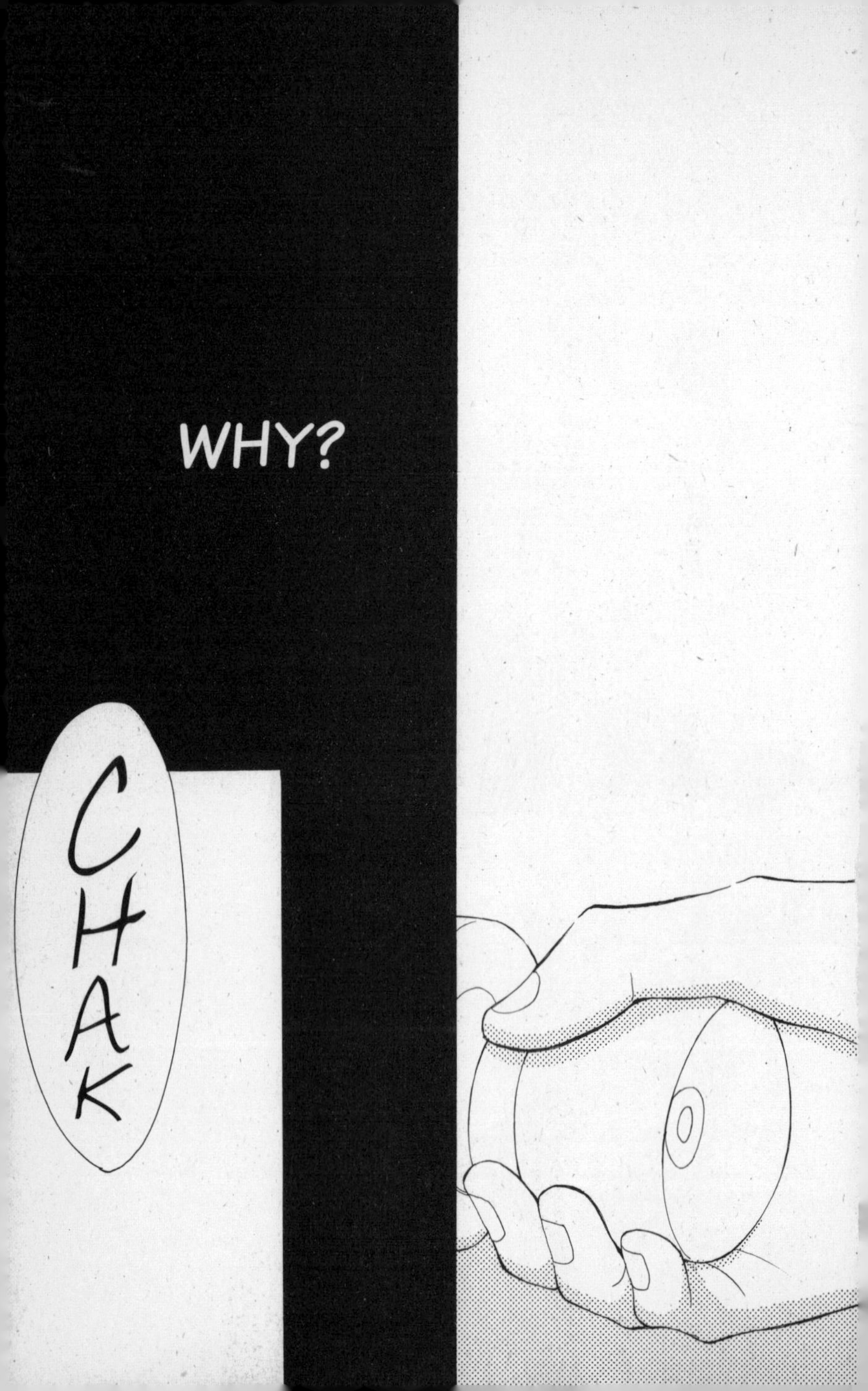
WHY?
CHAK

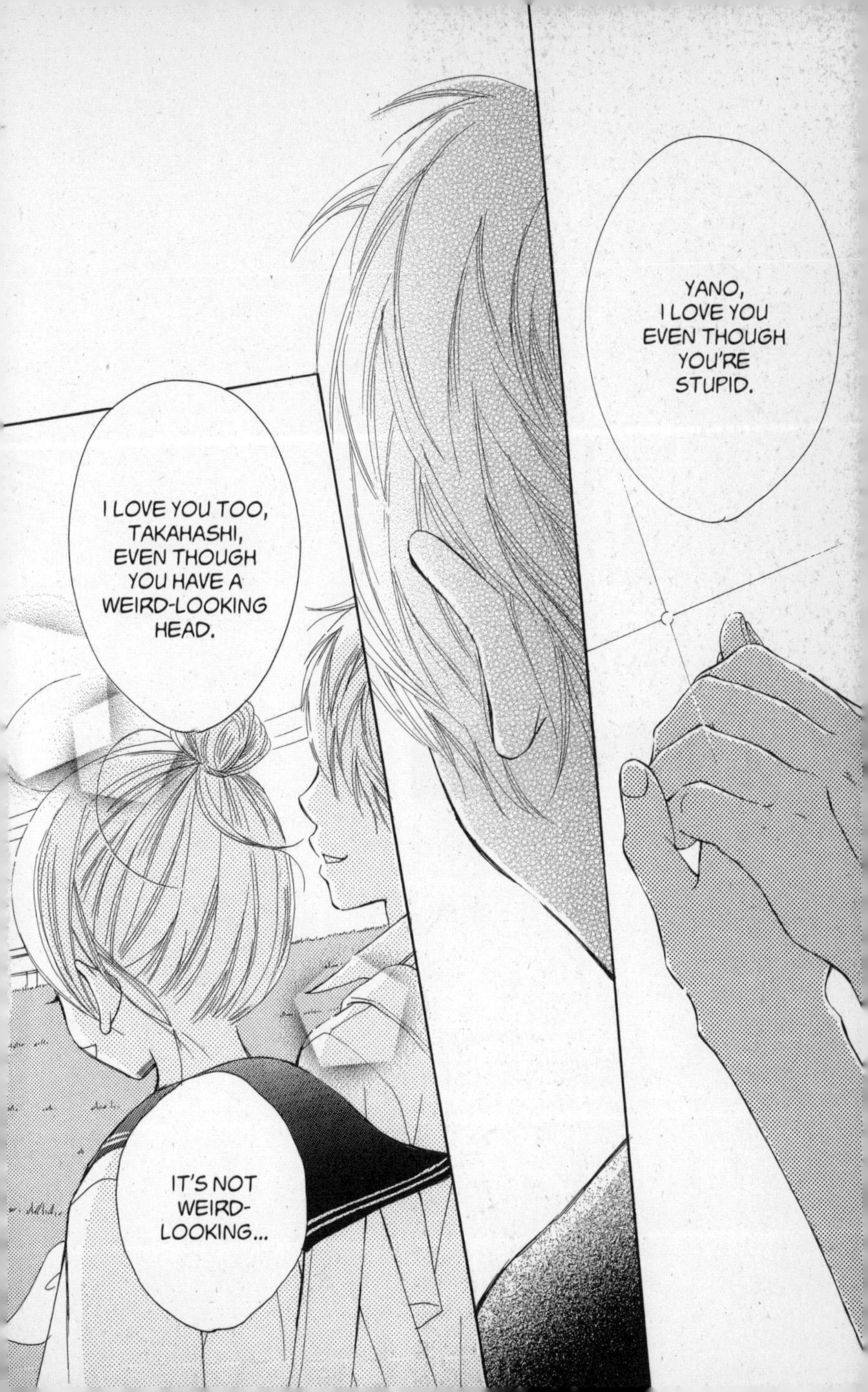
YANO, I LOVE YOU EVEN THOUGH YOU'RE STUPID.
I LOVE YOU TOO, TAKAHASHI, EVEN THOUGH YOU HAVE A WEIRD-LOOKING HEAD.
IT'S NOT WEIRD-LOOKING...

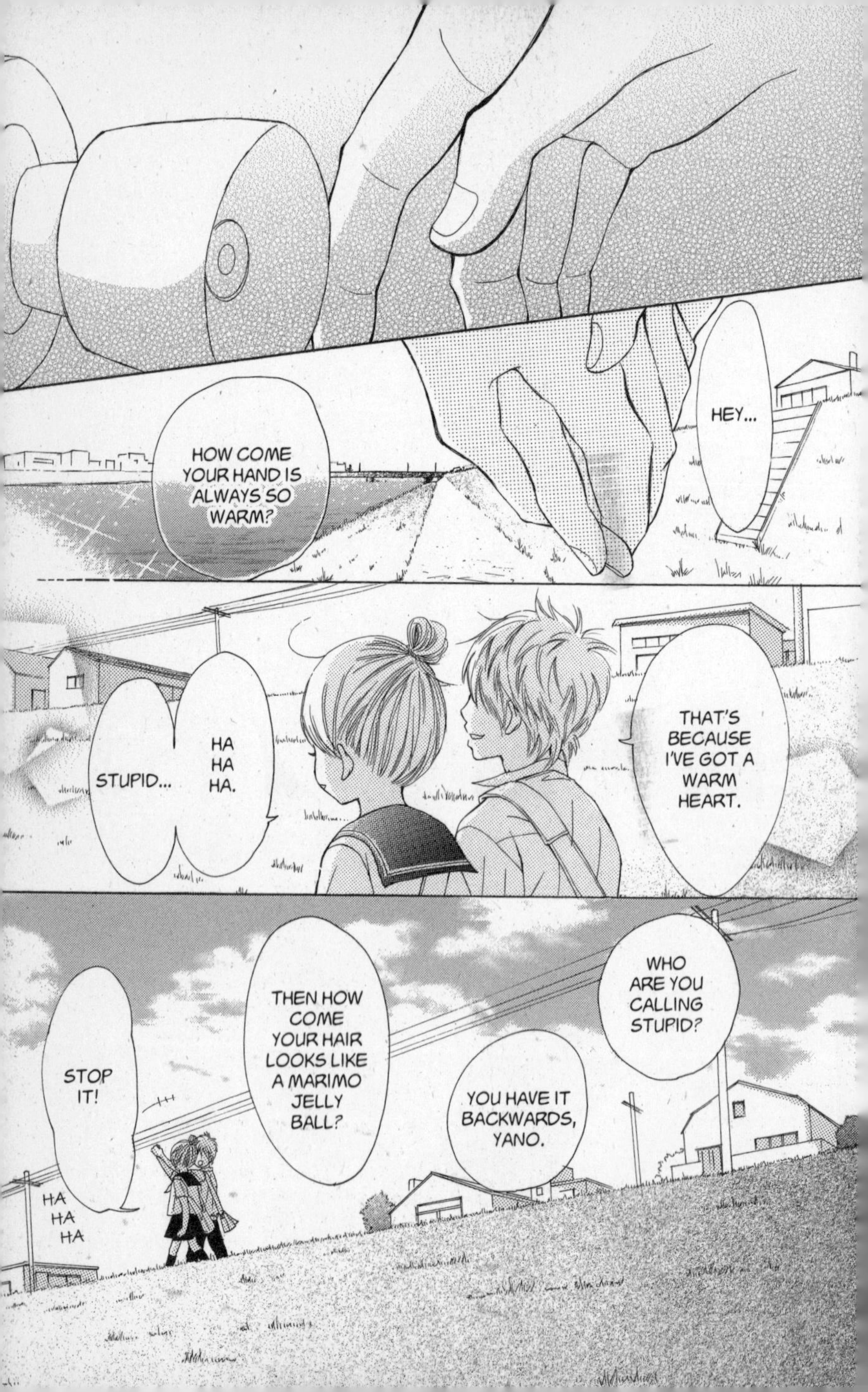
HEY...
HOW COME YOUR HAND IS ALWAYS SO WARM?
THAT'S BECAUSE I'VE GOT A WARM HEART.
HA HA HA.
STUPID...
WHO ARE YOU CALLING STUPID?
YOU HAVE IT BACKWARDS, YANO.
THEN HOW COME YOUR HAIR LOOKS LIKE A MARIMO JELLY BALL?
STOP IT!
HA HA HA

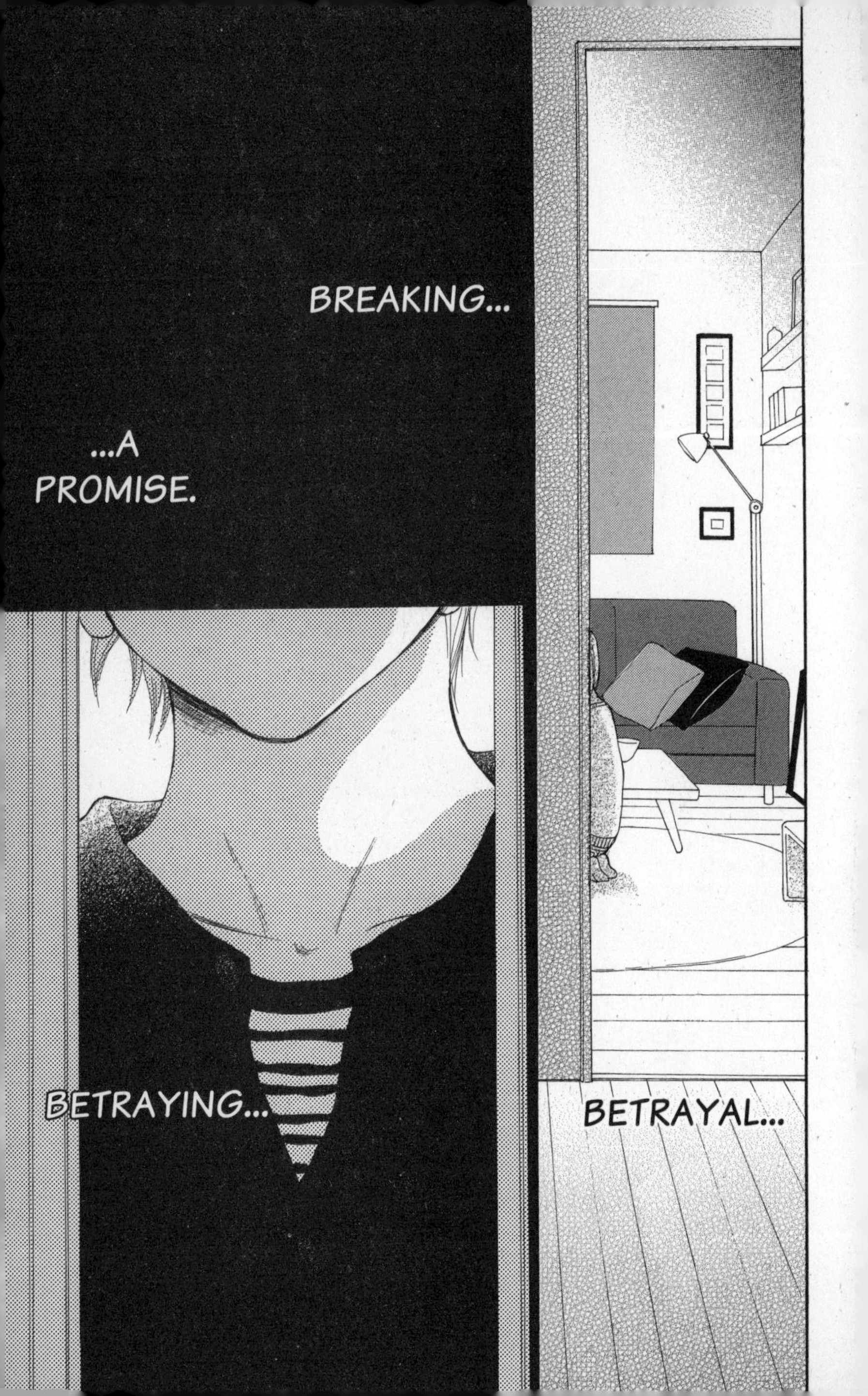

BREAKING...

...A PROMISE.

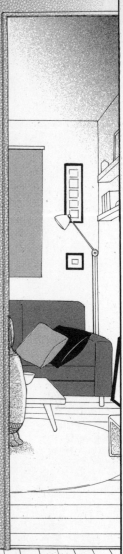

BETRAYING...

BETRAYAL...

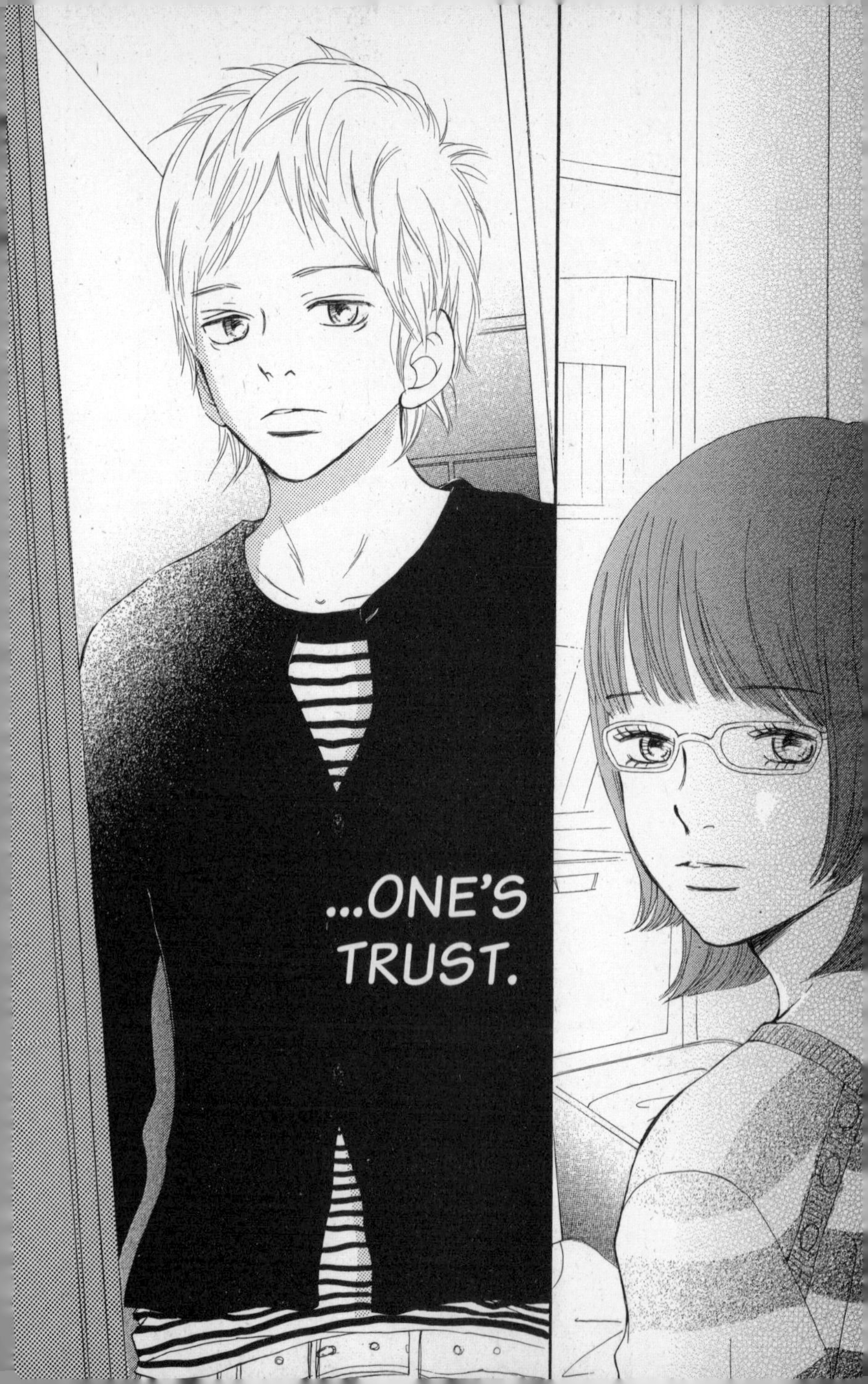
...ONE'S TRUST.

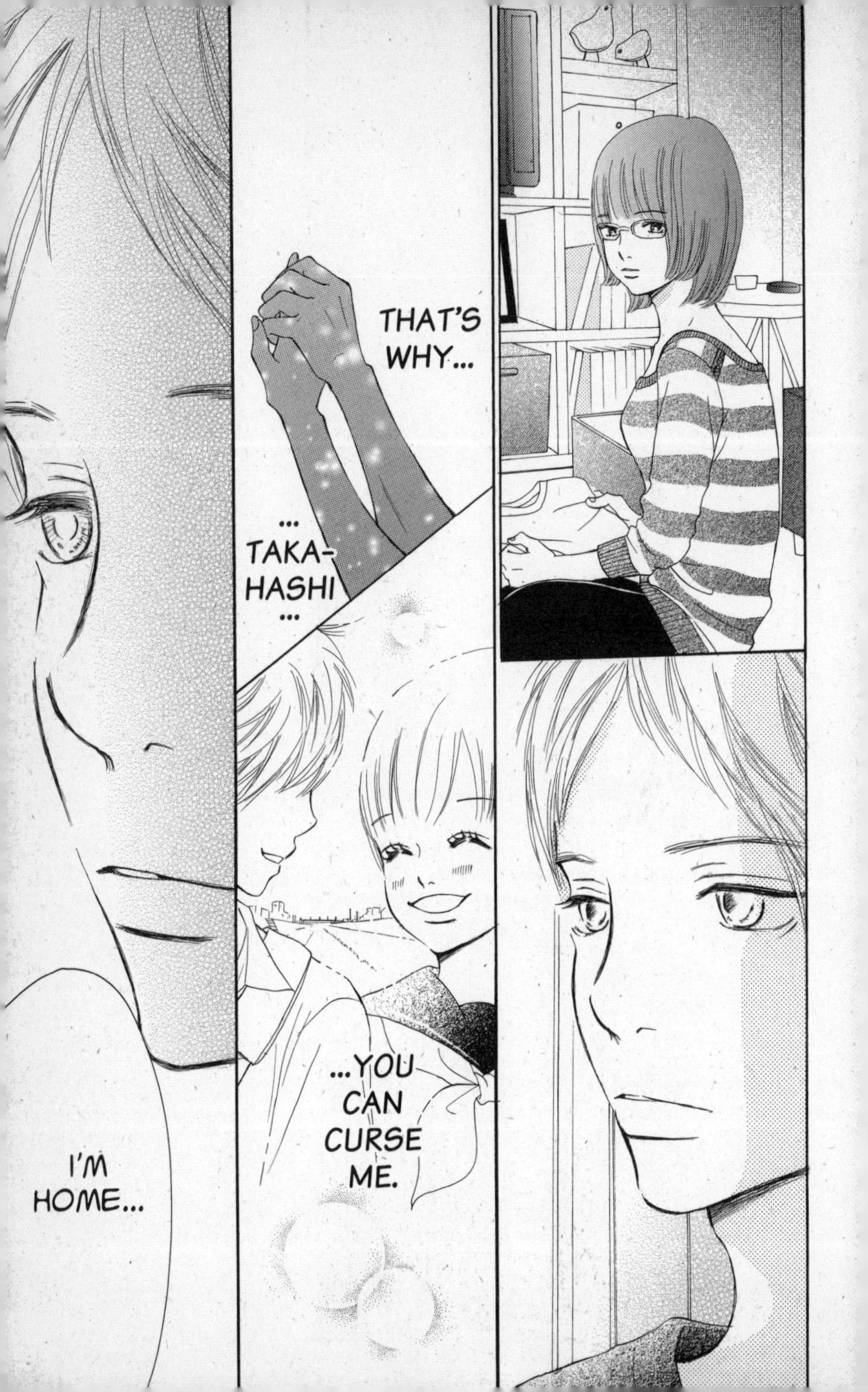
THAT'S WHY...
... TAKA-HASHI ...
...YOU CAN CURSE ME.
I'M HOME...

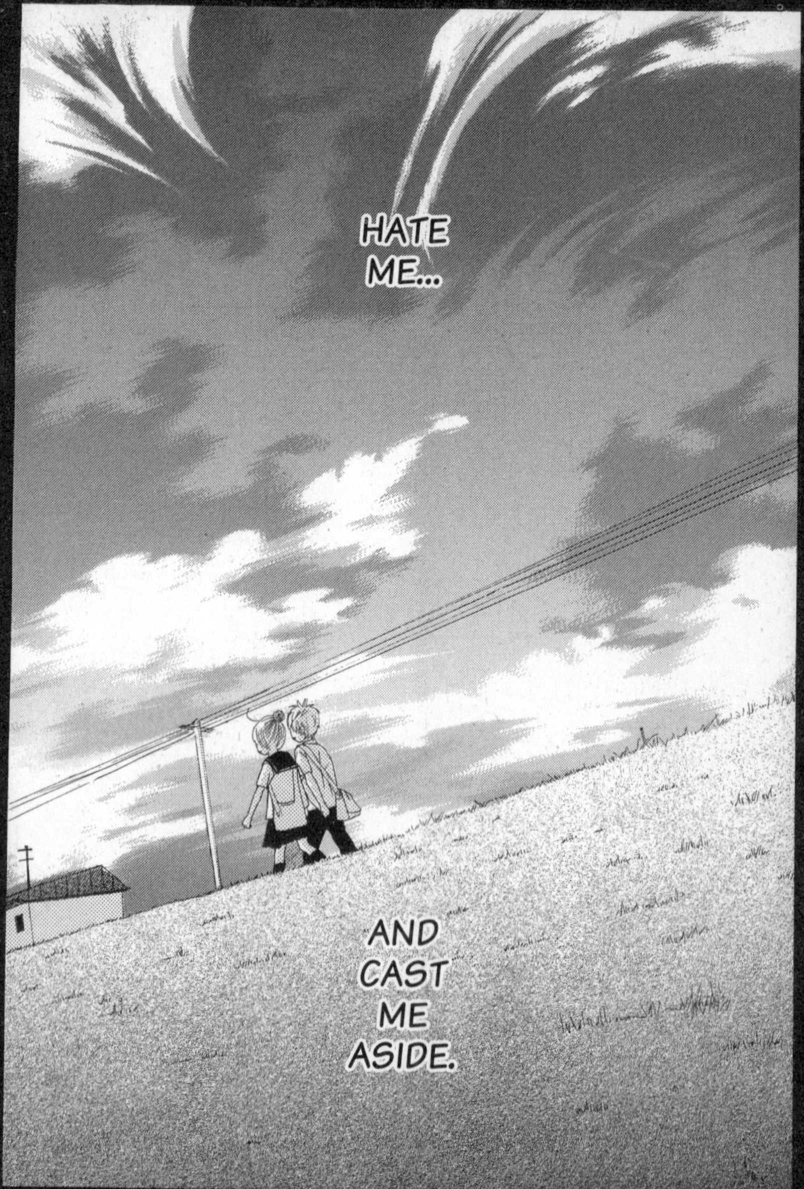
HATE ME...
AND CAST ME ASIDE.

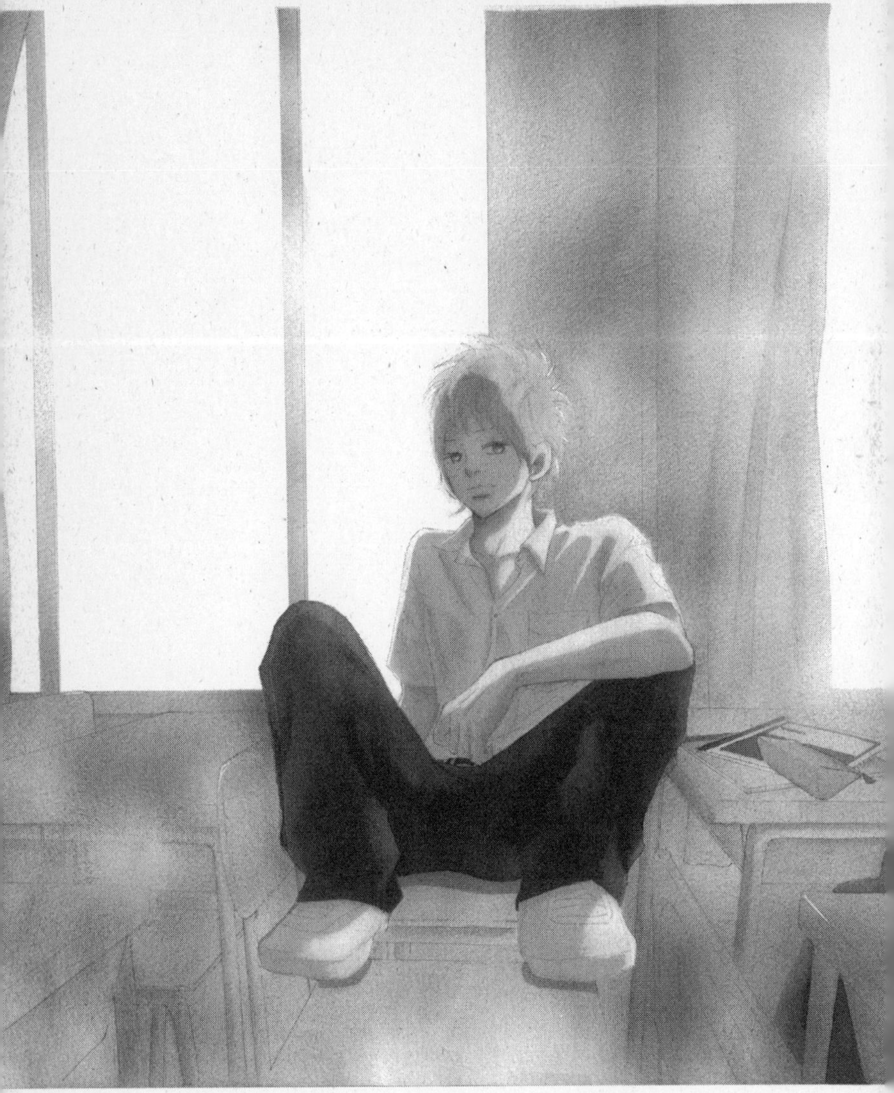

Chapter 46

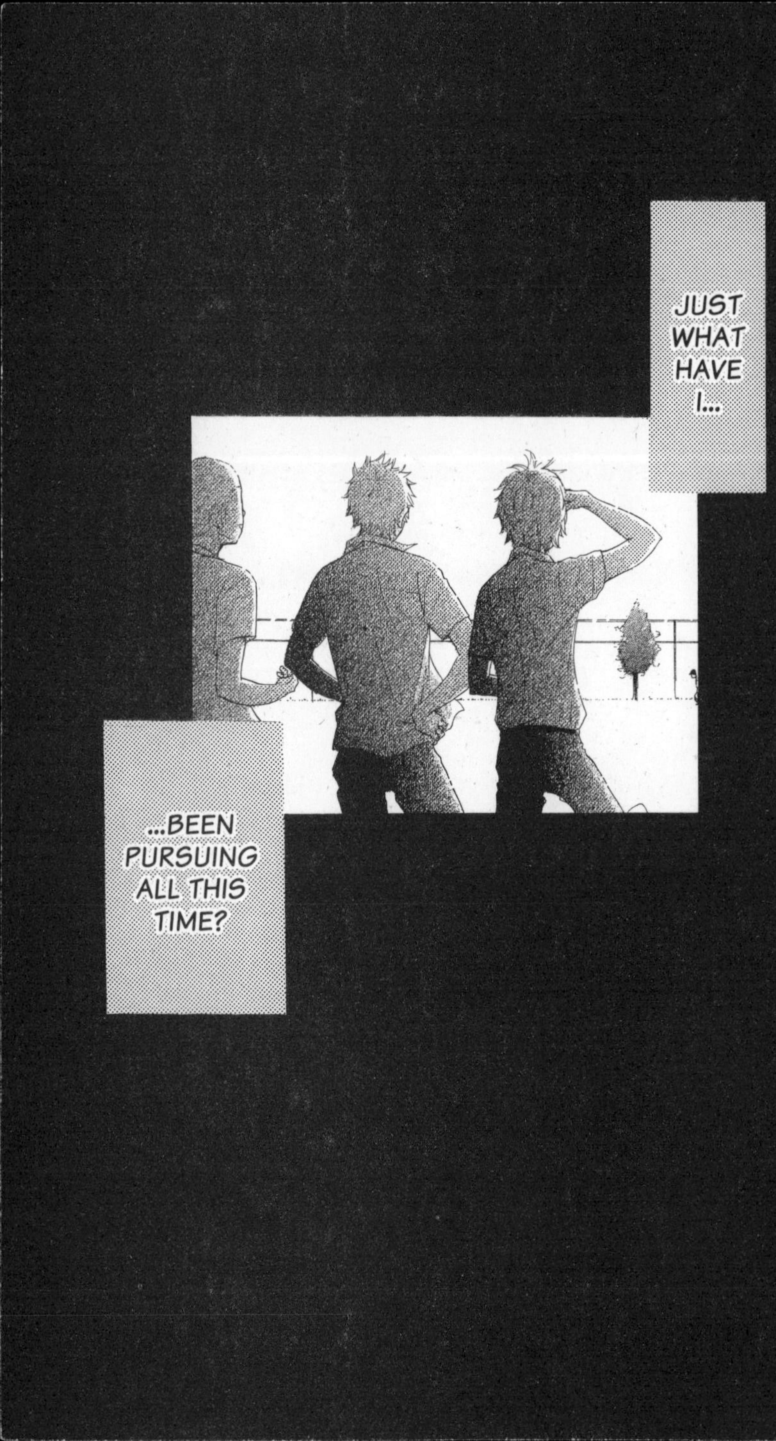
JUST WHAT HAVE I...
...BEEN PURSUING ALL THIS TIME?

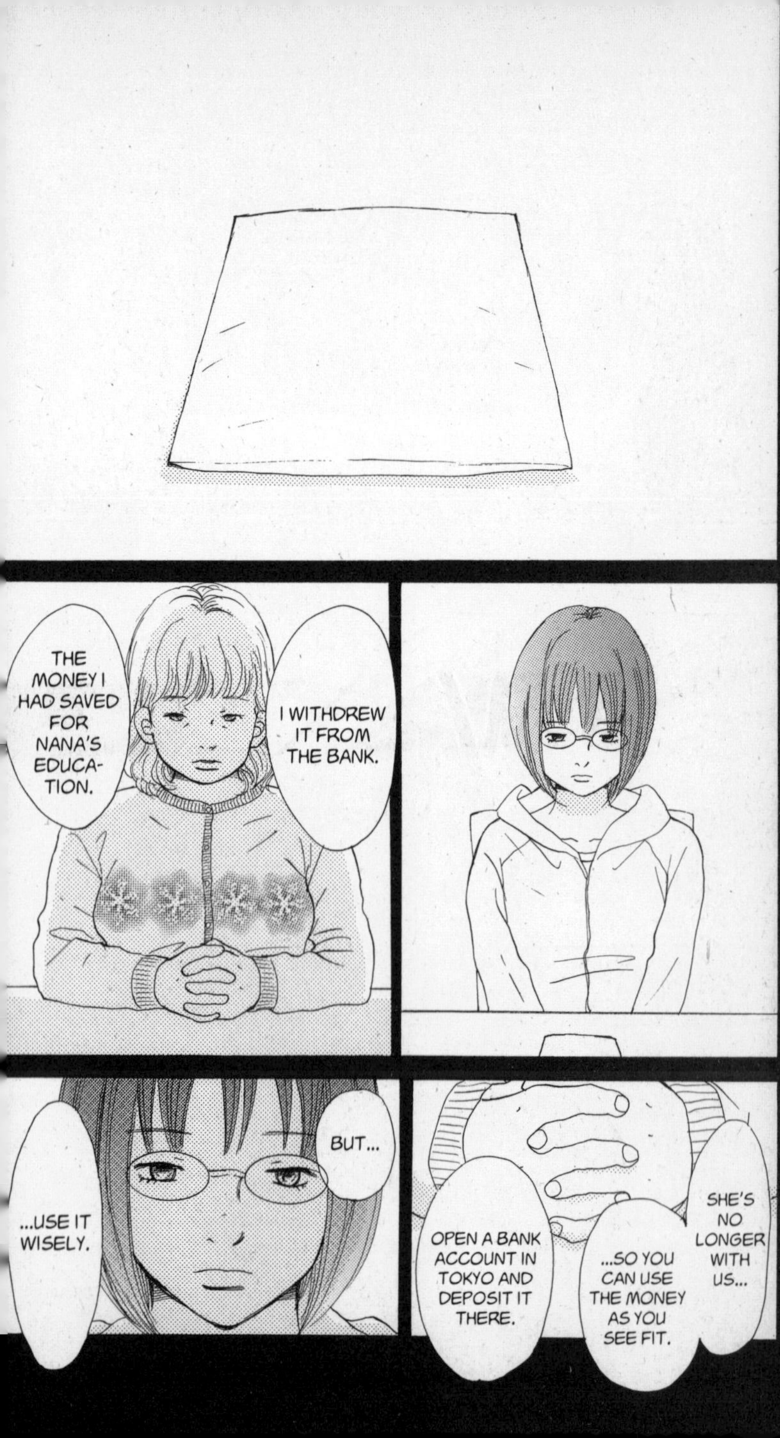
THE MONEY I HAD SAVED FOR NANA'S EDUCATION.
I WITHDREW IT FROM THE BANK.
SHE'S NO LONGER WITH US...
...SO YOU CAN USE THE MONEY AS YOU SEE FIT.
OPEN A BANK ACCOUNT IN TOKYO AND DEPOSIT IT THERE.
BUT...
...USE IT WISELY.

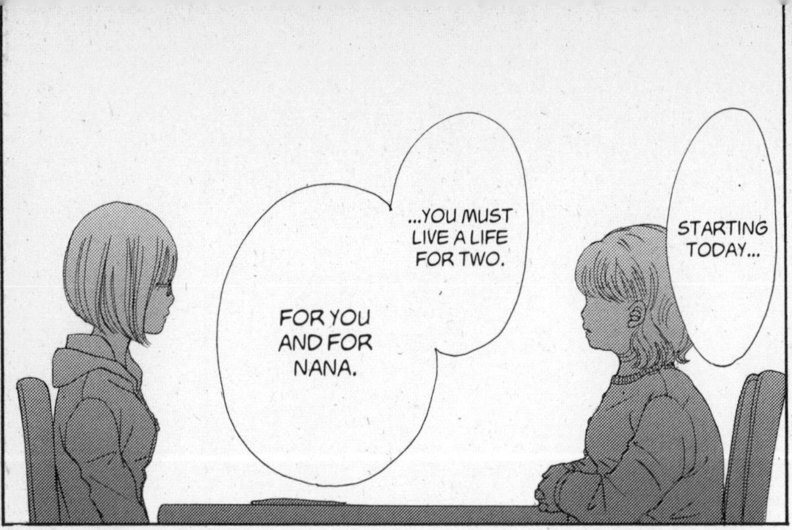
STARTING TODAY...
...YOU MUST LIVE A LIFE FOR TWO.
FOR YOU AND FOR NANA.

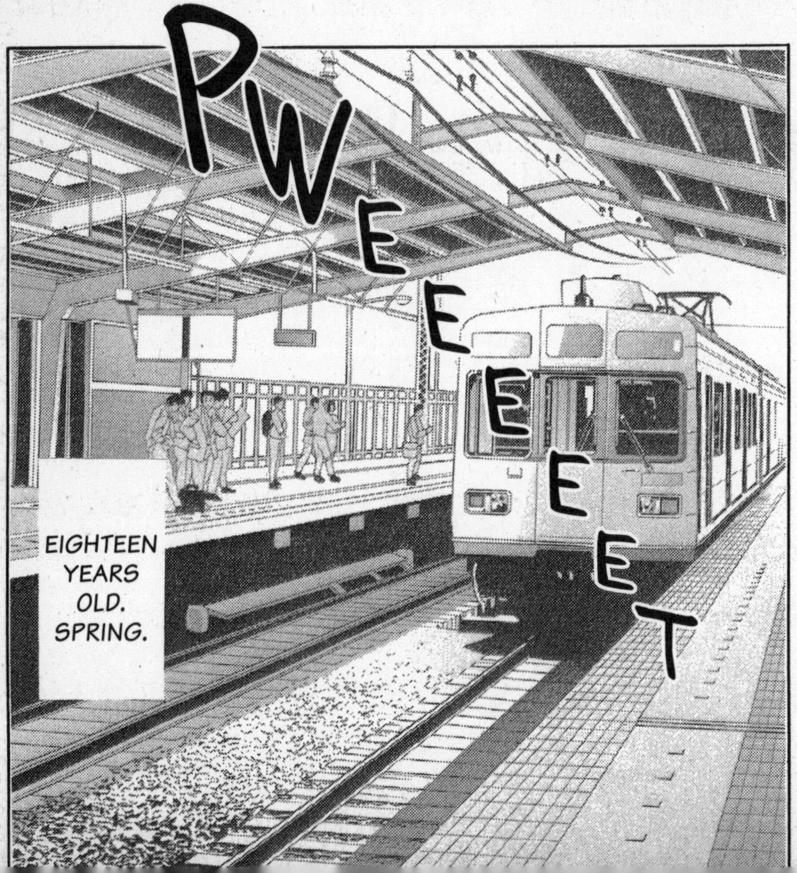
PWEEEEET
EIGHTEEN YEARS OLD. SPRING.

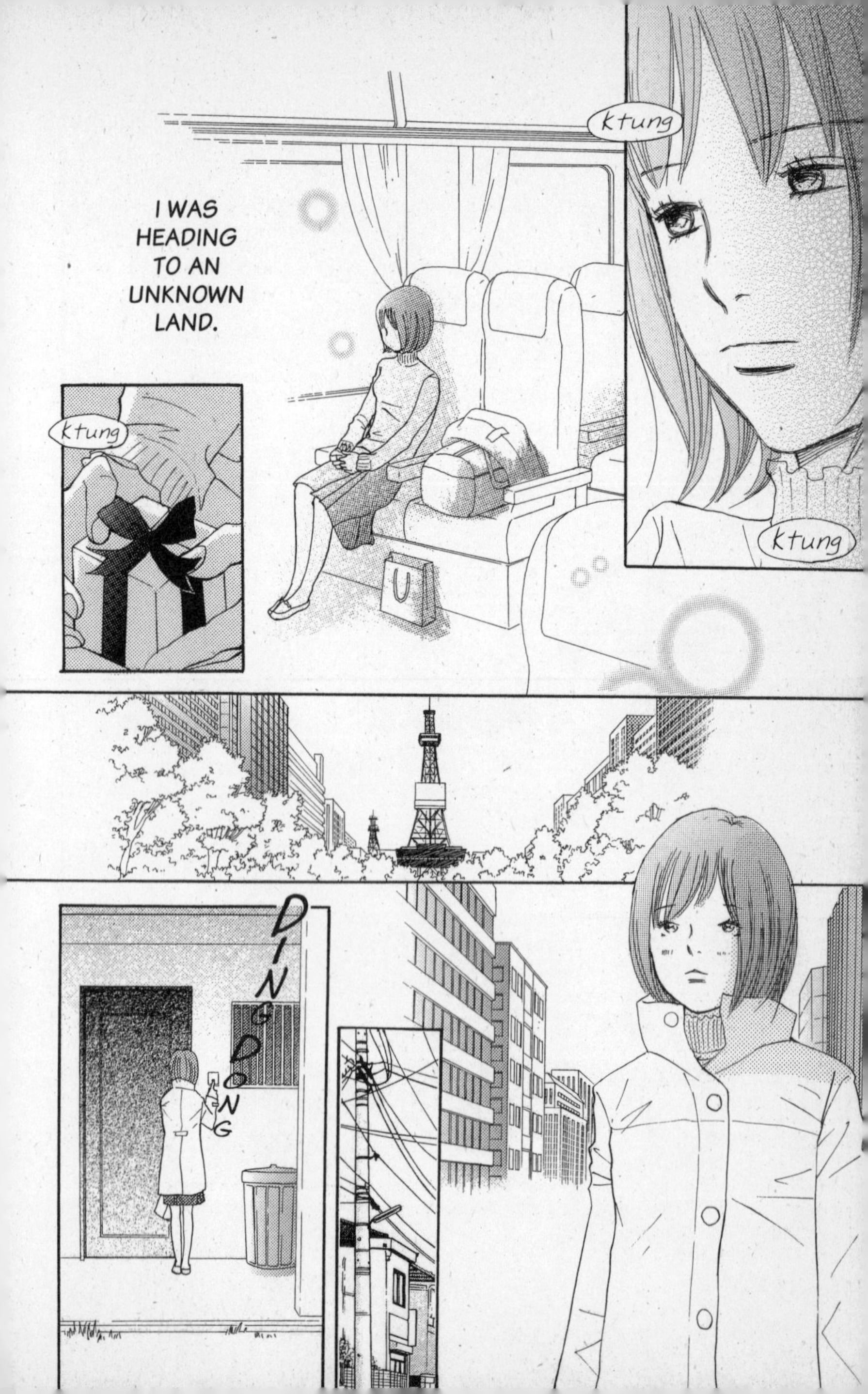
Ktung
Ktung
I WAS HEADING TO AN UNKNOWN LAND.
Ktung
DING DONG

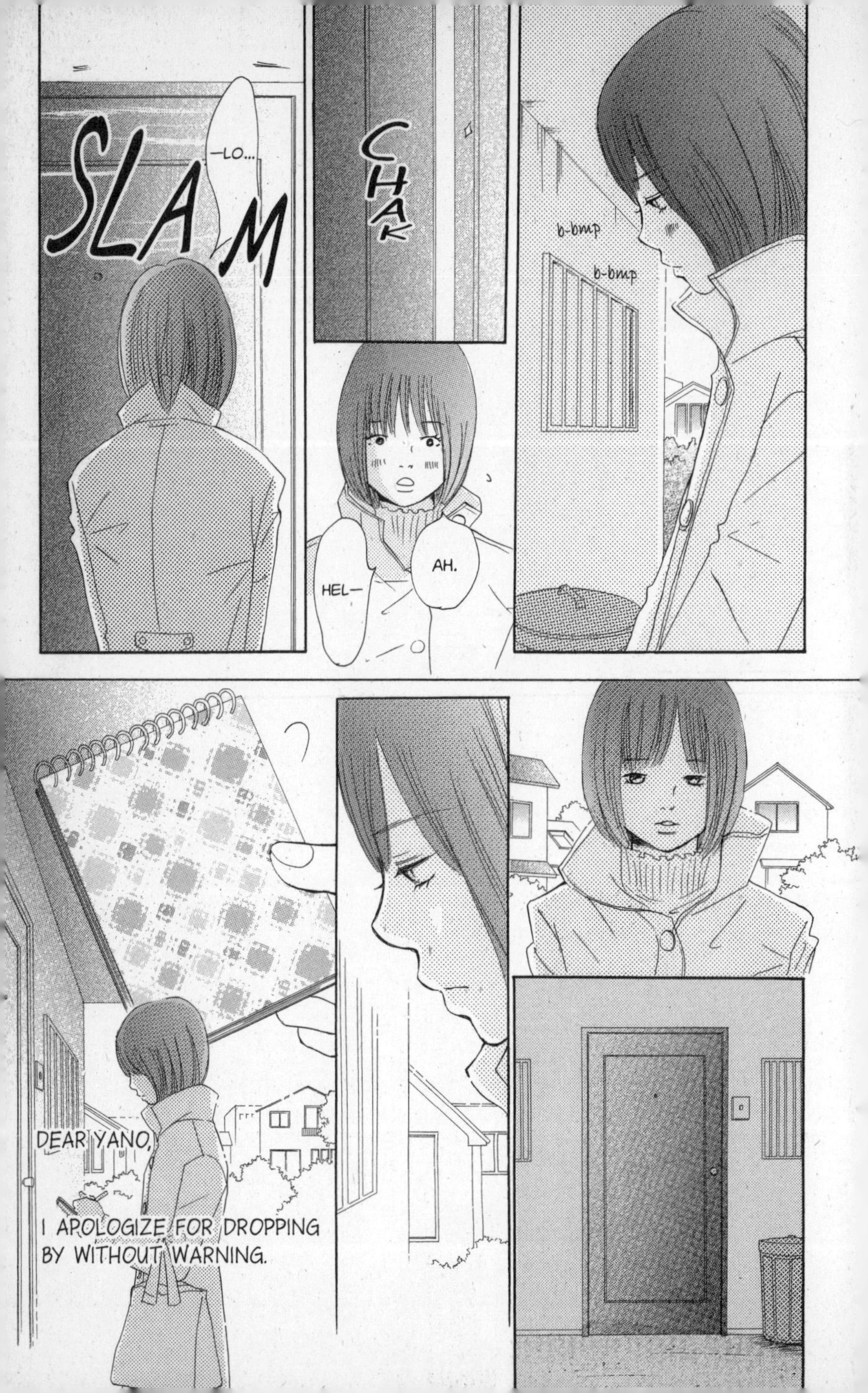
b-bmp
b-bmp
CHAK
AH.
HEL—
—LO...
SLAM
DEAR YANO,
I APOLOGIZE FOR DROPPING BY WITHOUT WARNING.

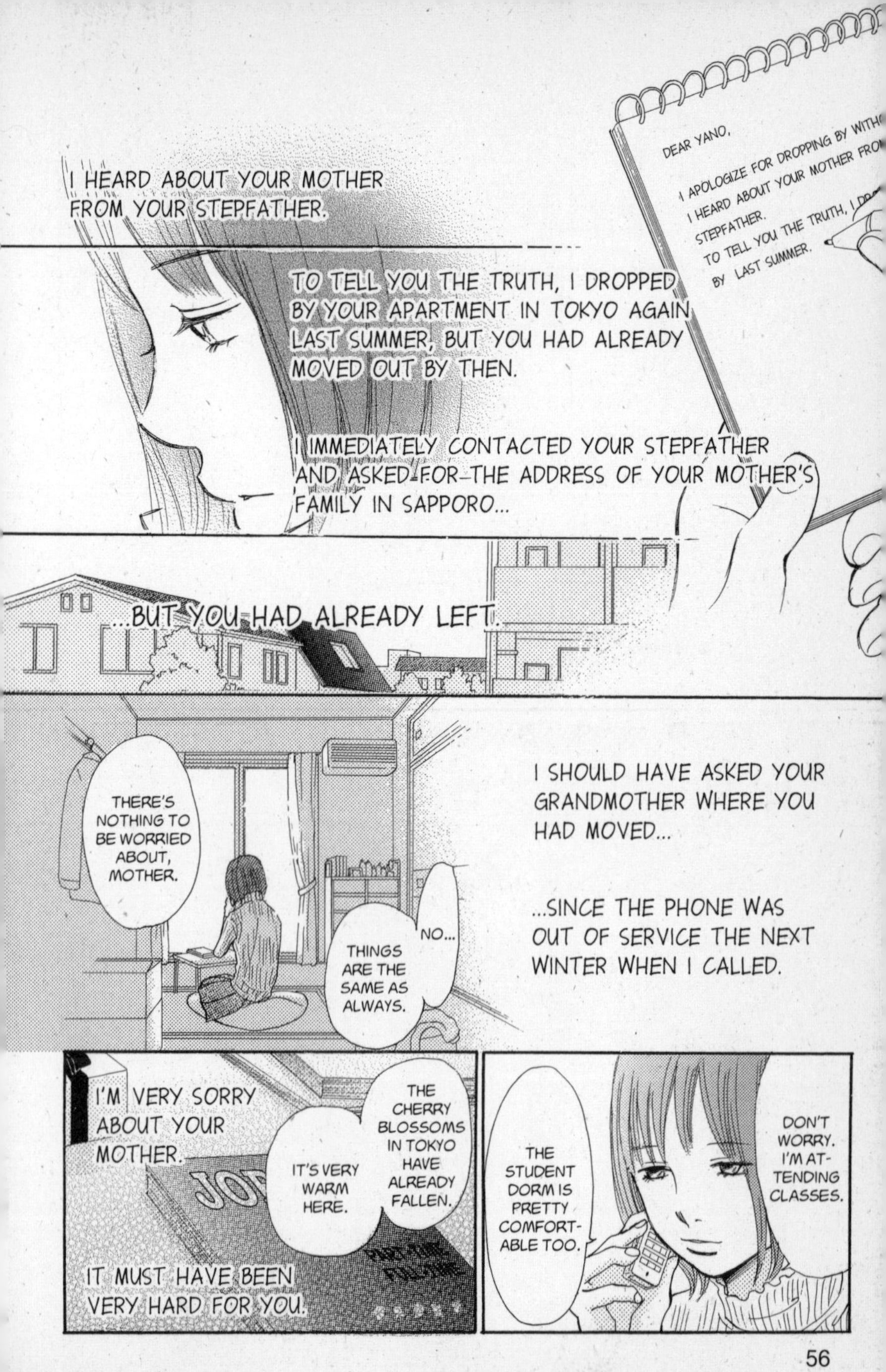
DEAR YANO,
I APOLOGIZE FOR DROPPING BY WITH
I HEARD ABOUT YOUR MOTHER FRO
STEPFATHER.
TO TELL YOU THE TRUTH, I
BY LAST SUMMER.
I HEARD ABOUT YOUR MOTHER FROM YOUR STEPFATHER.
TO TELL YOU THE TRUTH, I DROPPED BY YOUR APARTMENT IN TOKYO AGAIN LAST SUMMER, BUT YOU HAD ALREADY MOVED OUT BY THEN.
I IMMEDIATELY CONTACTED YOUR STEPFATHER AND ASKED FOR THE ADDRESS OF YOUR MOTHER'S FAMILY IN SAPPORO...
...BUT YOU HAD ALREADY LEFT.
I SHOULD HAVE ASKED YOUR GRANDMOTHER WHERE YOU HAD MOVED...
...SINCE THE PHONE WAS OUT OF SERVICE THE NEXT WINTER WHEN I CALLED.
NO... THINGS ARE THE SAME AS ALWAYS.
THERE'S NOTHING TO BE WORRIED ABOUT, MOTHER.
DON'T WORRY. I'M ATTENDING CLASSES.
THE STUDENT DORM IS PRETTY COMFORTABLE TOO.
THE CHERRY BLOSSOMS IN TOKYO HAVE ALREADY FALLEN.
IT'S VERY WARM HERE.
I'M VERY SORRY ABOUT YOUR MOTHER.
IT MUST HAVE BEEN VERY HARD FOR YOU.

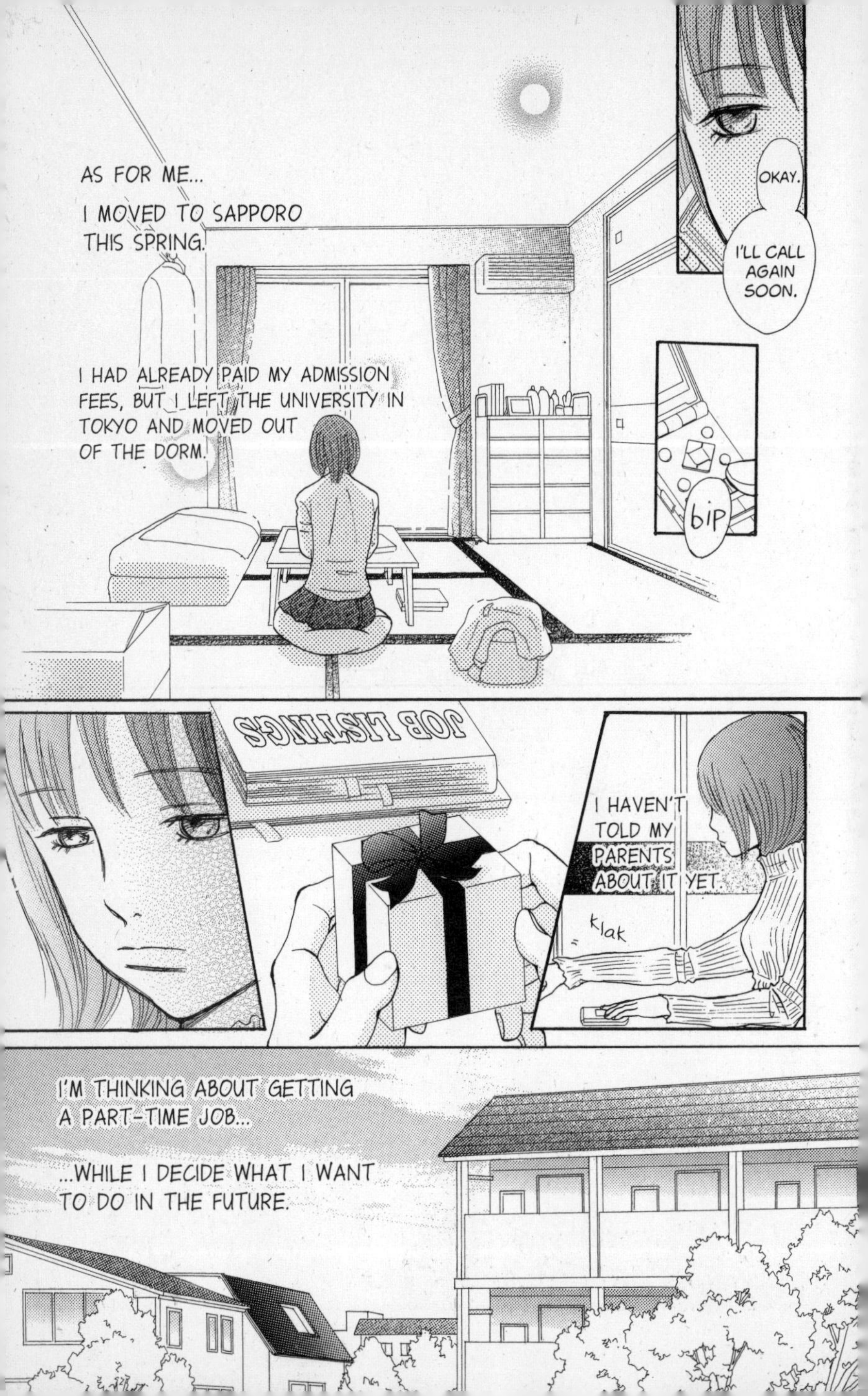
OKAY.
I'LL CALL AGAIN SOON.
bip
AS FOR ME...
I MOVED TO SAPPORO THIS SPRING.
I HAD ALREADY PAID MY ADMISSION FEES, BUT I LEFT THE UNIVERSITY IN TOKYO AND MOVED OUT OF THE DORM.
I HAVEN'T TOLD MY PARENTS ABOUT IT YET.
klak
JOB LISTINGS
I'M THINKING ABOUT GETTING A PART-TIME JOB...
...WHILE I DECIDE WHAT I WANT TO DO IN THE FUTURE.

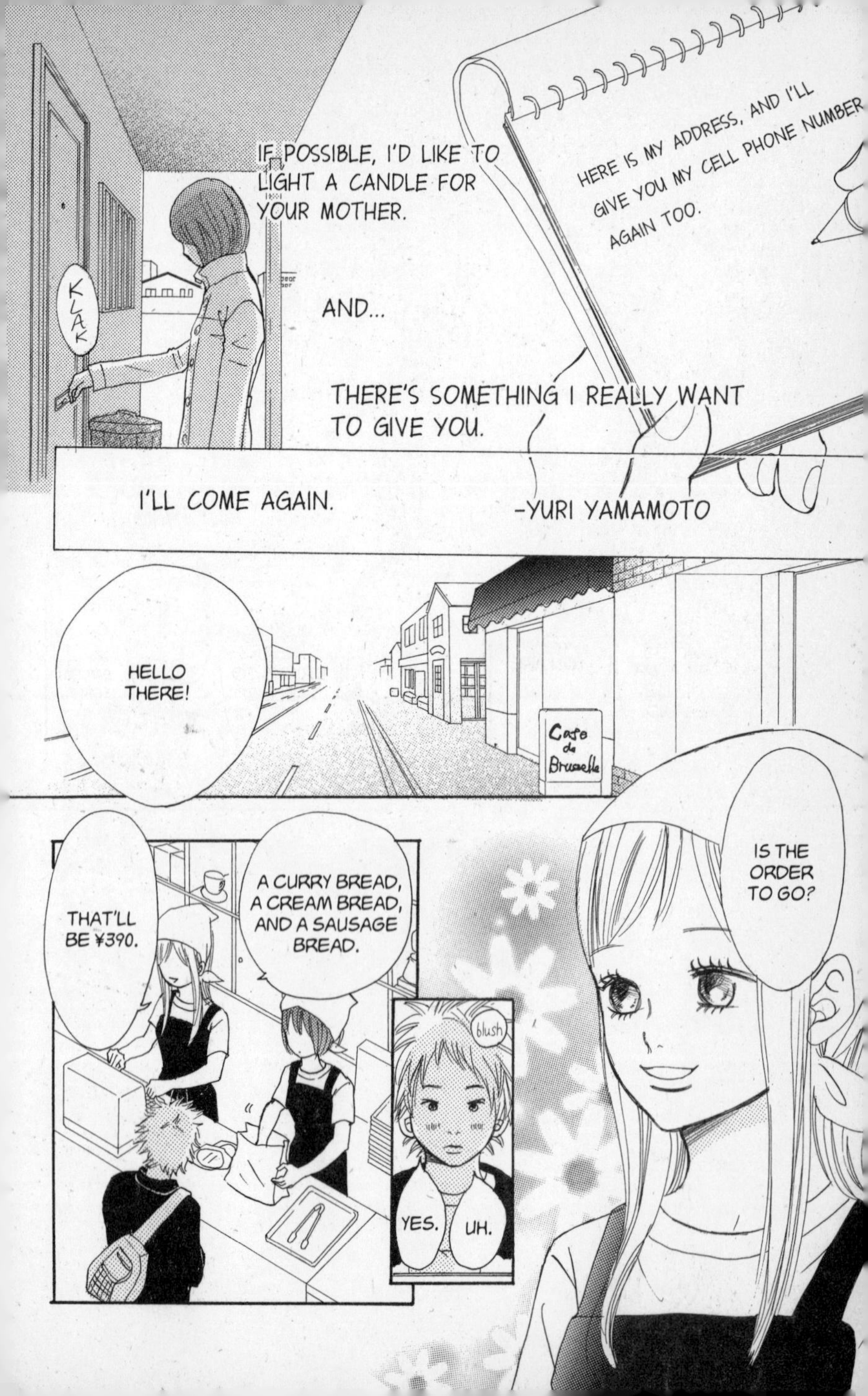
HERE IS MY ADDRESS, AND I'LL GIVE YOU MY CELL PHONE NUMBER AGAIN TOO.
IF POSSIBLE, I'D LIKE TO LIGHT A CANDLE FOR YOUR MOTHER.
KLAK
AND...
THERE'S SOMETHING I REALLY WANT TO GIVE YOU.
I'LL COME AGAIN. -YURI YAMAMOTO
Cafe de Bruxelle
HELLO THERE!
IS THE ORDER TO GO?
blush
UH.
YES.
A CURRY BREAD, A CREAM BREAD, AND A SAUSAGE BREAD.
THAT'LL BE ¥390.

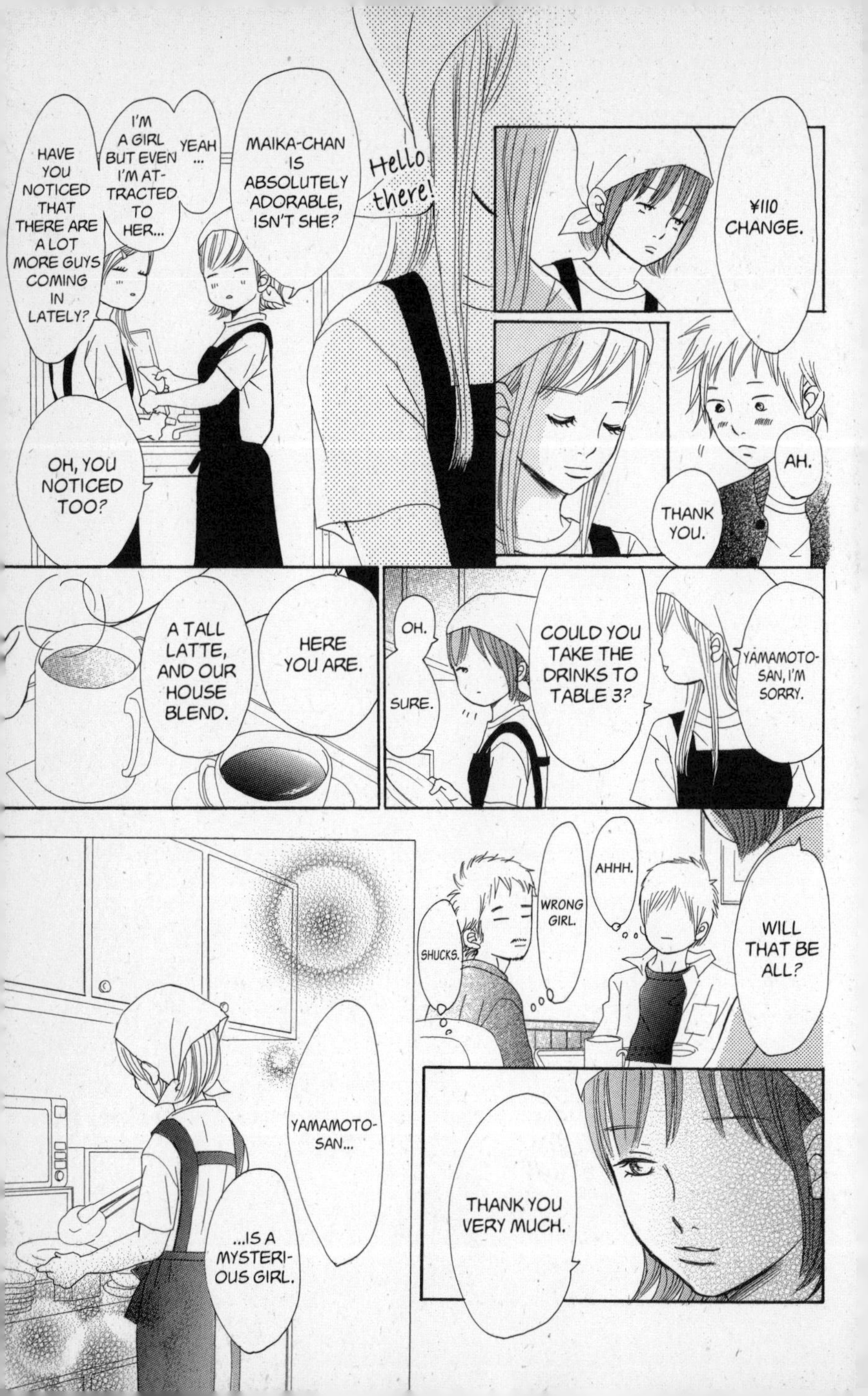
¥110 CHANGE.
AH.
THANK YOU.
Hello there!
MAIKA-CHAN IS ABSOLUTELY ADORABLE, ISN'T SHE?
YEAH...
I'M A GIRL BUT EVEN I'M ATTRACTED TO HER...
HAVE YOU NOTICED THAT THERE ARE A LOT MORE GUYS COMING IN LATELY?
OH, YOU NOTICED TOO?
YAMAMOTO-SAN, I'M SORRY.
COULD YOU TAKE THE DRINKS TO TABLE 3?
OH.
SURE.
HERE YOU ARE.
A TALL LATTE, AND OUR HOUSE BLEND.
WILL THAT BE ALL?
AHHH.
WRONG GIRL.
SHUCKS.
THANK YOU VERY MUCH.
YAMAMOTO-SAN...
...IS A MYSTERIOUS GIRL.

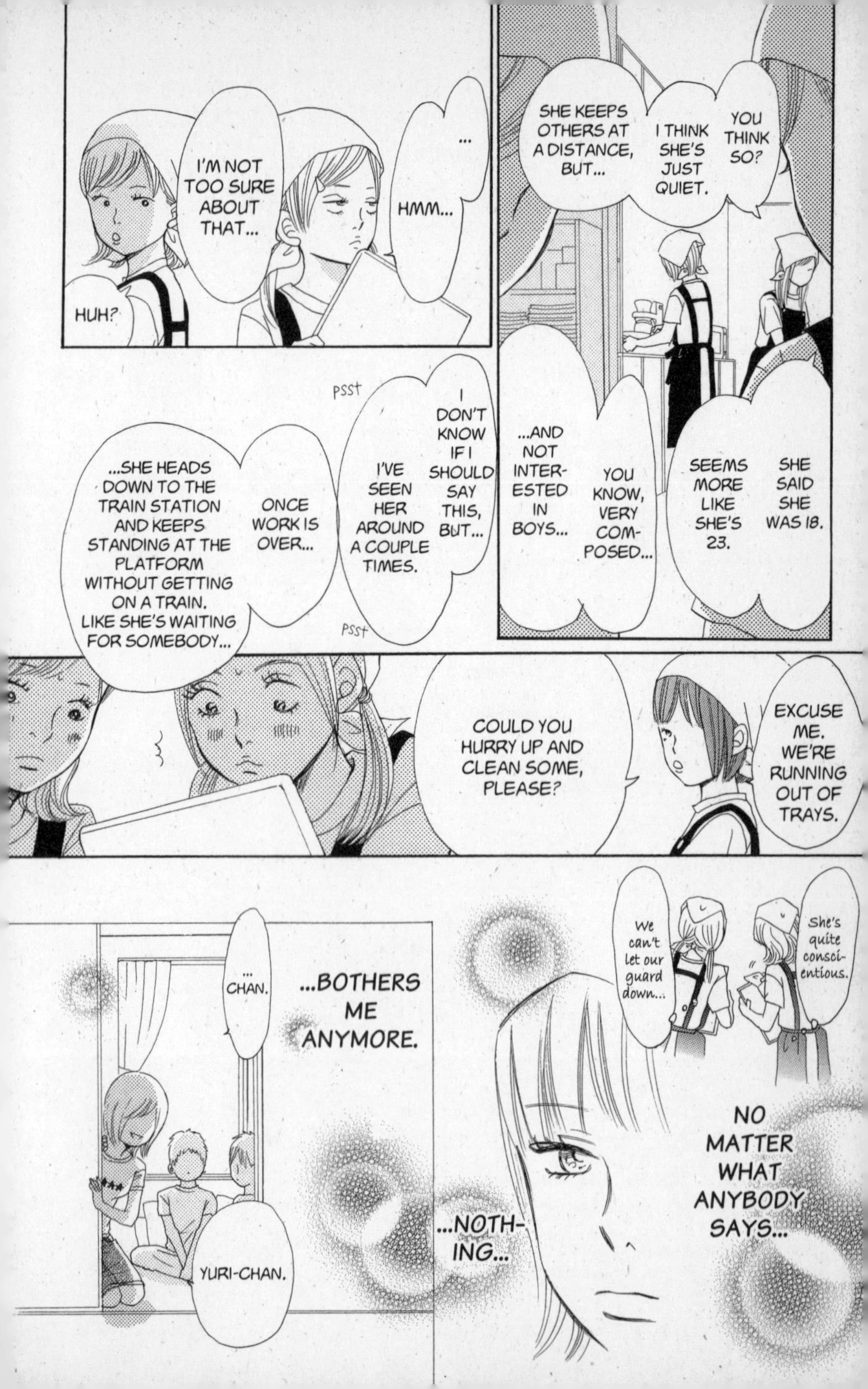
YOU THINK SO?
I THINK SHE'S JUST QUIET.
SHE KEEPS OTHERS AT A DISTANCE, BUT...
SHE SAID SHE WAS 18.
SEEMS MORE LIKE SHE'S 23.
YOU KNOW, VERY COMPOSED...
...AND NOT INTERESTED IN BOYS...
...
HMM...
I'M NOT TOO SURE ABOUT THAT...
HUH?
psst
I DON'T KNOW IF I SHOULD SAY THIS, BUT...
I'VE SEEN HER AROUND A COUPLE TIMES.
ONCE WORK IS OVER...
...SHE HEADS DOWN TO THE TRAIN STATION AND KEEPS STANDING AT THE PLATFORM WITHOUT GETTING ON A TRAIN. LIKE SHE'S WAITING FOR SOMEBODY...
psst
EXCUSE ME. WE'RE RUNNING OUT OF TRAYS.
COULD YOU HURRY UP AND CLEAN SOME, PLEASE?
She's quite conscientious.
We can't let our guard down...
NO MATTER WHAT ANYBODY SAYS...
...NOTHING...
...BOTHERS ME ANYMORE.
...CHAN.
YURI-CHAN.

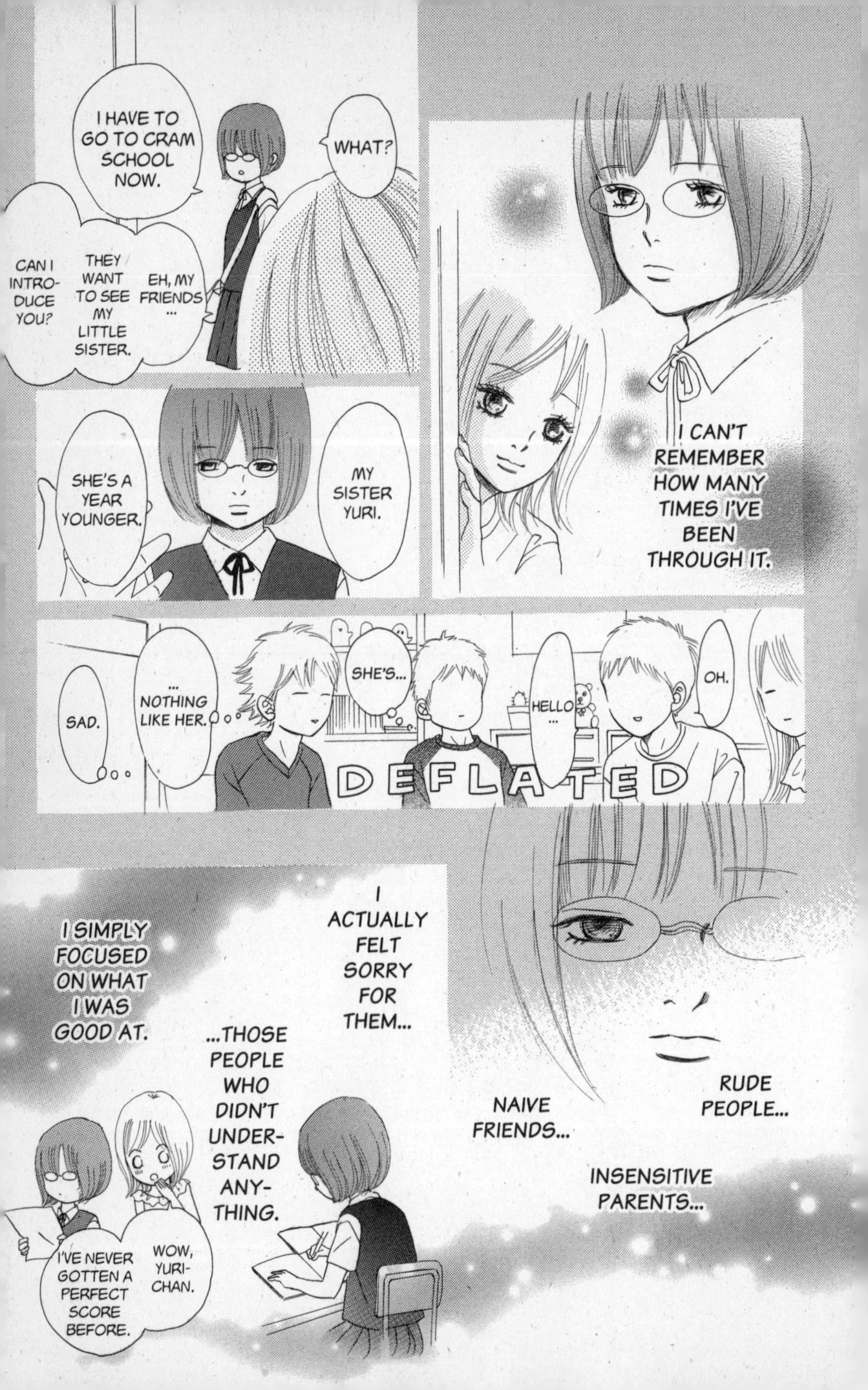
I CAN'T REMEMBER HOW MANY TIMES I'VE BEEN THROUGH IT.
WHAT?
I HAVE TO GO TO CRAM SCHOOL NOW.
EH, MY FRIENDS ...
THEY WANT TO SEE MY LITTLE SISTER.
CAN I INTRO-DUCE YOU?
MY SISTER YURI.
SHE'S A YEAR YOUNGER.
OH.
HELLO ...
SHE'S...
... NOTHING LIKE HER.
SAD.
DEFLATED
RUDE PEOPLE...
NAIVE FRIENDS...
INSENSITIVE PARENTS...
I ACTUALLY FELT SORRY FOR THEM...
...THOSE PEOPLE WHO DIDN'T UNDER-STAND ANY-THING.
I SIMPLY FOCUSED ON WHAT I WAS GOOD AT.
WOW, YURI-CHAN.
I'VE NEVER GOTTEN A PERFECT SCORE BEFORE.

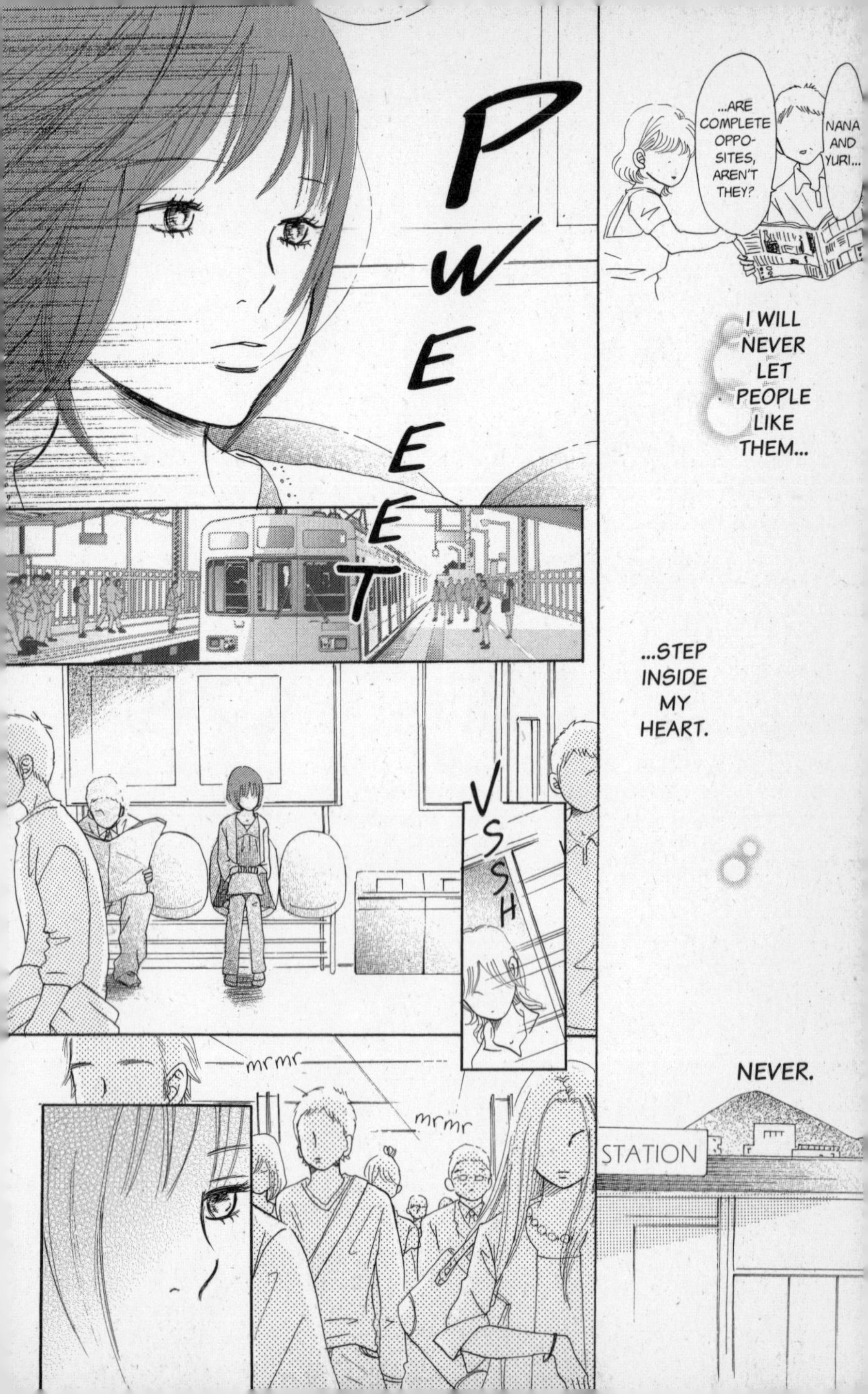
NANA AND YURI...
...ARE COMPLETE OPPO-SITES, AREN'T THEY?
I WILL NEVER LET PEOPLE LIKE THEM...
...STEP INSIDE MY HEART.
NEVER.
STATION
PWEEEET
VSSH
mrmr
mrmr

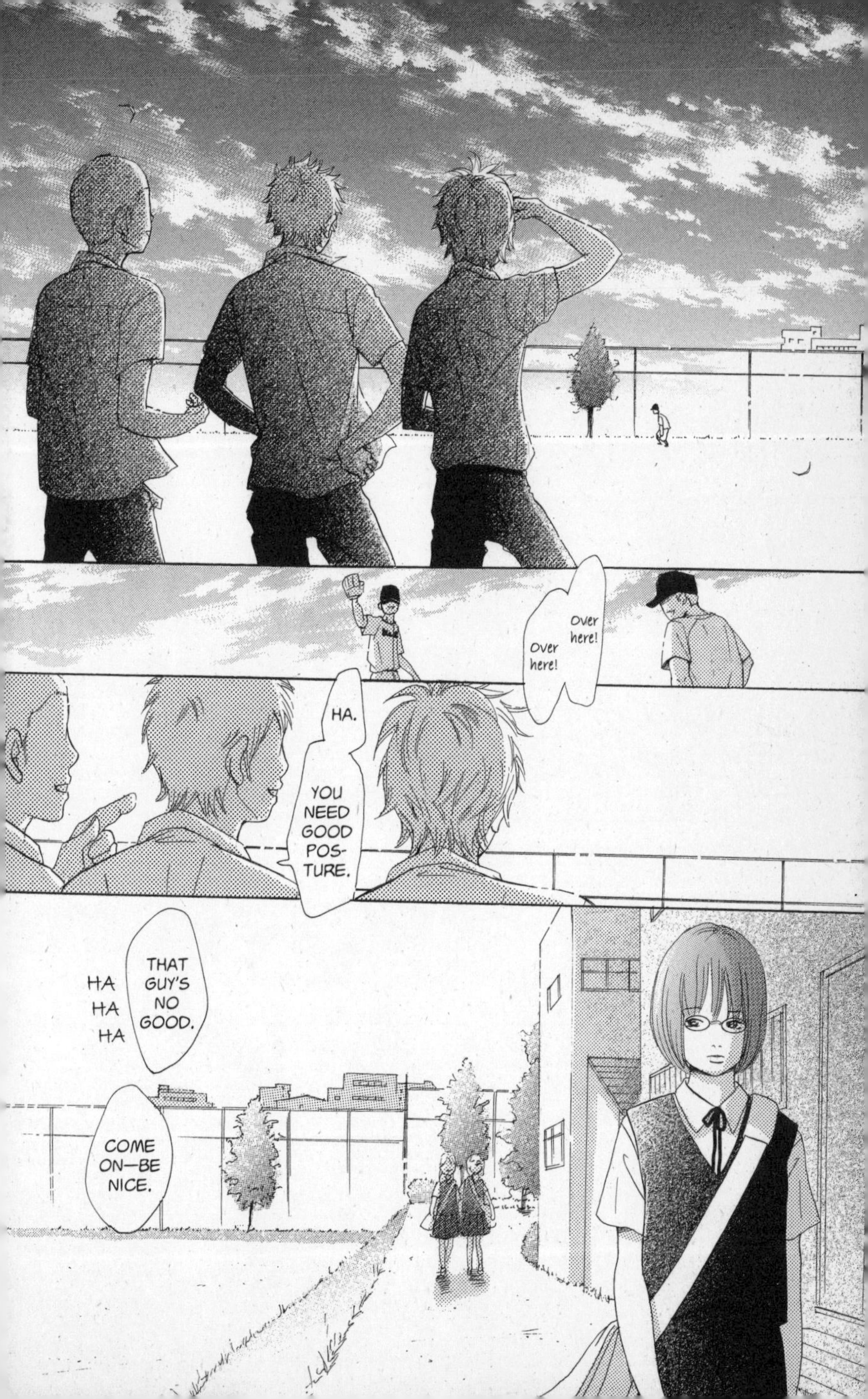
Over here! Over here!
HA.
YOU NEED GOOD POS-TURE.
THAT GUY'S NO GOOD.
HA HA HA
COME ON—BE NICE.

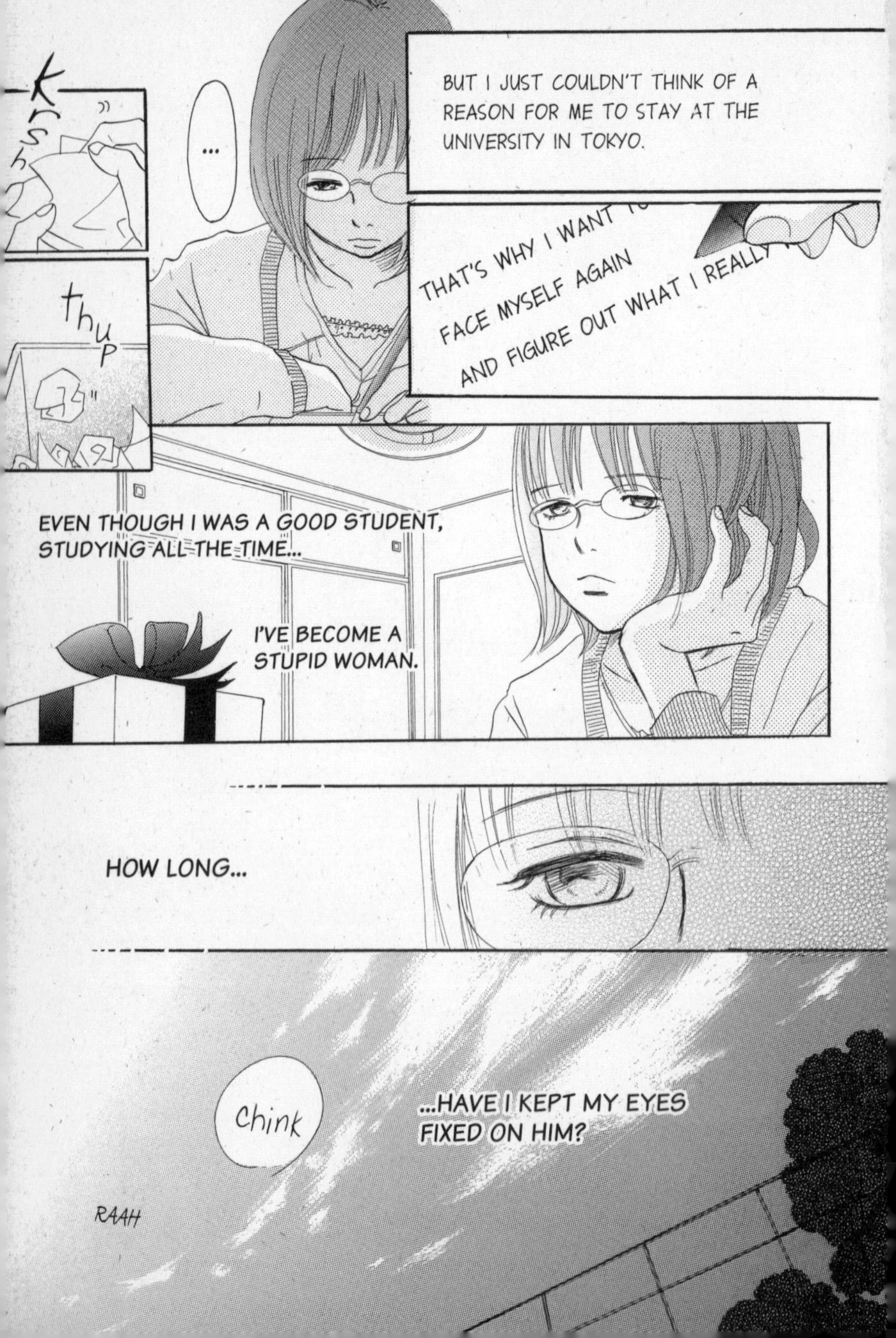
BUT I JUST COULDN'T THINK OF A REASON FOR ME TO STAY AT THE UNIVERSITY IN TOKYO.
THAT'S WHY I WANT
FACE MYSELF AGAIN
AND FIGURE OUT WHAT I REALL
...
Krsh
thup
EVEN THOUGH I WAS A GOOD STUDENT, STUDYING ALL THE TIME...
I'VE BECOME A STUPID WOMAN.
HOW LONG...
...HAVE I KEPT MY EYES FIXED ON HIM?
Chink
RAAH

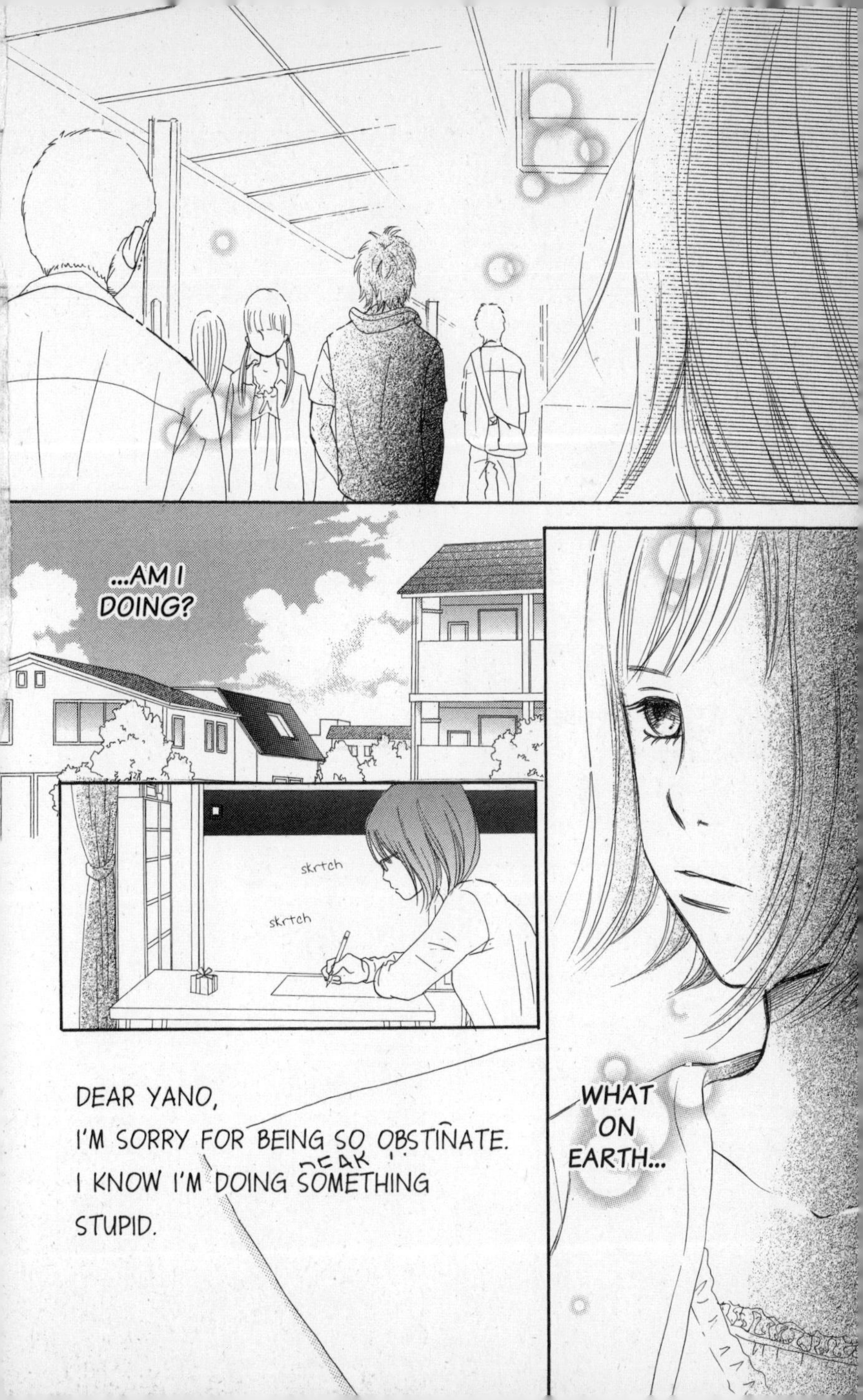
WHAT ON EARTH...
...AM I DOING?
skrtch
skrtch
DEAR YANO,
I'M SORRY FOR BEING SO OBSTINATE.
I KNOW I'M DOING SOMETHING
STUPID.

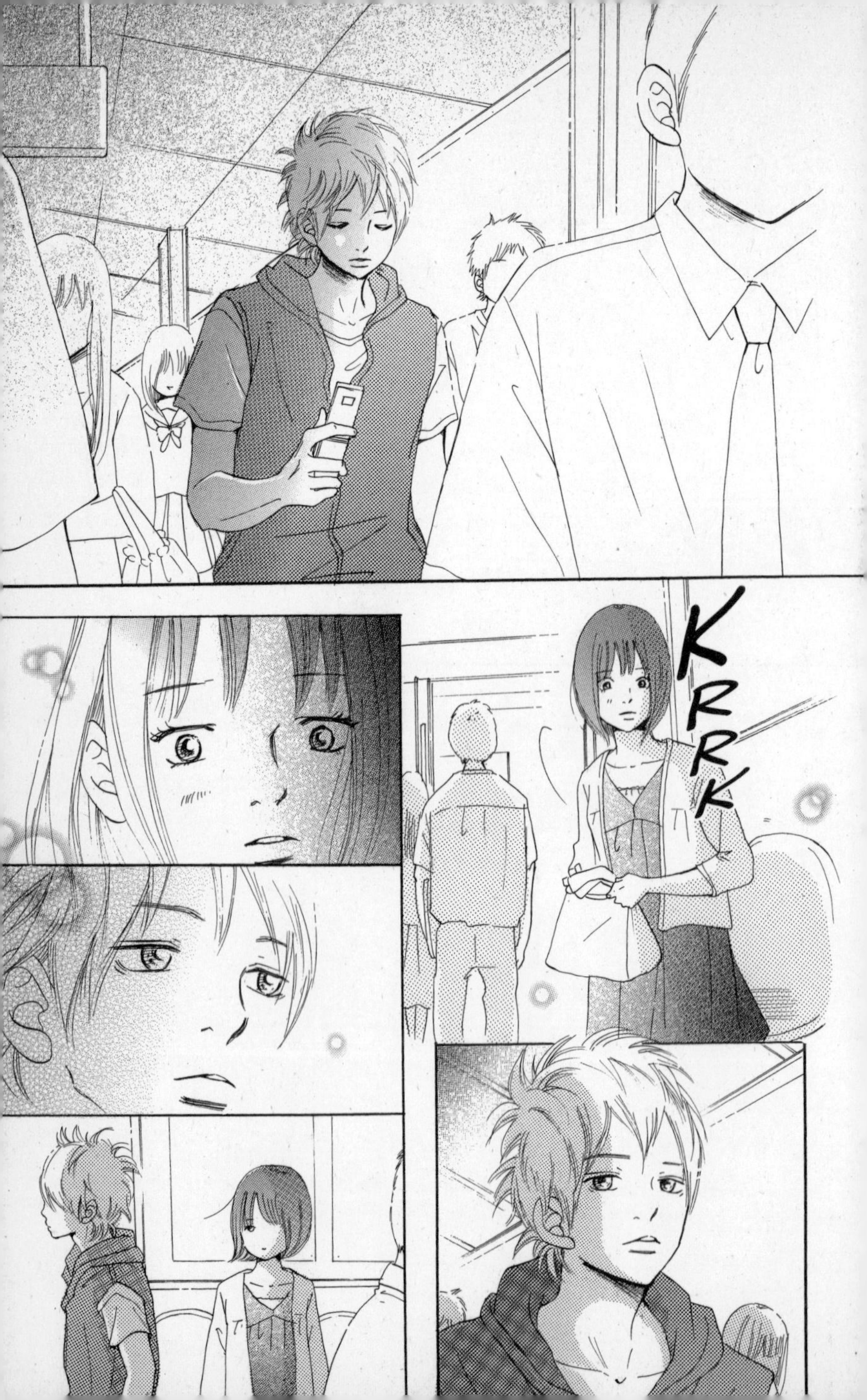
KRRRK

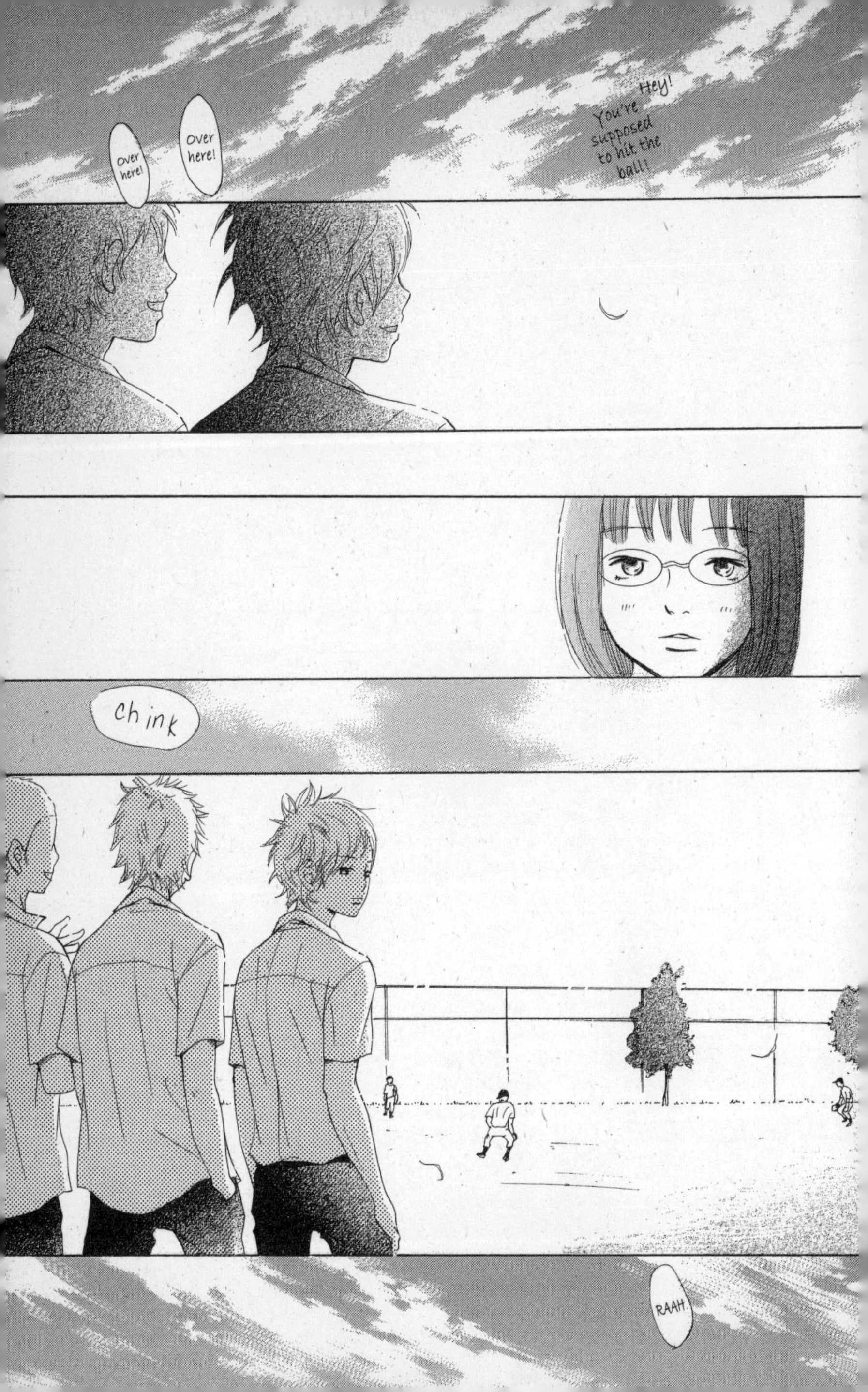
Hey! You're supposed to hit the ball!
Over here!
Over here!
Chink
RAAH.

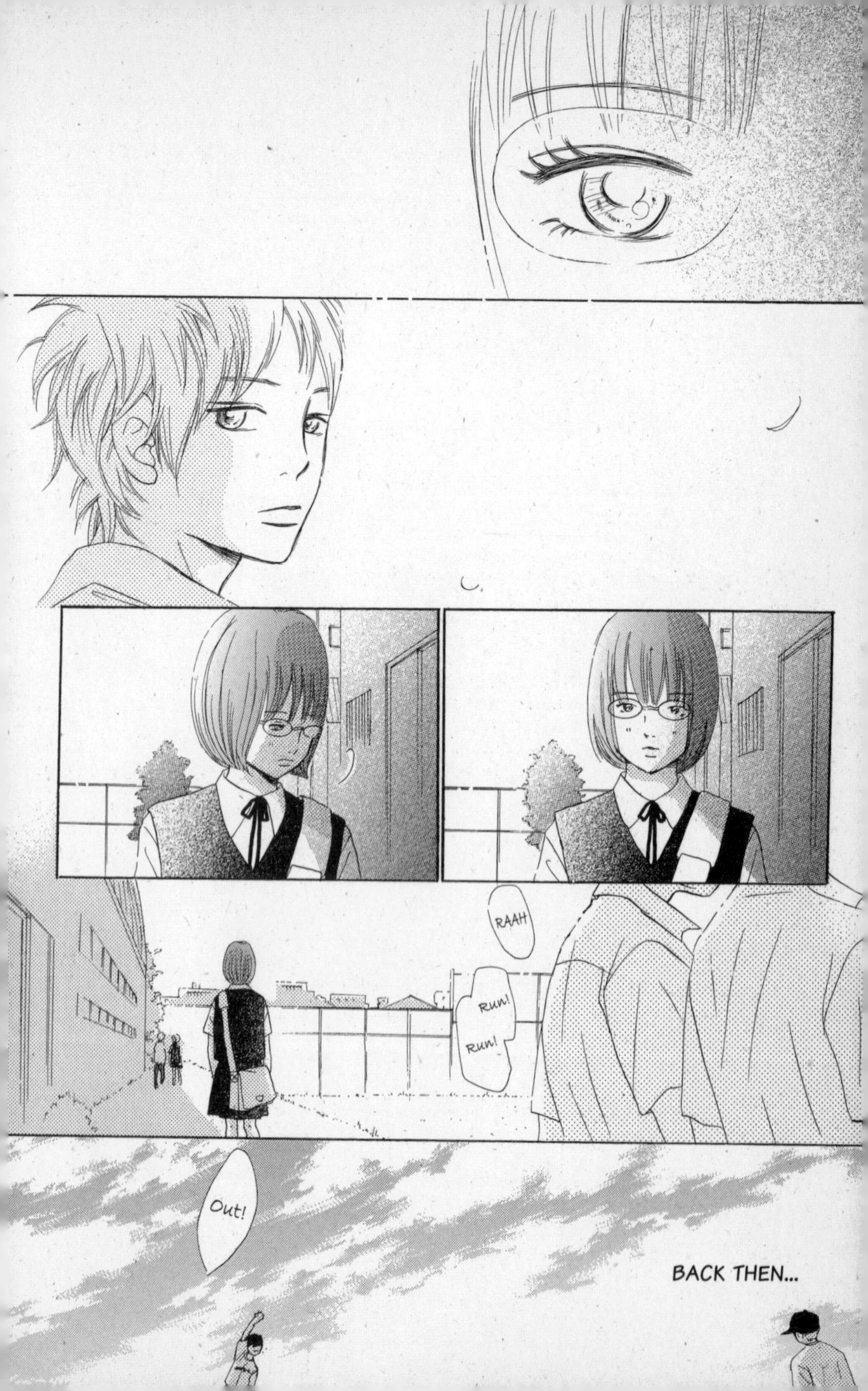
RAAH
Run! Run!
BACK THEN...
Out!

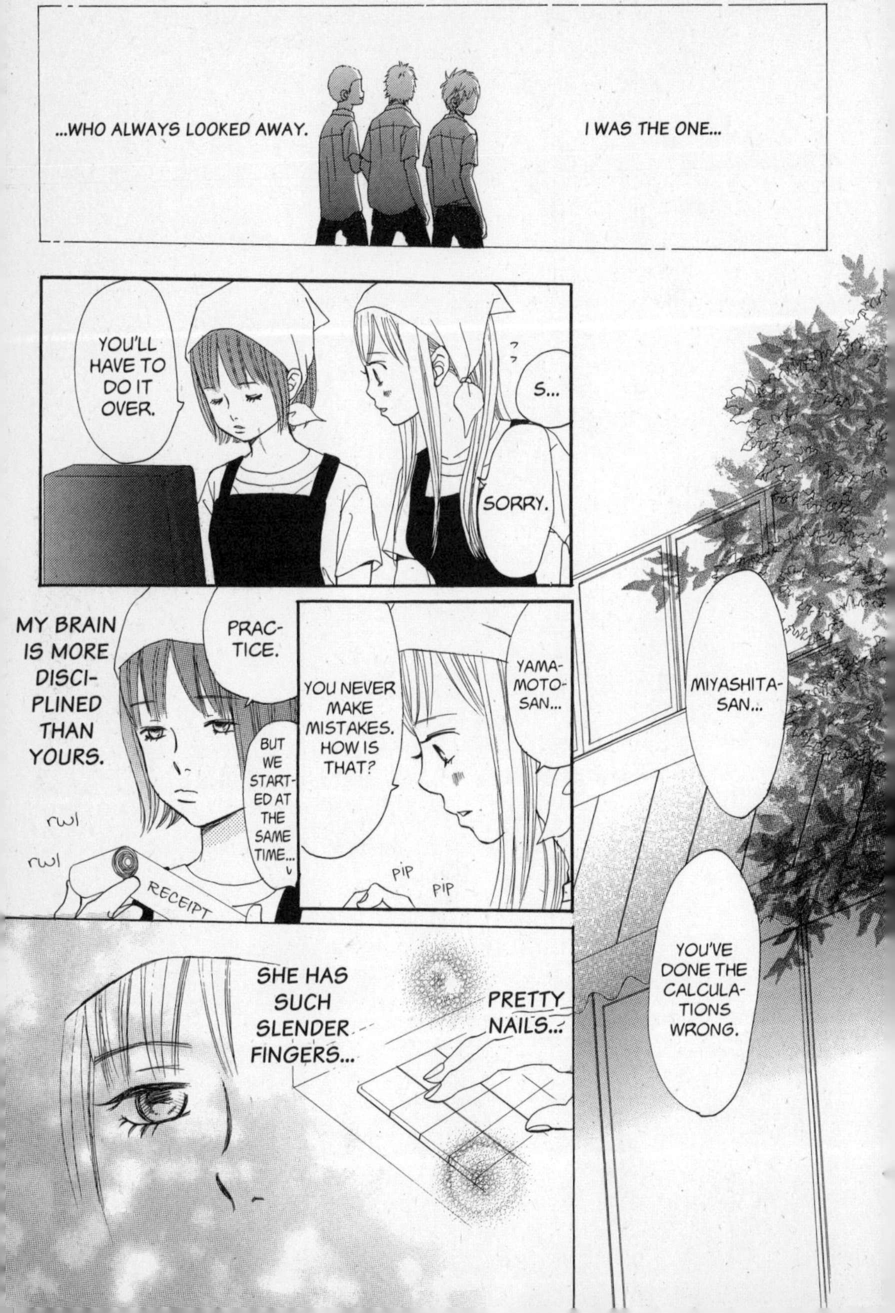

I WAS THE ONE...
...WHO ALWAYS LOOKED AWAY.
MIYASHITA-SAN...
YOU'VE DONE THE CALCULATIONS WRONG.
S...
SORRY.
YOU'LL HAVE TO DO IT OVER.
YAMAMOTO-SAN...
YOU NEVER MAKE MISTAKES. HOW IS THAT?
BUT WE STARTED AT THE SAME TIME...
PIP
PIP
PRACTICE.
MY BRAIN IS MORE DISCIPLINED THAN YOURS.
RWL
RWL
RECEIPT
PRETTY NAILS...
SHE HAS SUCH SLENDER FINGERS...

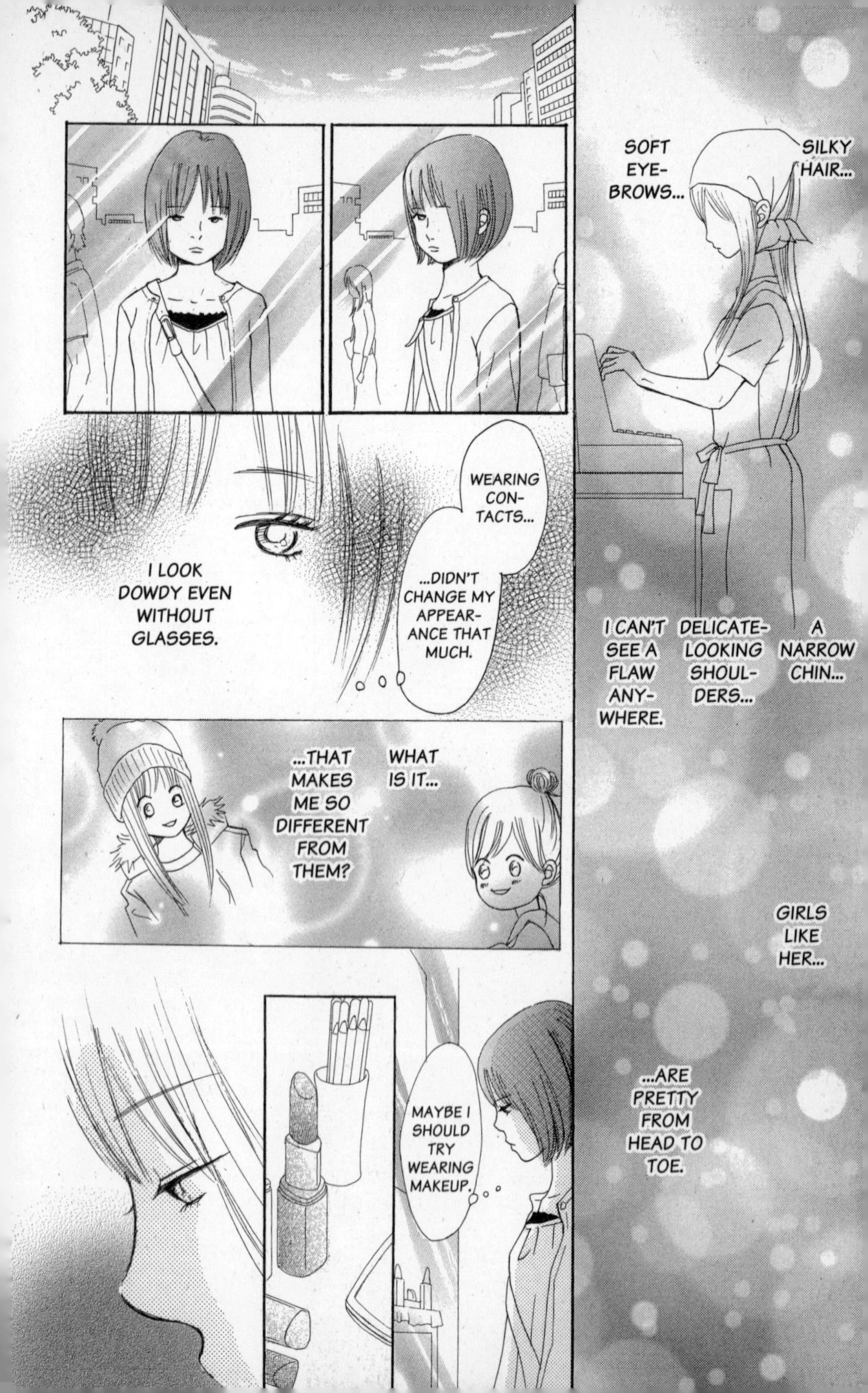
SILKY HAIR...
SOFT EYE-BROWS...
A NARROW CHIN...
DELICATE-LOOKING SHOULDERS...
I CAN'T SEE A FLAW ANYWHERE.
GIRLS LIKE HER...
...ARE PRETTY FROM HEAD TO TOE.
WEARING CONTACTS...
...DIDN'T CHANGE MY APPEARANCE THAT MUCH.
I LOOK DOWDY EVEN WITHOUT GLASSES.
WHAT IS IT...
...THAT MAKES ME SO DIFFERENT FROM THEM?
MAYBE I SHOULD TRY WEARING MAKEUP.

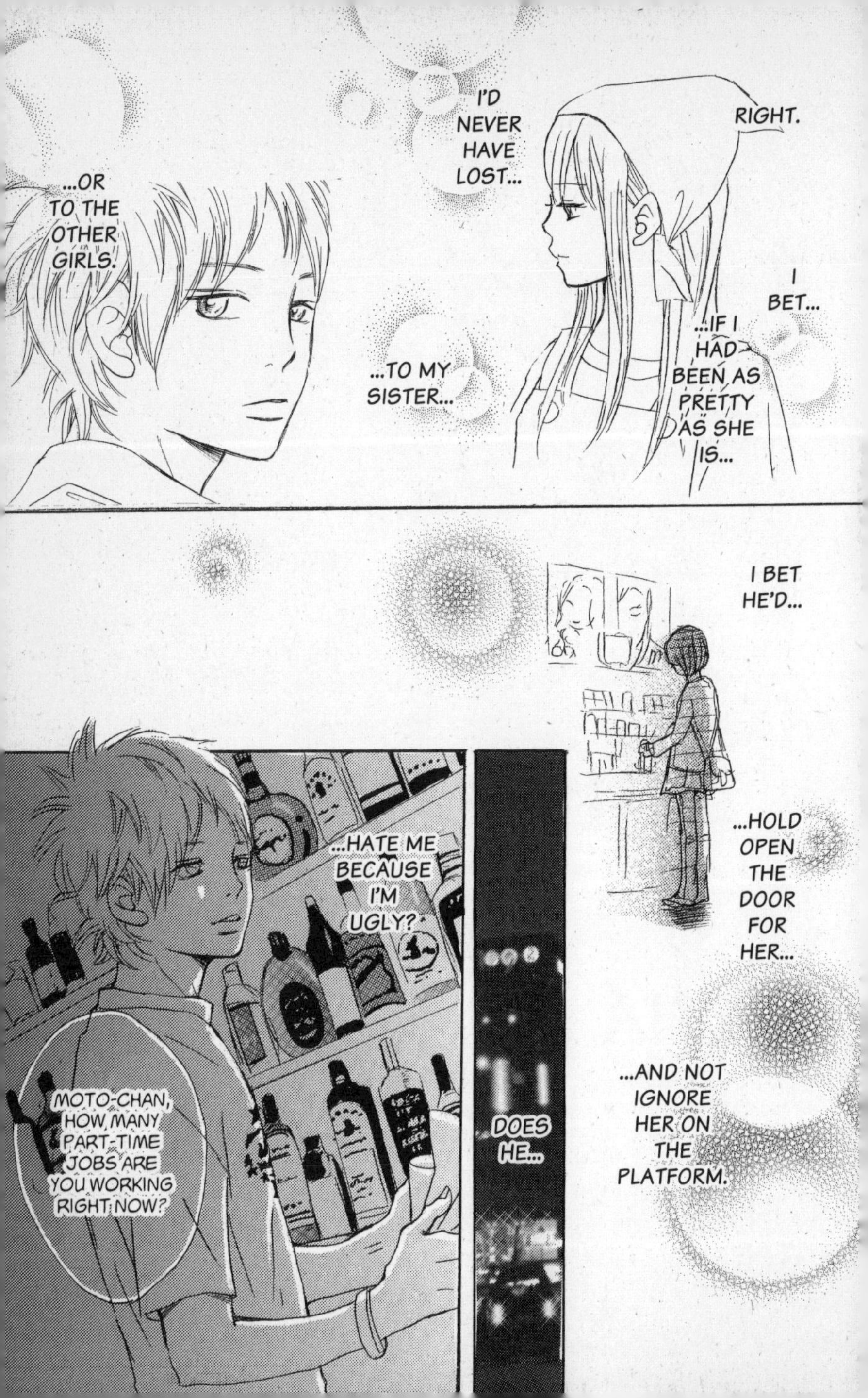
RIGHT.
I BET...
...IF I HAD BEEN AS PRETTY AS SHE IS...
I'D NEVER HAVE LOST...
...TO MY SISTER...
...OR TO THE OTHER GIRLS.
I BET HE'D...
...HOLD OPEN THE DOOR FOR HER...
...AND NOT IGNORE HER ON THE PLATFORM.
DOES HE...
...HATE ME BECAUSE I'M UGLY?
MOTO-CHAN, HOW MANY PART-TIME JOBS ARE YOU WORKING RIGHT NOW?

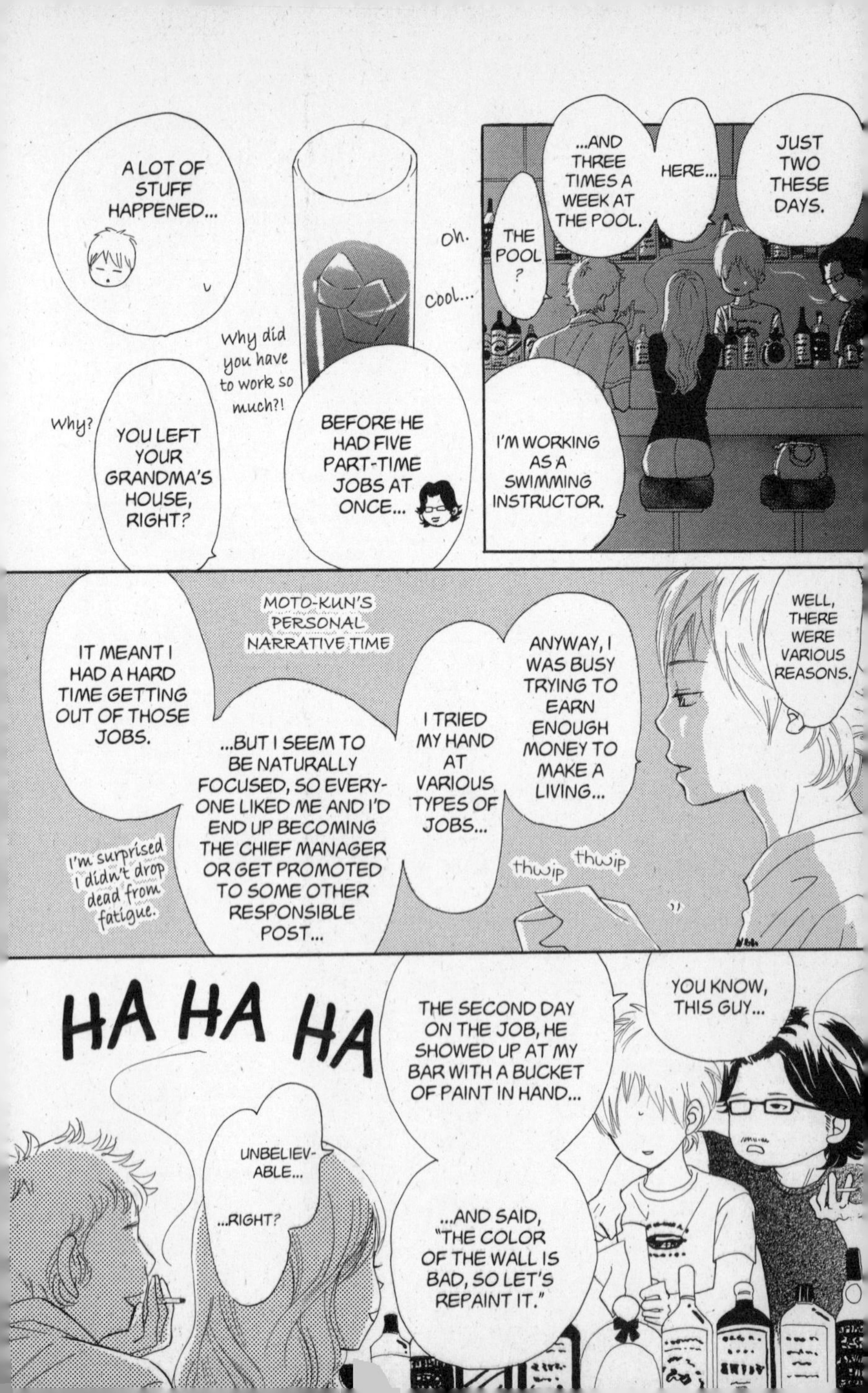
JUST TWO THESE DAYS.
HERE...
...AND THREE TIMES A WEEK AT THE POOL.
THE POOL?
I'M WORKING AS A SWIMMING INSTRUCTOR.
Oh.
cool...
BEFORE HE HAD FIVE PART-TIME JOBS AT ONCE...
Why did you have to work so much?!
A LOT OF STUFF HAPPENED...
YOU LEFT YOUR GRANDMA'S HOUSE, RIGHT?
Why?
WELL, THERE WERE VARIOUS REASONS.
ANYWAY, I WAS BUSY TRYING TO EARN ENOUGH MONEY TO MAKE A LIVING...
thwip
thwip
I TRIED MY HAND AT VARIOUS TYPES OF JOBS...
MOTO-KUN'S PERSONAL NARRATIVE TIME
...BUT I SEEM TO BE NATURALLY FOCUSED, SO EVERY-ONE LIKED ME AND I'D END UP BECOMING THE CHIEF MANAGER OR GET PROMOTED TO SOME OTHER RESPONSIBLE POST...
IT MEANT I HAD A HARD TIME GETTING OUT OF THOSE JOBS.
I'm surprised I didn't drop dead from fatigue.
YOU KNOW, THIS GUY...
THE SECOND DAY ON THE JOB, HE SHOWED UP AT MY BAR WITH A BUCKET OF PAINT IN HAND...
...AND SAID, "THE COLOR OF THE WALL IS BAD, SO LET'S REPAINT IT."
HA HA HA
UNBELIEV-ABLE...
...RIGHT?

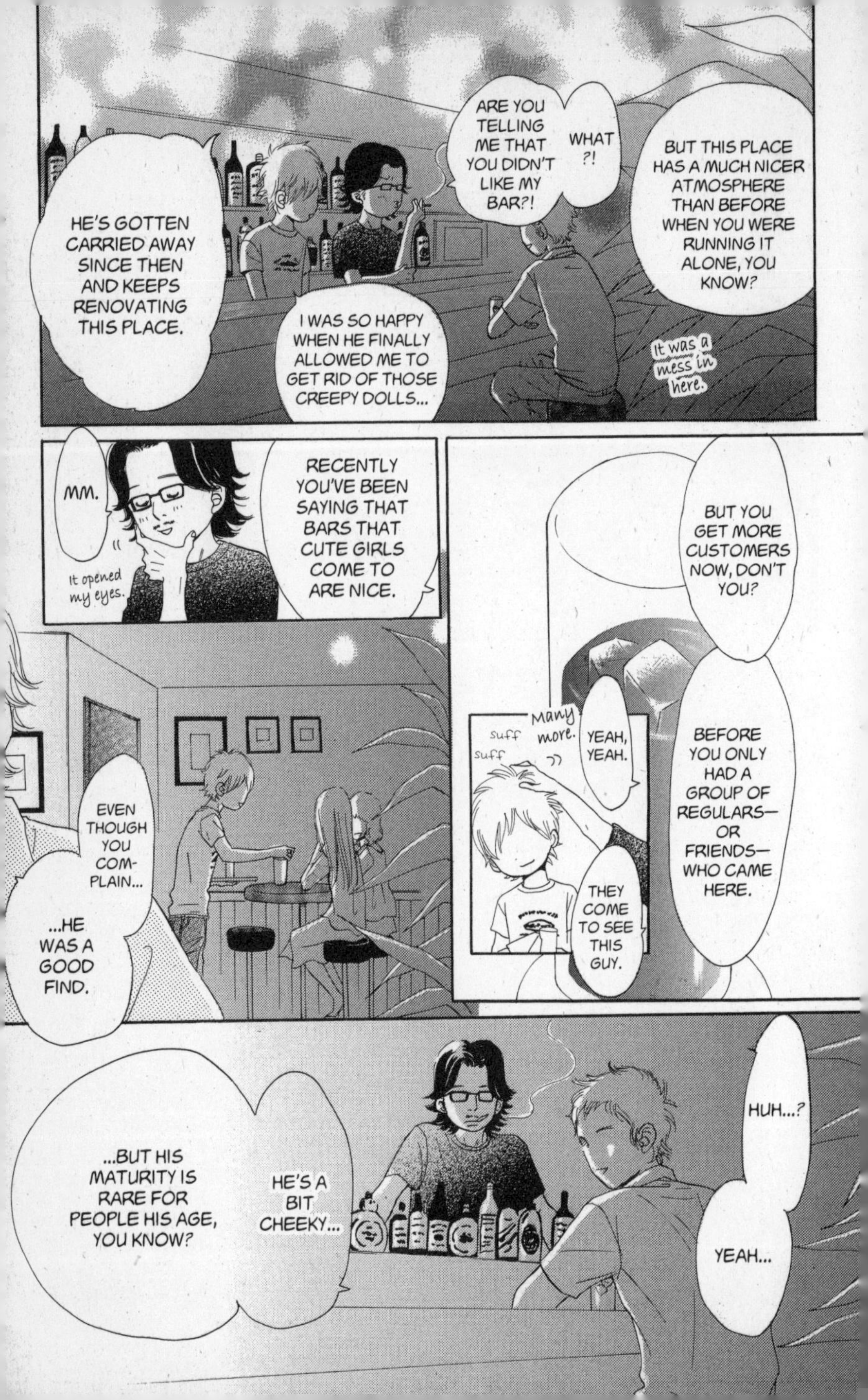
BUT THIS PLACE HAS A MUCH NICER ATMOSPHERE THAN BEFORE WHEN YOU WERE RUNNING IT ALONE, YOU KNOW?
WHAT?!
ARE YOU TELLING ME THAT YOU DIDN'T LIKE MY BAR?!
It was a mess in here.
HE'S GOTTEN CARRIED AWAY SINCE THEN AND KEEPS RENOVATING THIS PLACE.
I WAS SO HAPPY WHEN HE FINALLY ALLOWED ME TO GET RID OF THOSE CREEPY DOLLS...
BUT YOU GET MORE CUSTOMERS NOW, DON'T YOU?
BEFORE YOU ONLY HAD A GROUP OF REGULARS—OR FRIENDS—WHO CAME HERE.
YEAH, YEAH.
Many more.
suff suff
THEY COME TO SEE THIS GUY.
RECENTLY YOU'VE BEEN SAYING THAT BARS THAT CUTE GIRLS COME TO ARE NICE.
MM.
It opened my eyes.
EVEN THOUGH YOU COM-PLAIN...
...HE WAS A GOOD FIND.
HUH...?
YEAH...
HE'S A BIT CHEEKY...
...BUT HIS MATURITY IS RARE FOR PEOPLE HIS AGE, YOU KNOW?

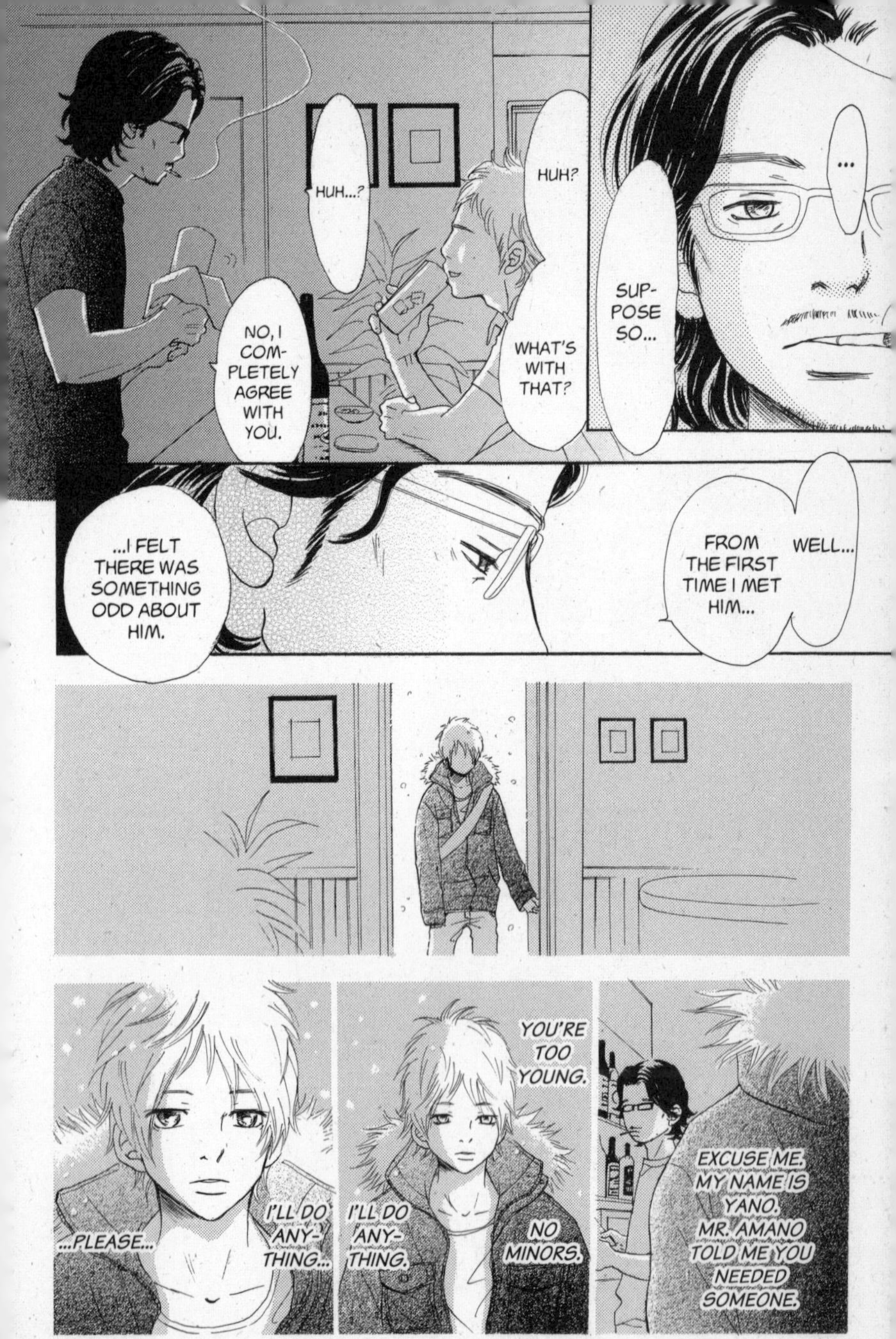
...
SUPPOSE SO...
HUH?
WHAT'S WITH THAT?
HUH...?
NO, I COMPLETELY AGREE WITH YOU.
WELL...
FROM THE FIRST TIME I MET HIM...
...I FELT THERE WAS SOMETHING ODD ABOUT HIM.
EXCUSE ME. MY NAME IS YANO. MR. AMANO TOLD ME YOU NEEDED SOMEONE.
YOU'RE TOO YOUNG.
NO MINORS.
I'LL DO ANYTHING.
I'LL DO ANYTHING...
...PLEASE...

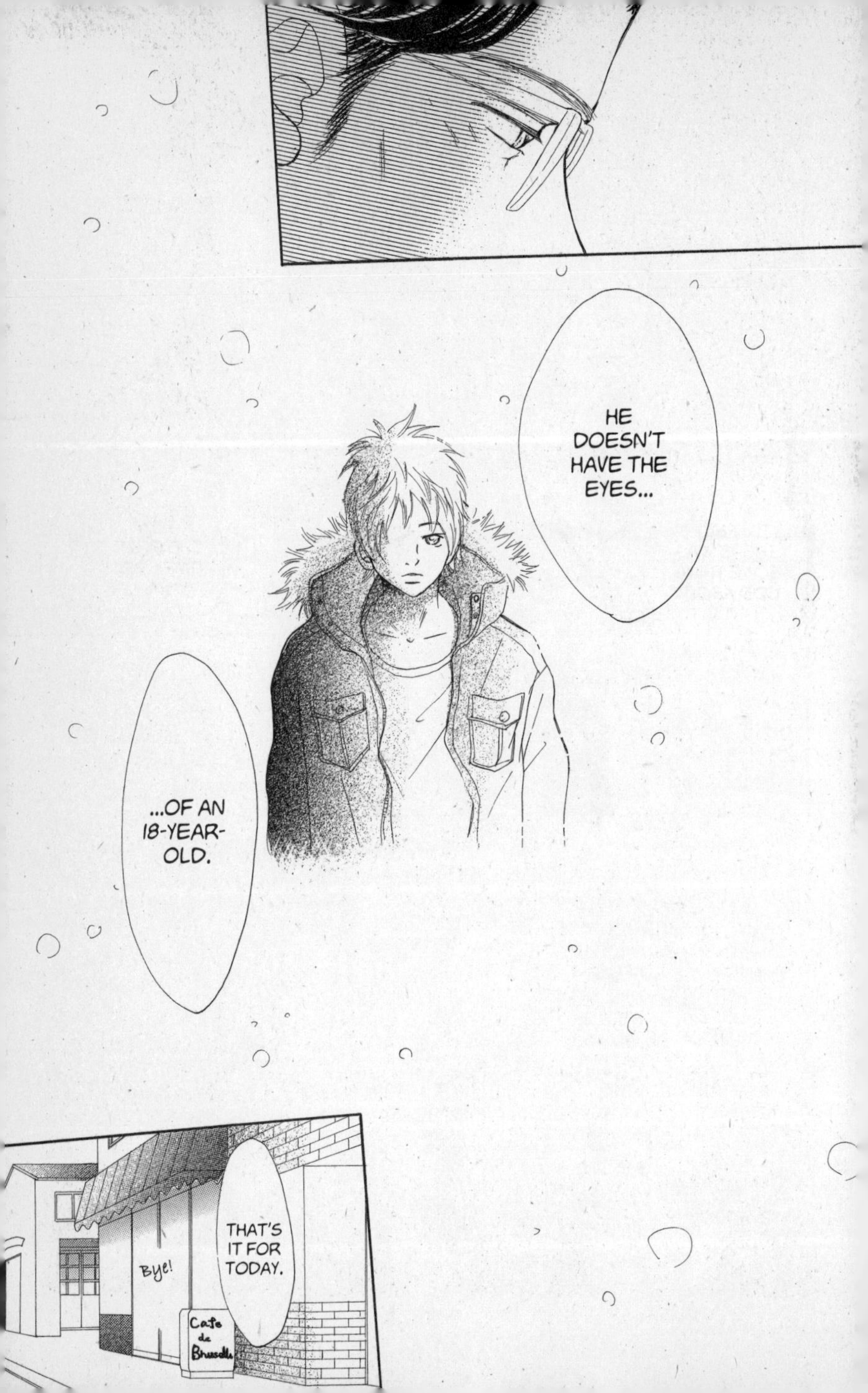
HE DOESN'T HAVE THE EYES...
...OF AN 18-YEAR-OLD.
THAT'S IT FOR TODAY.
Bye!
Cafe de Brussels

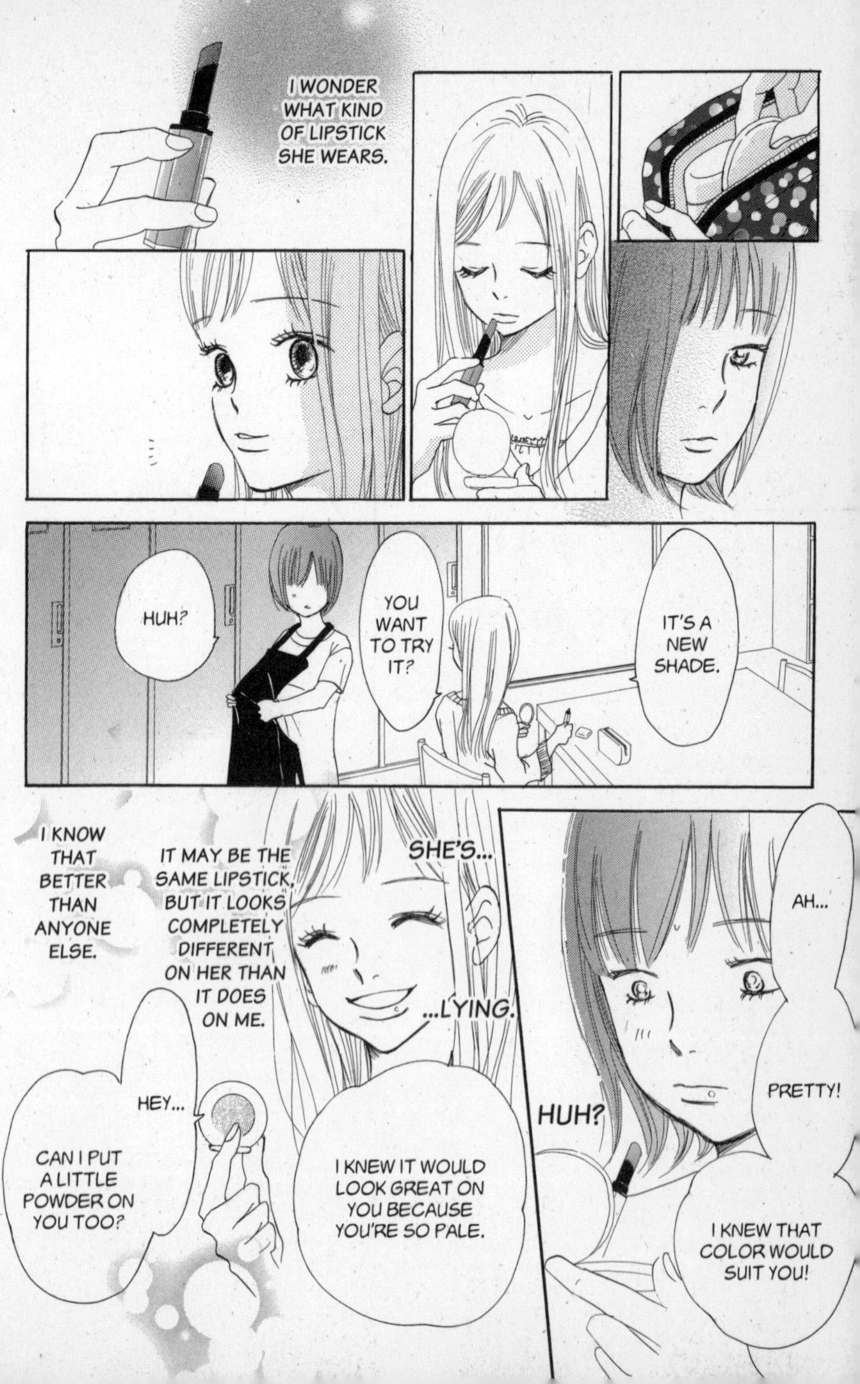
I WONDER WHAT KIND OF LIPSTICK SHE WEARS.
IT'S A NEW SHADE.
YOU WANT TO TRY IT?
HUH?
AH...
PRETTY!
I KNEW THAT COLOR WOULD SUIT YOU!
HUH?
SHE'S...
...LYING.
IT MAY BE THE SAME LIPSTICK, BUT IT LOOKS COMPLETELY DIFFERENT ON HER THAN IT DOES ON ME.
I KNOW THAT BETTER THAN ANYONE ELSE.
I KNEW IT WOULD LOOK GREAT ON YOU BECAUSE YOU'RE SO PALE.
HEY...
CAN I PUT A LITTLE POWDER ON YOU TOO?

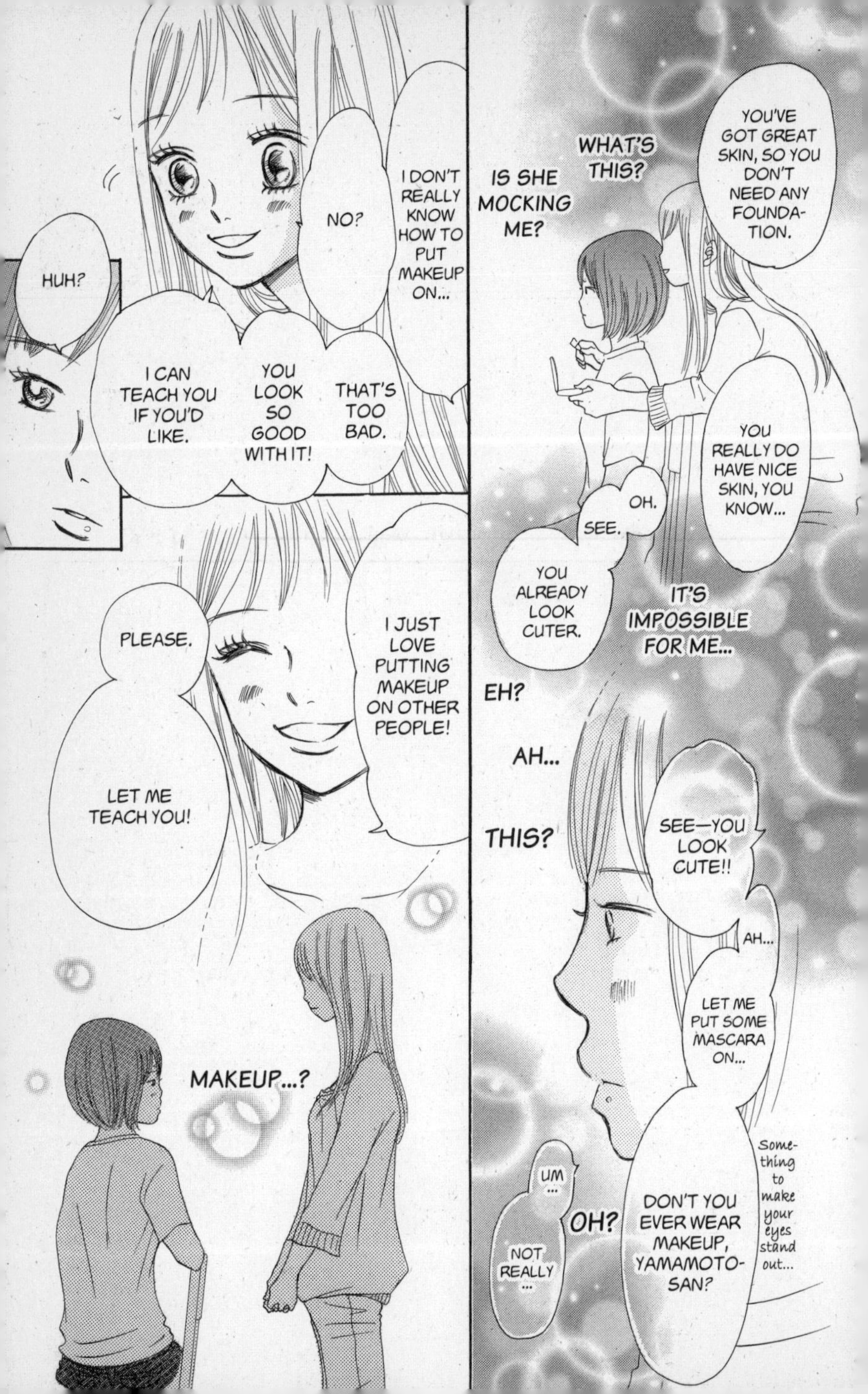
YOU'VE GOT GREAT SKIN, SO YOU DON'T NEED ANY FOUNDATION.
WHAT'S THIS?
IS SHE MOCKING ME?
YOU REALLY DO HAVE NICE SKIN, YOU KNOW...
OH.
SEE.
YOU ALREADY LOOK CUTER.
IT'S IMPOSSIBLE FOR ME...
SEE—YOU LOOK CUTE!!
EH?
AH...
THIS?
AH...
LET ME PUT SOME MASCARA ON...
Something to make your eyes stand out...
DON'T YOU EVER WEAR MAKEUP, YAMAMOTO-SAN?
OH?
UM...
NOT REALLY...
I DON'T REALLY KNOW HOW TO PUT MAKEUP ON...
NO?
THAT'S TOO BAD.
YOU LOOK SO GOOD WITH IT!
I CAN TEACH YOU IF YOU'D LIKE.
HUH?
I JUST LOVE PUTTING MAKEUP ON OTHER PEOPLE!
PLEASE.
LET ME TEACH YOU!
MAKEUP...?

Chapter 47

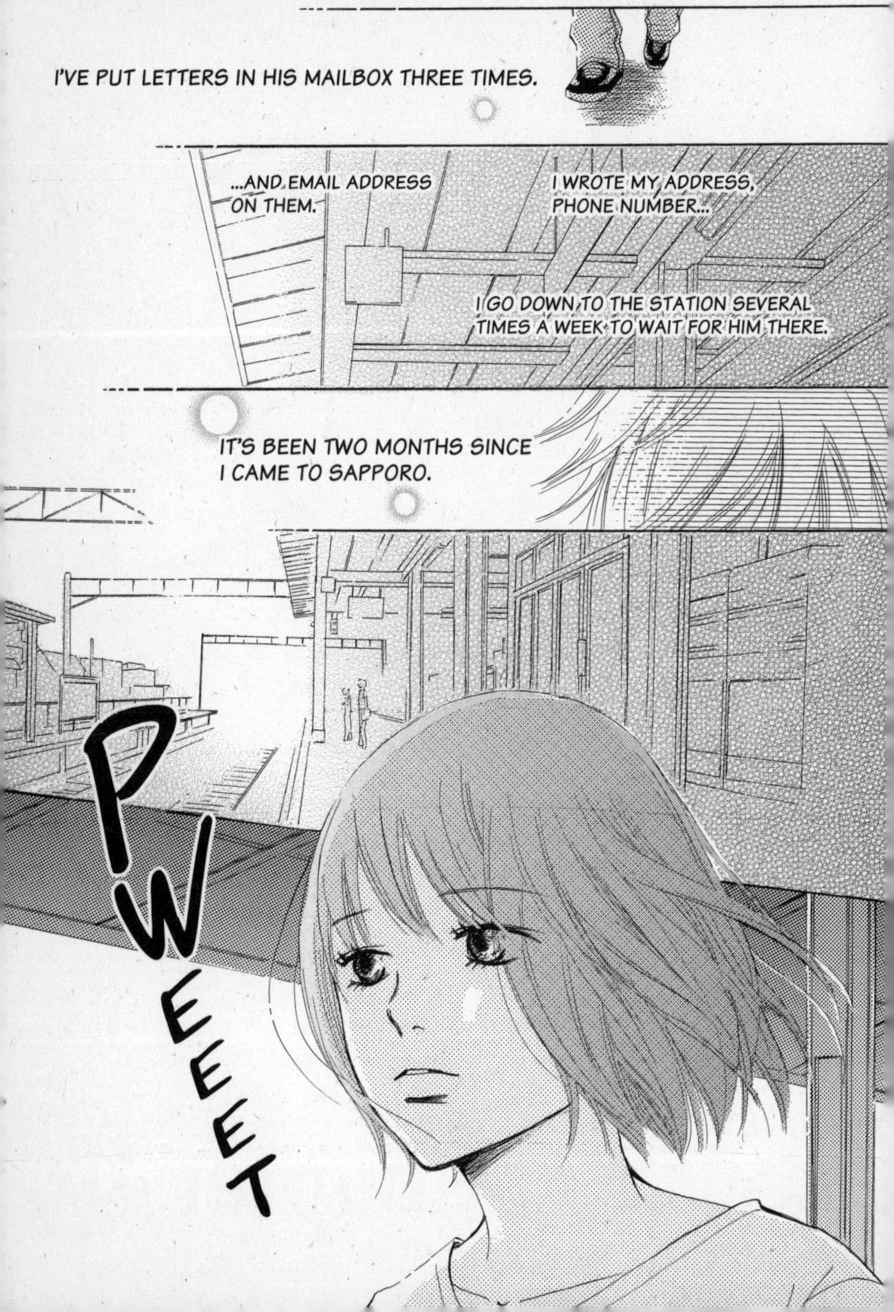
I'VE PUT LETTERS IN HIS MAILBOX THREE TIMES.
I WROTE MY ADDRESS, PHONE NUMBER...
...AND EMAIL ADDRESS ON THEM.
I GO DOWN TO THE STATION SEVERAL TIMES A WEEK TO WAIT FOR HIM THERE.
IT'S BEEN TWO MONTHS SINCE I CAME TO SAPPORO.
PWEEEET

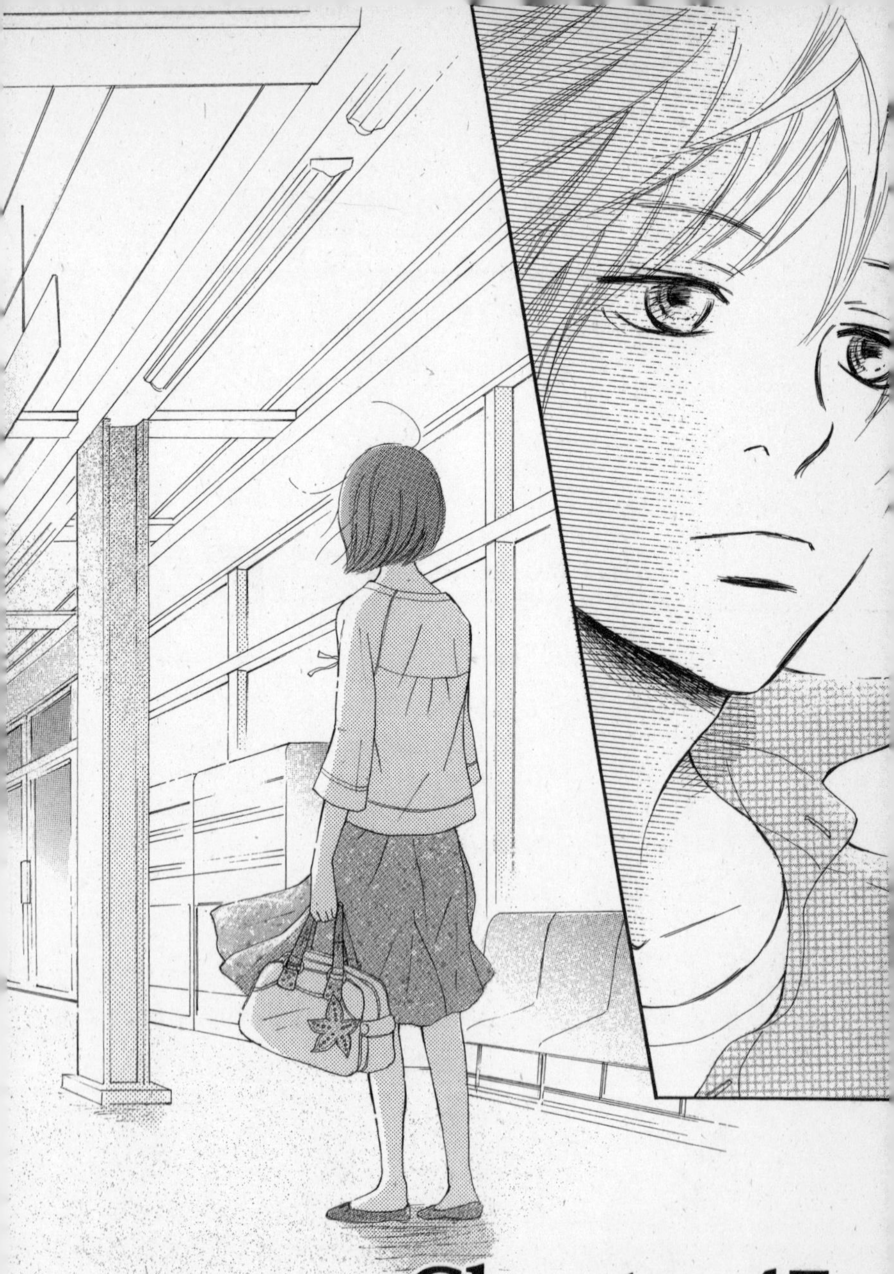

Chapter 47

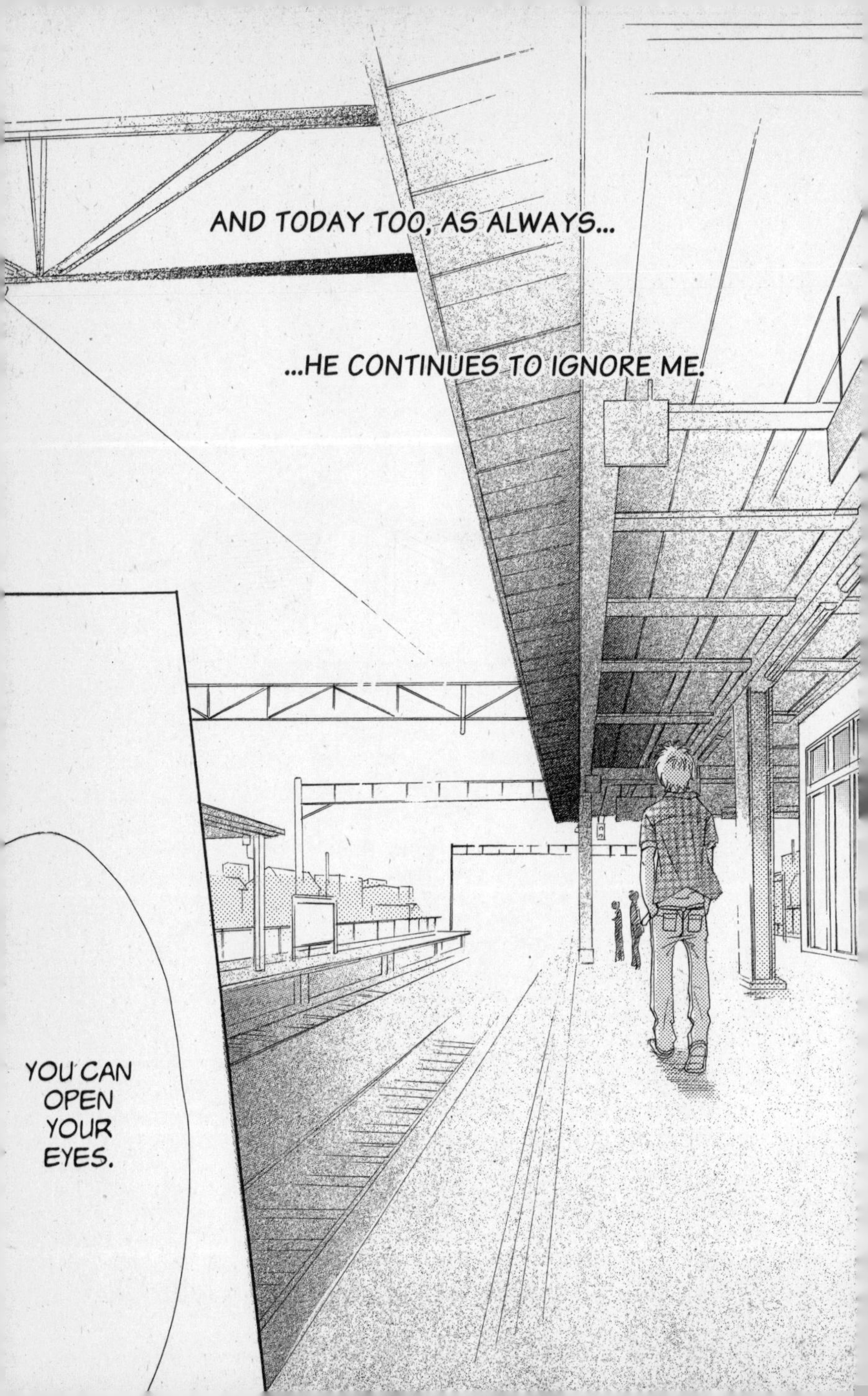
AND TODAY TOO, AS ALWAYS...
...HE CONTINUES TO IGNORE ME.
YOU CAN OPEN YOUR EYES.

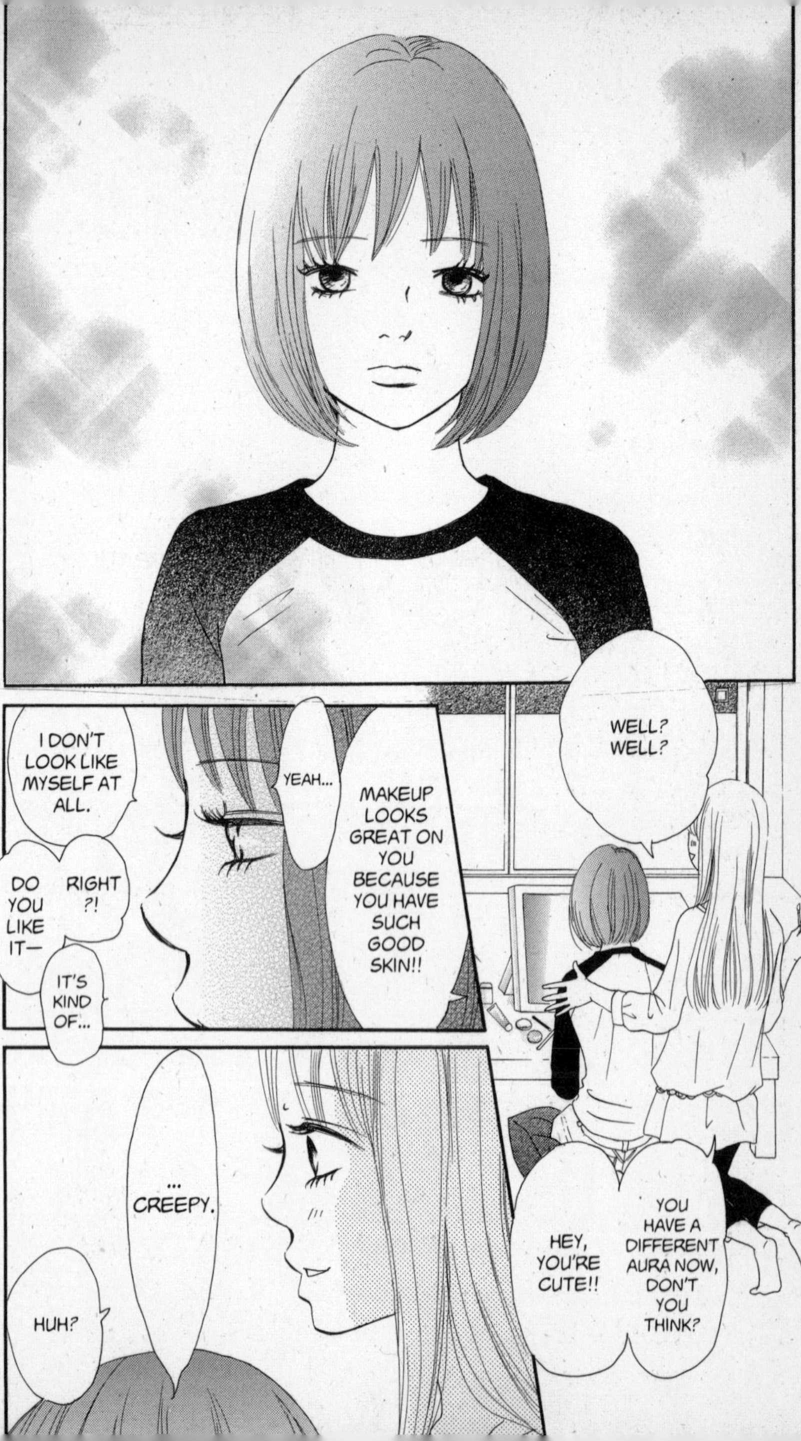
WELL? WELL?
YOU HAVE A DIFFERENT AURA NOW, DON'T YOU THINK?
HEY, YOU'RE CUTE!!
MAKEUP LOOKS GREAT ON YOU BECAUSE YOU HAVE SUCH GOOD SKIN!!
YEAH...
I DON'T LOOK LIKE MYSELF AT ALL.
RIGHT?!
DO YOU LIKE IT—
IT'S KIND OF...
... CREEPY.
HUH?

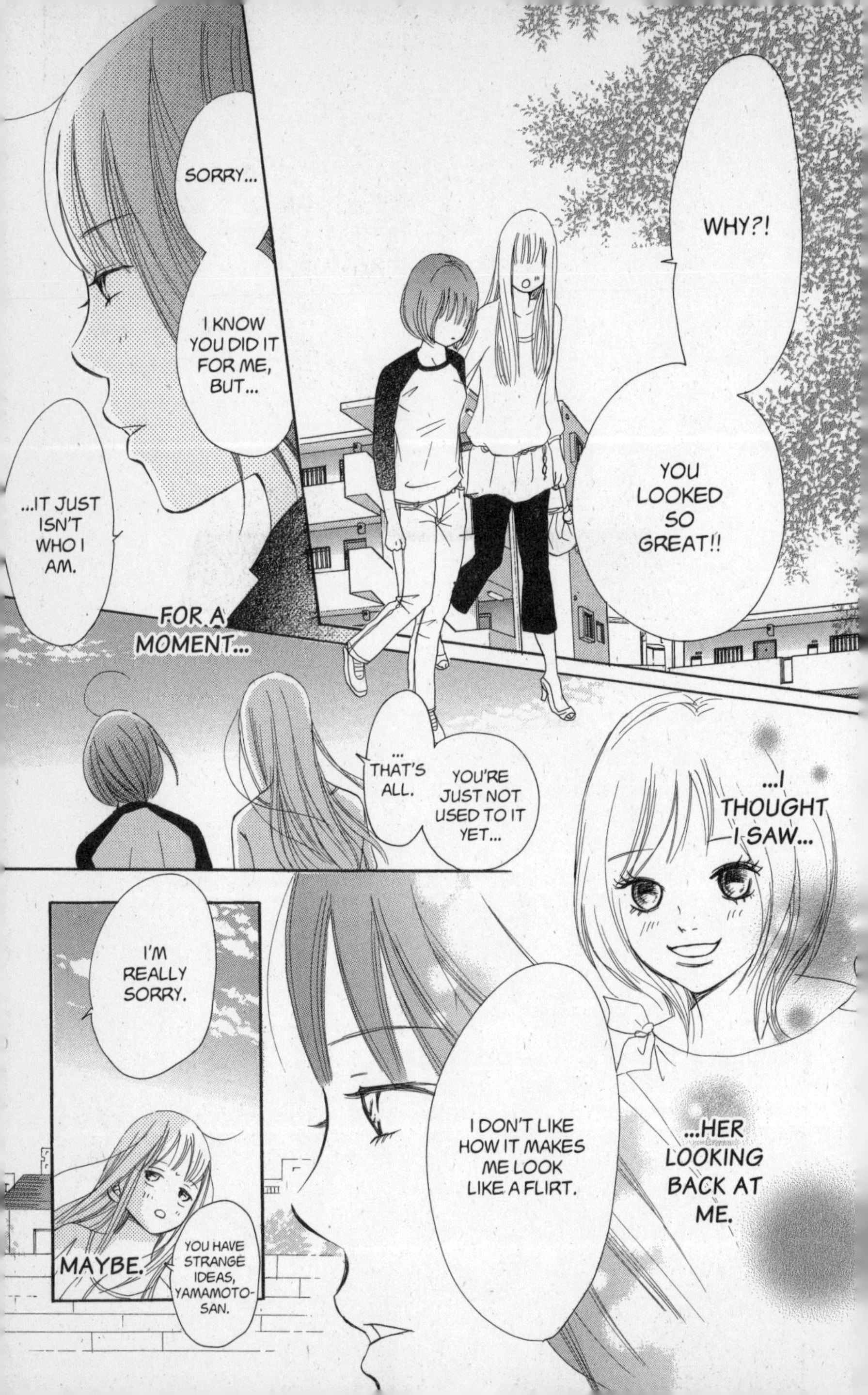
WHY?!
YOU LOOKED SO GREAT!!
SORRY...
I KNOW YOU DID IT FOR ME, BUT...
...IT JUST ISN'T WHO I AM.
... THAT'S ALL.
YOU'RE JUST NOT USED TO IT YET...
FOR A MOMENT...
...I THOUGHT I SAW...
I DON'T LIKE HOW IT MAKES ME LOOK LIKE A FLIRT.
...HER LOOKING BACK AT ME.
I'M REALLY SORRY.
YOU HAVE STRANGE IDEAS, YAMAMOTO-SAN.
MAYBE.

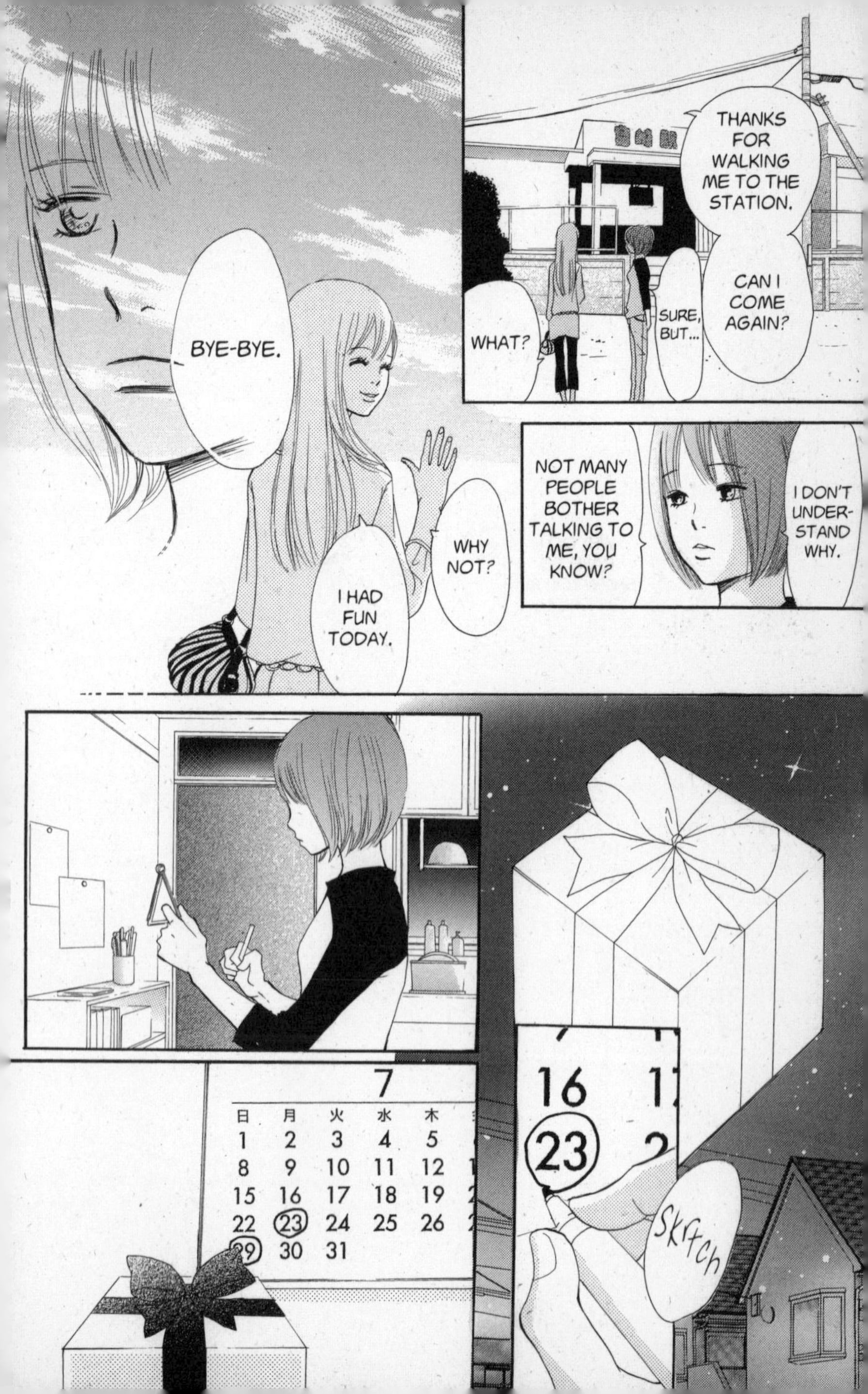
THANKS FOR WALKING ME TO THE STATION.
CAN I COME AGAIN?
SURE, BUT...
WHAT?
I DON'T UNDER-STAND WHY.
NOT MANY PEOPLE BOTHER TALKING TO ME, YOU KNOW?
WHY NOT?
I HAD FUN TODAY.
BYE-BYE.
Skrtch

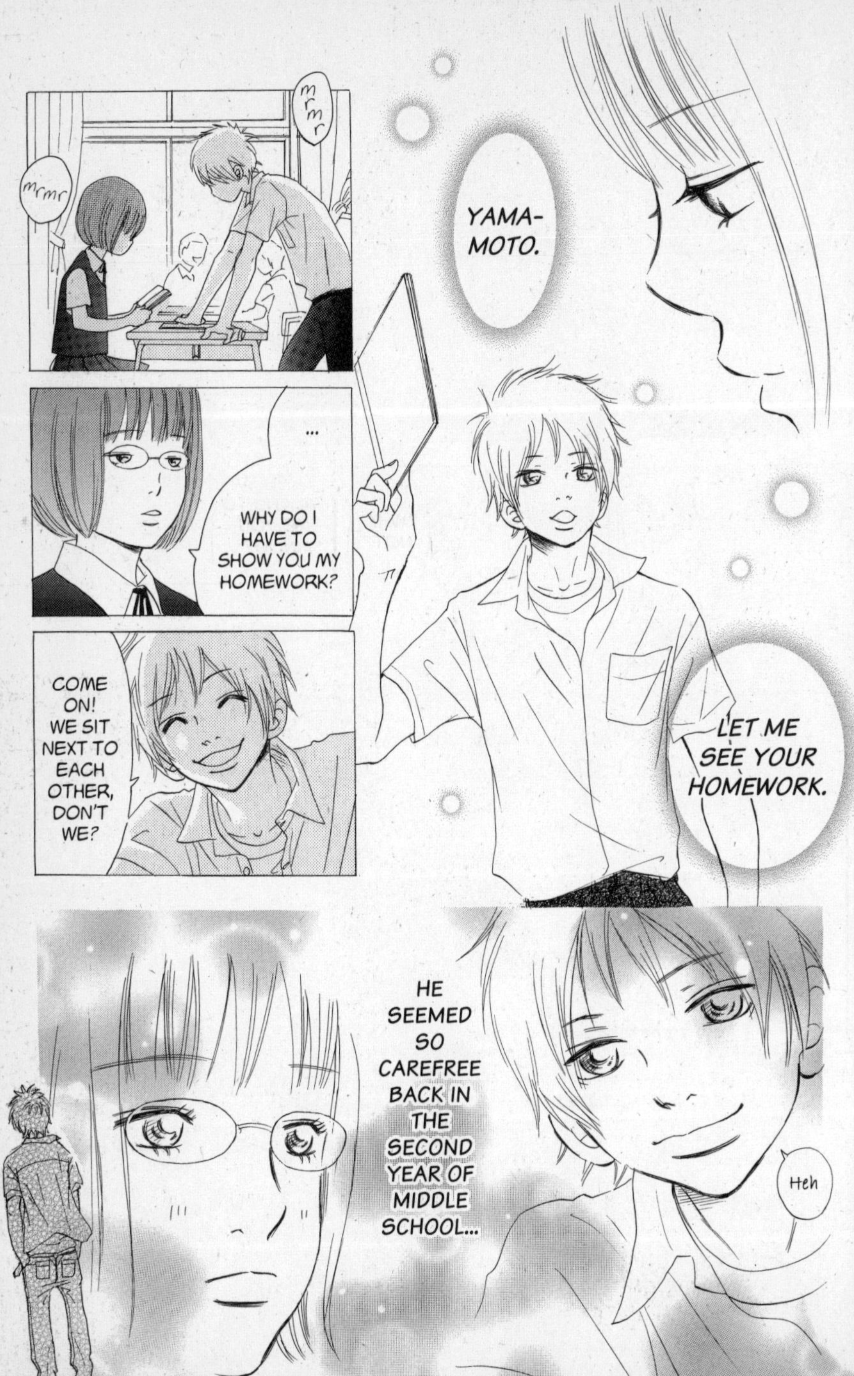
YAMA-MOTO.
LET ME SEE YOUR HOMEWORK.
mrmr
mrmr
...
WHY DO I HAVE TO SHOW YOU MY HOMEWORK?
COME ON! WE SIT NEXT TO EACH OTHER, DON'T WE?
Heh
HE SEEMED SO CAREFREE BACK IN THE SECOND YEAR OF MIDDLE SCHOOL...

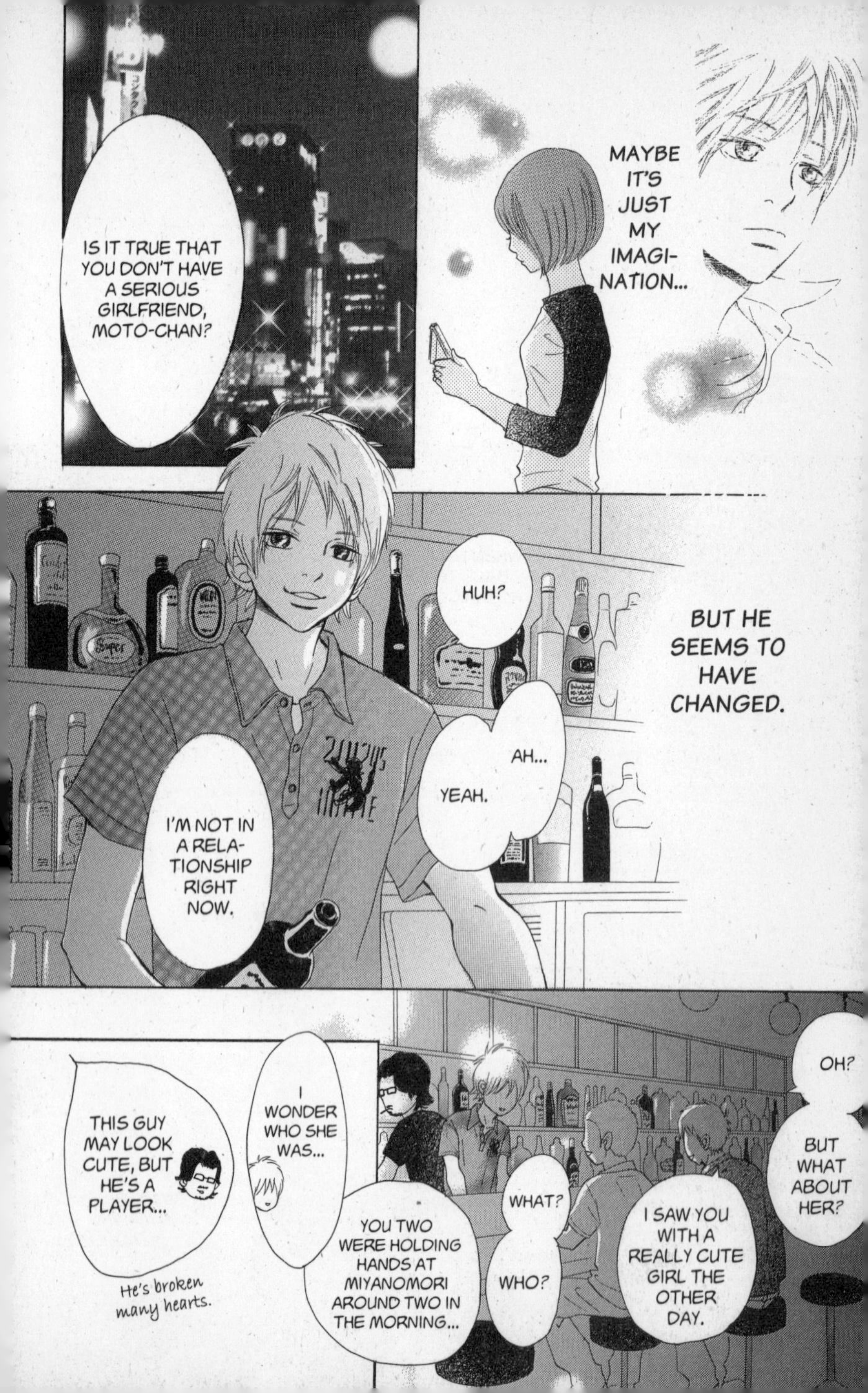
MAYBE IT'S JUST MY IMAGINATION...
IS IT TRUE THAT YOU DON'T HAVE A SERIOUS GIRLFRIEND, MOTO-CHAN?
BUT HE SEEMS TO HAVE CHANGED.
HUH?
AH... YEAH.
I'M NOT IN A RELATIONSHIP RIGHT NOW.
OH?
BUT WHAT ABOUT HER?
I SAW YOU WITH A REALLY CUTE GIRL THE OTHER DAY.
WHAT?
WHO?
YOU TWO WERE HOLDING HANDS AT MIYANOMORI AROUND TWO IN THE MORNING...
I WONDER WHO SHE WAS...
THIS GUY MAY LOOK CUTE, BUT HE'S A PLAYER...
He's broken many hearts.

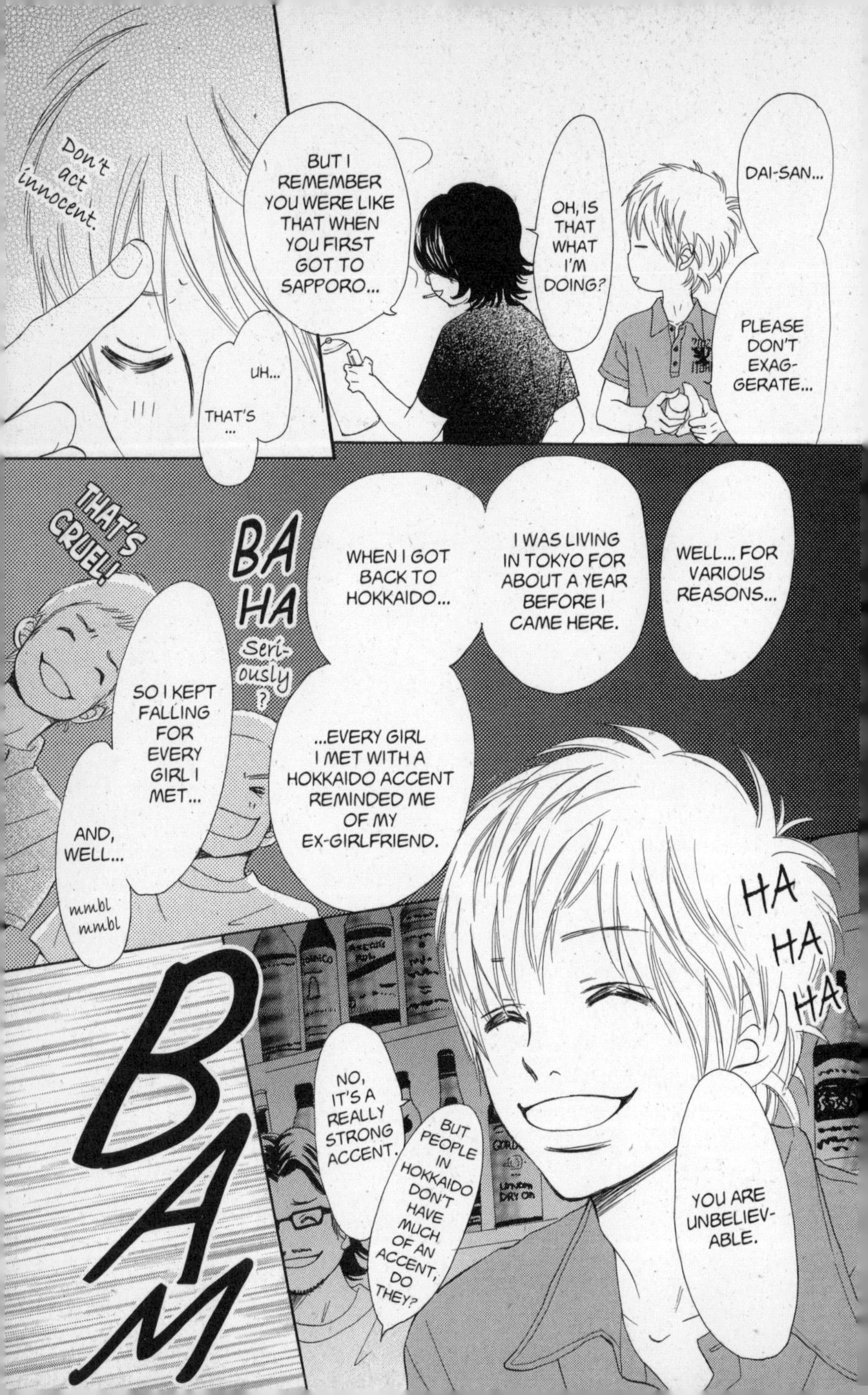
DAI-SAN...
PLEASE DON'T EXAG-GERATE...
OH, IS THAT WHAT I'M DOING?
BUT I REMEMBER YOU WERE LIKE THAT WHEN YOU FIRST GOT TO SAPPORO...
Don't act innocent.
UH...
THAT'S ...
WELL... FOR VARIOUS REASONS...
I WAS LIVING IN TOKYO FOR ABOUT A YEAR BEFORE I CAME HERE.
WHEN I GOT BACK TO HOKKAIDO...
...EVERY GIRL I MET WITH A HOKKAIDO ACCENT REMINDED ME OF MY EX-GIRLFRIEND.
BA HA
Seri-ously?
SO I KEPT FALLING FOR EVERY GIRL I MET...
AND, WELL...
mmbl mmbl
THAT'S CRUEL!
HA HA HA
YOU ARE UNBELIEV-ABLE.
NO, IT'S A REALLY STRONG ACCENT.
BUT PEOPLE IN HOKKAIDO DON'T HAVE MUCH OF AN ACCENT, DO THEY?
BAM

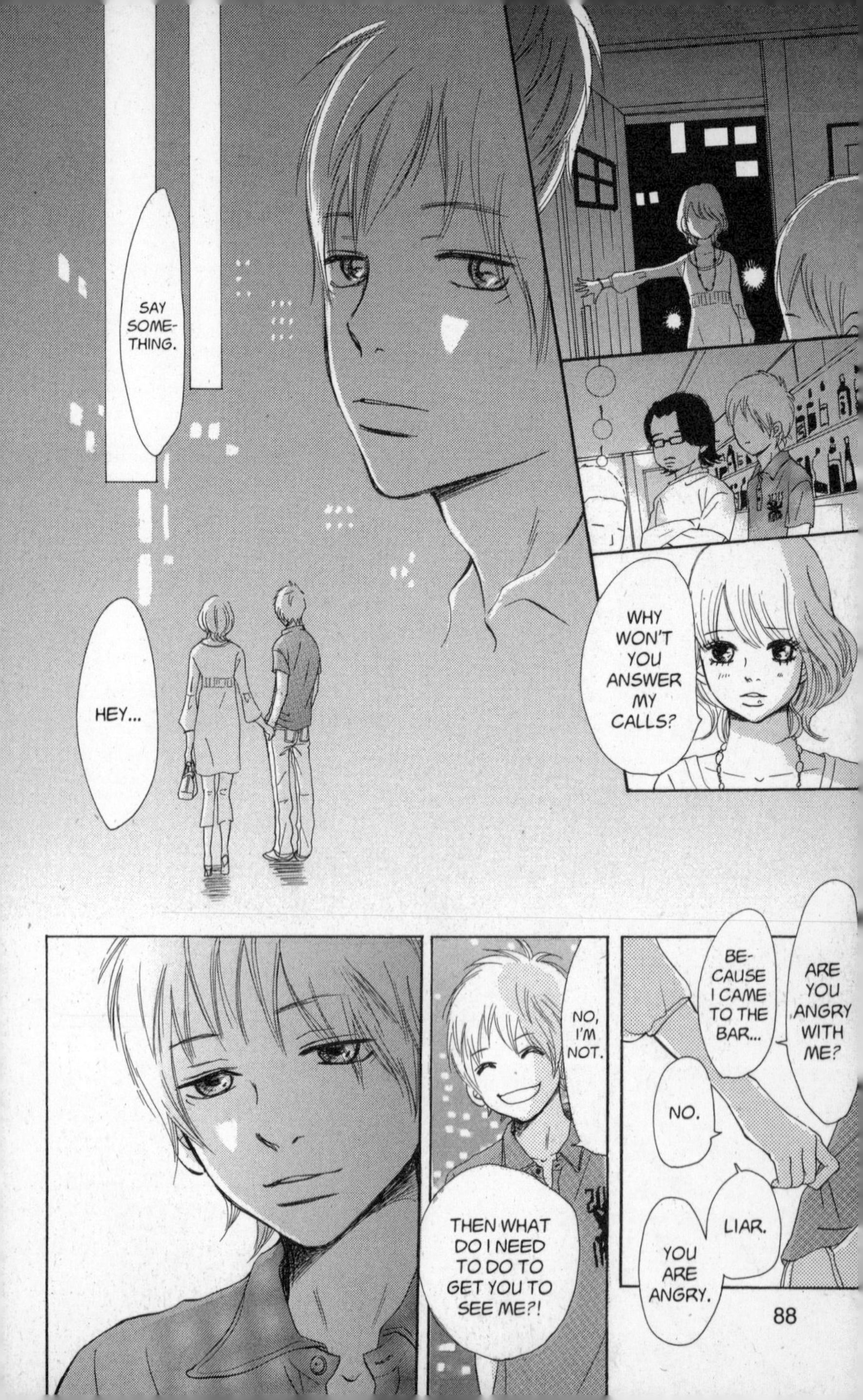
WHY WON'T YOU ANSWER MY CALLS?
SAY SOMETHING.
HEY...
ARE YOU ANGRY WITH ME?
BECAUSE I CAME TO THE BAR...
NO.
LIAR.
YOU ARE ANGRY.
NO, I'M NOT.
THEN WHAT DO I NEED TO DO TO GET YOU TO SEE ME?!

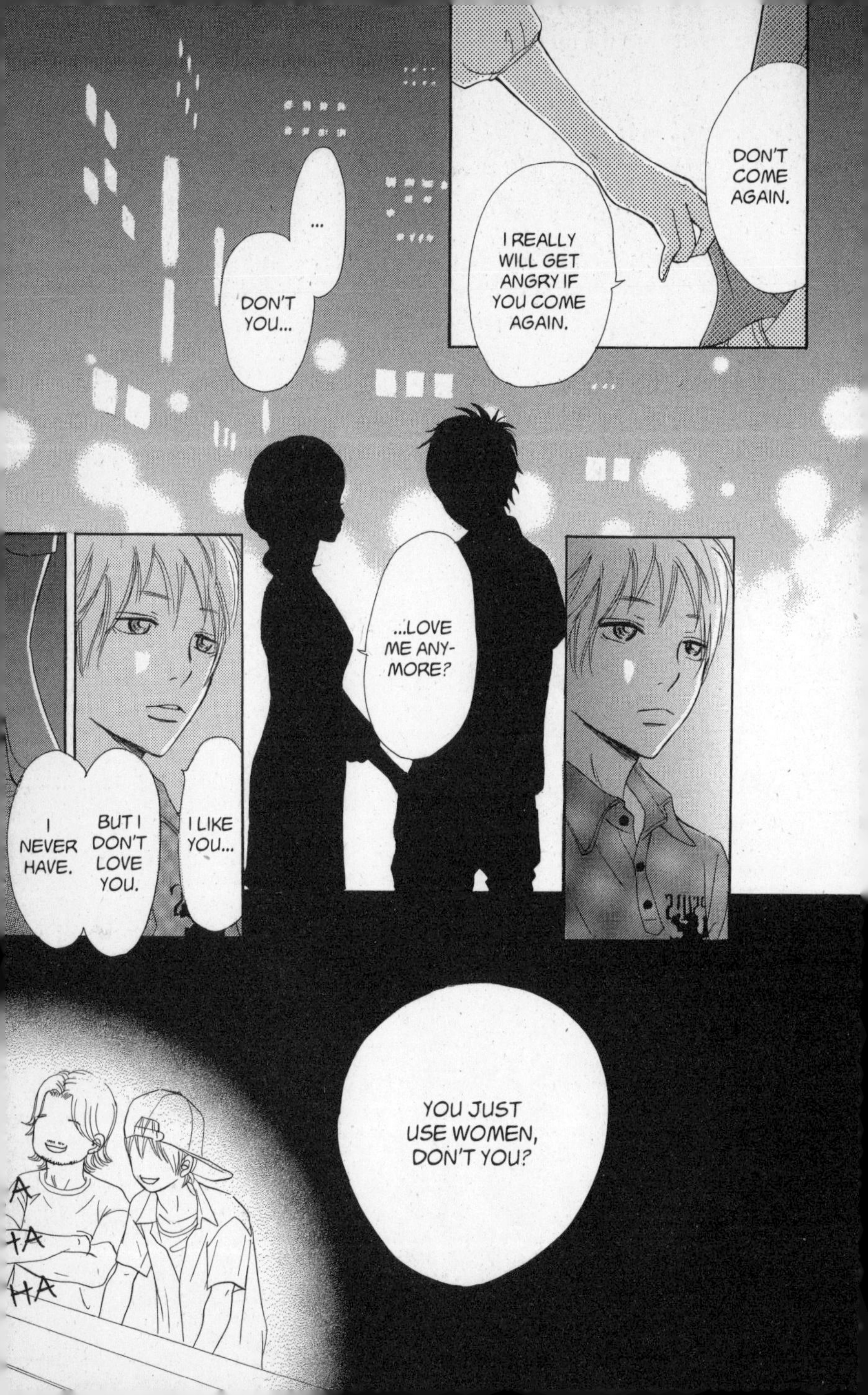
DON'T COME AGAIN.
I REALLY WILL GET ANGRY IF YOU COME AGAIN.
...
DON'T YOU...
...LOVE ME ANY-MORE?
I LIKE YOU...
BUT I DON'T LOVE YOU.
I NEVER HAVE.
YOU JUST USE WOMEN, DON'T YOU?
A HA HA

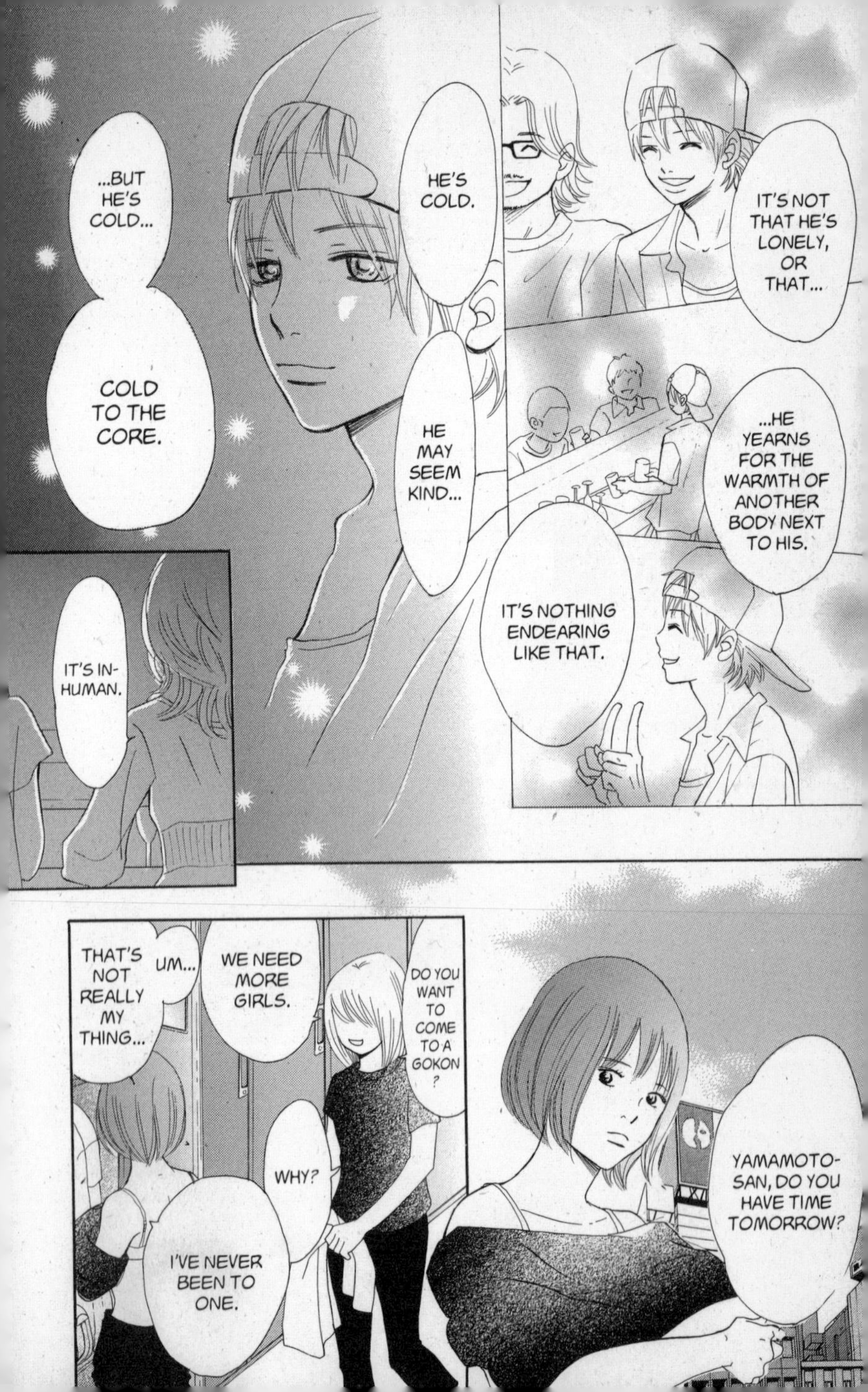
IT'S NOT THAT HE'S LONELY, OR THAT...
...HE YEARNS FOR THE WARMTH OF ANOTHER BODY NEXT TO HIS.
IT'S NOTHING ENDEARING LIKE THAT.
HE'S COLD.
HE MAY SEEM KIND...
...BUT HE'S COLD...
COLD TO THE CORE.
IT'S IN-HUMAN.
YAMAMOTO-SAN, DO YOU HAVE TIME TOMORROW?
DO YOU WANT TO COME TO A GOKON?
WE NEED MORE GIRLS.
UM...
THAT'S NOT REALLY MY THING...
WHY?
I'VE NEVER BEEN TO ONE.

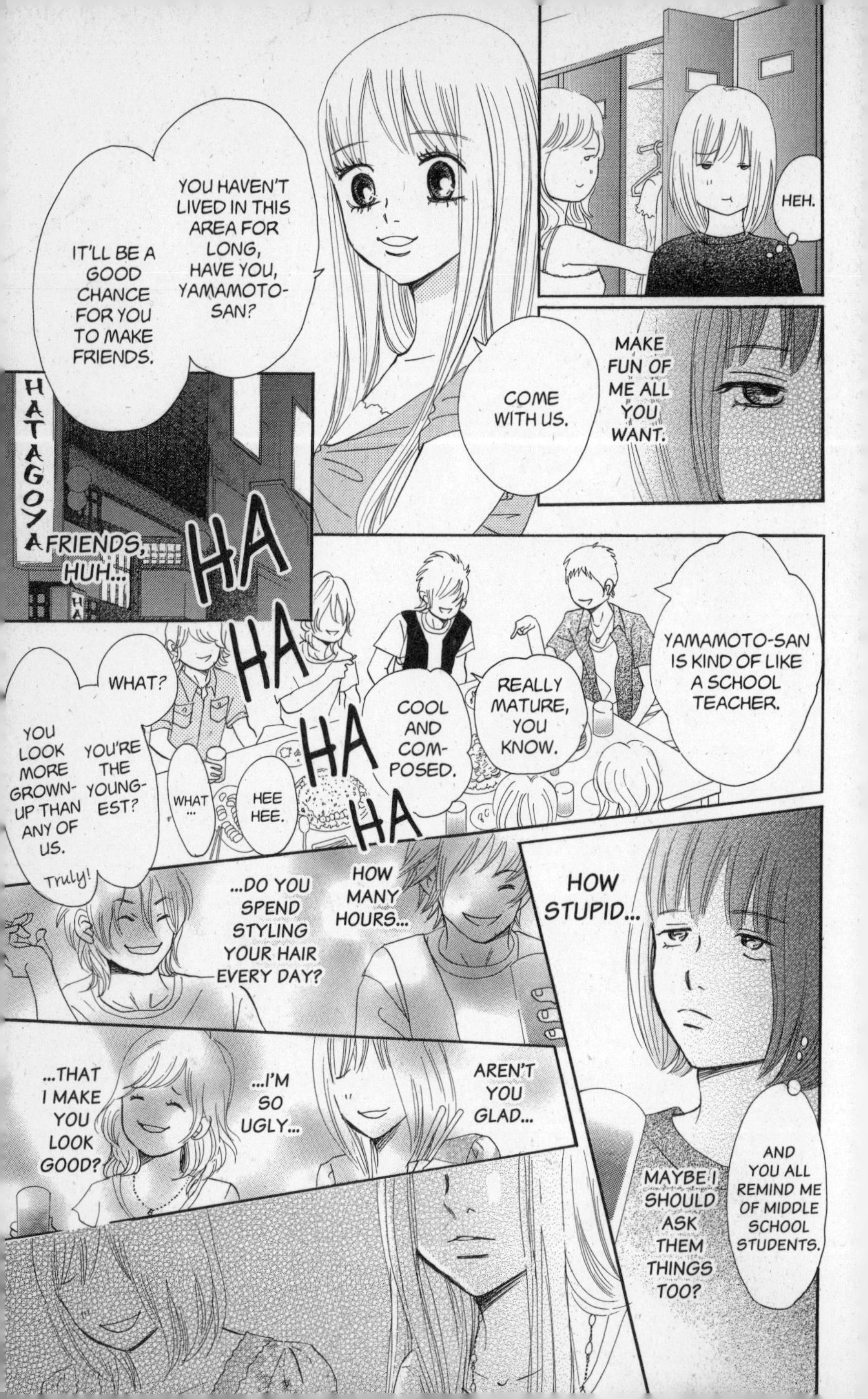
HEH.
MAKE FUN OF ME ALL YOU WANT.
YOU HAVEN'T LIVED IN THIS AREA FOR LONG, HAVE YOU, YAMAMOTO-SAN?
IT'LL BE A GOOD CHANCE FOR YOU TO MAKE FRIENDS.
COME WITH US.
HATAGOYA
FRIENDS, HUH...
HA HA HA HA
YAMAMOTO-SAN IS KIND OF LIKE A SCHOOL TEACHER.
REALLY MATURE, YOU KNOW.
COOL AND COM-POSED.
WHAT?
YOU'RE THE YOUNG-EST?
YOU LOOK MORE GROWN-UP THAN ANY OF US.
HEE HEE.
WHAT...
HOW STUPID...
AND YOU ALL REMIND ME OF MIDDLE SCHOOL STUDENTS.
MAYBE I SHOULD ASK THEM THINGS TOO?
HOW MANY HOURS...
...DO YOU SPEND STYLING YOUR HAIR EVERY DAY?
Truly!
AREN'T YOU GLAD...
...I'M SO UGLY...
...THAT I MAKE YOU LOOK GOOD?

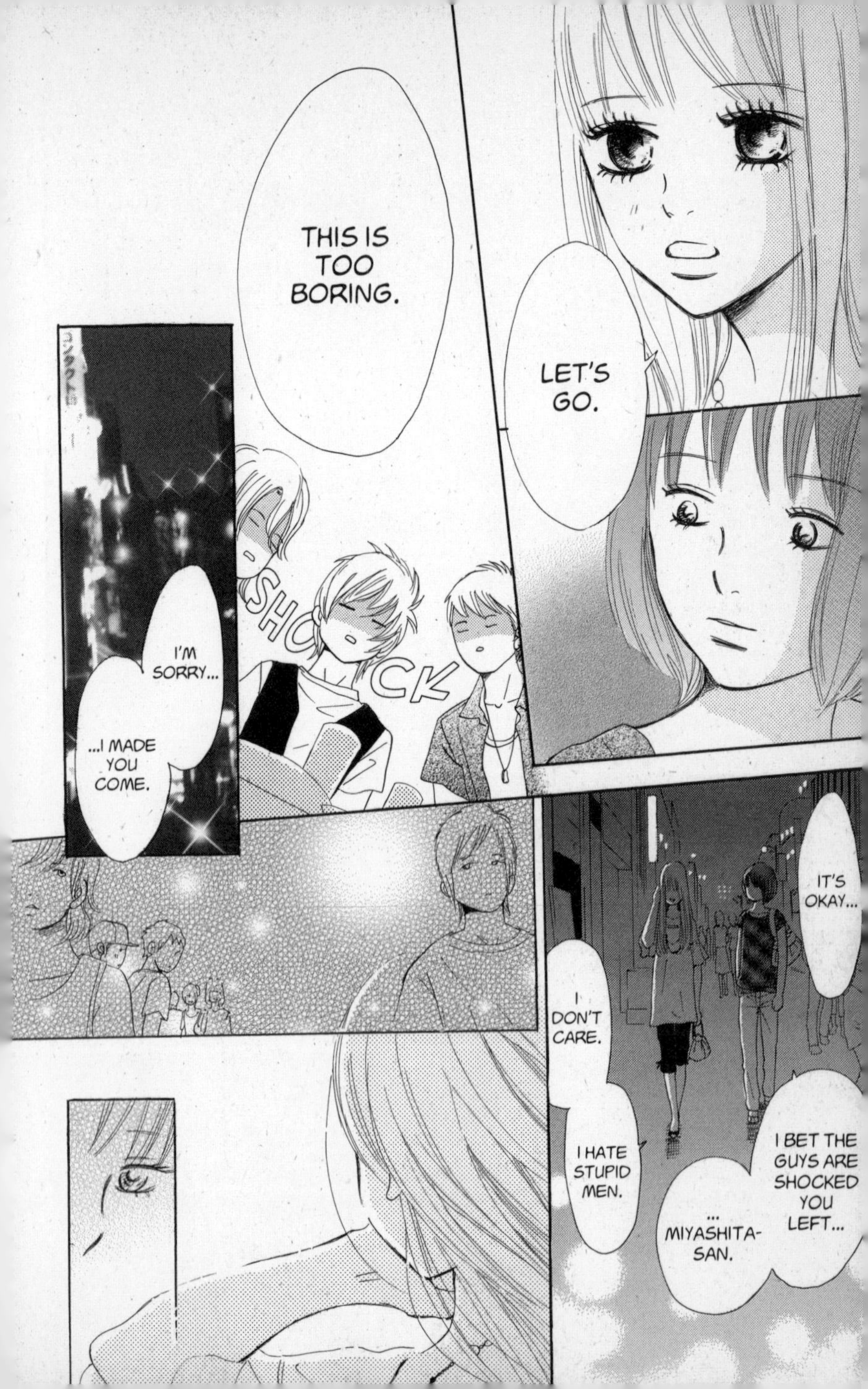
LET'S GO.
THIS IS TOO BORING.
SHOCK
I'M SORRY...
...I MADE YOU COME.
IT'S OKAY...
I DON'T CARE.
I BET THE GUYS ARE SHOCKED YOU LEFT...
...MIYASHITA-SAN.
I HATE STUPID MEN.

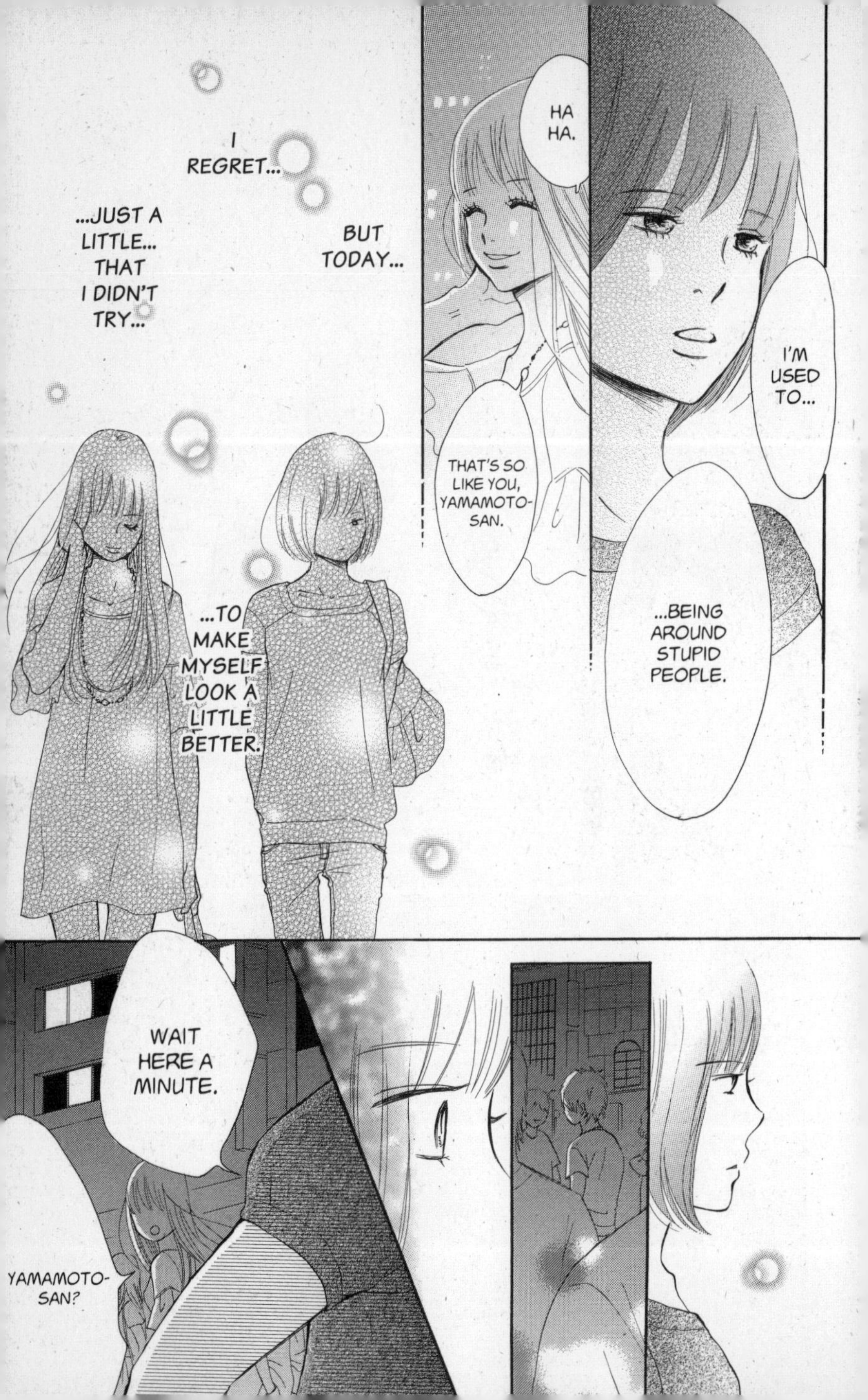
I'M USED TO...
...BEING AROUND STUPID PEOPLE.
HA HA.
THAT'S SO LIKE YOU, YAMAMOTO-SAN.
BUT TODAY...
I REGRET...
...JUST A LITTLE... THAT I DIDN'T TRY...
...TO MAKE MYSELF LOOK A LITTLE BETTER.
WAIT HERE A MINUTE.
YAMAMOTO-SAN?

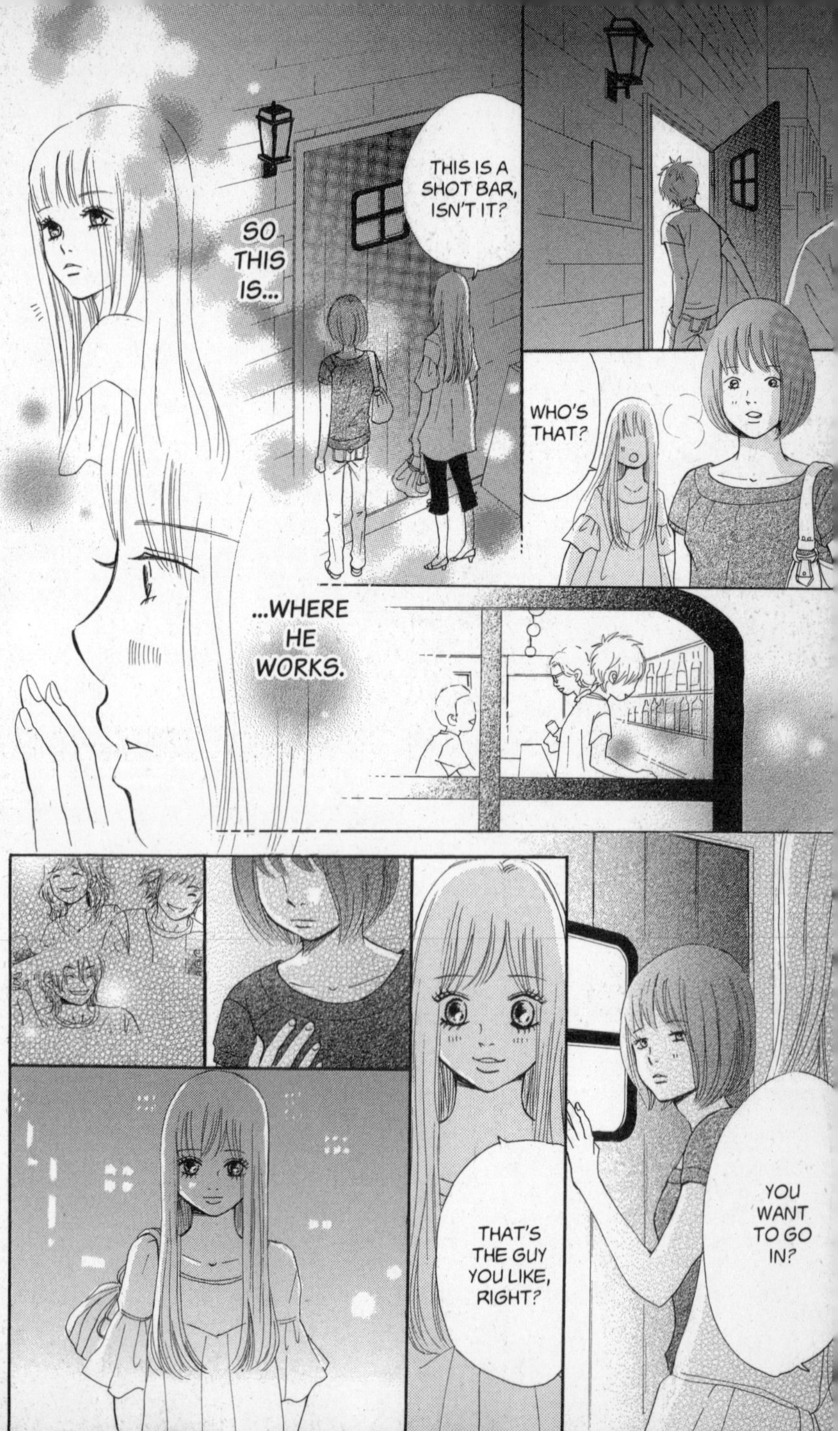
THIS IS A SHOT BAR, ISN'T IT?
SO THIS IS...
WHO'S THAT?
...WHERE HE WORKS.
THAT'S THE GUY YOU LIKE, RIGHT?
YOU WANT TO GO IN?

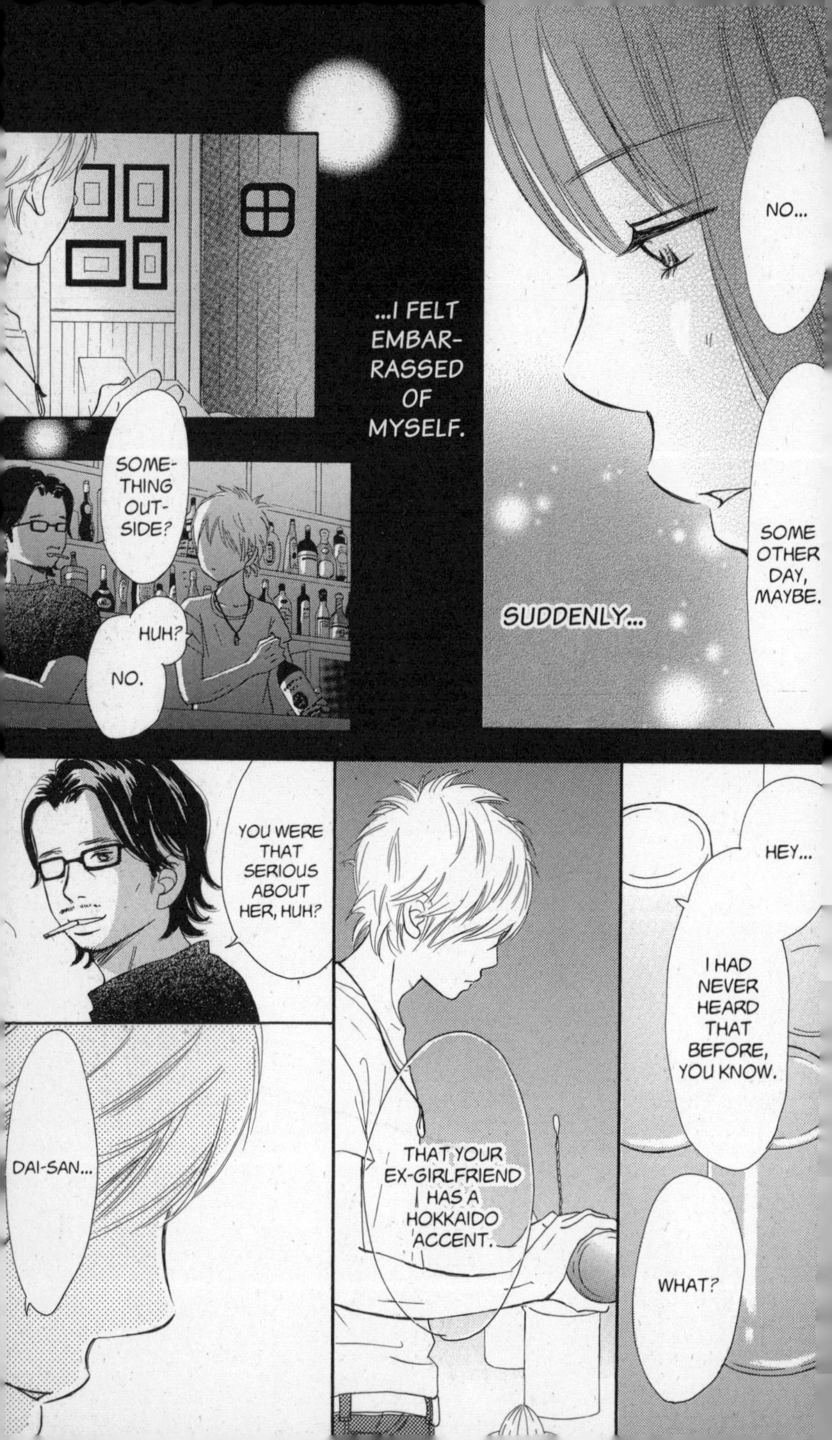
NO...
SOME OTHER DAY, MAYBE.
SUDDENLY...
...I FELT EMBARRASSED OF MYSELF.
SOMETHING OUTSIDE?
HUH?
NO.
HEY...
I HAD NEVER HEARD THAT BEFORE, YOU KNOW.
WHAT?
THAT YOUR EX-GIRLFRIEND HAS A HOKKAIDO ACCENT.
YOU WERE THAT SERIOUS ABOUT HER, HUH?
DAI-SAN...

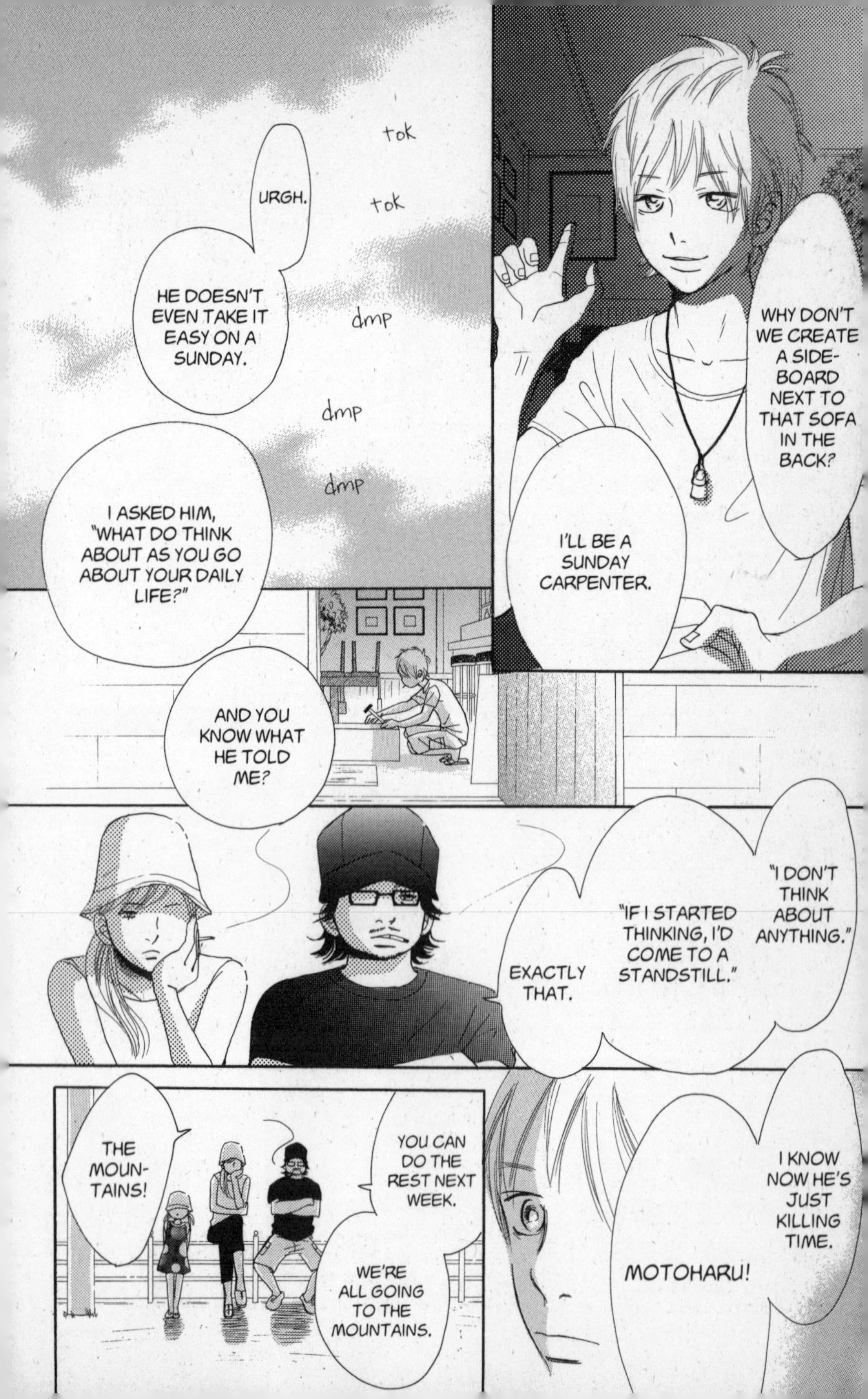
WHY DON'T WE CREATE A SIDE-BOARD NEXT TO THAT SOFA IN THE BACK?
I'LL BE A SUNDAY CARPENTER.
tok
tok
URGH.
HE DOESN'T EVEN TAKE IT EASY ON A SUNDAY.
dmp
dmp
dmp
I ASKED HIM, "WHAT DO THINK ABOUT AS YOU GO ABOUT YOUR DAILY LIFE?"
AND YOU KNOW WHAT HE TOLD ME?
"I DON'T THINK ABOUT ANYTHING."
"IF I STARTED THINKING, I'D COME TO A STANDSTILL."
EXACTLY THAT.
I KNOW NOW HE'S JUST KILLING TIME.
MOTOHARU!
YOU CAN DO THE REST NEXT WEEK.
WE'RE ALL GOING TO THE MOUNTAINS.
THE MOUN-TAINS!

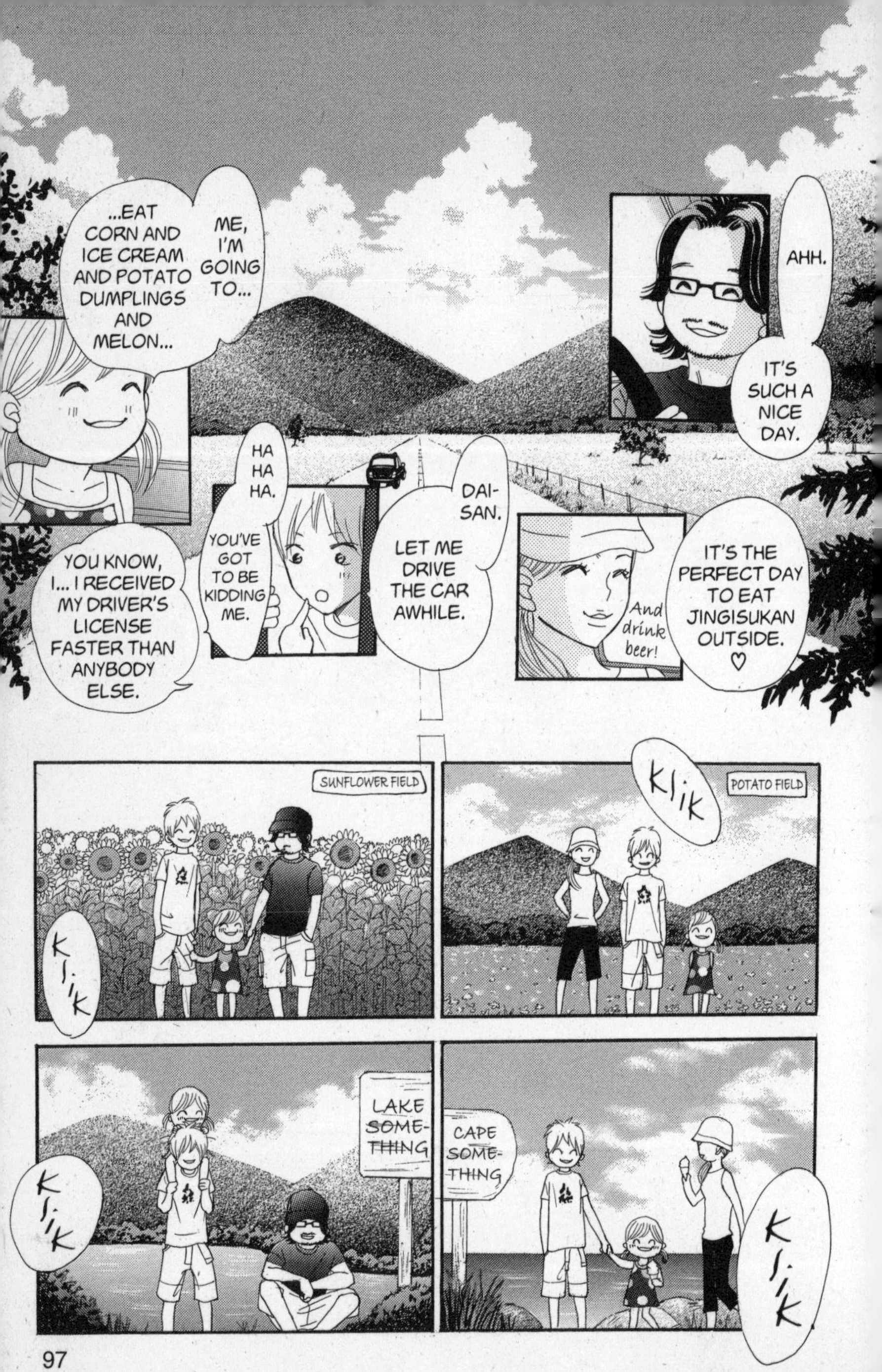
AHH.
IT'S SUCH A NICE DAY.
ME, I'M GOING TO...
...EAT CORN AND ICE CREAM AND POTATO DUMPLINGS AND MELON...
IT'S THE PERFECT DAY TO EAT JINGISUKAN OUTSIDE. ♡
And drink beer!
DAI-SAN.
LET ME DRIVE THE CAR AWHILE.
HA HA HA.
YOU'VE GOT TO BE KIDDING ME.
YOU KNOW, I... I RECEIVED MY DRIVER'S LICENSE FASTER THAN ANYBODY ELSE.
POTATO FIELD
Klik
SUNFLOWER FIELD
Klik
CAPE SOME-THING
Klik.
LAKE SOME-THING
Klik

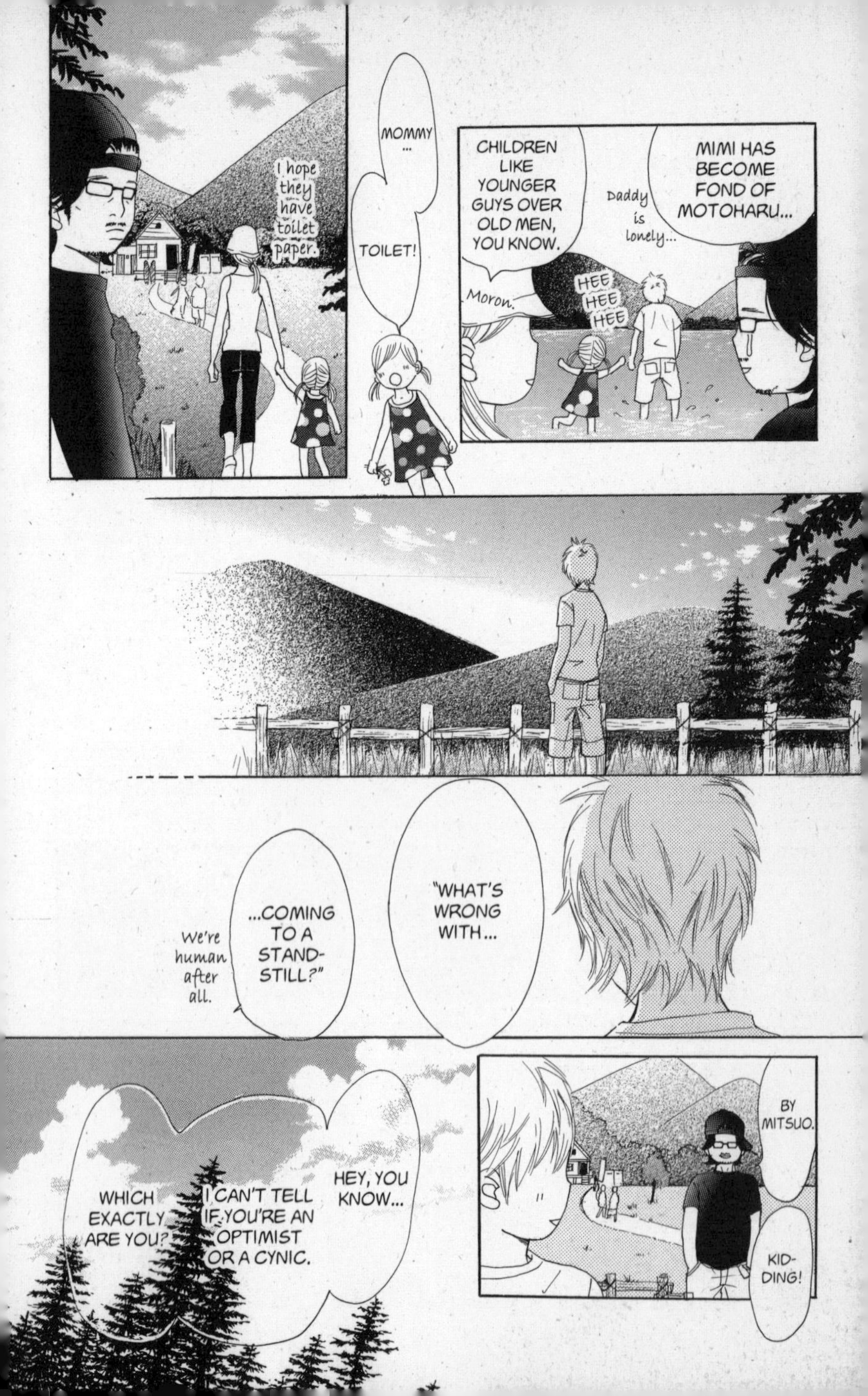
MIMI HAS BECOME FOND OF MOTOHARU...
Daddy is lonely...
CHILDREN LIKE YOUNGER GUYS OVER OLD MEN, YOU KNOW.
HEE HEE HEE
Moron.
MOMMY ...
TOILET!
I hope they have toilet paper.
"WHAT'S WRONG WITH...
...COMING TO A STAND-STILL?"
We're human after all.
BY MITSUO.
KID-DING!
HEY, YOU KNOW...
I CAN'T TELL IF YOU'RE AN OPTIMIST OR A CYNIC.
WHICH EXACTLY ARE YOU?

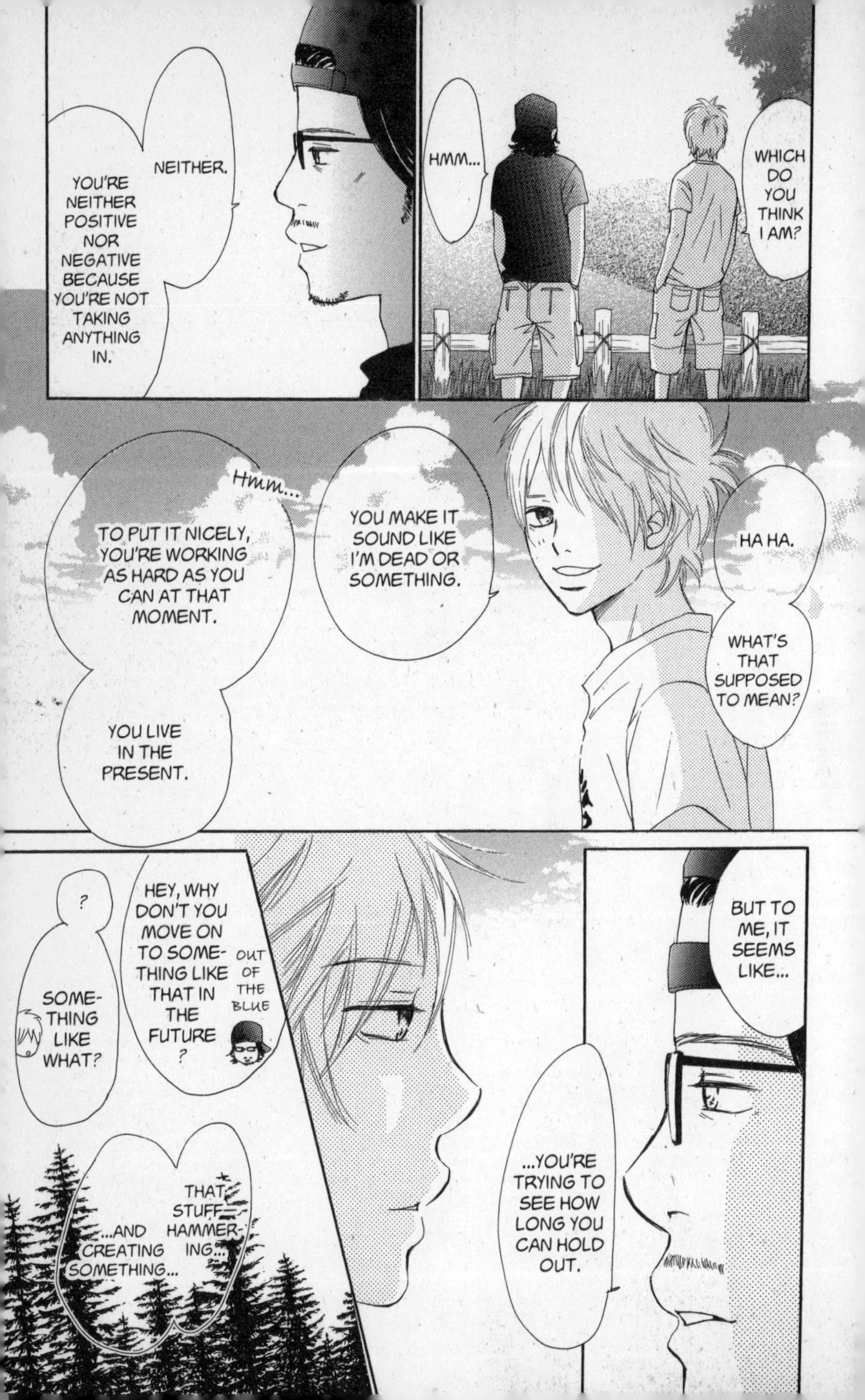
WHICH DO YOU THINK I AM?
HMM...
NEITHER.
YOU'RE NEITHER POSITIVE NOR NEGATIVE BECAUSE YOU'RE NOT TAKING ANYTHING IN.
HA HA.
WHAT'S THAT SUPPOSED TO MEAN?
YOU MAKE IT SOUND LIKE I'M DEAD OR SOMETHING.
Hmm...
TO PUT IT NICELY, YOU'RE WORKING AS HARD AS YOU CAN AT THAT MOMENT.
YOU LIVE IN THE PRESENT.
BUT TO ME, IT SEEMS LIKE...
...YOU'RE TRYING TO SEE HOW LONG YOU CAN HOLD OUT.
HEY, WHY DON'T YOU MOVE ON TO SOME-THING LIKE THAT IN THE FUTURE?
OUT OF THE BLUE
?
SOME-THING LIKE WHAT?
THAT STUFF— HAMMER-ING...
...AND CREATING SOMETHING...

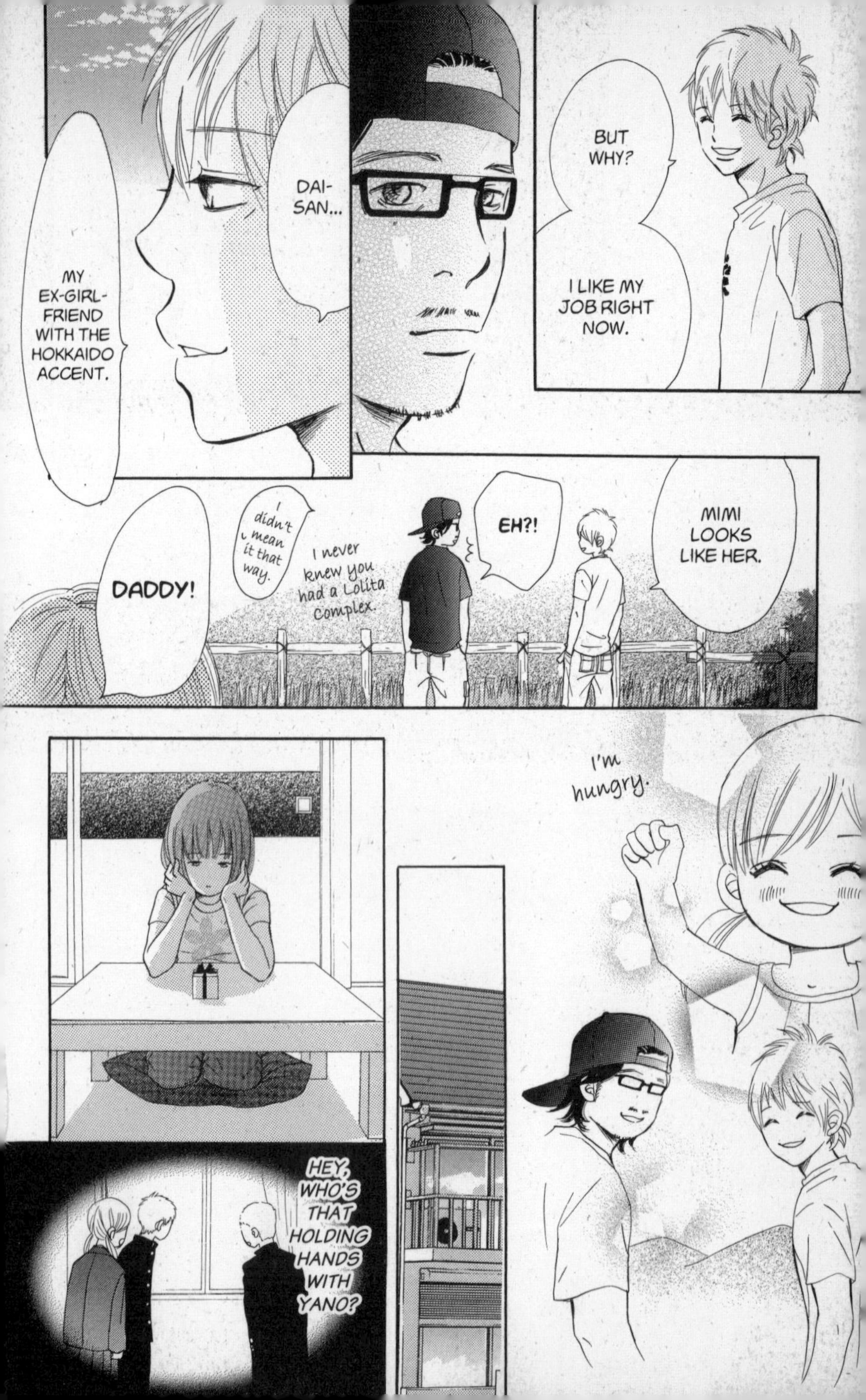
BUT WHY?
I LIKE MY JOB RIGHT NOW.
DAI-SAN...
MY EX-GIRLFRIEND WITH THE HOKKAIDO ACCENT.
MIMI LOOKS LIKE HER.
EH?!
I never knew you had a Lolita complex.
I didn't mean it that way.
DADDY!
I'm hungry.
HEY, WHO'S THAT HOLDING HANDS WITH YANO?

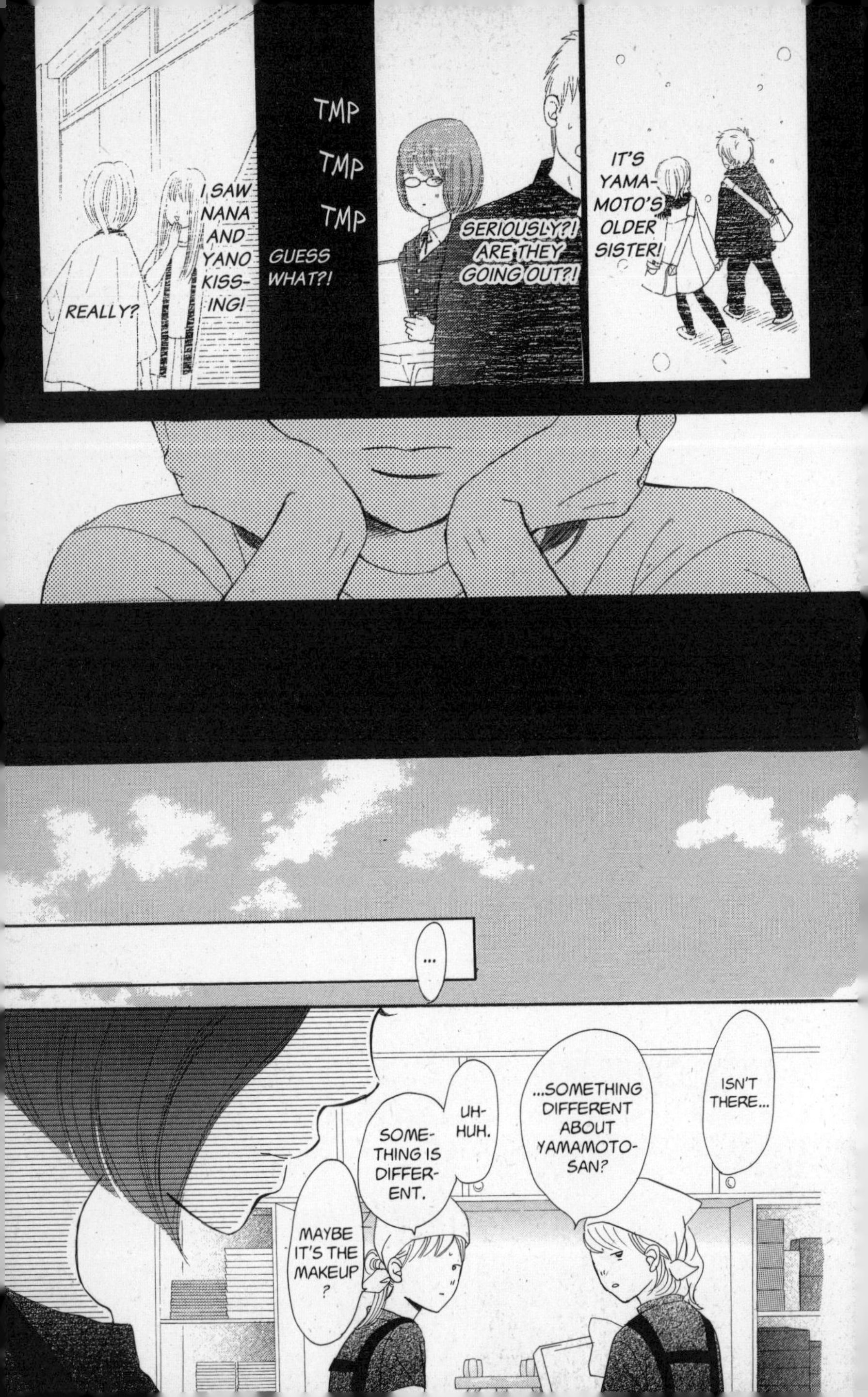
IT'S YAMAMOTO'S OLDER SISTER!
SERIOUSLY?! ARE THEY GOING OUT?!
TMP
TMP
TMP
GUESS WHAT?!
I SAW NANA AND YANO KISSING!
REALLY?
...
ISN'T THERE...
...SOMETHING DIFFERENT ABOUT YAMAMOTO-SAN?
UH-HUH.
SOMETHING IS DIFFERENT.
MAYBE IT'S THE MAKEUP?

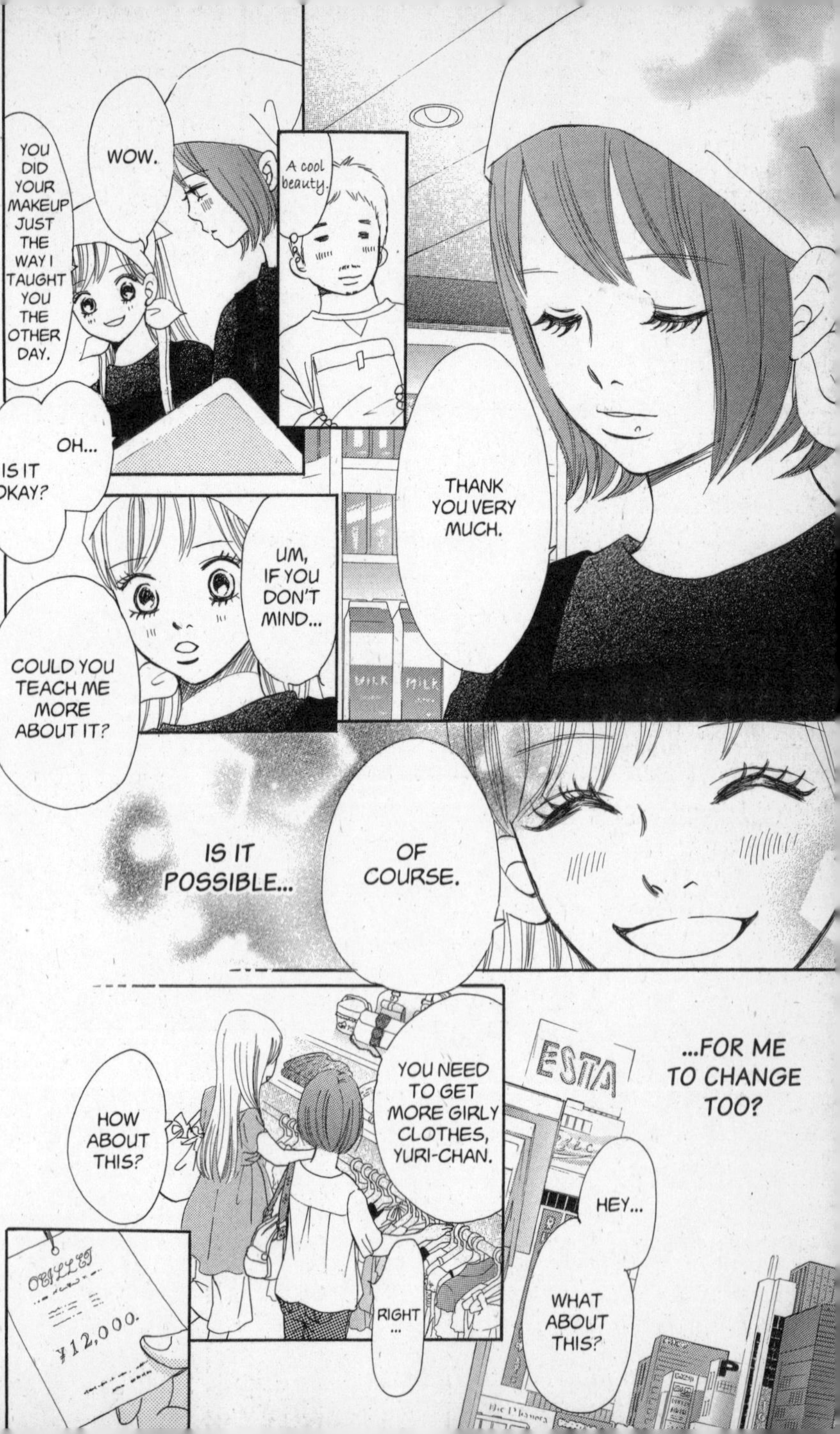
THANK YOU VERY MUCH.
A cool beauty.
WOW.
YOU DID YOUR MAKEUP JUST THE WAY I TAUGHT YOU THE OTHER DAY.
OH... IS IT OKAY?
UM, IF YOU DON'T MIND...
COULD YOU TEACH ME MORE ABOUT IT?
OF COURSE.
IS IT POSSIBLE...
...FOR ME TO CHANGE TOO?
HEY...
WHAT ABOUT THIS?
ESTA
YOU NEED TO GET MORE GIRLY CLOTHES, YURI-CHAN.
HOW ABOUT THIS?
RIGHT...
¥12,000.

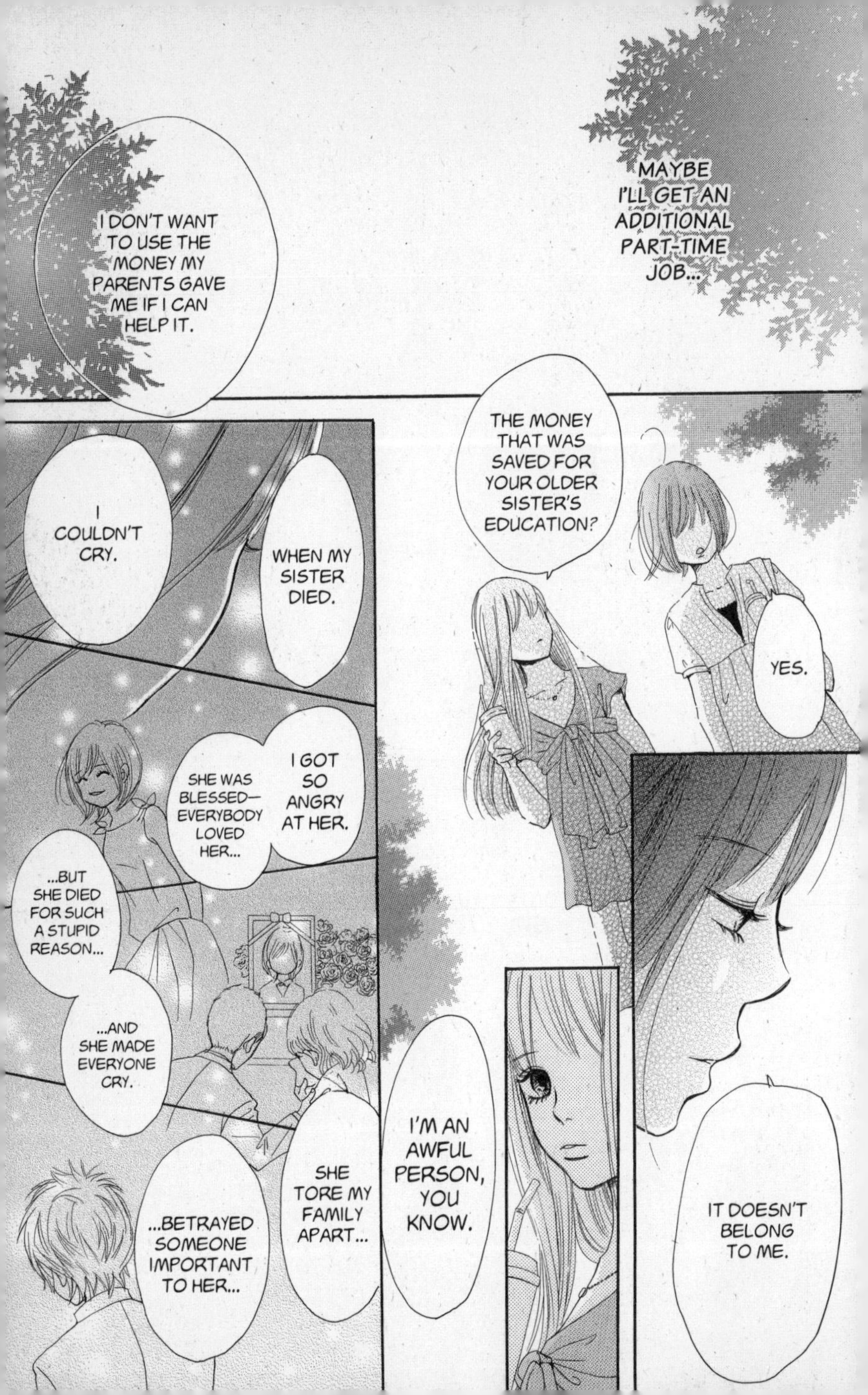
MAYBE I'LL GET AN ADDITIONAL PART-TIME JOB...
I DON'T WANT TO USE THE MONEY MY PARENTS GAVE ME IF I CAN HELP IT.
THE MONEY THAT WAS SAVED FOR YOUR OLDER SISTER'S EDUCATION?
YES.
IT DOESN'T BELONG TO ME.
I'M AN AWFUL PERSON, YOU KNOW.
WHEN MY SISTER DIED.
I COULDN'T CRY.
I GOT SO ANGRY AT HER.
SHE WAS BLESSED—EVERYBODY LOVED HER...
...BUT SHE DIED FOR SUCH A STUPID REASON...
...AND SHE MADE EVERYONE CRY.
SHE TORE MY FAMILY APART...
...BETRAYED SOMEONE IMPORTANT TO HER...

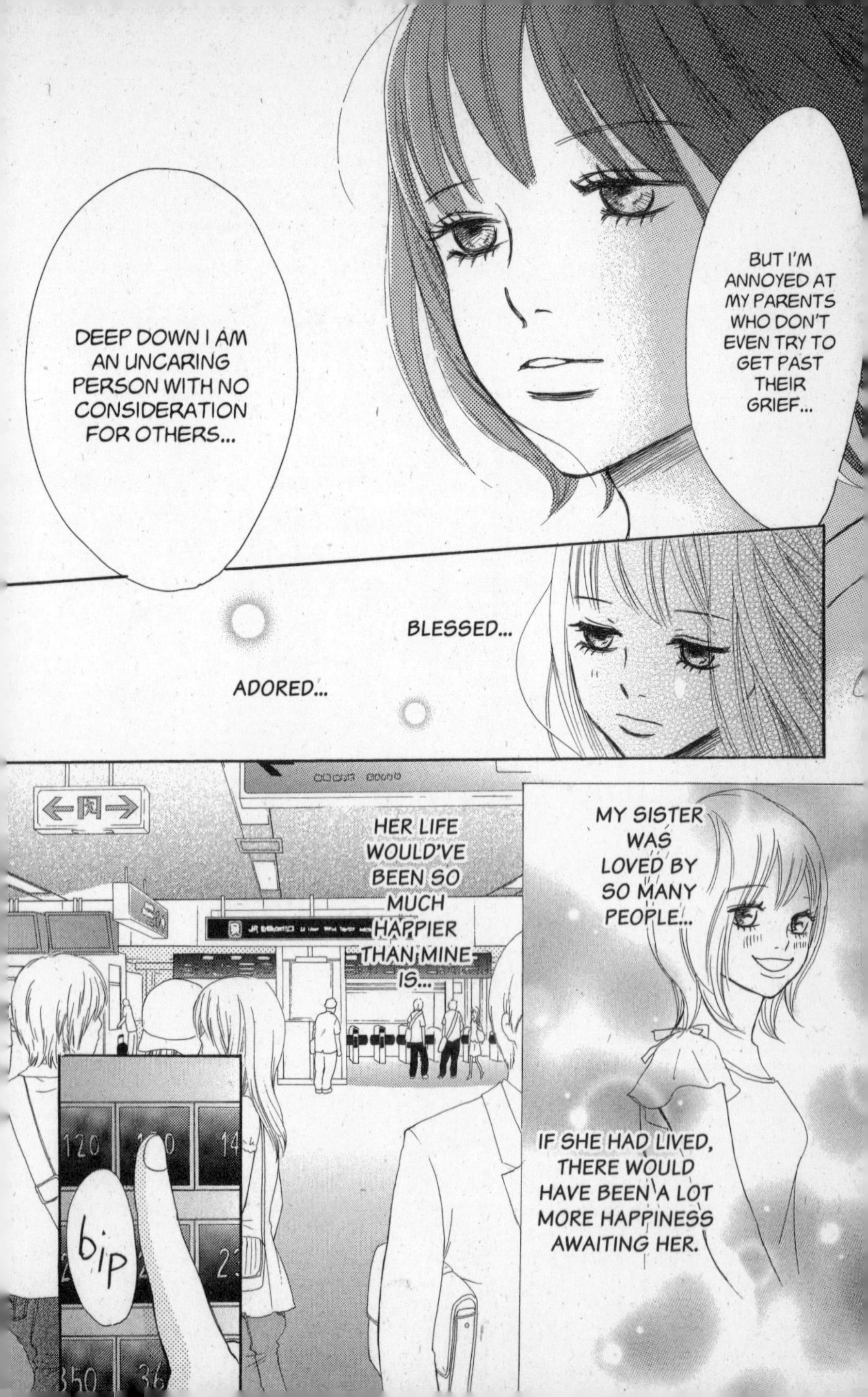
BUT I'M ANNOYED AT MY PARENTS WHO DON'T EVEN TRY TO GET PAST THEIR GRIEF...
DEEP DOWN I AM AN UNCARING PERSON WITH NO CONSIDERATION FOR OTHERS...
BLESSED...
ADORED...
MY SISTER WAS LOVED BY SO MANY PEOPLE...
IF SHE HAD LIVED, THERE WOULD HAVE BEEN A LOT MORE HAPPINESS AWAITING HER.
HER LIFE WOULD'VE BEEN SO MUCH HAPPIER THAN MINE IS...
bip

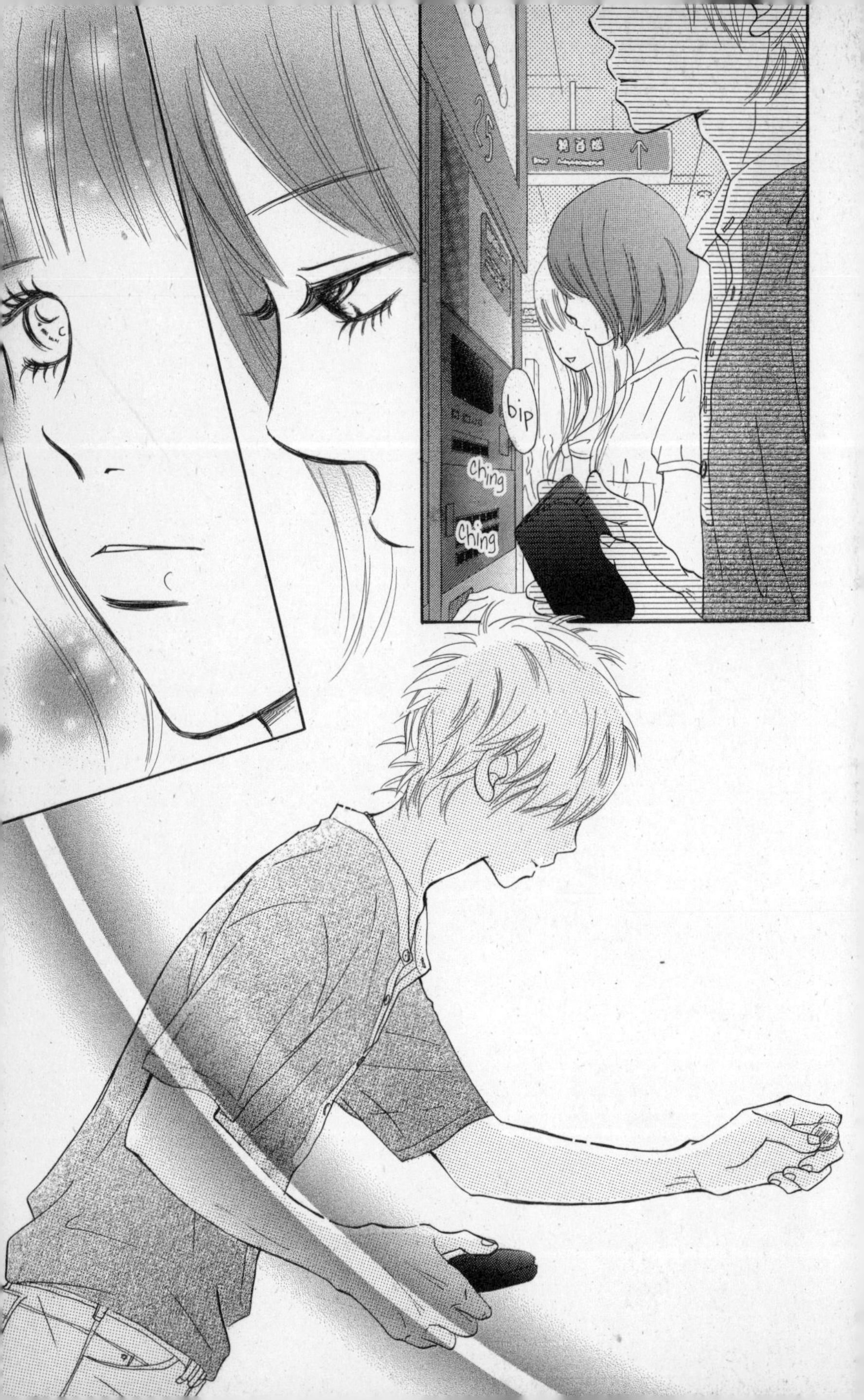
bip
Ching
Ching

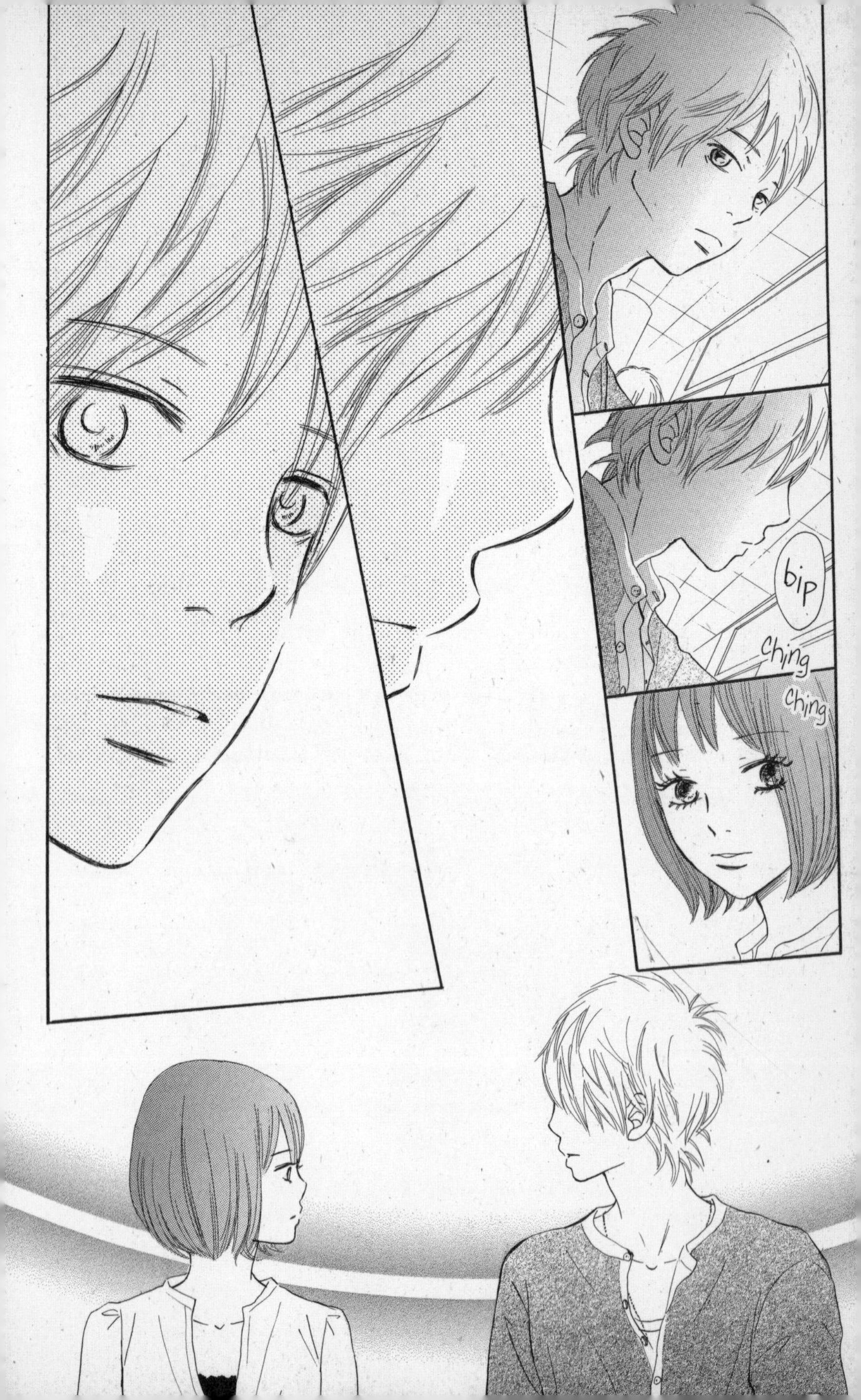
bip
ching
ching

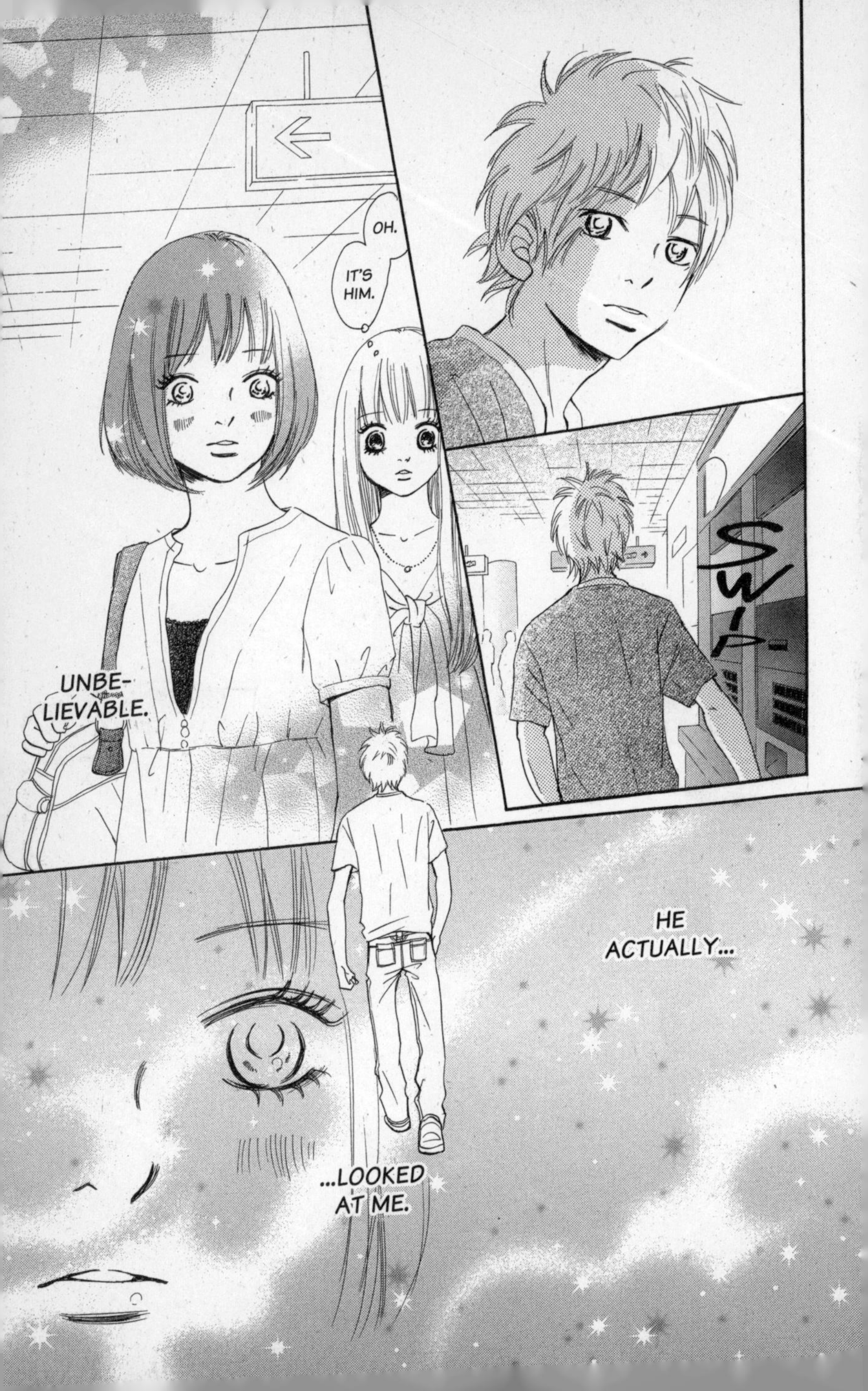
SWIP
OH.
IT'S HIM.
UNBE-LIEVABLE.
HE ACTUALLY...
...LOOKED AT ME.

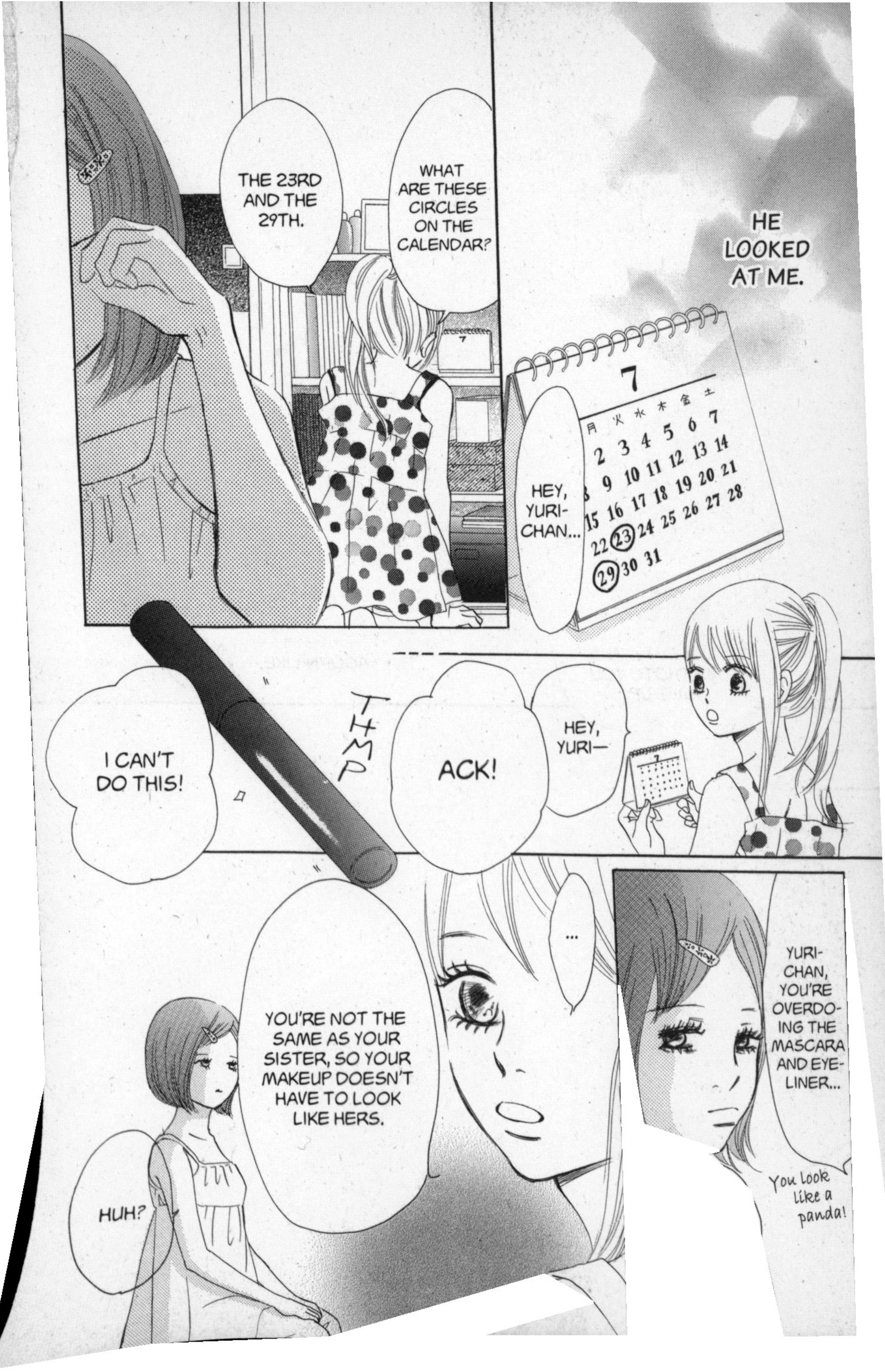
HE LOOKED AT ME.
HEY, YURI-CHAN...
WHAT ARE THESE CIRCLES ON THE CALENDAR?
THE 23RD AND THE 29TH.
HEY, YURI—
ACK!
THMP
I CAN'T DO THIS!
YURI-CHAN, YOU'RE OVERDO-ING THE MASCARA AND EYE-LINER...
You look like a panda!
...
YOU'RE NOT THE SAME AS YOUR SISTER, SO YOUR MAKEUP DOESN'T HAVE TO LOOK LIKE HERS.
HUH?

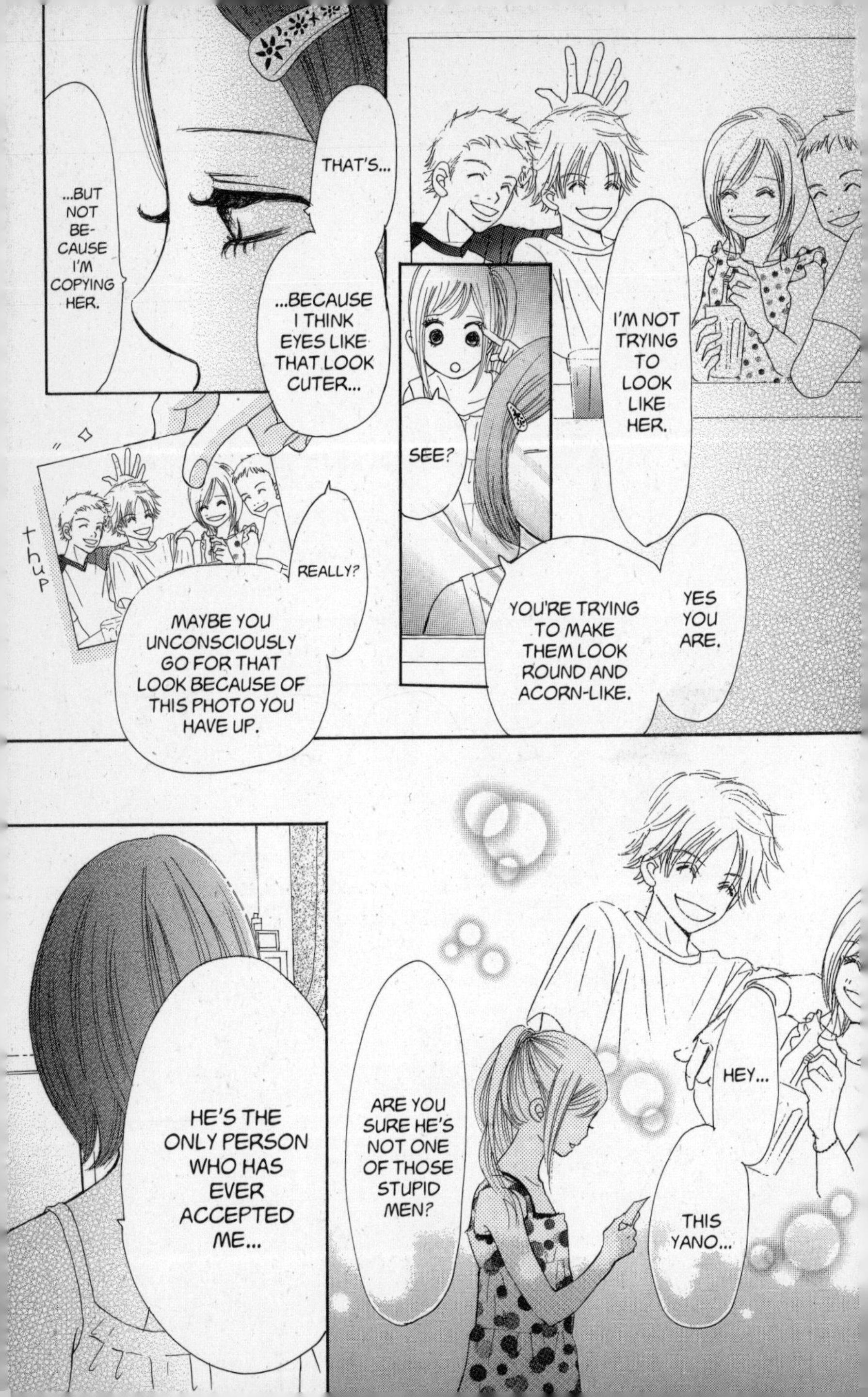
I'M NOT TRYING TO LOOK LIKE HER.
SEE?
YES YOU ARE.
YOU'RE TRYING TO MAKE THEM LOOK ROUND AND ACORN-LIKE.
THAT'S...
...BUT NOT BE-CAUSE I'M COPYING HER.
...BECAUSE I THINK EYES LIKE THAT LOOK CUTER...
thup
REALLY?
MAYBE YOU UNCONSCIOUSLY GO FOR THAT LOOK BECAUSE OF THIS PHOTO YOU HAVE UP.
HEY...
THIS YANO...
ARE YOU SURE HE'S NOT ONE OF THOSE STUPID MEN?
HE'S THE ONLY PERSON WHO HAS EVER ACCEPTED ME...

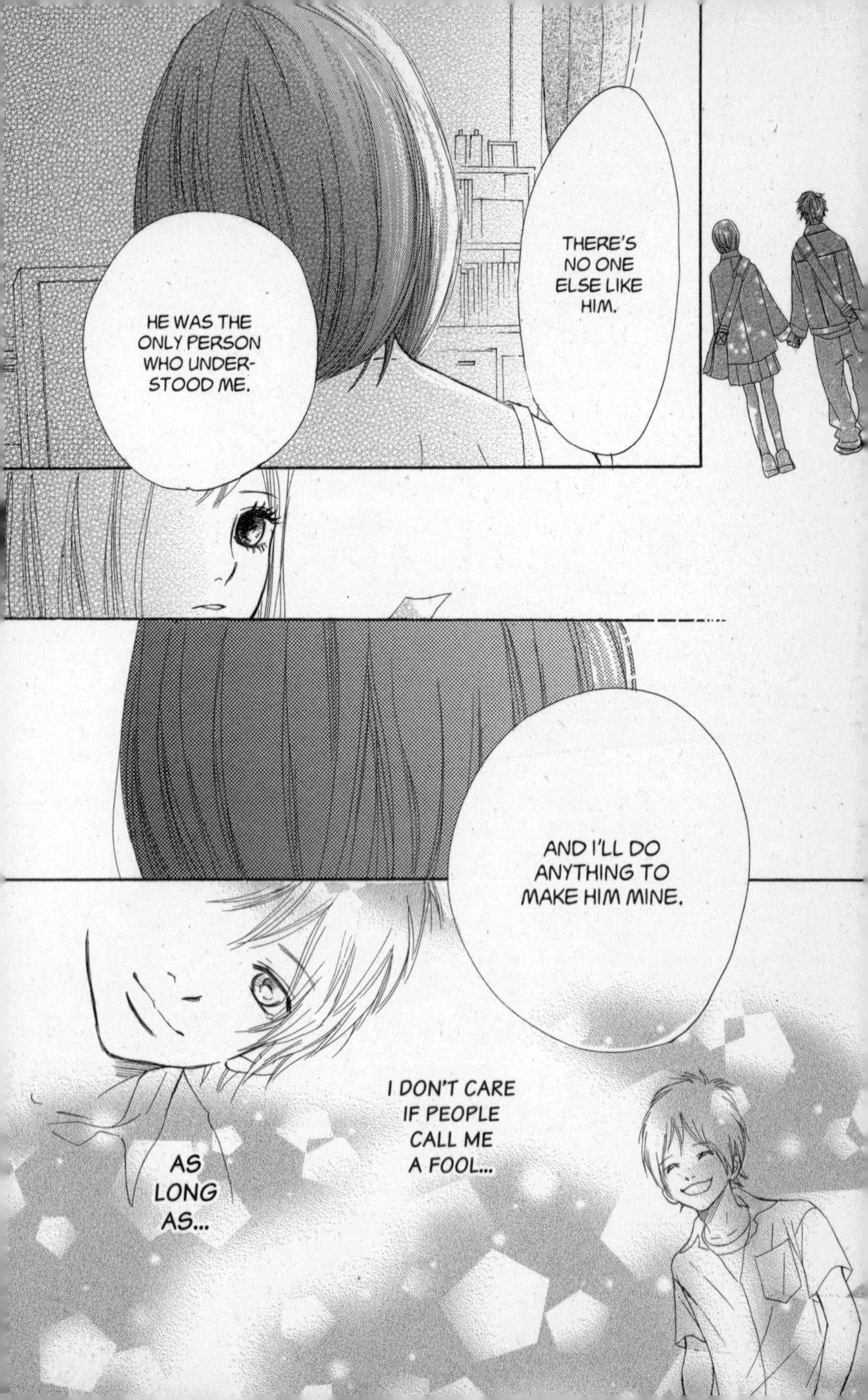
THERE'S NO ONE ELSE LIKE HIM.
HE WAS THE ONLY PERSON WHO UNDER-STOOD ME.
AND I'LL DO ANYTHING TO MAKE HIM MINE.
I DON'T CARE IF PEOPLE CALL ME A FOOL...
AS LONG AS...

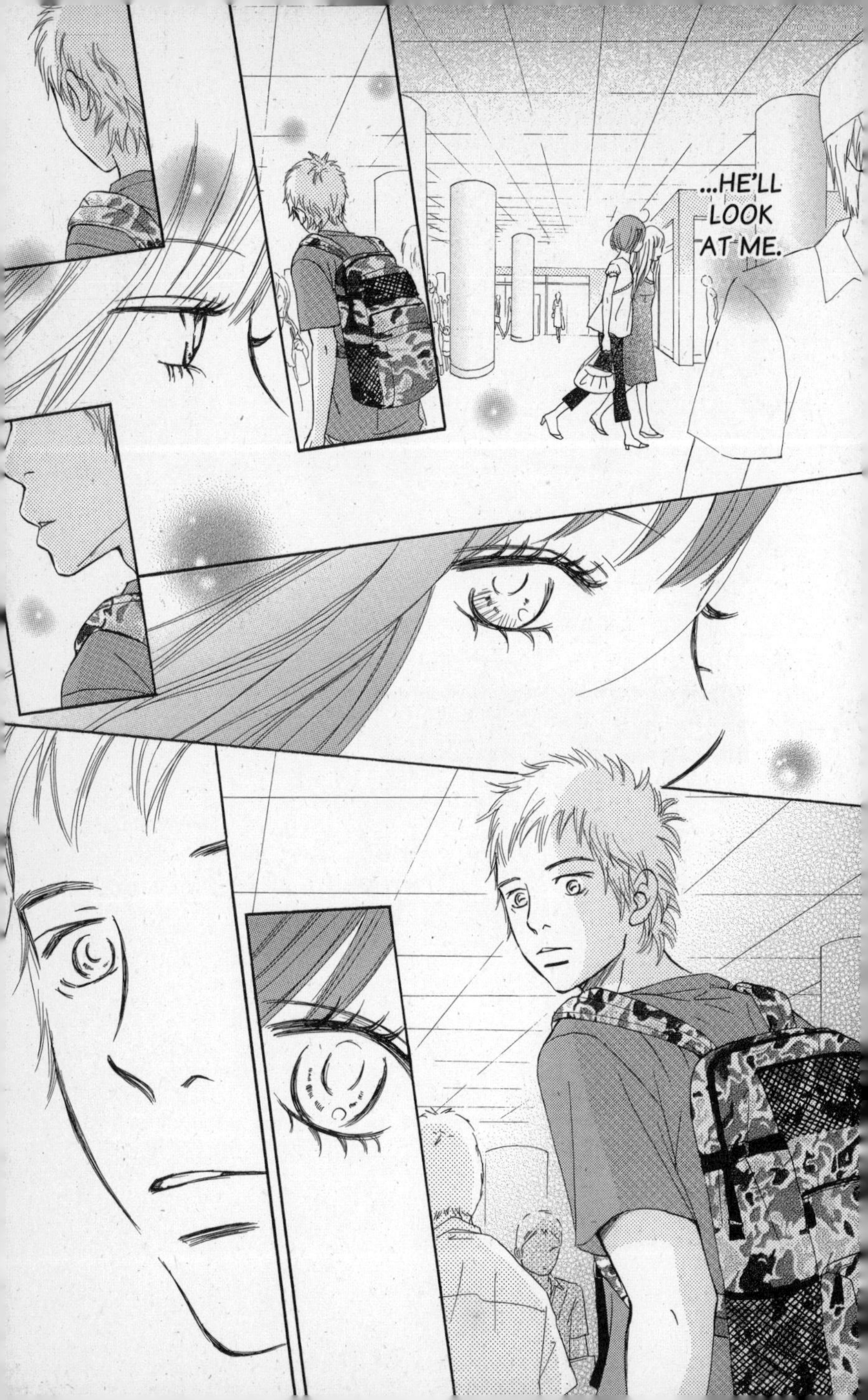
...HE'LL LOOK AT ME.

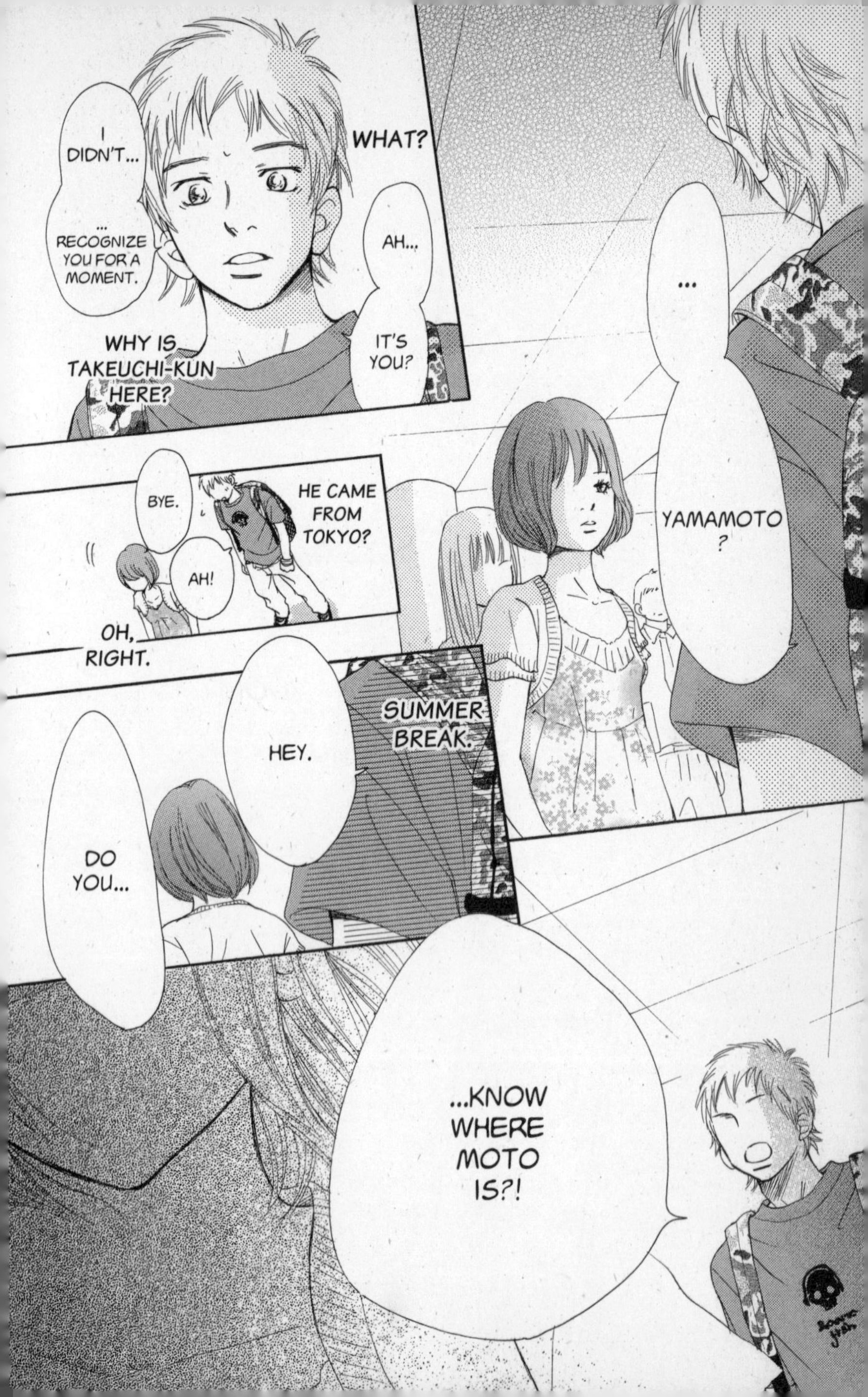
...
YAMAMOTO?
WHAT?
AH...
IT'S YOU?
I DIDN'T...
... RECOGNIZE YOU FOR A MOMENT.
WHY IS TAKEUCHI-KUN HERE?
HE CAME FROM TOKYO?
BYE.
AH!
OH, RIGHT.
SUMMER BREAK.
HEY.
DO YOU...
...KNOW WHERE MOTO IS?!

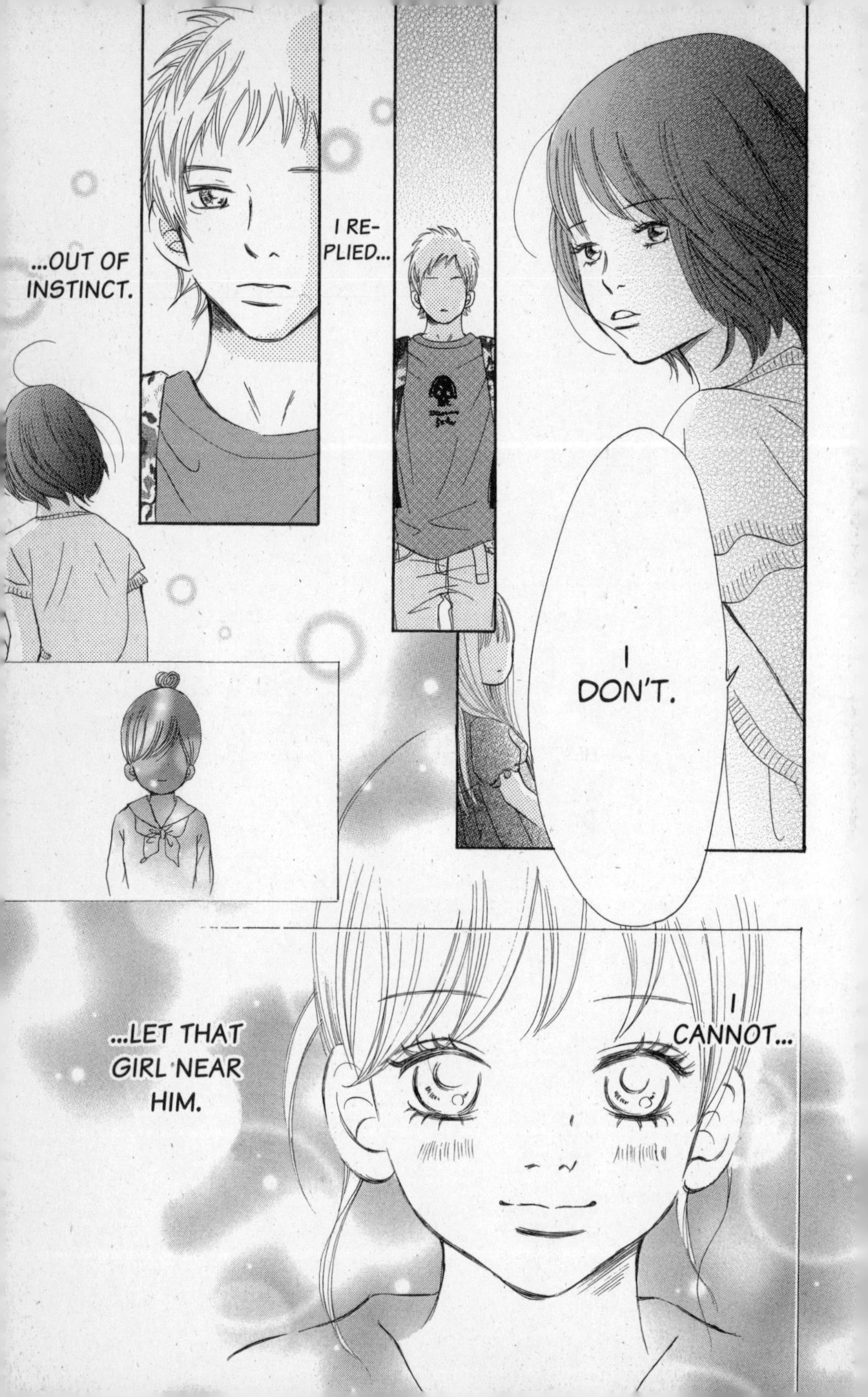
I DON'T.
I RE-PLIED...
...OUT OF INSTINCT.
I CANNOT...
...LET THAT GIRL NEAR HIM.

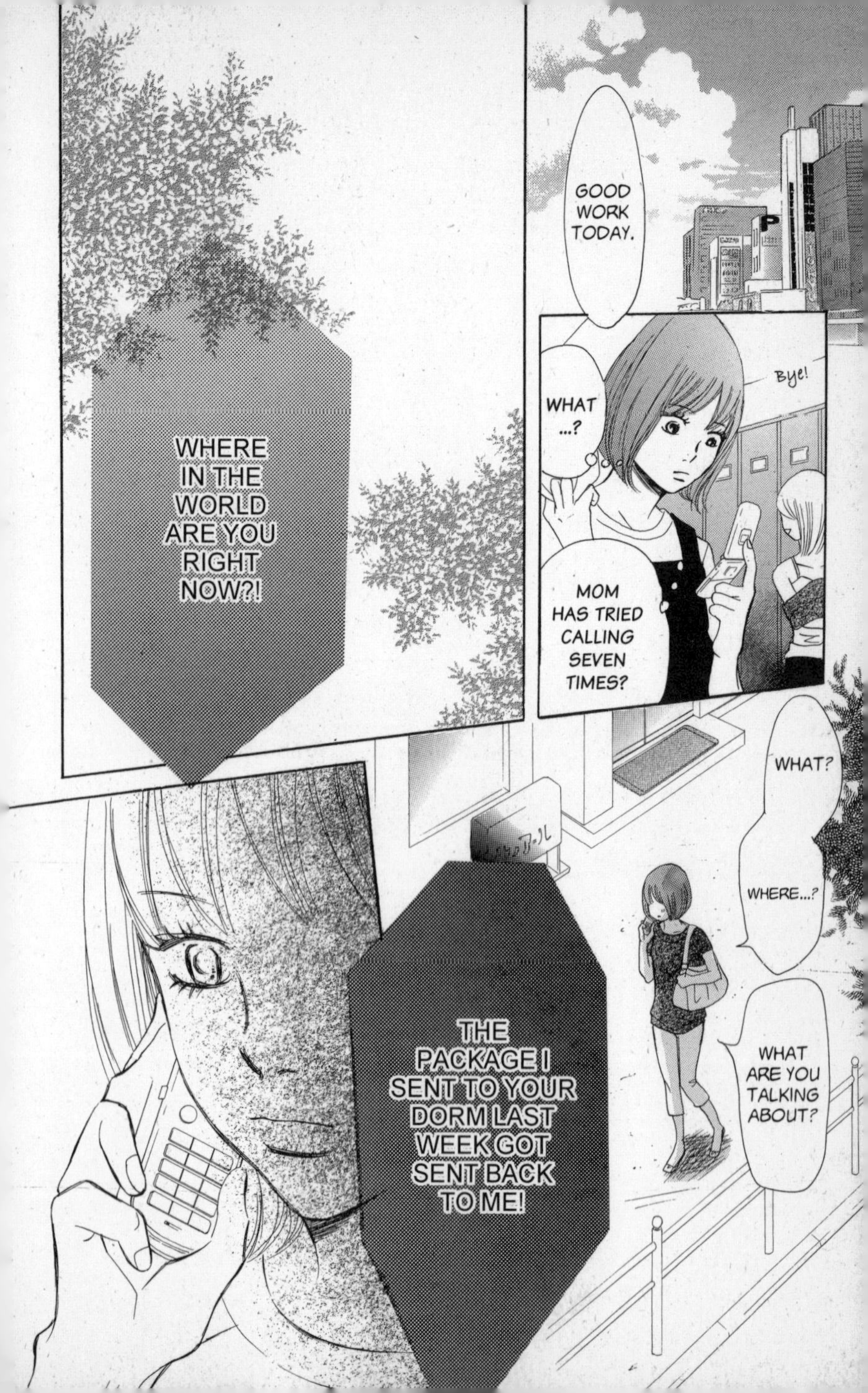
GOOD WORK TODAY.
Bye!
WHAT ...?
MOM HAS TRIED CALLING SEVEN TIMES?
WHERE IN THE WORLD ARE YOU RIGHT NOW?!
WHAT?
WHERE...?
WHAT ARE YOU TALKING ABOUT?
THE PACKAGE I SENT TO YOUR DORM LAST WEEK GOT SENT BACK TO ME!

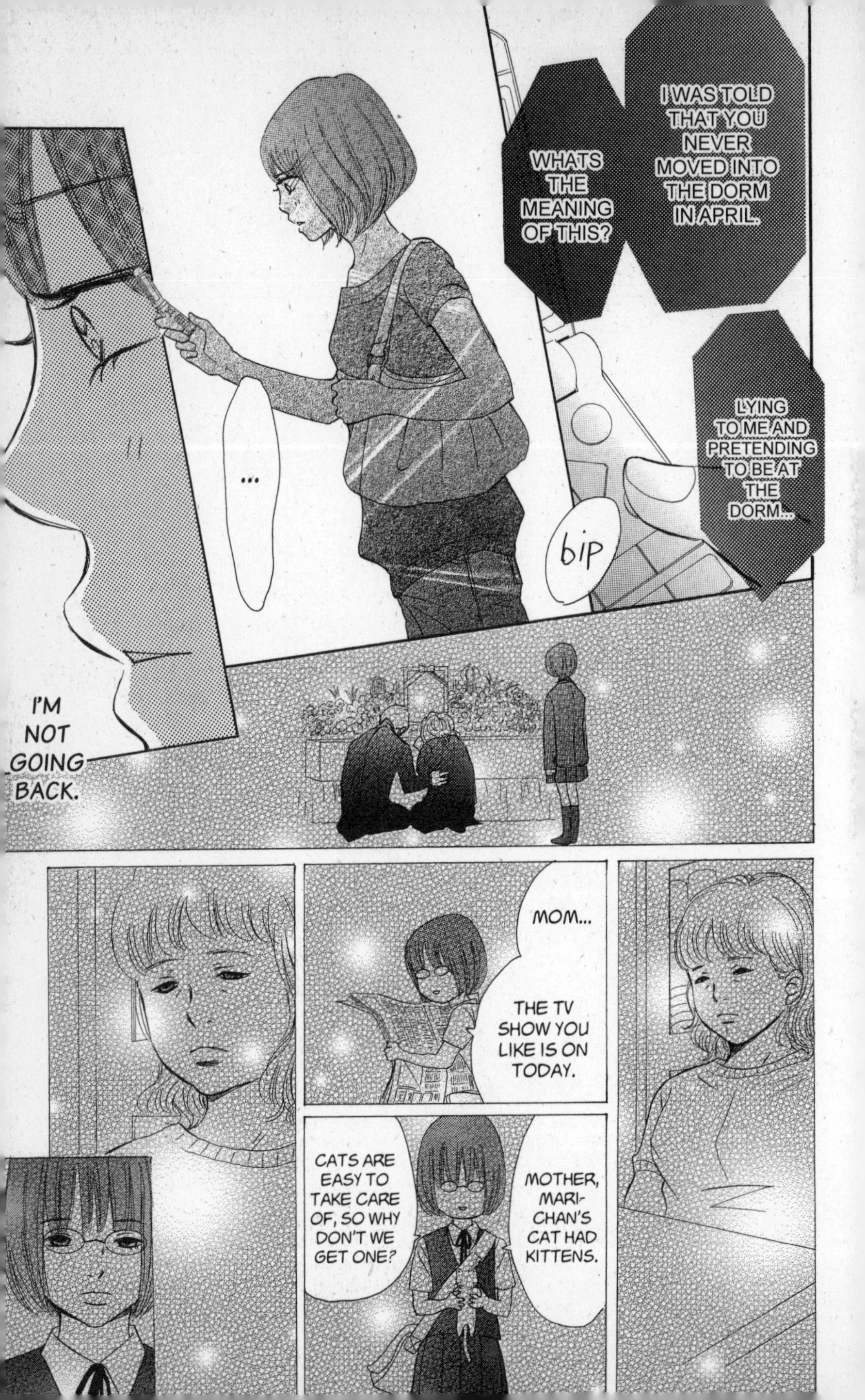
I WAS TOLD THAT YOU NEVER MOVED INTO THE DORM IN APRIL.
WHATS THE MEANING OF THIS?
LYING TO ME AND PRETENDING TO BE AT THE DORM...
bip
...
I'M NOT GOING BACK.
MOM...
THE TV SHOW YOU LIKE IS ON TODAY.
MOTHER, MARI-CHAN'S CAT HAD KITTENS.
CATS ARE EASY TO TAKE CARE OF, SO WHY DON'T WE GET ONE?

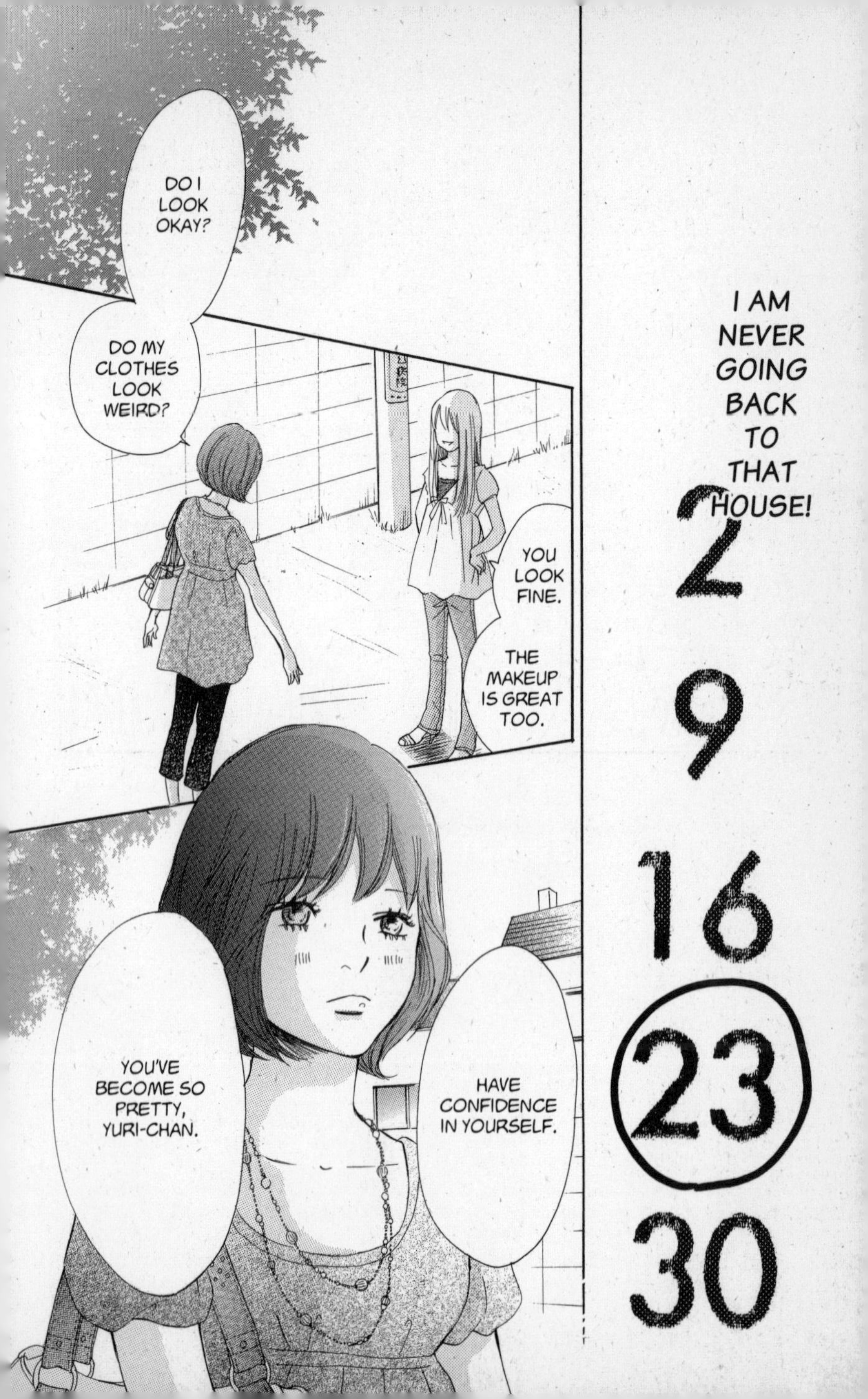
I AM NEVER GOING BACK TO THAT HOUSE!
2
9
16
23
30
DO I LOOK OKAY?
DO MY CLOTHES LOOK WEIRD?
YOU LOOK FINE.
THE MAKEUP IS GREAT TOO.
HAVE CONFIDENCE IN YOURSELF.
YOU'VE BECOME SO PRETTY, YURI-CHAN.

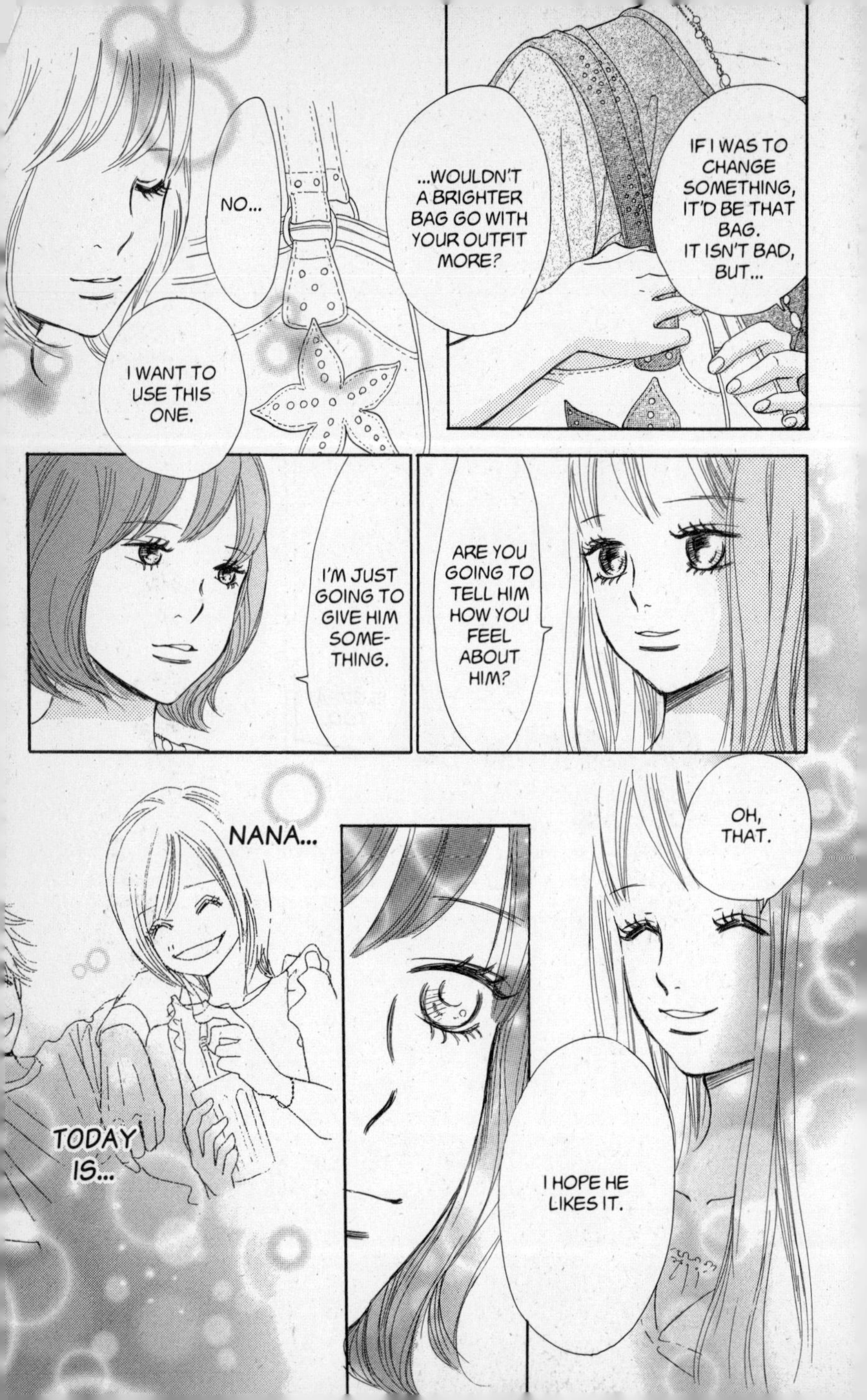
IF I WAS TO CHANGE SOMETHING, IT'D BE THAT BAG. IT ISN'T BAD, BUT...
...WOULDN'T A BRIGHTER BAG GO WITH YOUR OUTFIT MORE?
NO...
I WANT TO USE THIS ONE.
ARE YOU GOING TO TELL HIM HOW YOU FEEL ABOUT HIM?
I'M JUST GOING TO GIVE HIM SOME-THING.
OH, THAT.
I HOPE HE LIKES IT.
NANA...
TODAY IS...

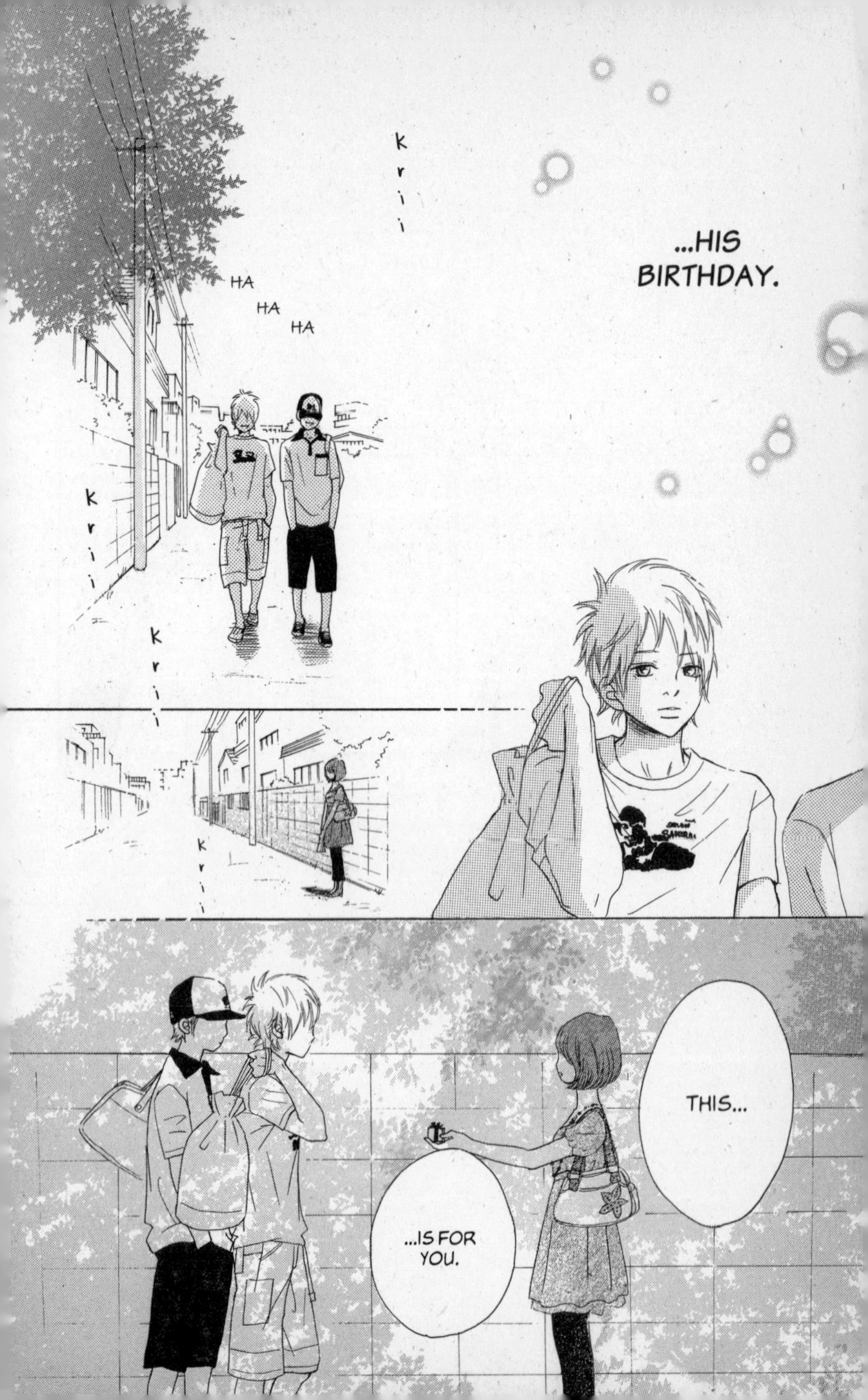
...HIS BIRTHDAY.
Krii
HA HA HA
Krii
Krii
Krii
THIS...
...IS FOR YOU.

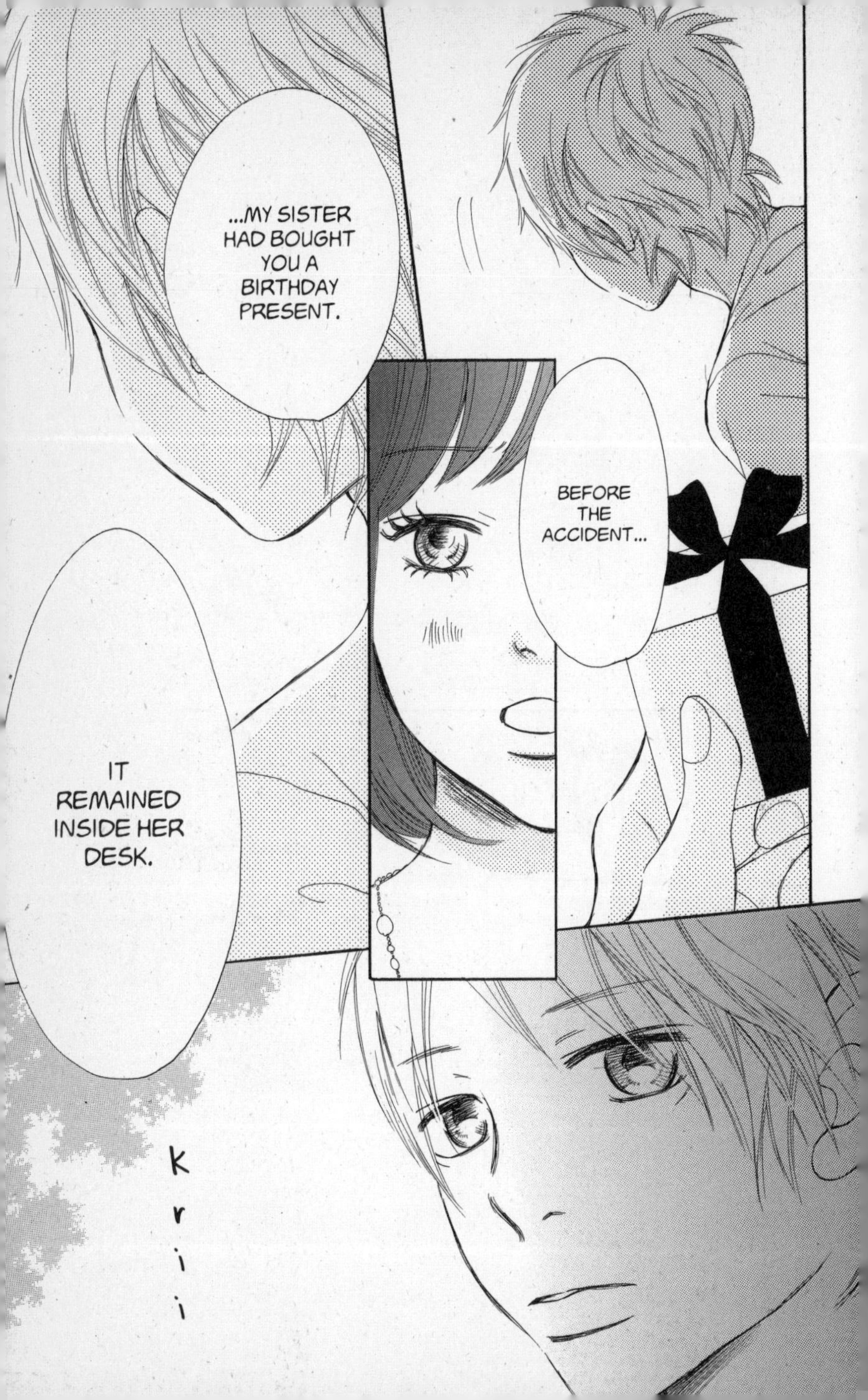
BEFORE THE ACCIDENT...
...MY SISTER HAD BOUGHT YOU A BIRTHDAY PRESENT.
IT REMAINED INSIDE HER DESK.
Krii

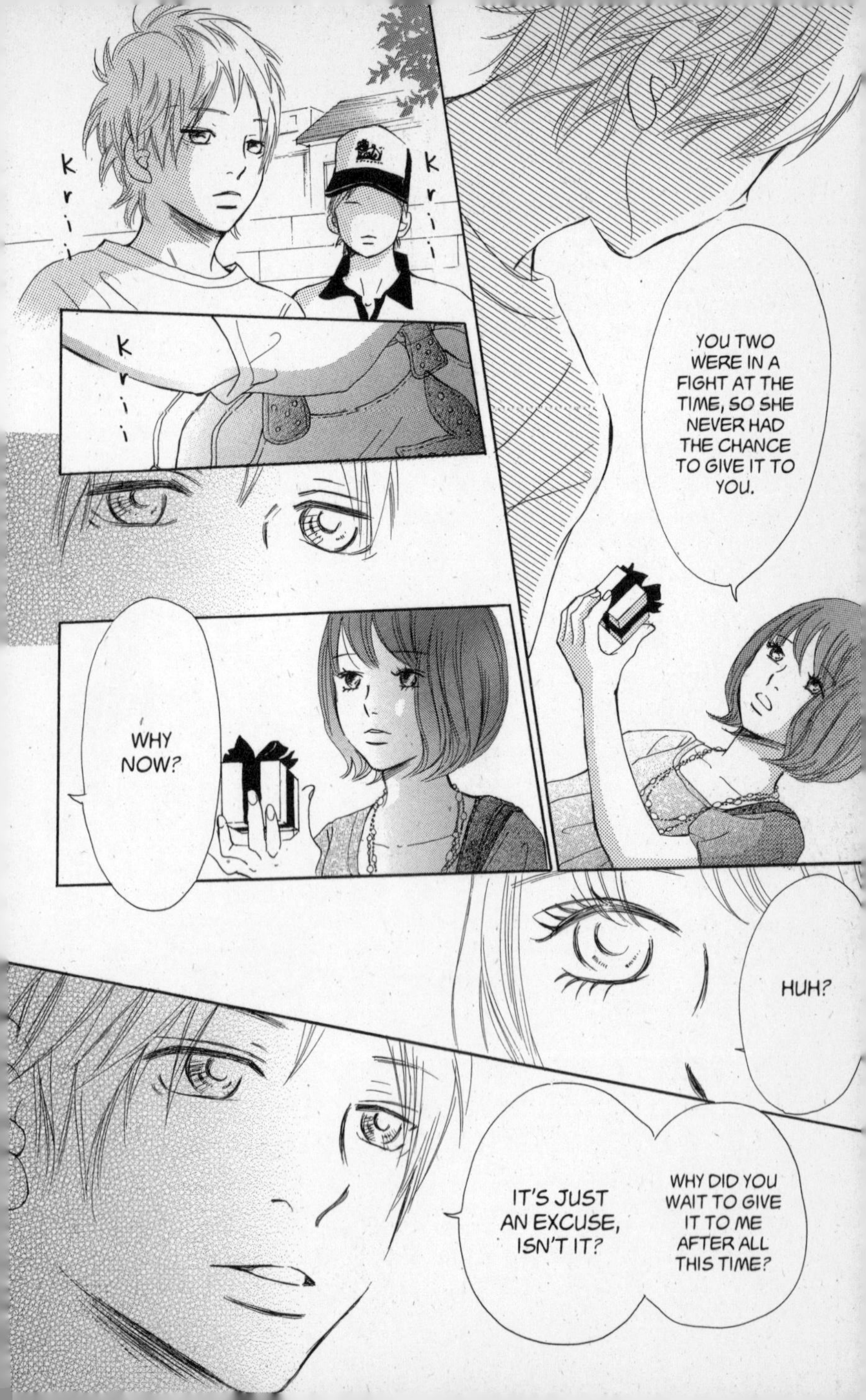
YOU TWO WERE IN A FIGHT AT THE TIME, SO SHE NEVER HAD THE CHANCE TO GIVE IT TO YOU.
Kri...
Kri...
Kri...
WHY NOW?
HUH?
WHY DID YOU WAIT TO GIVE IT TO ME AFTER ALL THIS TIME?
IT'S JUST AN EXCUSE, ISN'T IT?

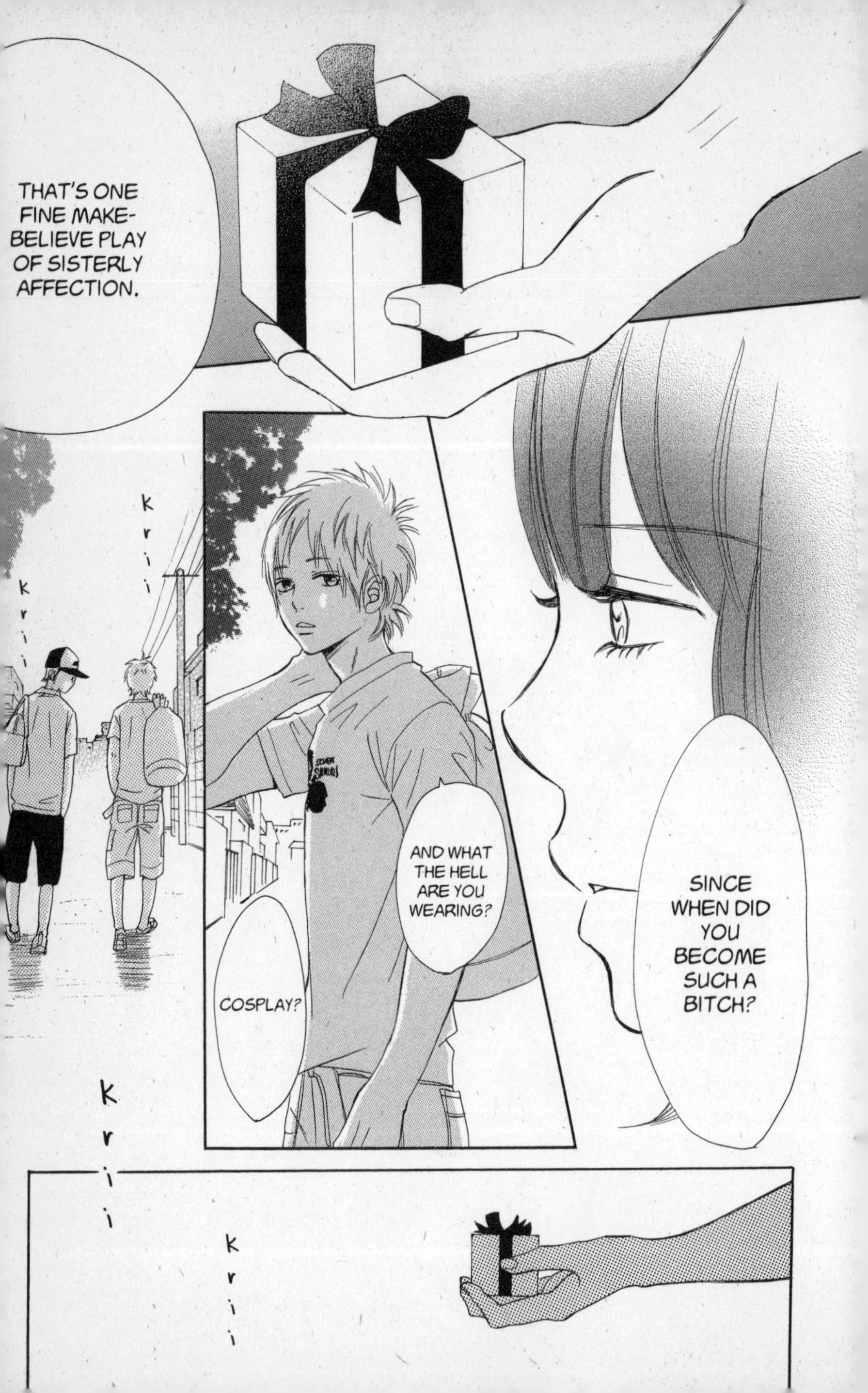
THAT'S ONE FINE MAKE-BELIEVE PLAY OF SISTERLY AFFECTION.
SINCE WHEN DID YOU BECOME SUCH A BITCH?
AND WHAT THE HELL ARE YOU WEARING?
COSPLAY?
Krii
Krii
Krii
Krii

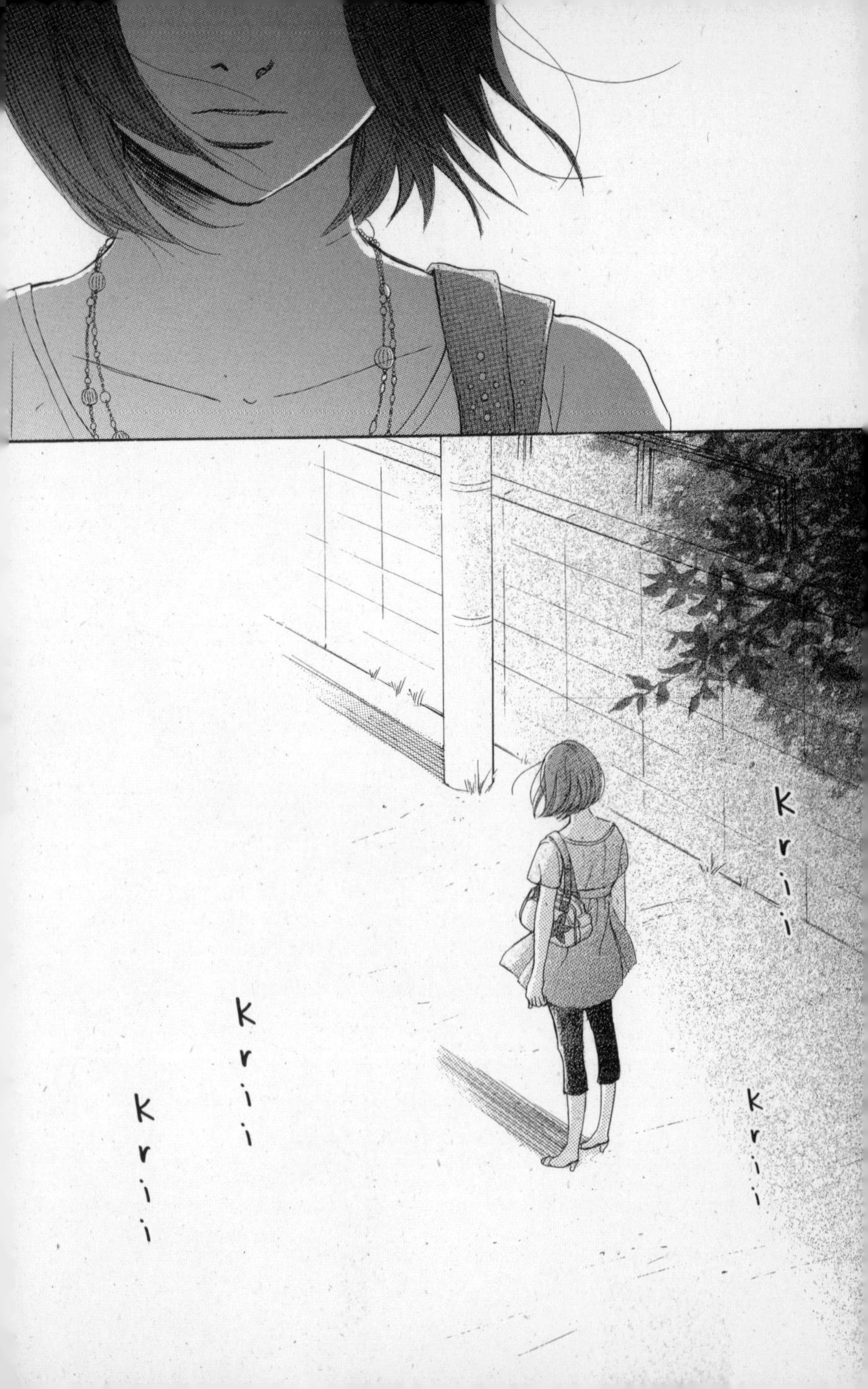
Kri..i
Kri..i
Kri
Kri..i

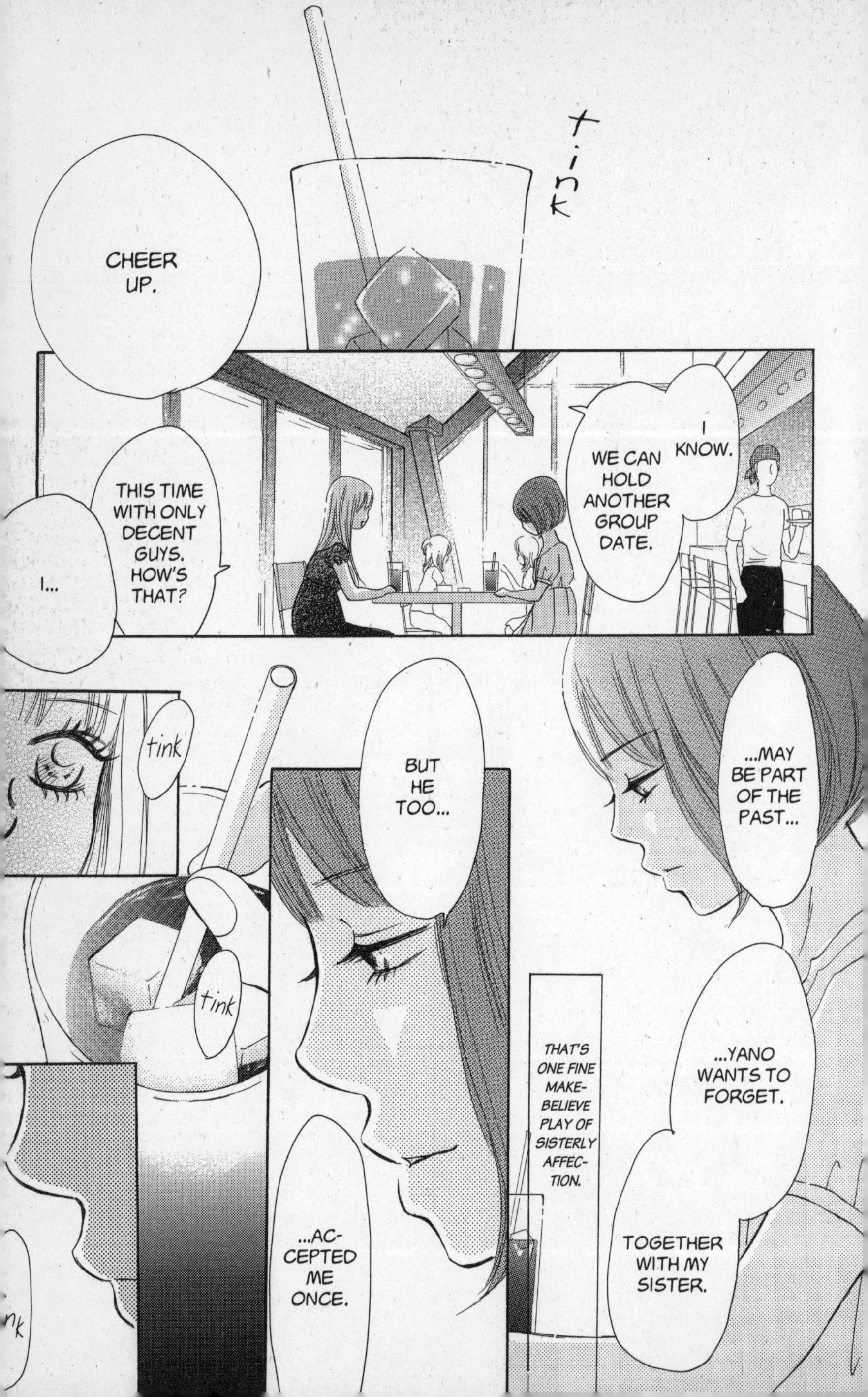
tink
CHEER UP.
I KNOW.
WE CAN HOLD ANOTHER GROUP DATE.
THIS TIME WITH ONLY DECENT GUYS. HOW'S THAT?
I...
...MAY BE PART OF THE PAST...
...YANO WANTS TO FORGET.
TOGETHER WITH MY SISTER.
THAT'S ONE FINE MAKE-BELIEVE PLAY OF SISTERLY AFFECTION.
BUT HE TOO...
...ACCEPTED ME ONCE.
tink
tink
nk

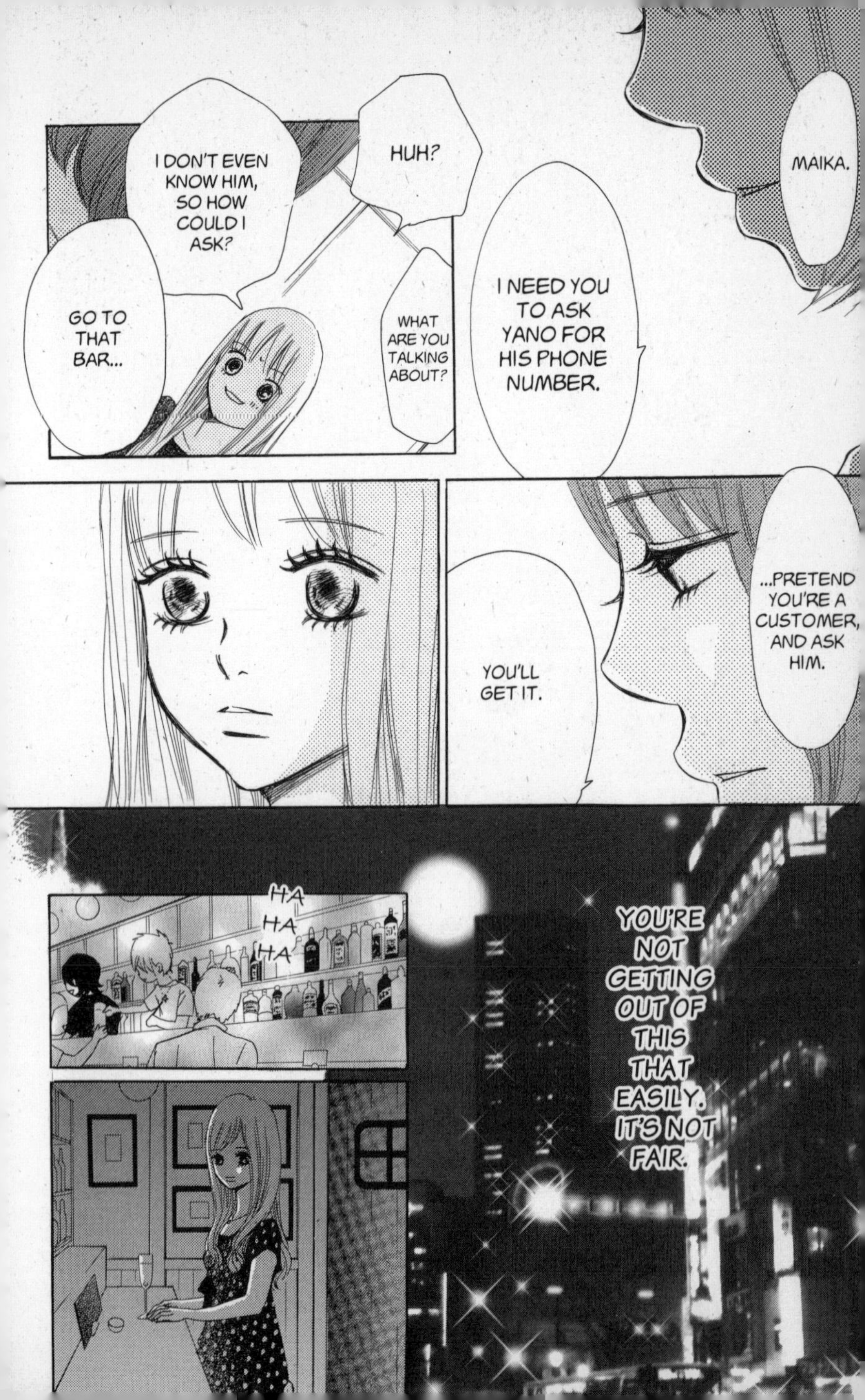
MAIKA.
I NEED YOU TO ASK YANO FOR HIS PHONE NUMBER.
HUH?
WHAT ARE YOU TALKING ABOUT?
I DON'T EVEN KNOW HIM, SO HOW COULD I ASK?
GO TO THAT BAR...
...PRETEND YOU'RE A CUSTOMER, AND ASK HIM.
YOU'LL GET IT.
YOU'RE NOT GETTING OUT OF THIS THAT EASILY. IT'S NOT FAIR.
HA HA HA

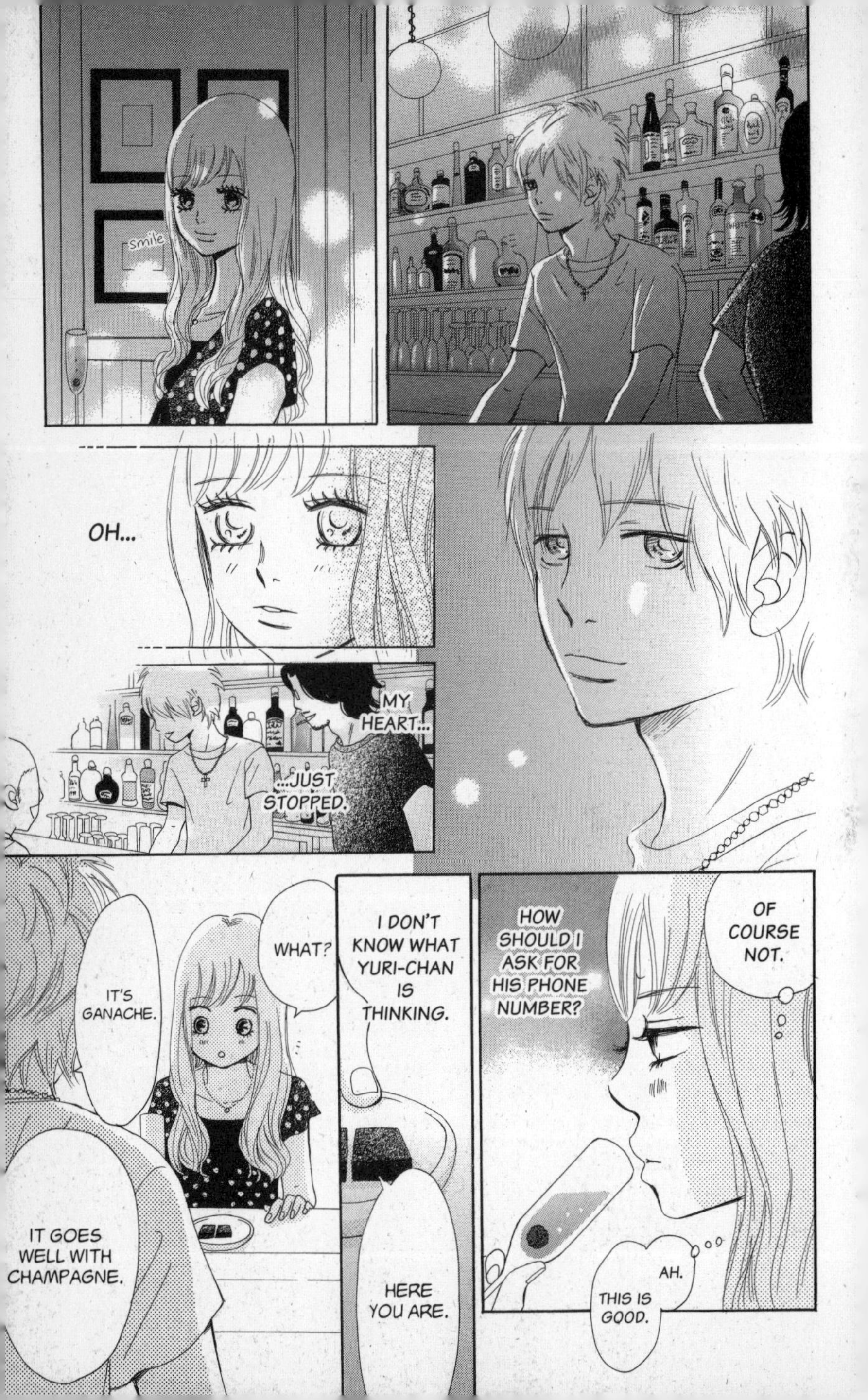
smile
OH...
MY HEART...
...JUST STOPPED.
OF COURSE NOT.
HOW SHOULD I ASK FOR HIS PHONE NUMBER?
AH.
THIS IS GOOD.
I DON'T KNOW WHAT YURI-CHAN IS THINKING.
HERE YOU ARE.
WHAT?
IT'S GANACHE.
IT GOES WELL WITH CHAMPAGNE.

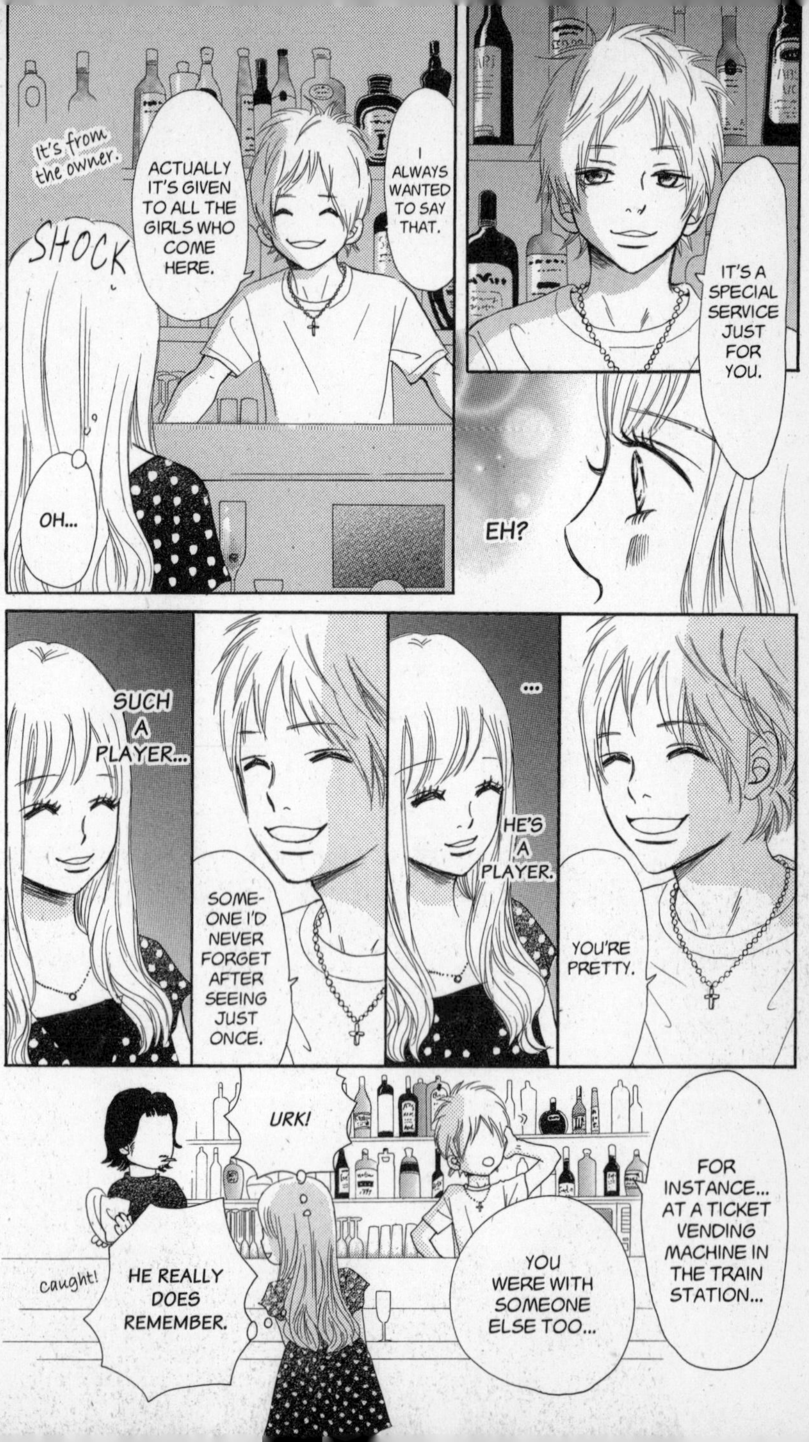
IT'S A SPECIAL SERVICE JUST FOR YOU.
EH?
I ALWAYS WANTED TO SAY THAT.
ACTUALLY IT'S GIVEN TO ALL THE GIRLS WHO COME HERE.
It's from the owner.
SHOCK
OH...
YOU'RE PRETTY.
HE'S A PLAYER.
...
SOME-ONE I'D NEVER FORGET AFTER SEEING JUST ONCE.
SUCH A PLAYER...
FOR INSTANCE... AT A TICKET VENDING MACHINE IN THE TRAIN STATION...
YOU WERE WITH SOMEONE ELSE TOO...
URK!
HE REALLY DOES REMEMBER.
caught!

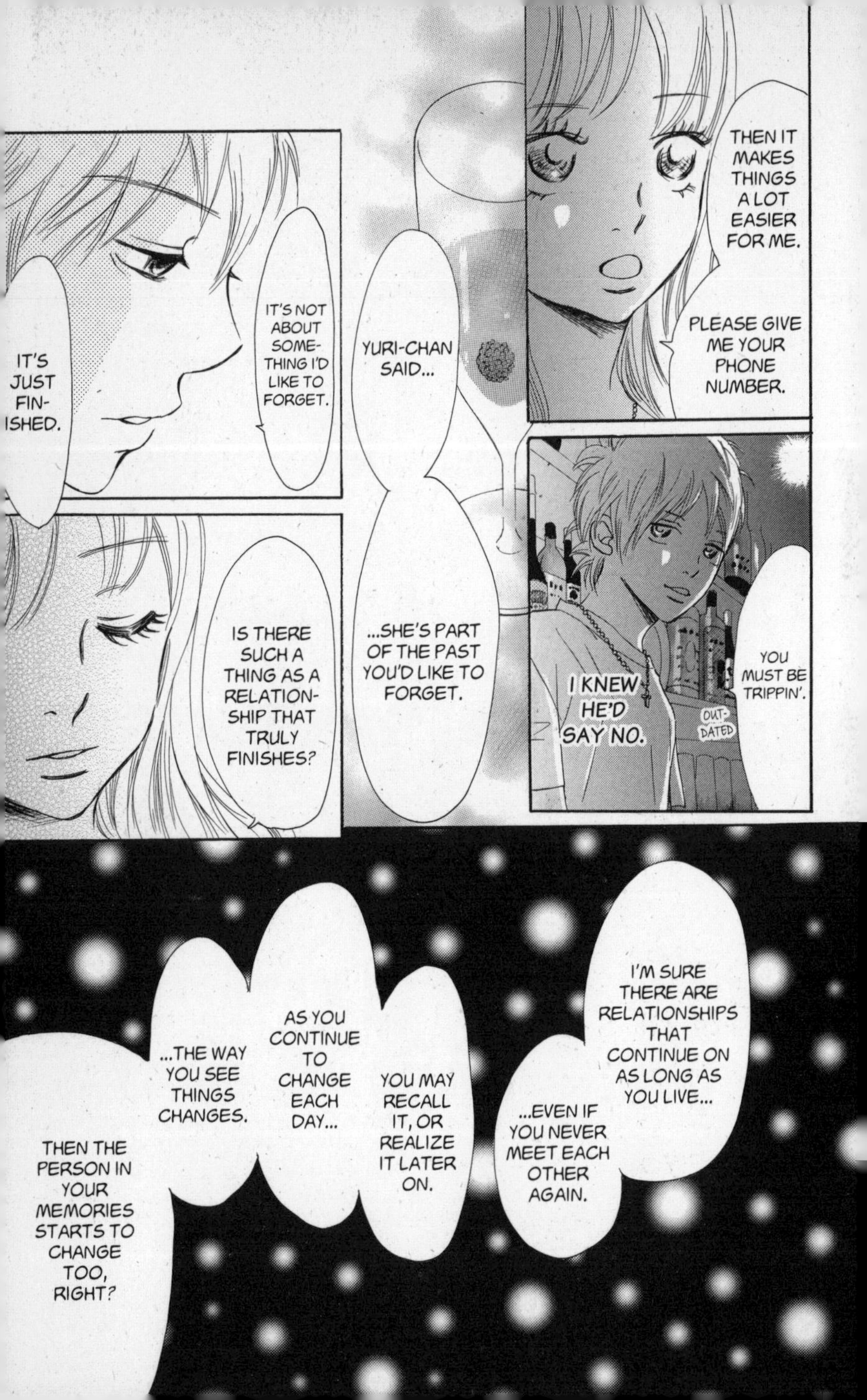
THEN IT MAKES THINGS A LOT EASIER FOR ME.
PLEASE GIVE ME YOUR PHONE NUMBER.
YOU MUST BE TRIPPIN'.
OUT-DATED
I KNEW HE'D SAY NO.
YURI-CHAN SAID...
...SHE'S PART OF THE PAST YOU'D LIKE TO FORGET.
IT'S NOT ABOUT SOMETHING I'D LIKE TO FORGET.
IT'S JUST FINISHED.
IS THERE SUCH A THING AS A RELATIONSHIP THAT TRULY FINISHES?
I'M SURE THERE ARE RELATIONSHIPS THAT CONTINUE ON AS LONG AS YOU LIVE...
...EVEN IF YOU NEVER MEET EACH OTHER AGAIN.
YOU MAY RECALL IT, OR REALIZE IT LATER ON.
AS YOU CONTINUE TO CHANGE EACH DAY...
...THE WAY YOU SEE THINGS CHANGES.
THEN THE PERSON IN YOUR MEMORIES STARTS TO CHANGE TOO, RIGHT?

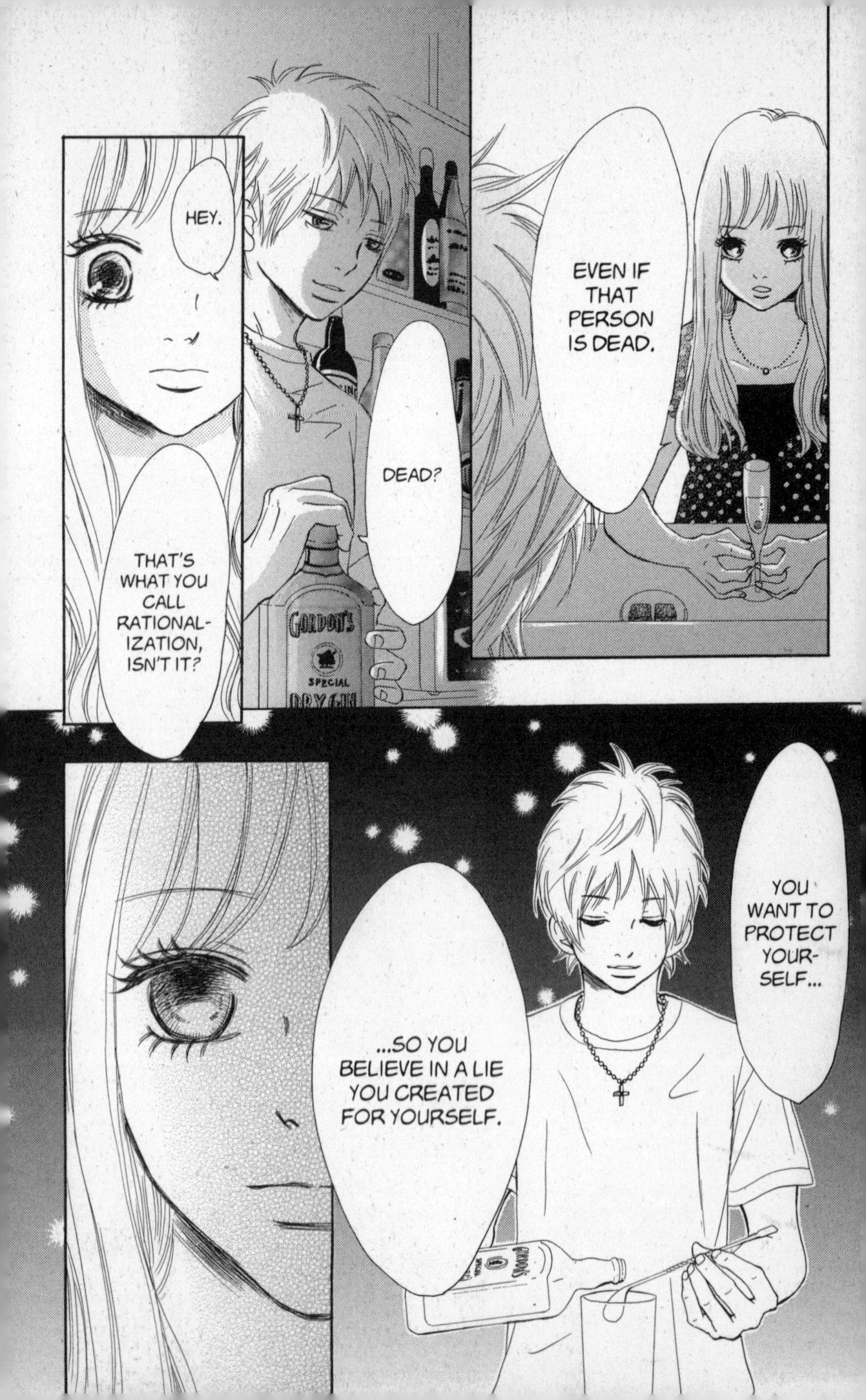
EVEN IF THAT PERSON IS DEAD.
DEAD?
HEY.
THAT'S WHAT YOU CALL RATIONALIZATION, ISN'T IT?
YOU WANT TO PROTECT YOURSELF...
...SO YOU BELIEVE IN A LIE YOU CREATED FOR YOURSELF.

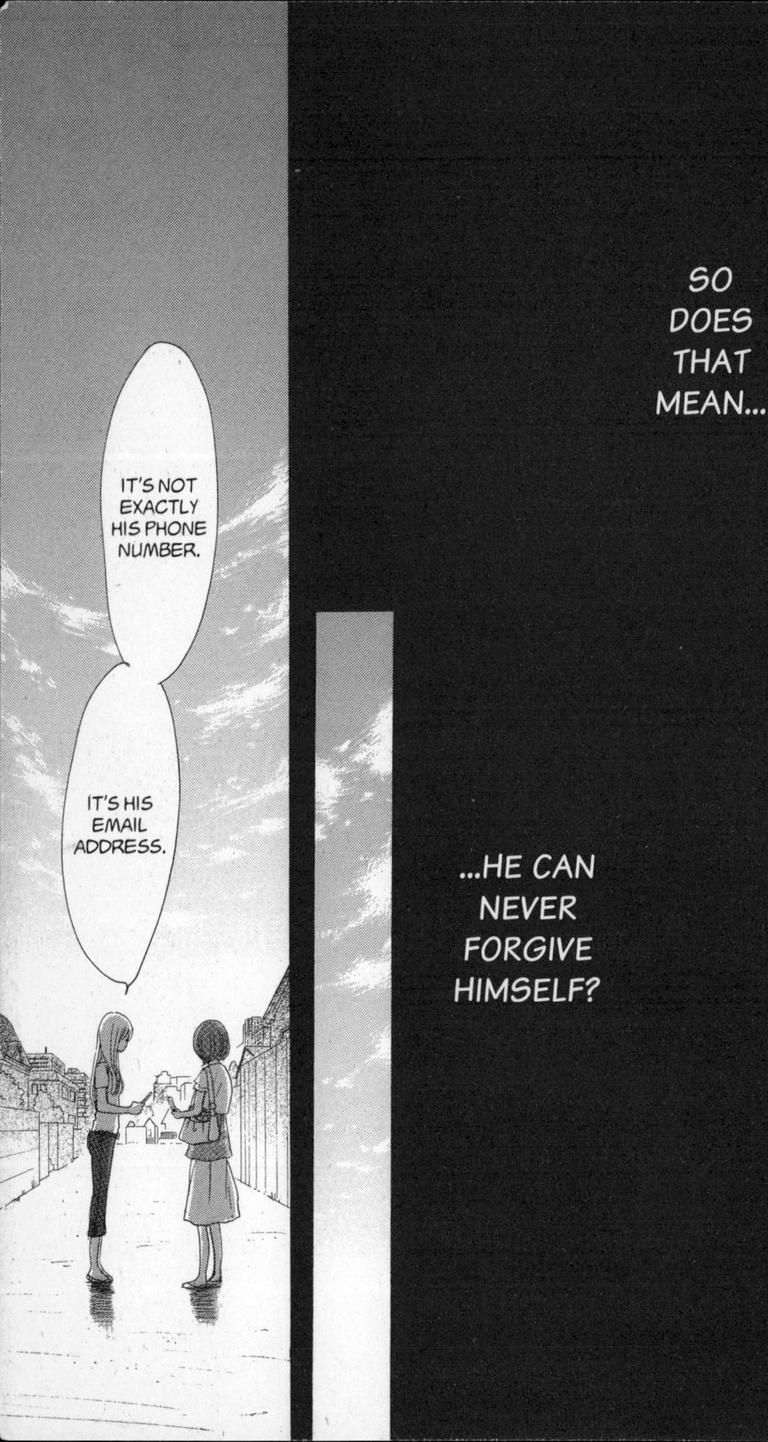
SO DOES THAT MEAN...
...HE CAN NEVER FORGIVE HIMSELF?
IT'S NOT EXACTLY HIS PHONE NUMBER.
IT'S HIS EMAIL ADDRESS.

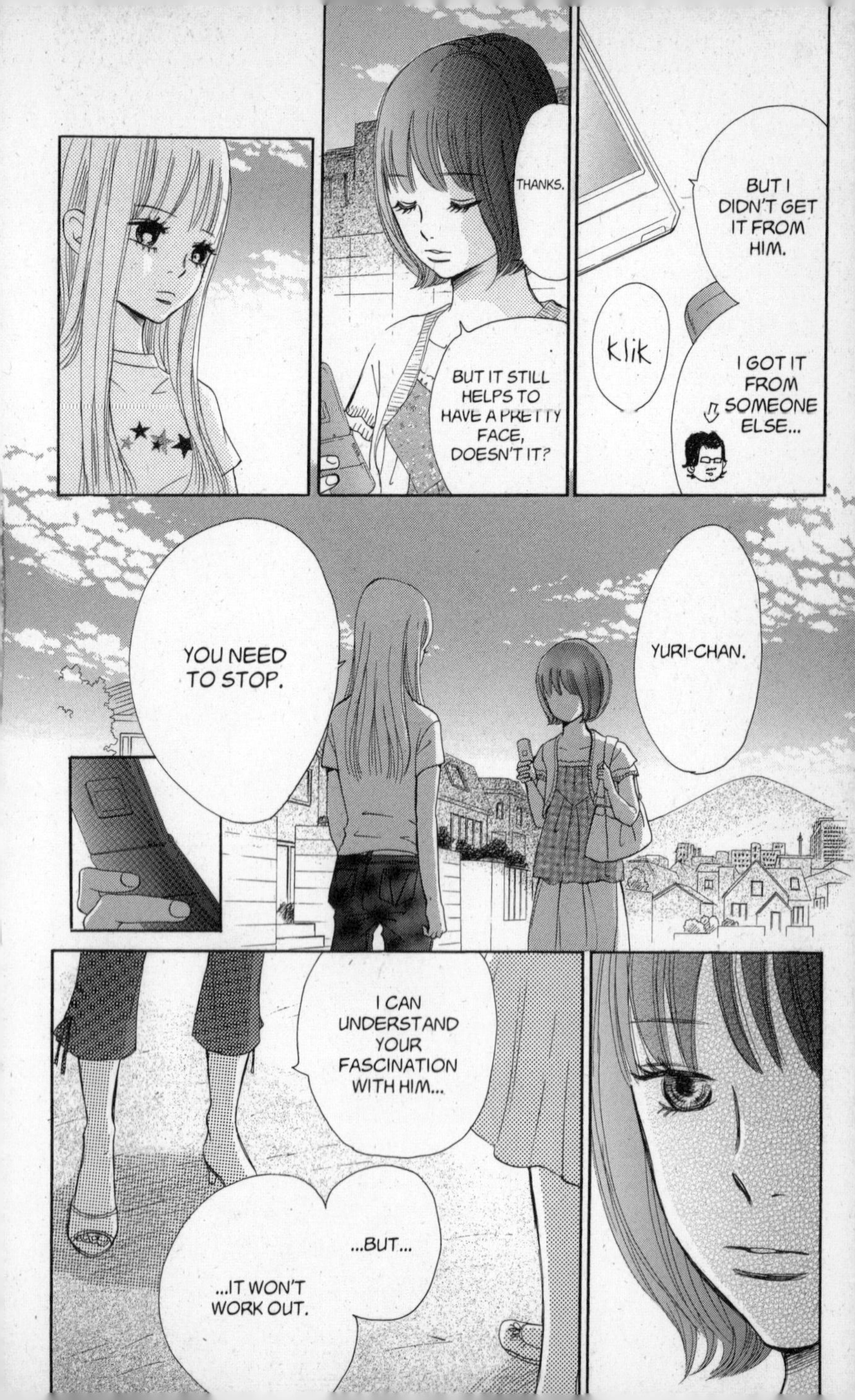

BUT I DIDN'T GET IT FROM HIM.
Klik
I GOT IT FROM SOMEONE ELSE...
THANKS.
BUT IT STILL HELPS TO HAVE A PRETTY FACE, DOESN'T IT?
YURI-CHAN.
YOU NEED TO STOP.
I CAN UNDERSTAND YOUR FASCINATION WITH HIM...
...BUT...
...IT WON'T WORK OUT.

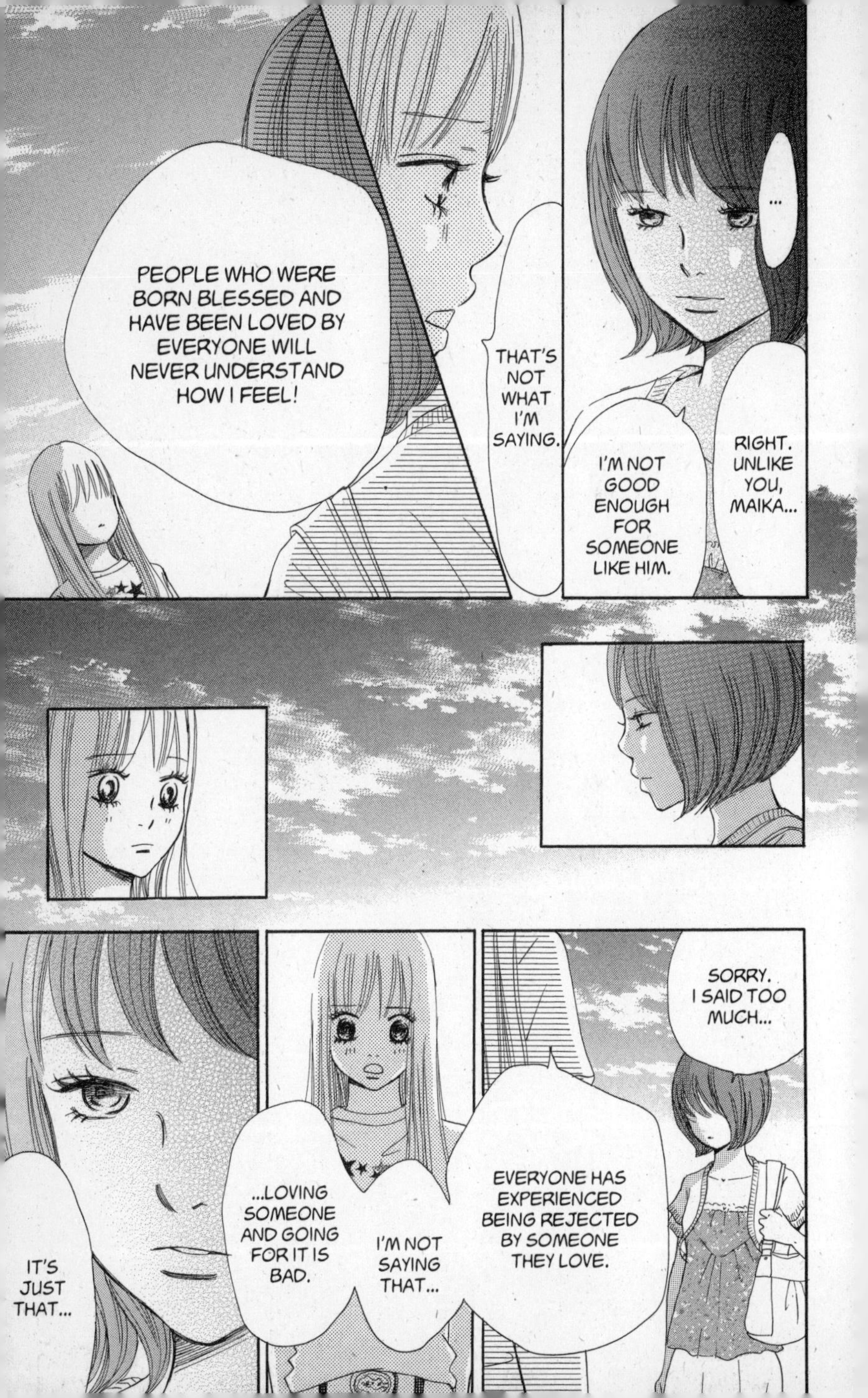
...
RIGHT. UNLIKE YOU, MAIKA...
I'M NOT GOOD ENOUGH FOR SOMEONE LIKE HIM.
THAT'S NOT WHAT I'M SAYING.
PEOPLE WHO WERE BORN BLESSED AND HAVE BEEN LOVED BY EVERYONE WILL NEVER UNDERSTAND HOW I FEEL!
SORRY. I SAID TOO MUCH...
EVERYONE HAS EXPERIENCED BEING REJECTED BY SOMEONE THEY LOVE.
I'M NOT SAYING THAT...
...LOVING SOMEONE AND GOING FOR IT IS BAD.
IT'S JUST THAT...

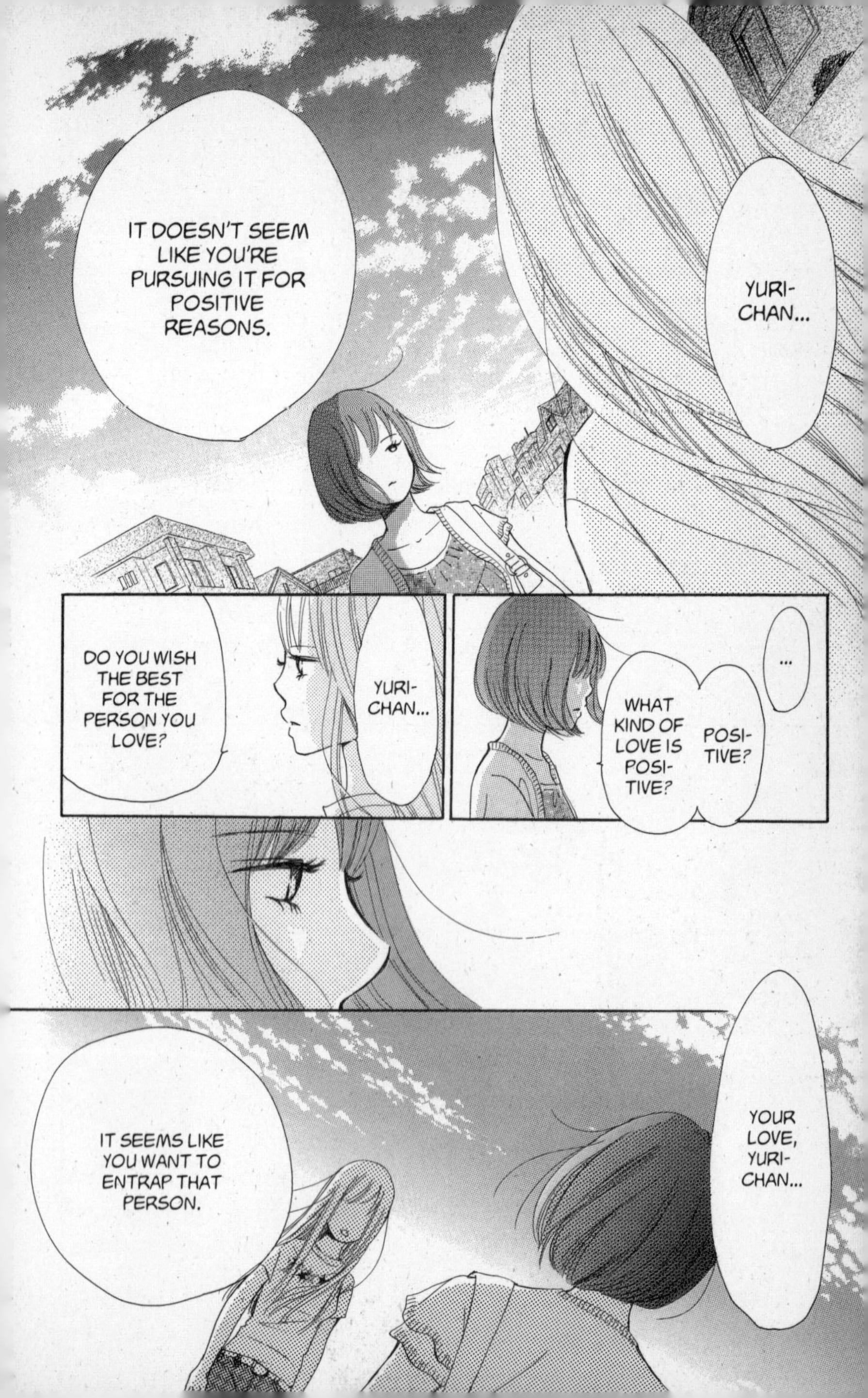
YURI-CHAN...
IT DOESN'T SEEM LIKE YOU'RE PURSUING IT FOR POSITIVE REASONS.
...
POSITIVE?
WHAT KIND OF LOVE IS POSITIVE?
YURI-CHAN...
DO YOU WISH THE BEST FOR THE PERSON YOU LOVE?
YOUR LOVE, YURI-CHAN...
IT SEEMS LIKE YOU WANT TO ENTRAP THAT PERSON.

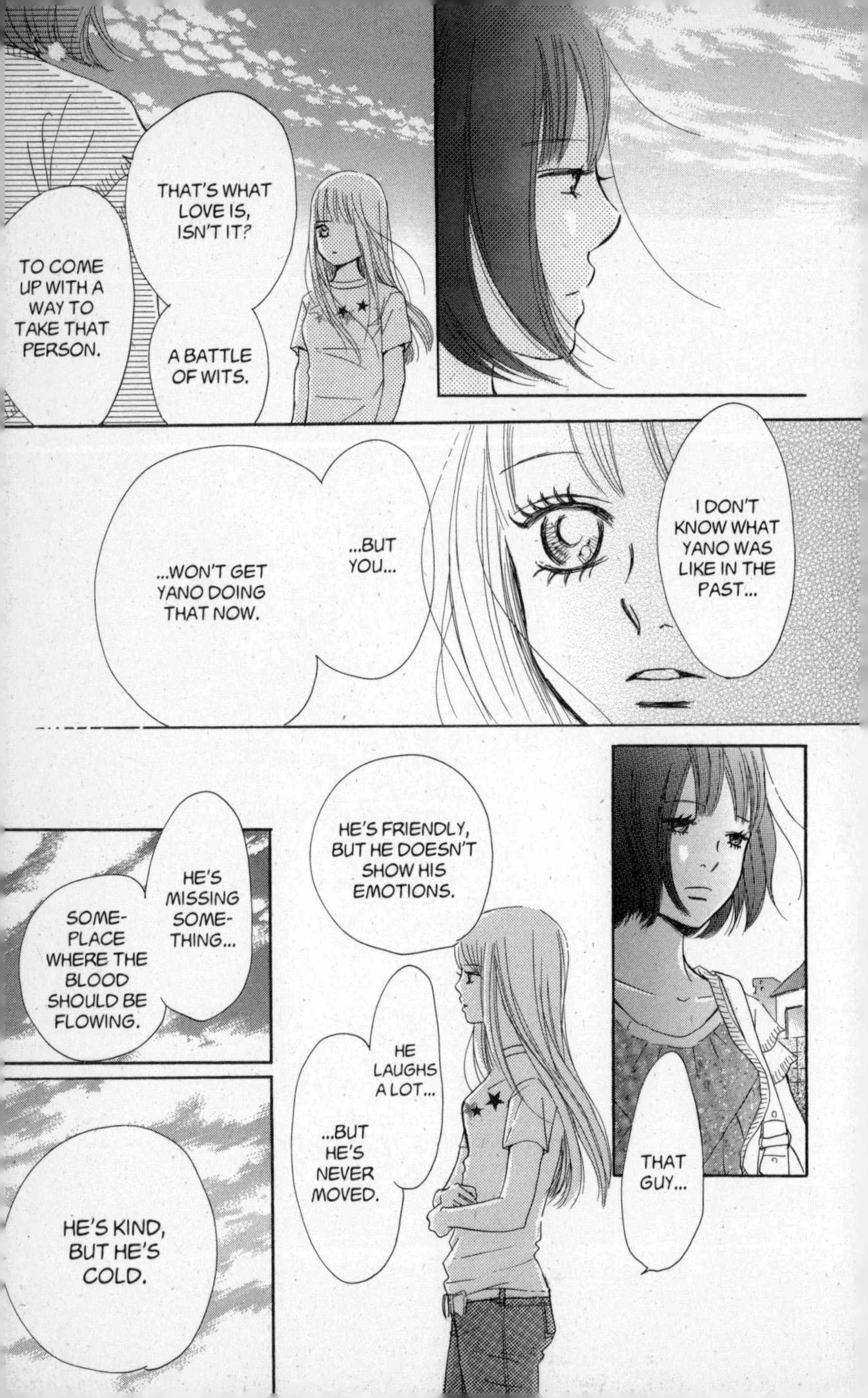
THAT'S WHAT LOVE IS, ISN'T IT?
A BATTLE OF WITS.
TO COME UP WITH A WAY TO TAKE THAT PERSON.
I DON'T KNOW WHAT YANO WAS LIKE IN THE PAST...
...BUT YOU...
...WON'T GET YANO DOING THAT NOW.
THAT GUY...
HE'S FRIENDLY, BUT HE DOESN'T SHOW HIS EMOTIONS.
HE LAUGHS A LOT...
...BUT HE'S NEVER MOVED.
HE'S MISSING SOME-THING...
SOME-PLACE WHERE THE BLOOD SHOULD BE FLOWING.
HE'S KIND, BUT HE'S COLD.

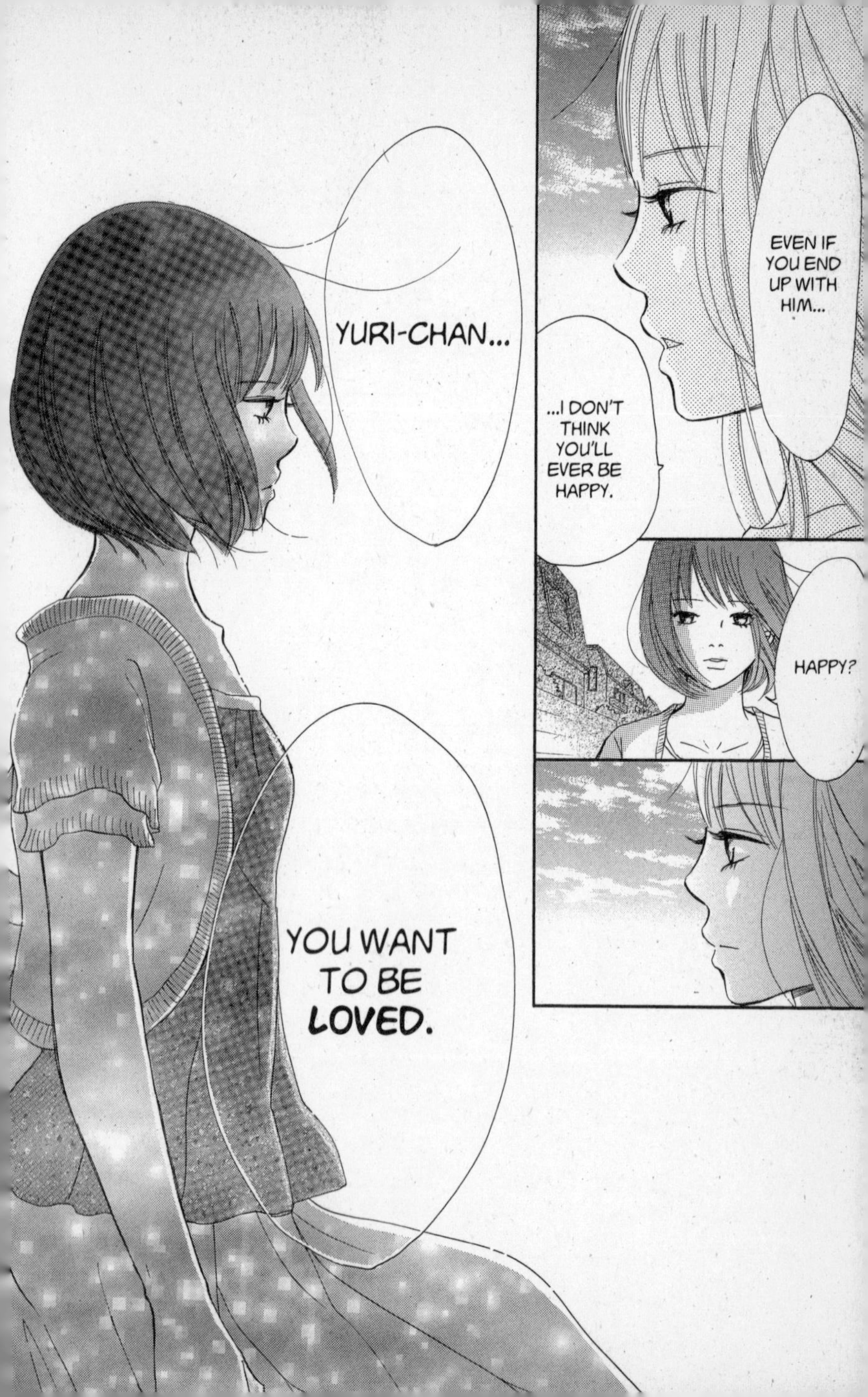
EVEN IF YOU END UP WITH HIM...
...I DON'T THINK YOU'LL EVER BE HAPPY.
HAPPY?
YURI-CHAN...
YOU WANT TO BE **LOVED**.

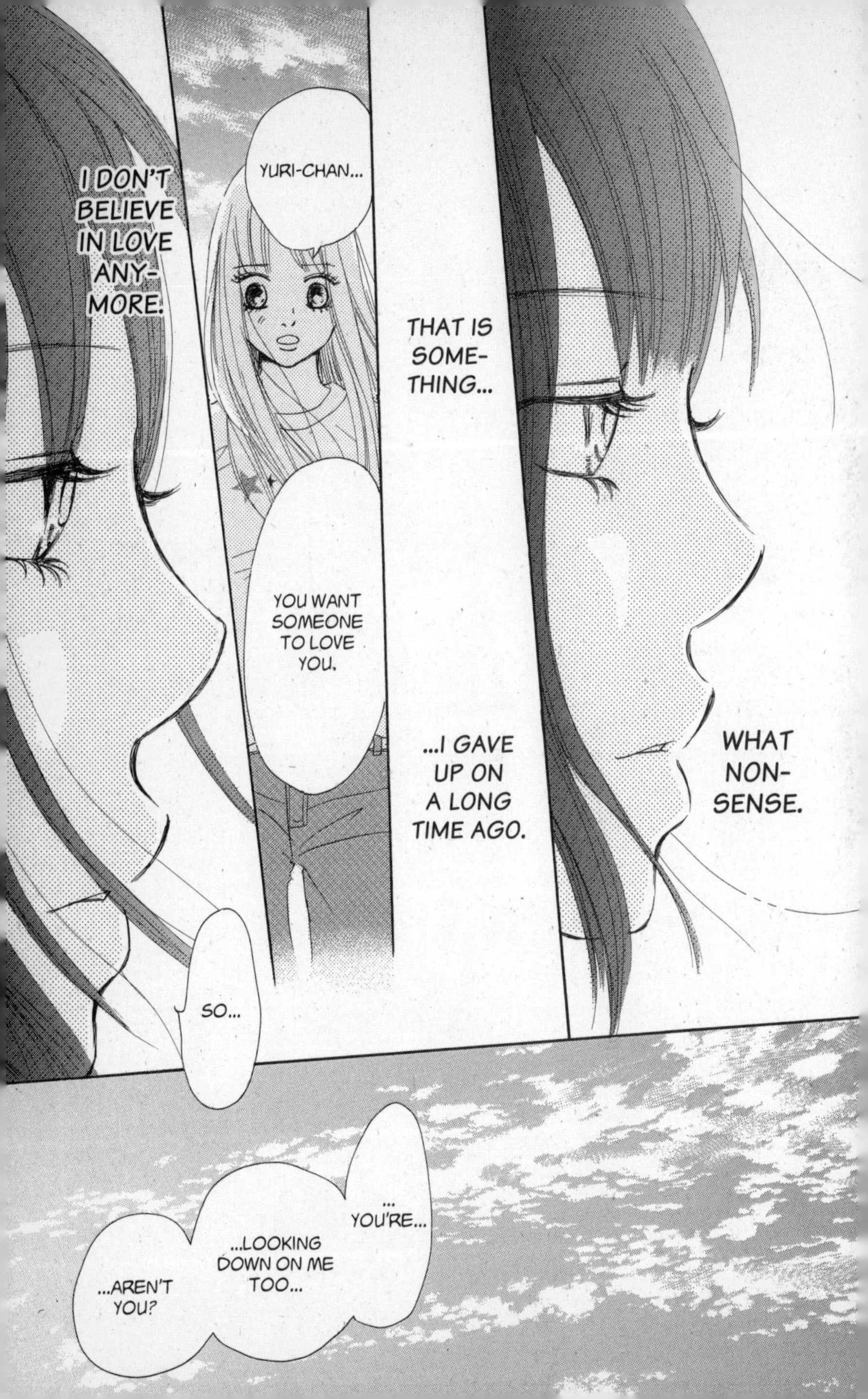
WHAT NON-SENSE.
THAT IS SOME-THING...
...I GAVE UP ON A LONG TIME AGO.
YURI-CHAN...
YOU WANT SOMEONE TO LOVE YOU.
I DON'T BELIEVE IN LOVE ANY-MORE.
SO...
...YOU'RE...
...LOOKING DOWN ON ME TOO...
...AREN'T YOU?

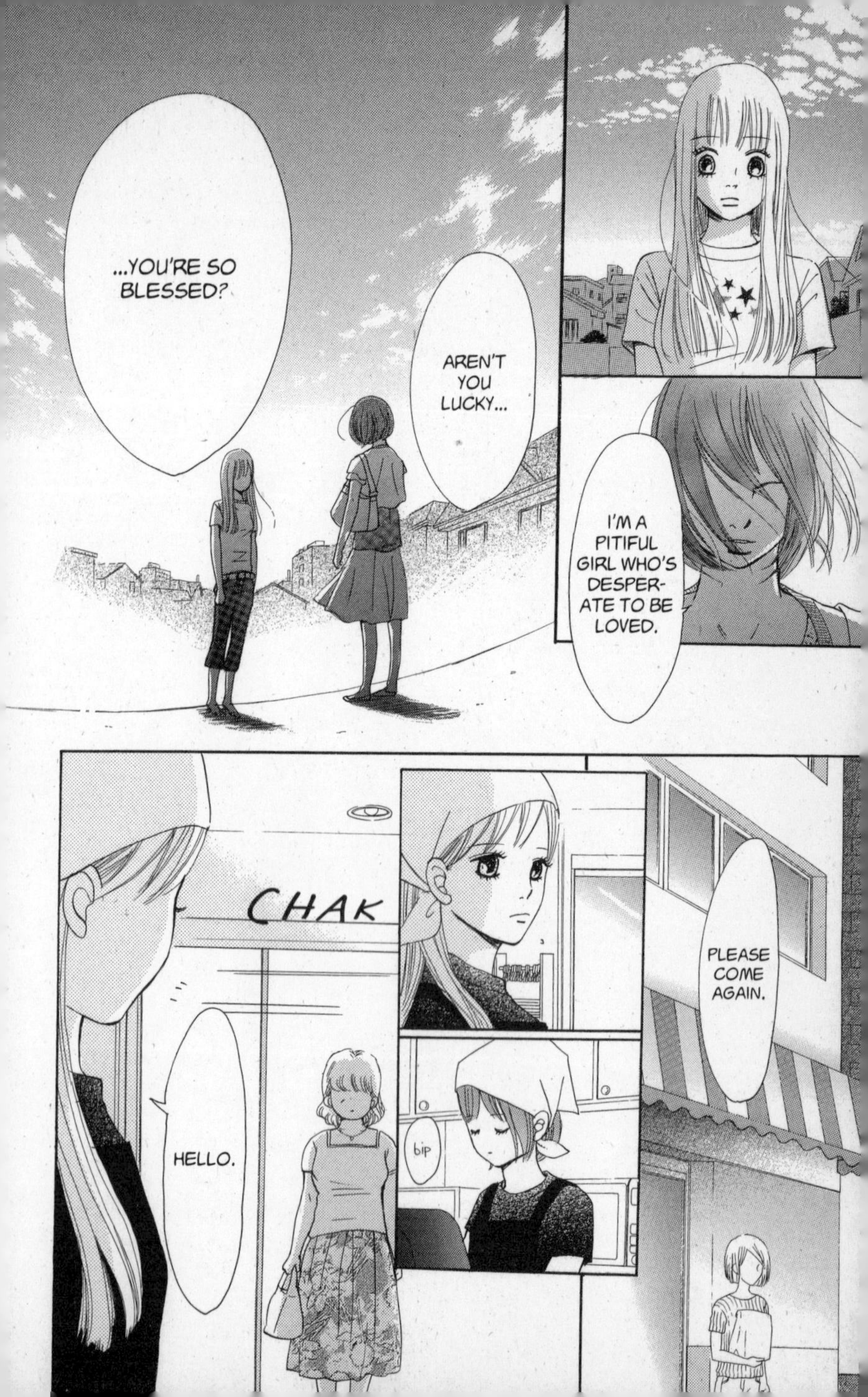
I'M A PITIFUL GIRL WHO'S DESPER-ATE TO BE LOVED.
AREN'T YOU LUCKY...
...YOU'RE SO BLESSED?
PLEASE COME AGAIN.
bip
CHAK
HELLO.

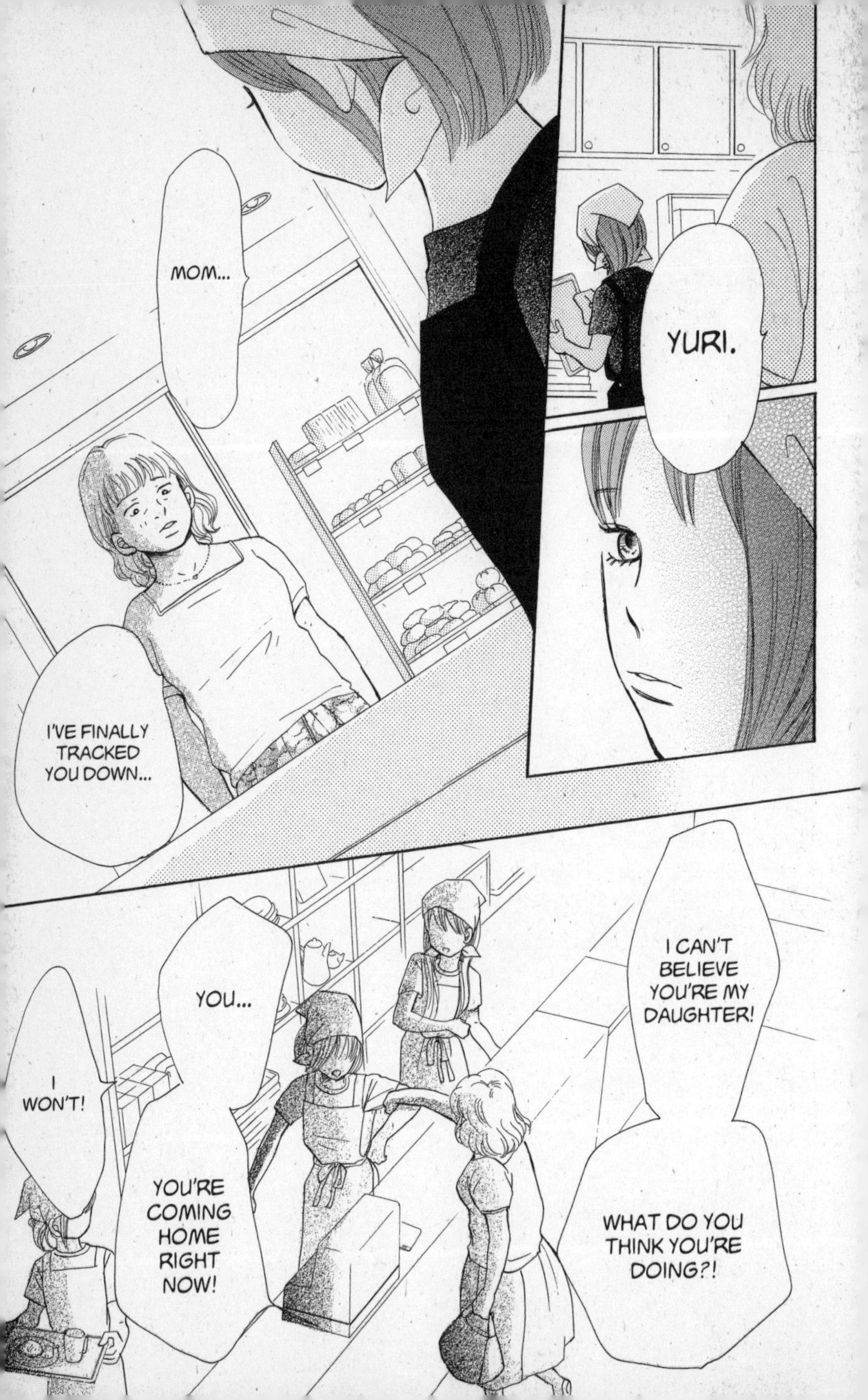
YURI.
MOM...
I'VE FINALLY TRACKED YOU DOWN...
I CAN'T BELIEVE YOU'RE MY DAUGHTER!
WHAT DO YOU THINK YOU'RE DOING?!
YOU...
YOU'RE COMING HOME RIGHT NOW!
I WON'T!

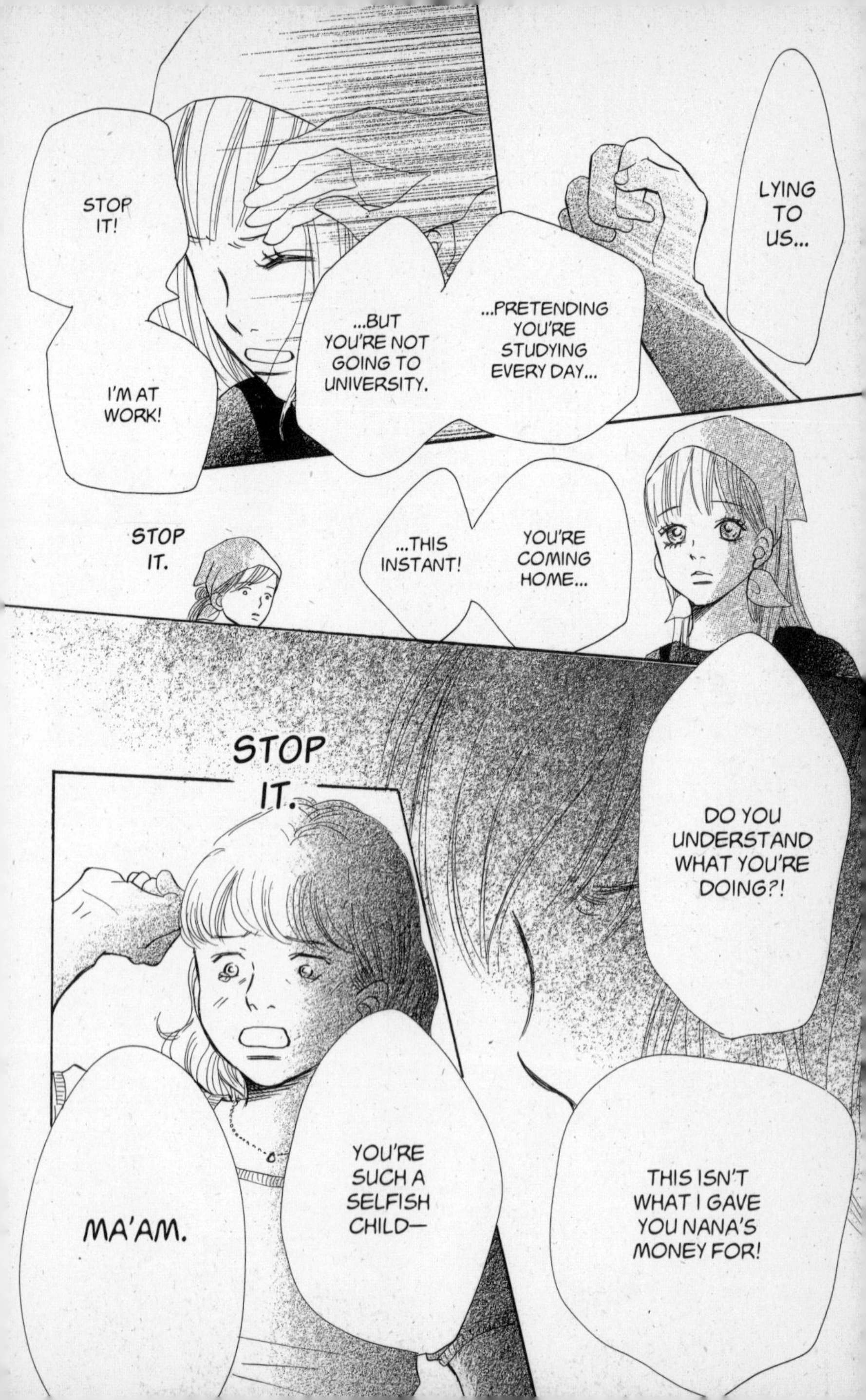
LYING TO US...
...PRETENDING YOU'RE STUDYING EVERY DAY...
...BUT YOU'RE NOT GOING TO UNIVERSITY.
STOP IT!
I'M AT WORK!
YOU'RE COMING HOME...
...THIS INSTANT!
STOP IT.
DO YOU UNDERSTAND WHAT YOU'RE DOING?!
THIS ISN'T WHAT I GAVE YOU NANA'S MONEY FOR!
YOU'RE SUCH A SELFISH CHILD—
STOP IT.
MA'AM.

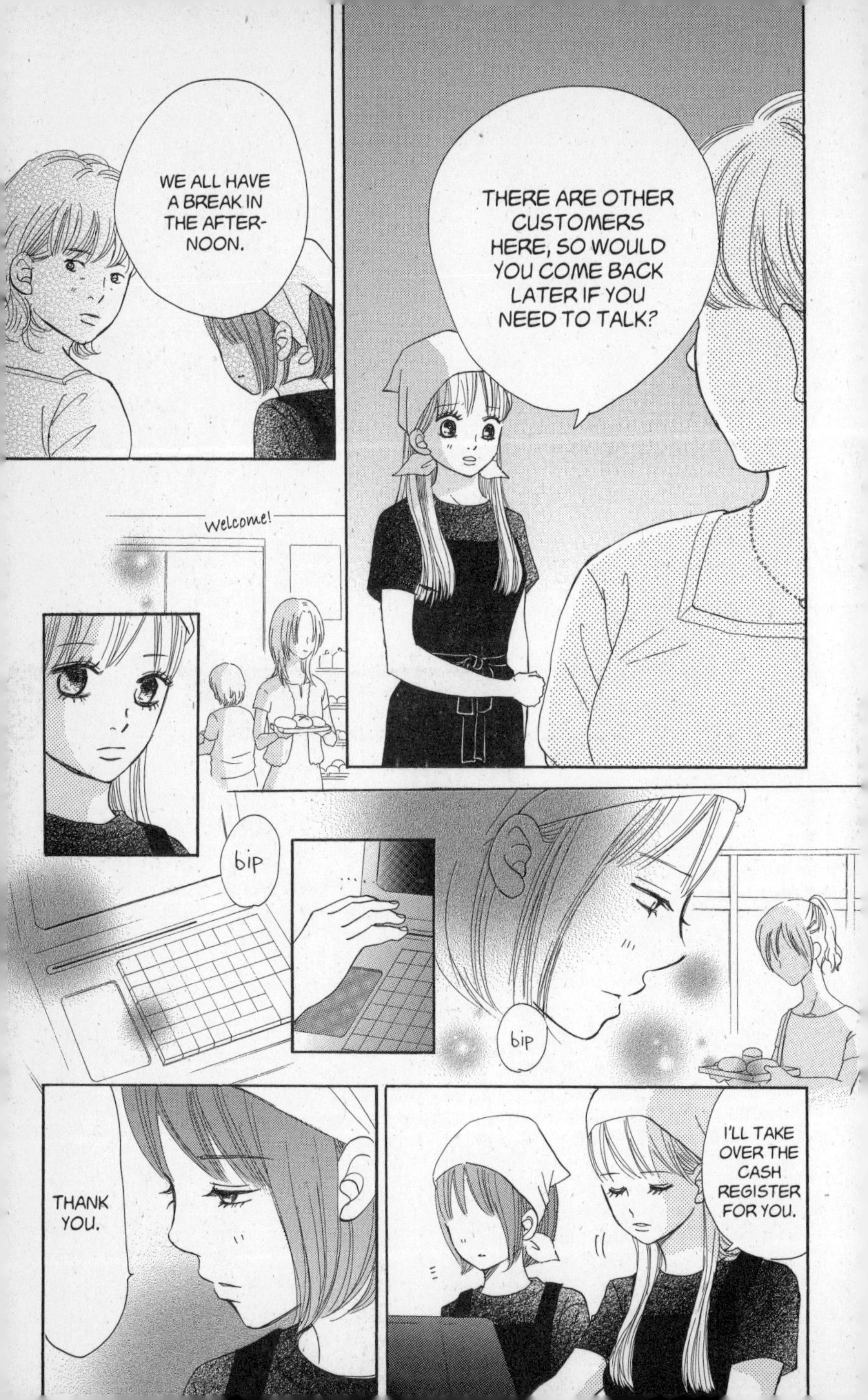
THERE ARE OTHER CUSTOMERS HERE, SO WOULD YOU COME BACK LATER IF YOU NEED TO TALK?
WE ALL HAVE A BREAK IN THE AFTER-NOON.
Welcome!
bip
...
bip
I'LL TAKE OVER THE CASH REGISTER FOR YOU.
THANK YOU.

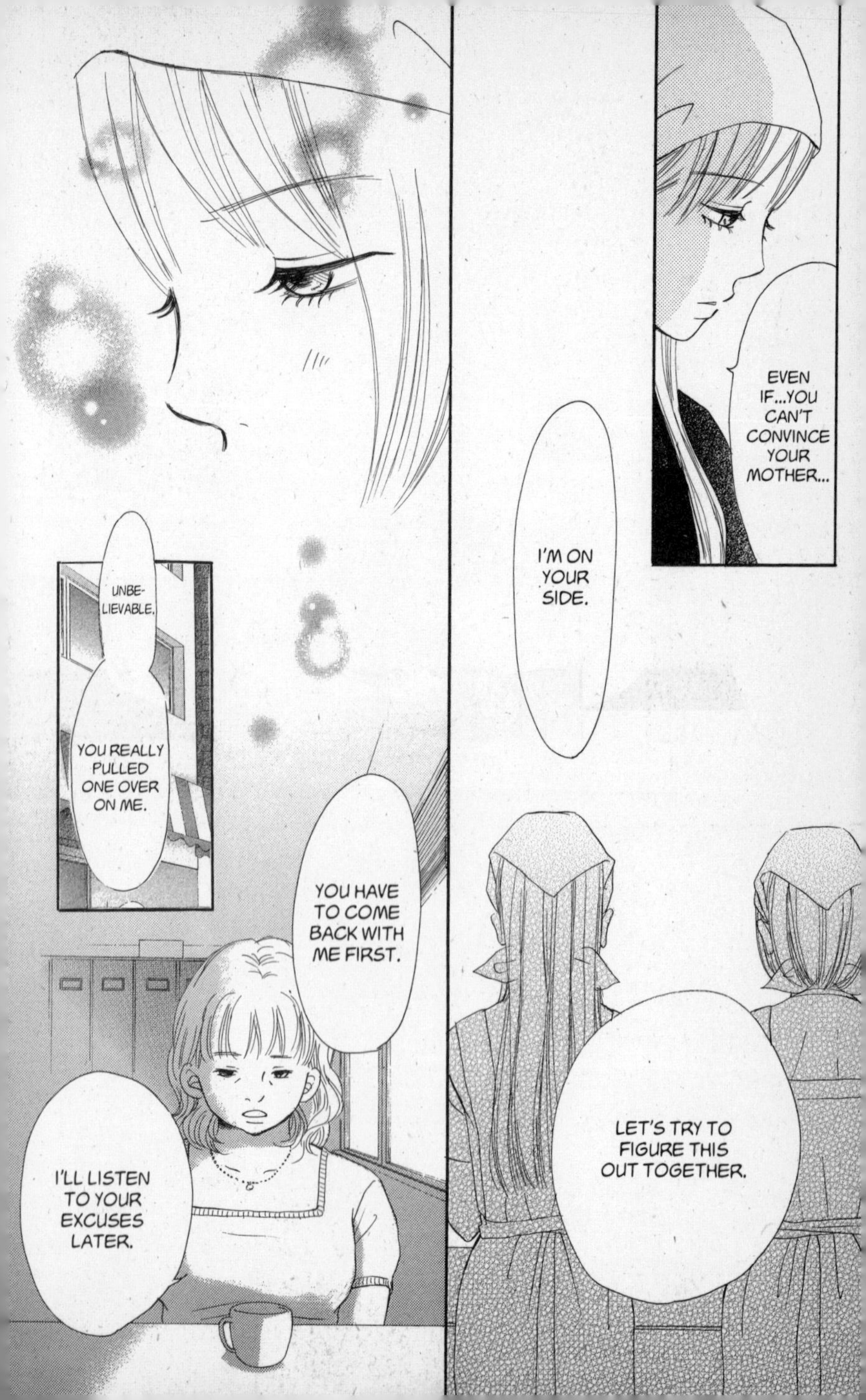
EVEN IF...YOU CAN'T CONVINCE YOUR MOTHER...
I'M ON YOUR SIDE.
LET'S TRY TO FIGURE THIS OUT TOGETHER.
UNBE-LIEVABLE.
YOU REALLY PULLED ONE OVER ON ME.
YOU HAVE TO COME BACK WITH ME FIRST.
I'LL LISTEN TO YOUR EXCUSES LATER.

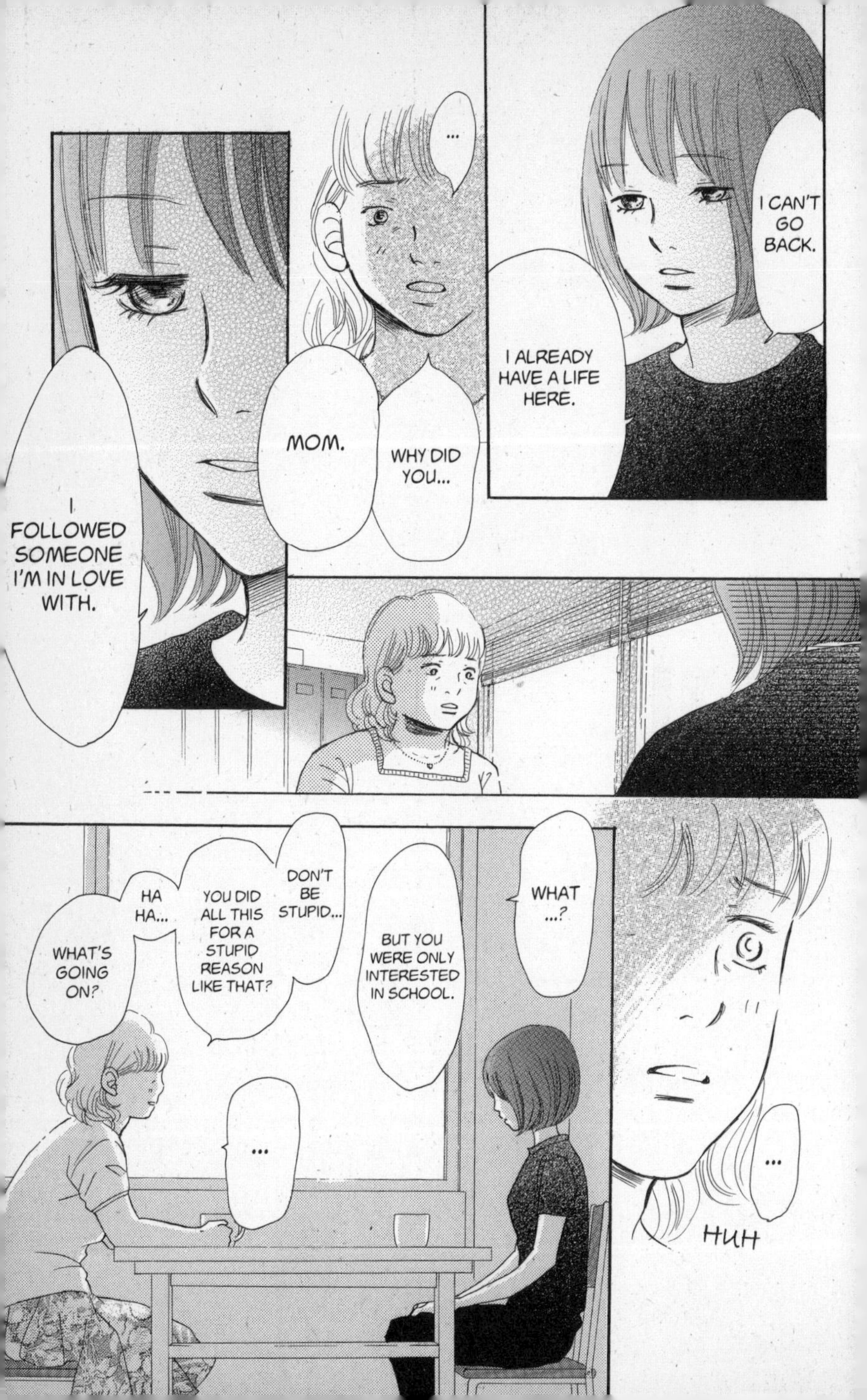
I CAN'T GO BACK.
I ALREADY HAVE A LIFE HERE.
...
MOM.
WHY DID YOU...
I FOLLOWED SOMEONE I'M IN LOVE WITH.
...
HUH
WHAT ...?
BUT YOU WERE ONLY INTERESTED IN SCHOOL.
DON'T BE STUPID...
YOU DID ALL THIS FOR A STUPID REASON LIKE THAT?
HA HA...
WHAT'S GOING ON?
...

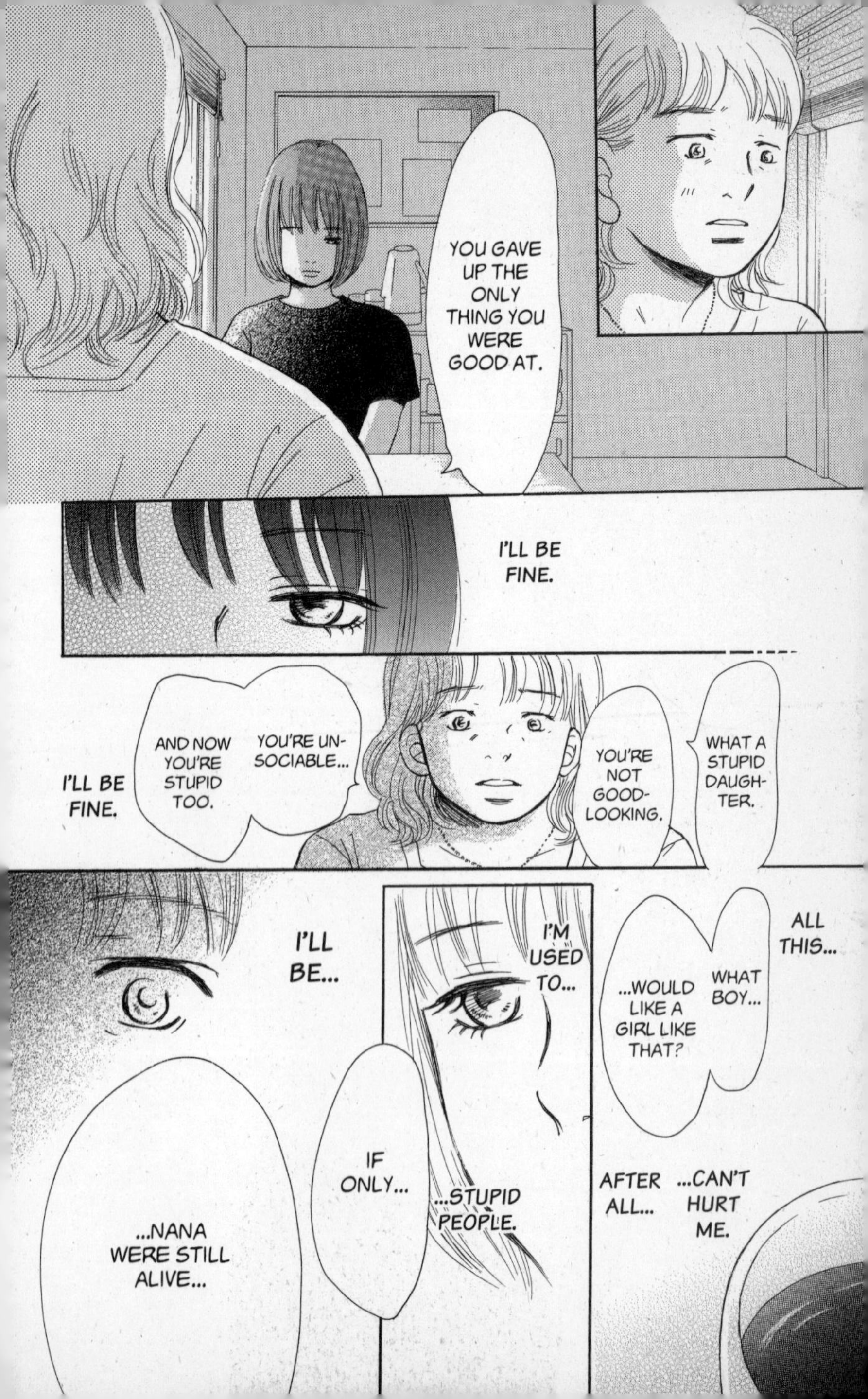
YOU GAVE UP THE ONLY THING YOU WERE GOOD AT.
I'LL BE FINE.
WHAT A STUPID DAUGHTER.
YOU'RE NOT GOOD-LOOKING.
YOU'RE UN-SOCIABLE...
AND NOW YOU'RE STUPID TOO.
I'LL BE FINE.
ALL THIS...
WHAT BOY...
...WOULD LIKE A GIRL LIKE THAT?
...CAN'T HURT ME.
AFTER ALL...
I'M USED TO...
...STUPID PEOPLE.
I'LL BE...
IF ONLY...
...NANA WERE STILL ALIVE...

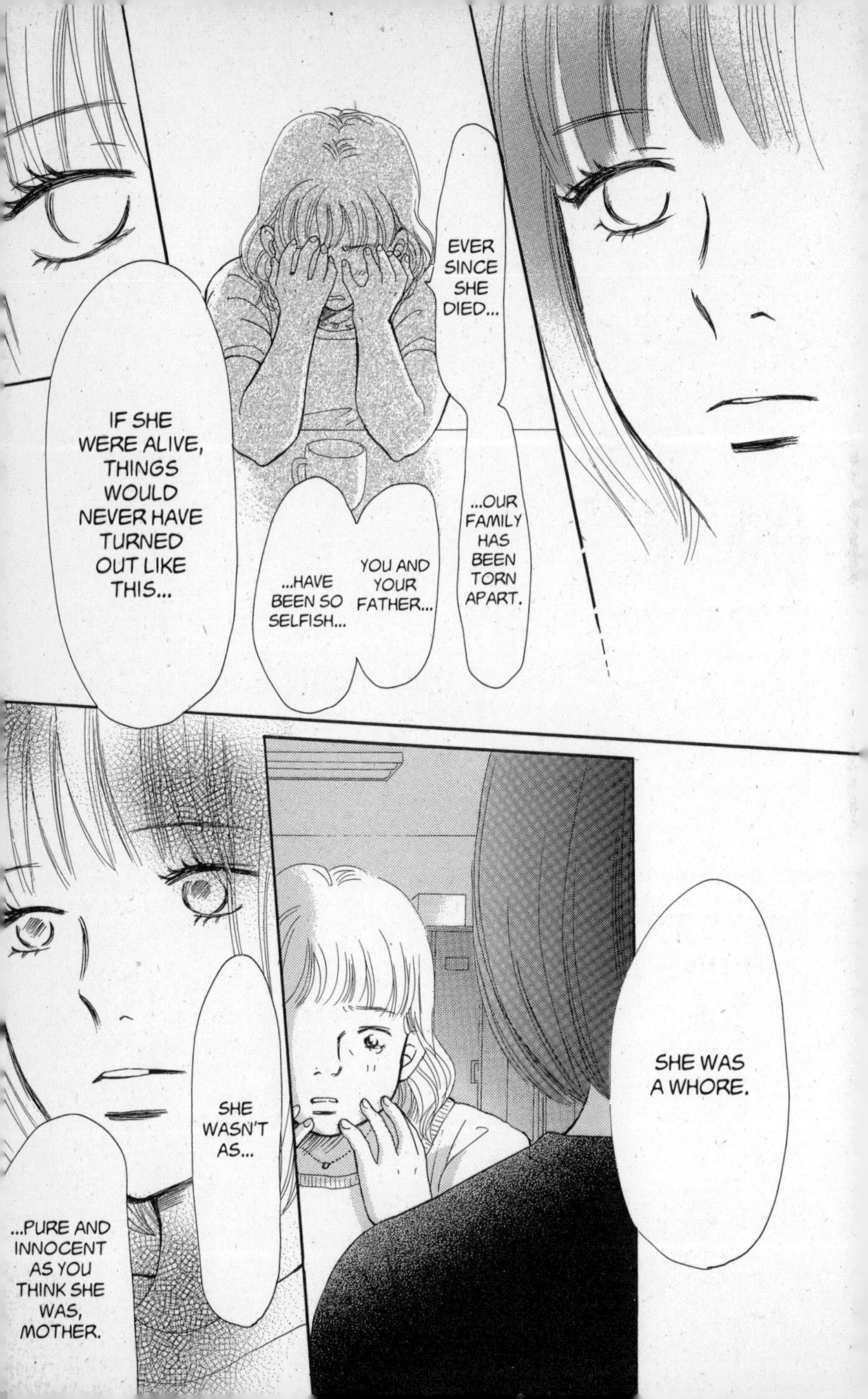
EVER SINCE SHE DIED...
...OUR FAMILY HAS BEEN TORN APART.
YOU AND YOUR FATHER...
...HAVE BEEN SO SELFISH...
IF SHE WERE ALIVE, THINGS WOULD NEVER HAVE TURNED OUT LIKE THIS...
SHE WAS A WHORE.
SHE WASN'T AS...
...PURE AND INNOCENT AS YOU THINK SHE WAS, MOTHER.

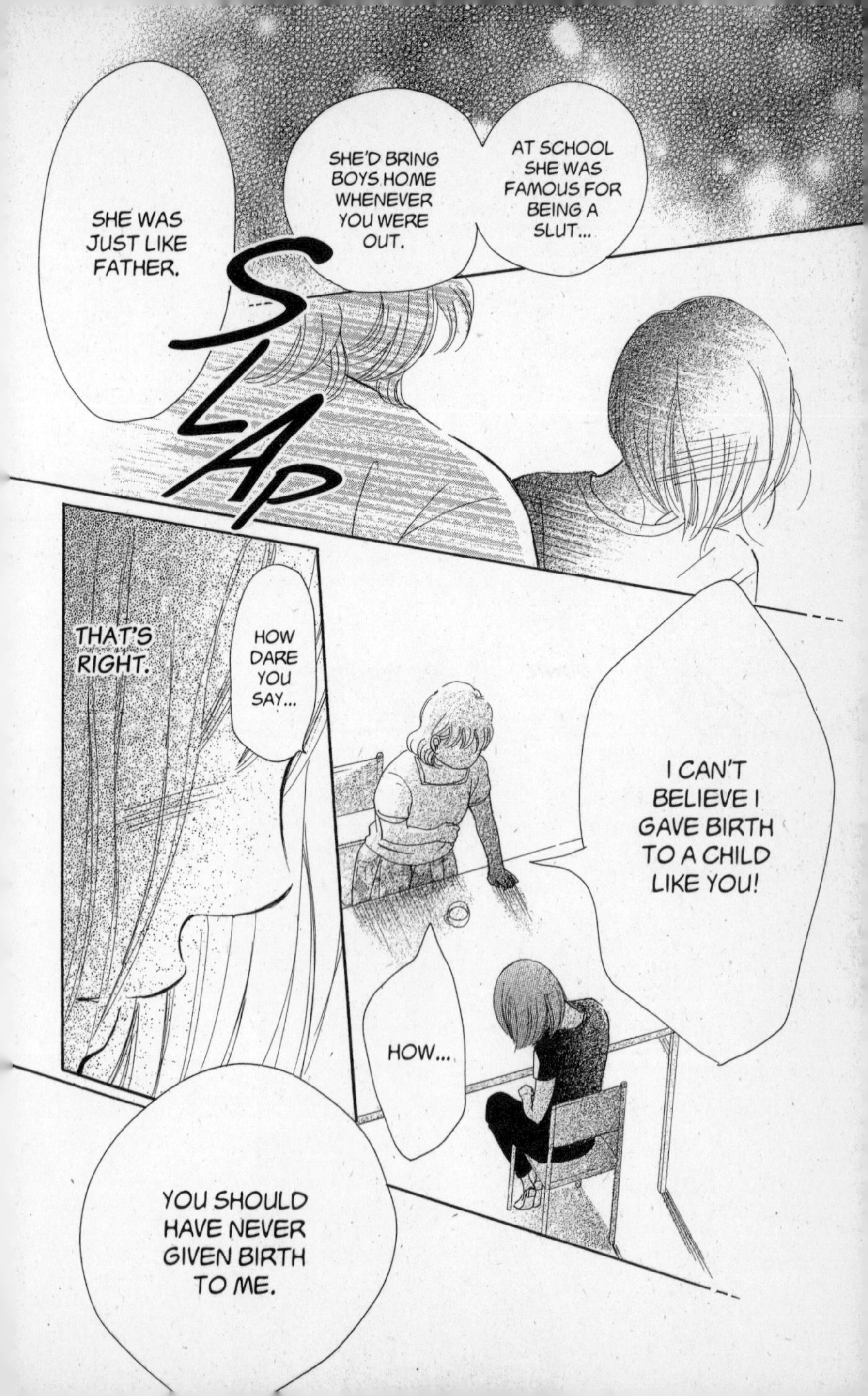
AT SCHOOL SHE WAS FAMOUS FOR BEING A SLUT...
SHE'D BRING BOYS HOME WHENEVER YOU WERE OUT.
SHE WAS JUST LIKE FATHER.
SLAP
I CAN'T BELIEVE I GAVE BIRTH TO A CHILD LIKE YOU!
HOW...
HOW DARE YOU SAY...
THAT'S RIGHT.
YOU SHOULD HAVE NEVER GIVEN BIRTH TO ME.

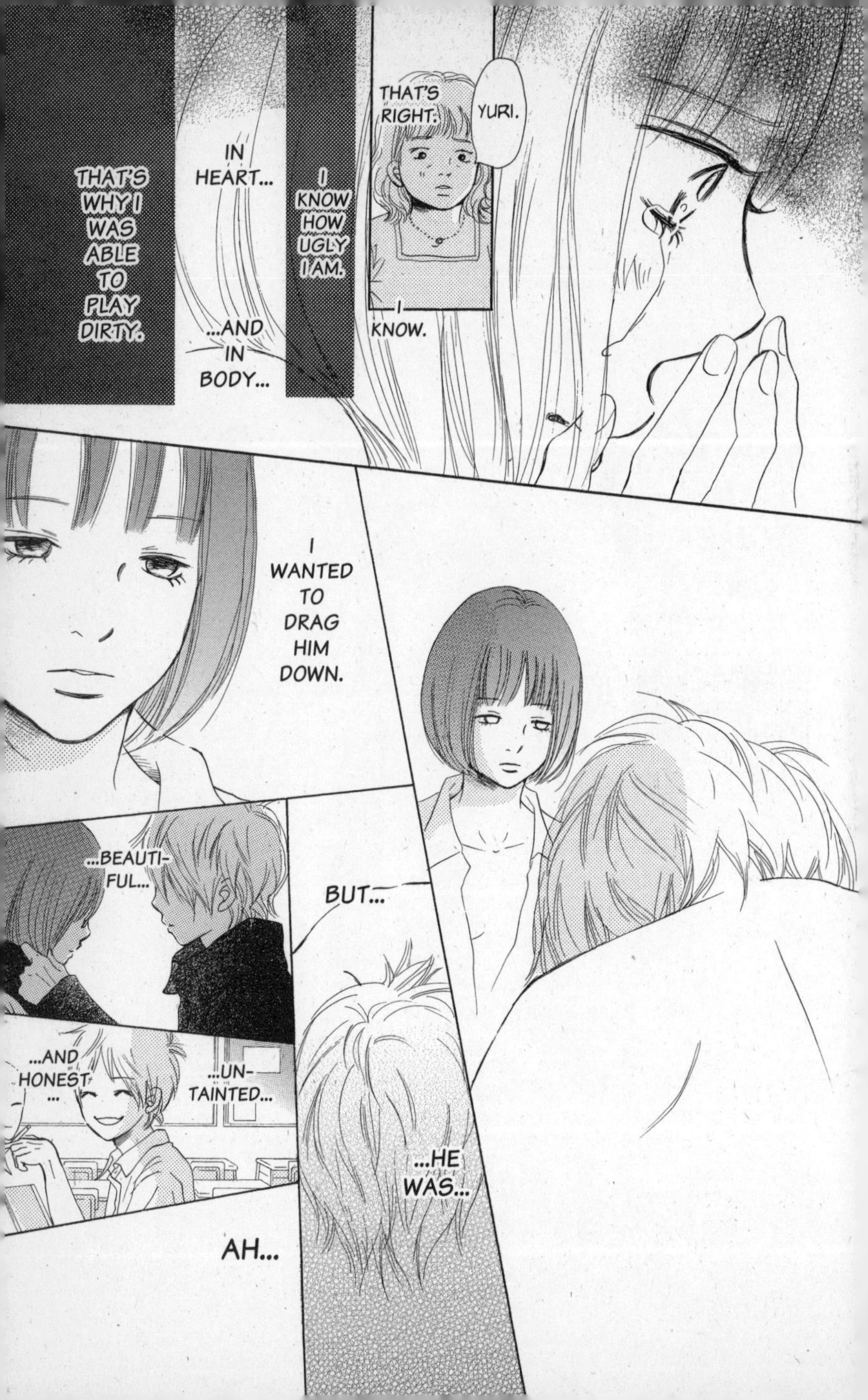
YURI.
THAT'S RIGHT.
I KNOW.
I KNOW HOW UGLY I AM.
IN HEART...
...AND IN BODY...
THAT'S WHY I WAS ABLE TO PLAY DIRTY.
I WANTED TO DRAG HIM DOWN.
BUT...
...HE WAS...
...BEAUTIFUL...
...UNTAINTED...
...AND HONEST...
AH...

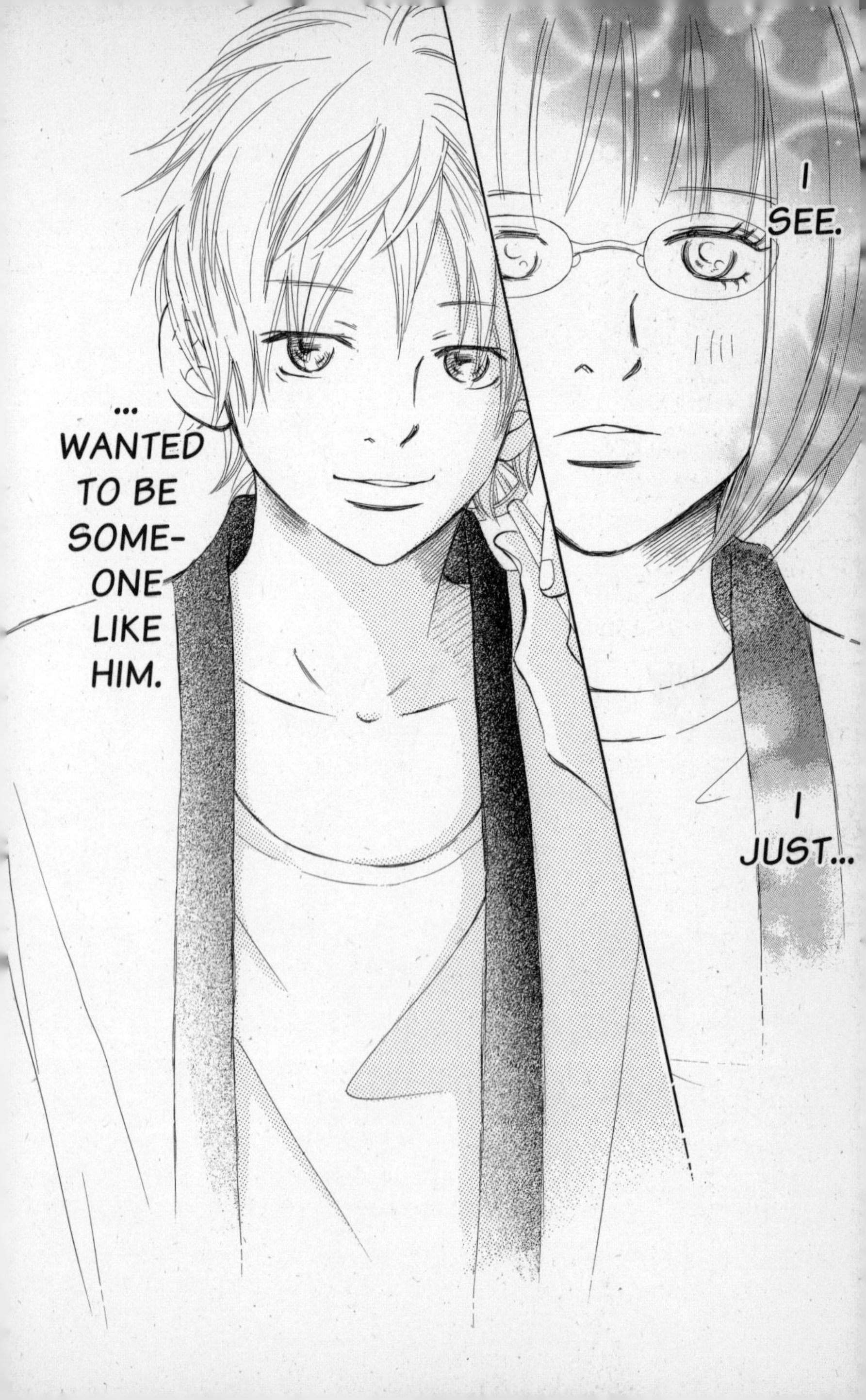
I SEE.
I JUST...
...WANTED TO BE SOMEONE LIKE HIM.

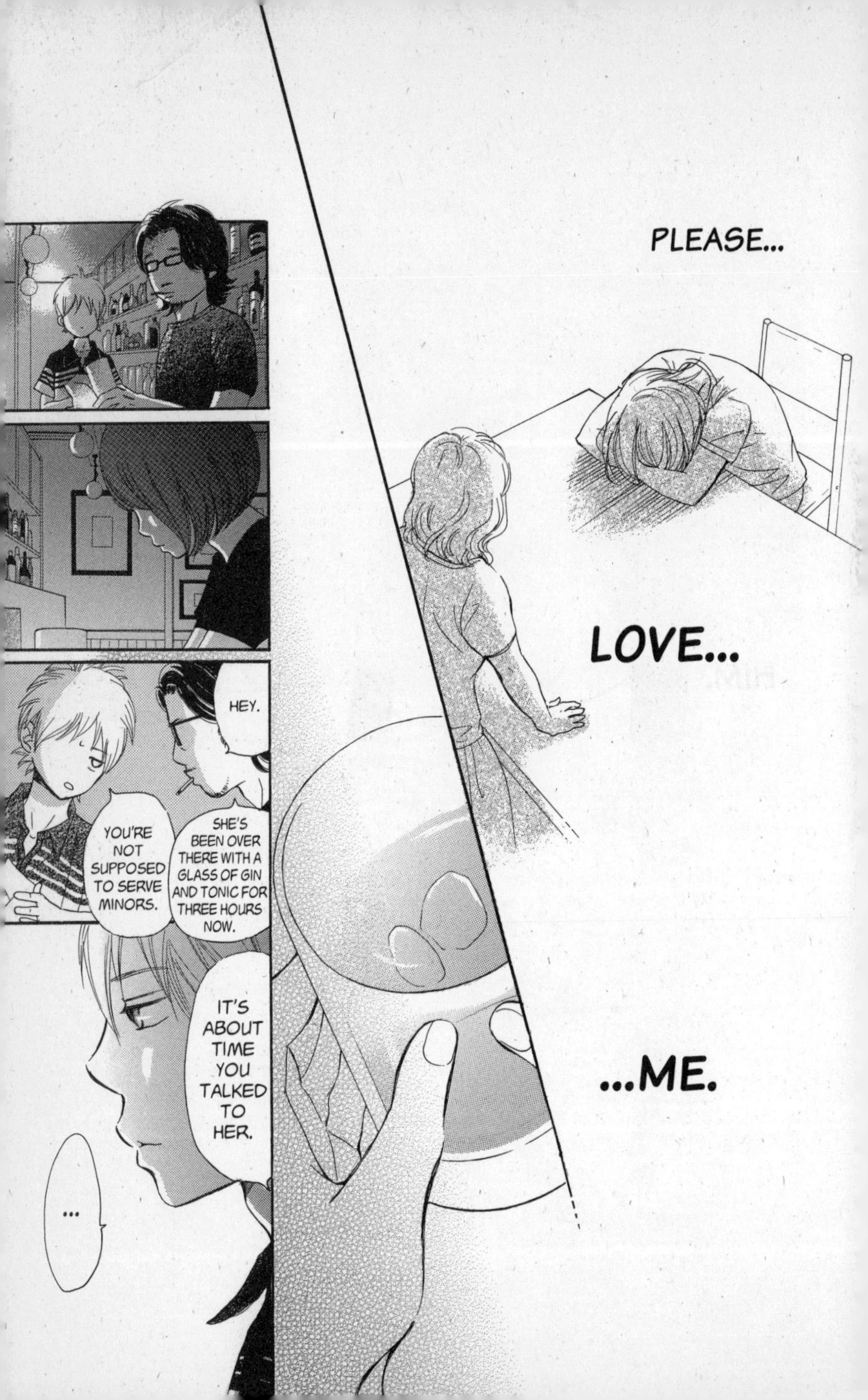
PLEASE...
LOVE...
...ME.
HEY.
SHE'S BEEN OVER THERE WITH A GLASS OF GIN AND TONIC FOR THREE HOURS NOW.
YOU'RE NOT SUPPOSED TO SERVE MINORS.
IT'S ABOUT TIME YOU TALKED TO HER.
...

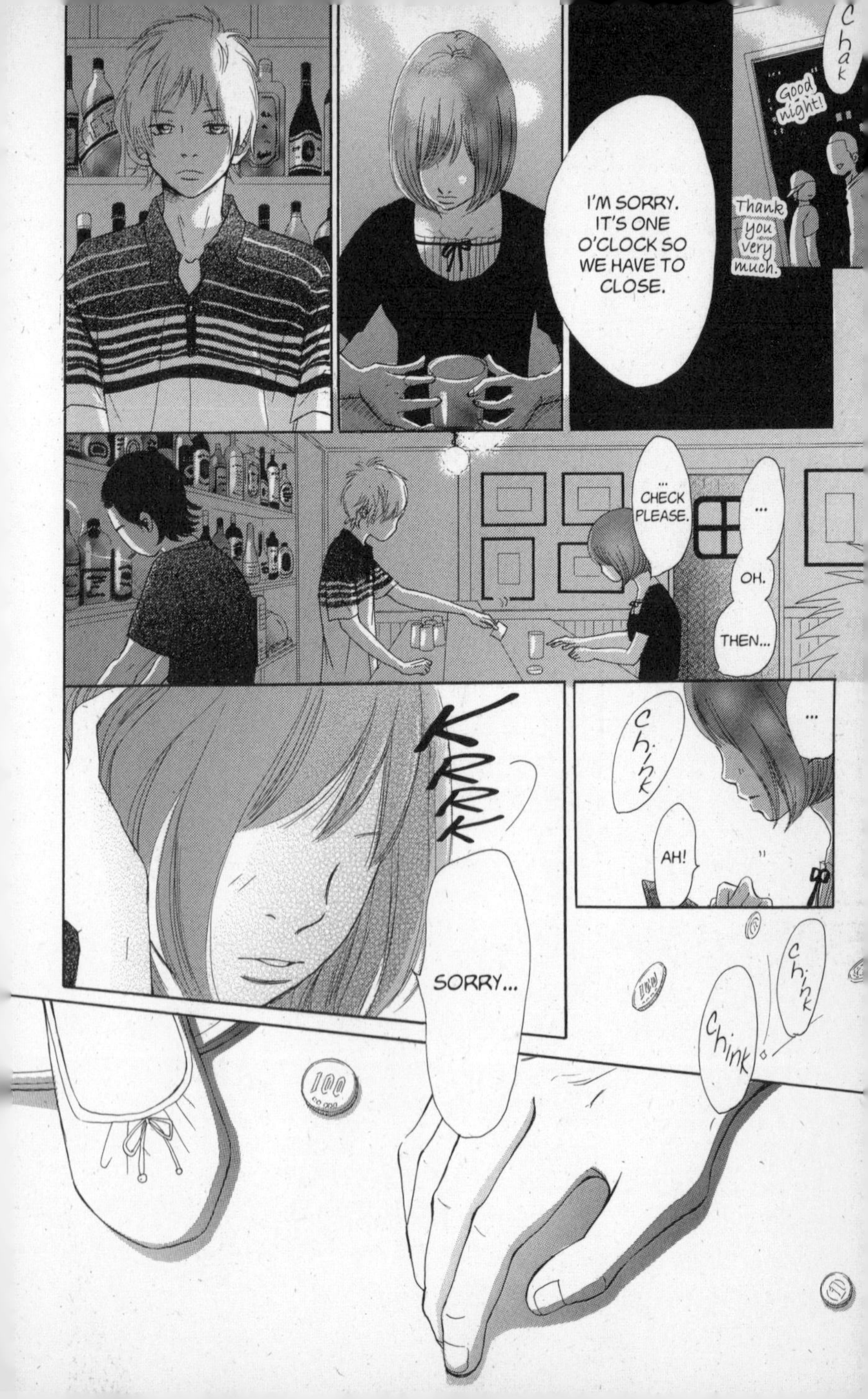
Chak
Good night!
Thank you very much.
I'M SORRY. IT'S ONE O'CLOCK SO WE HAVE TO CLOSE.
... OH. THEN...
... CHECK PLEASE.
...
Chink
AH!
KRRRK
SORRY...
Chink
Chink

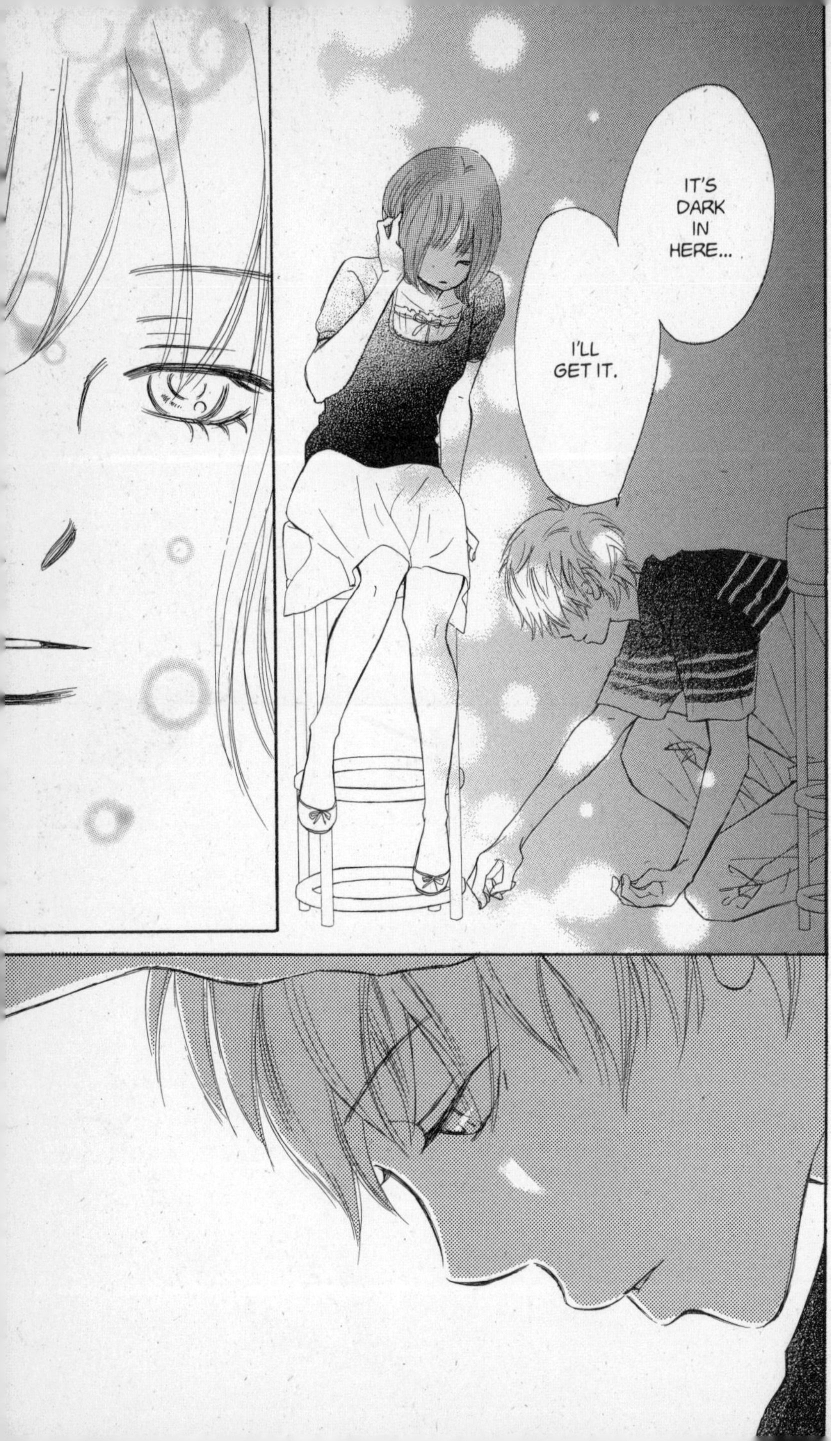
IT'S DARK IN HERE...
I'LL GET IT.

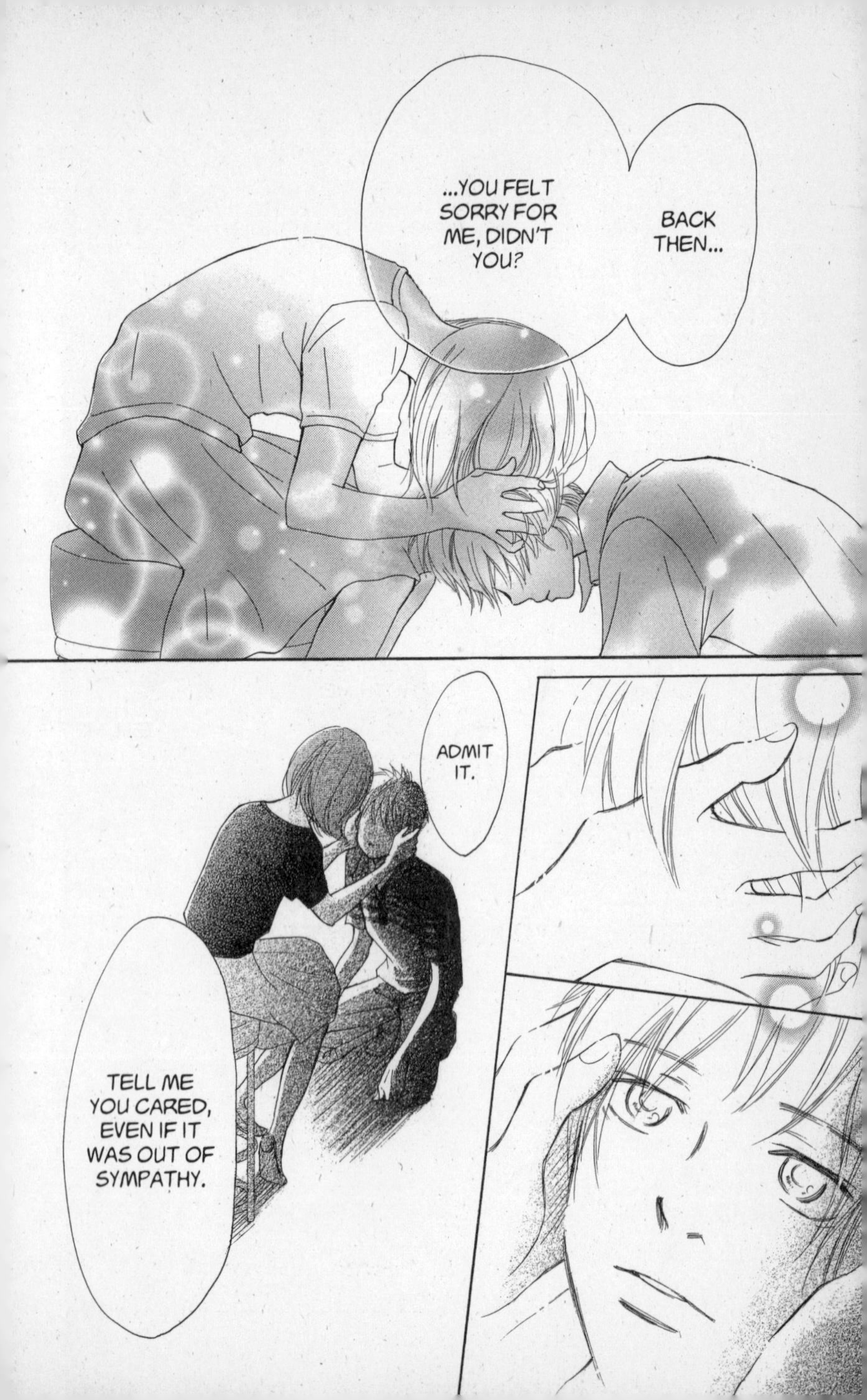
BACK THEN...
...YOU FELT SORRY FOR ME, DIDN'T YOU?
ADMIT IT.
TELL ME YOU CARED, EVEN IF IT WAS OUT OF SYMPATHY.

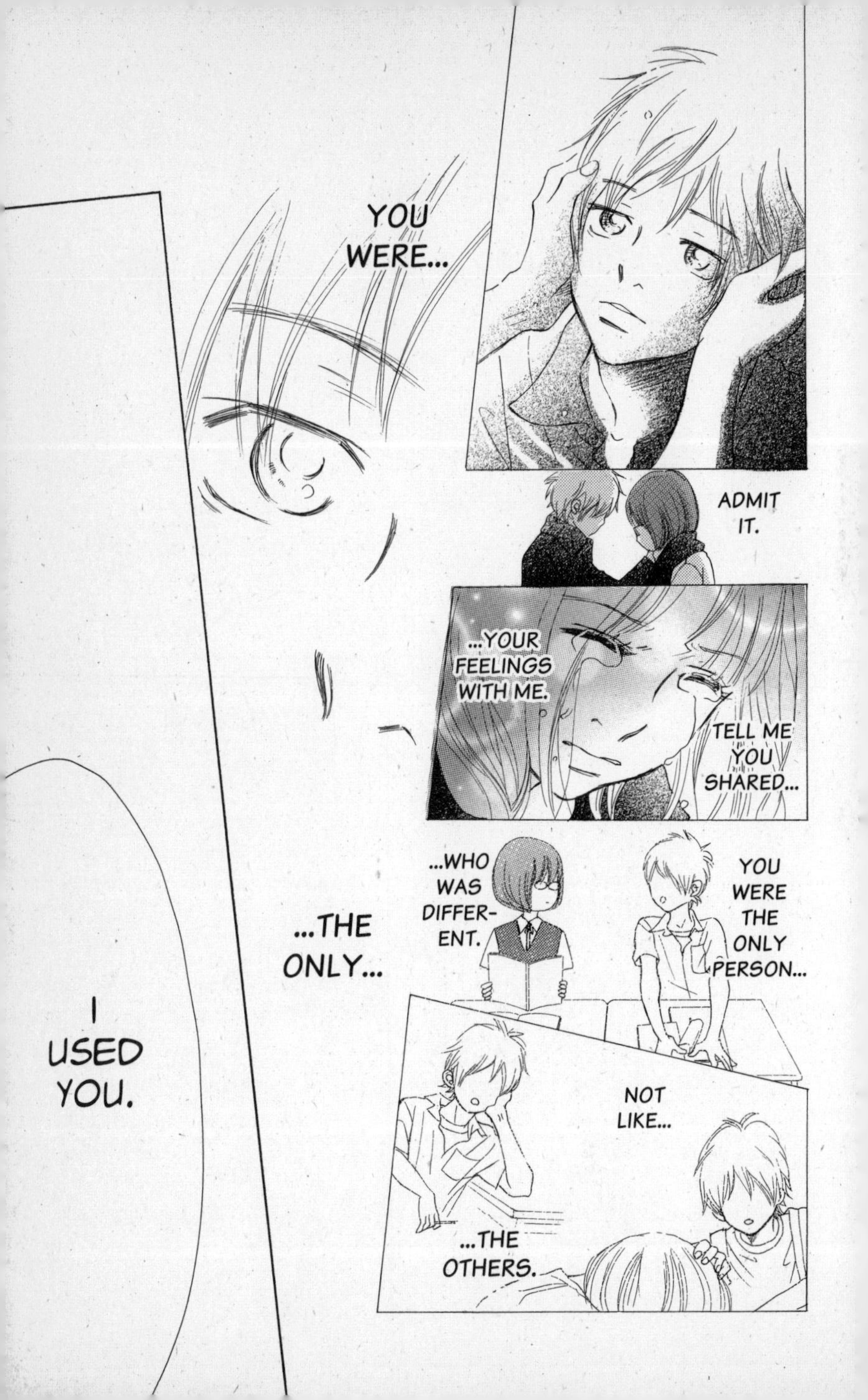
YOU WERE...
ADMIT IT.
TELL ME YOU SHARED...
...YOUR FEELINGS WITH ME.
YOU WERE THE ONLY PERSON...
...WHO WAS DIFFER-ENT.
...THE ONLY...
NOT LIKE...
...THE OTHERS.
I USED YOU.

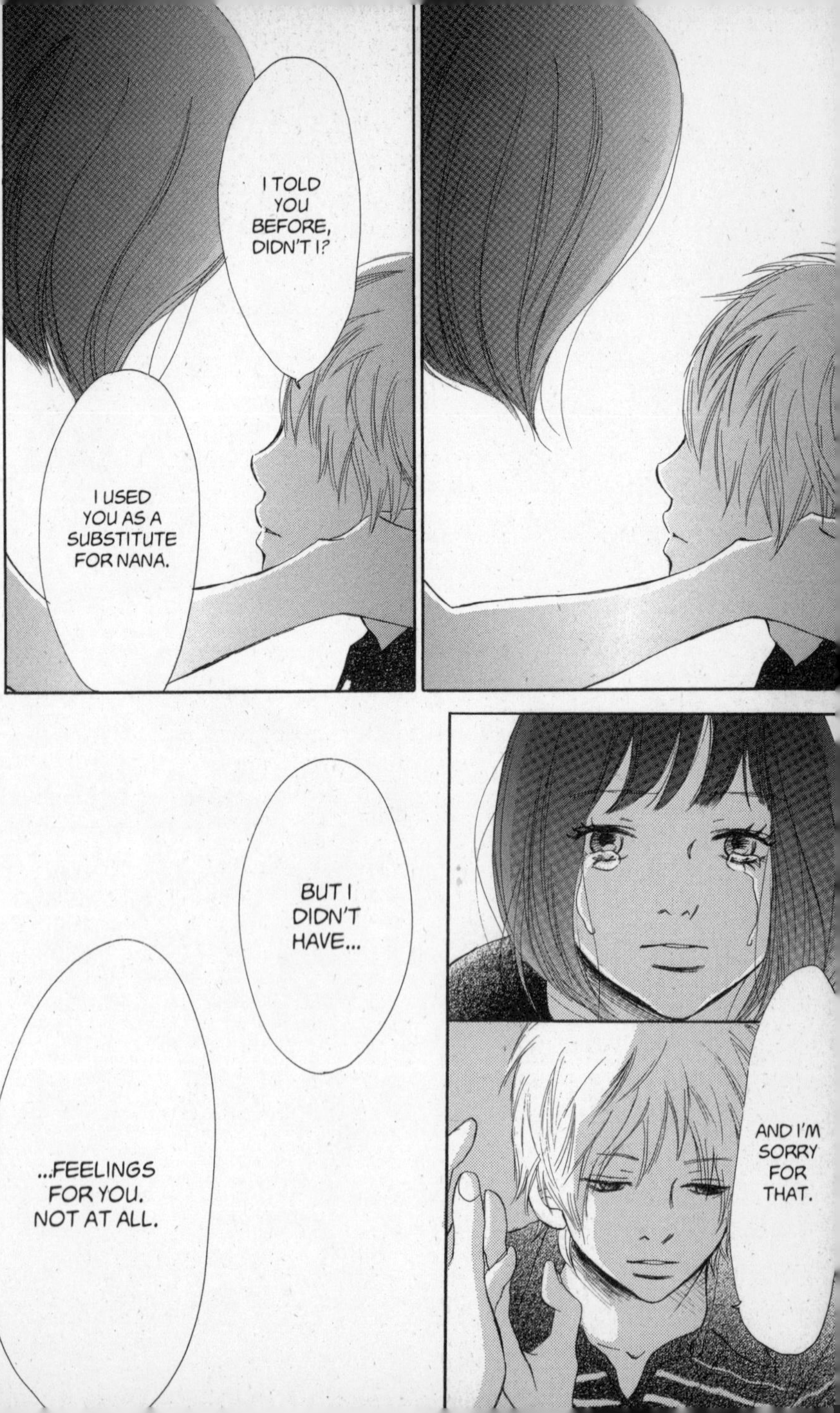
I TOLD YOU BEFORE, DIDN'T I?
I USED YOU AS A SUBSTITUTE FOR NANA.
AND I'M SORRY FOR THAT.
BUT I DIDN'T HAVE...
...FEELINGS FOR YOU. NOT AT ALL.

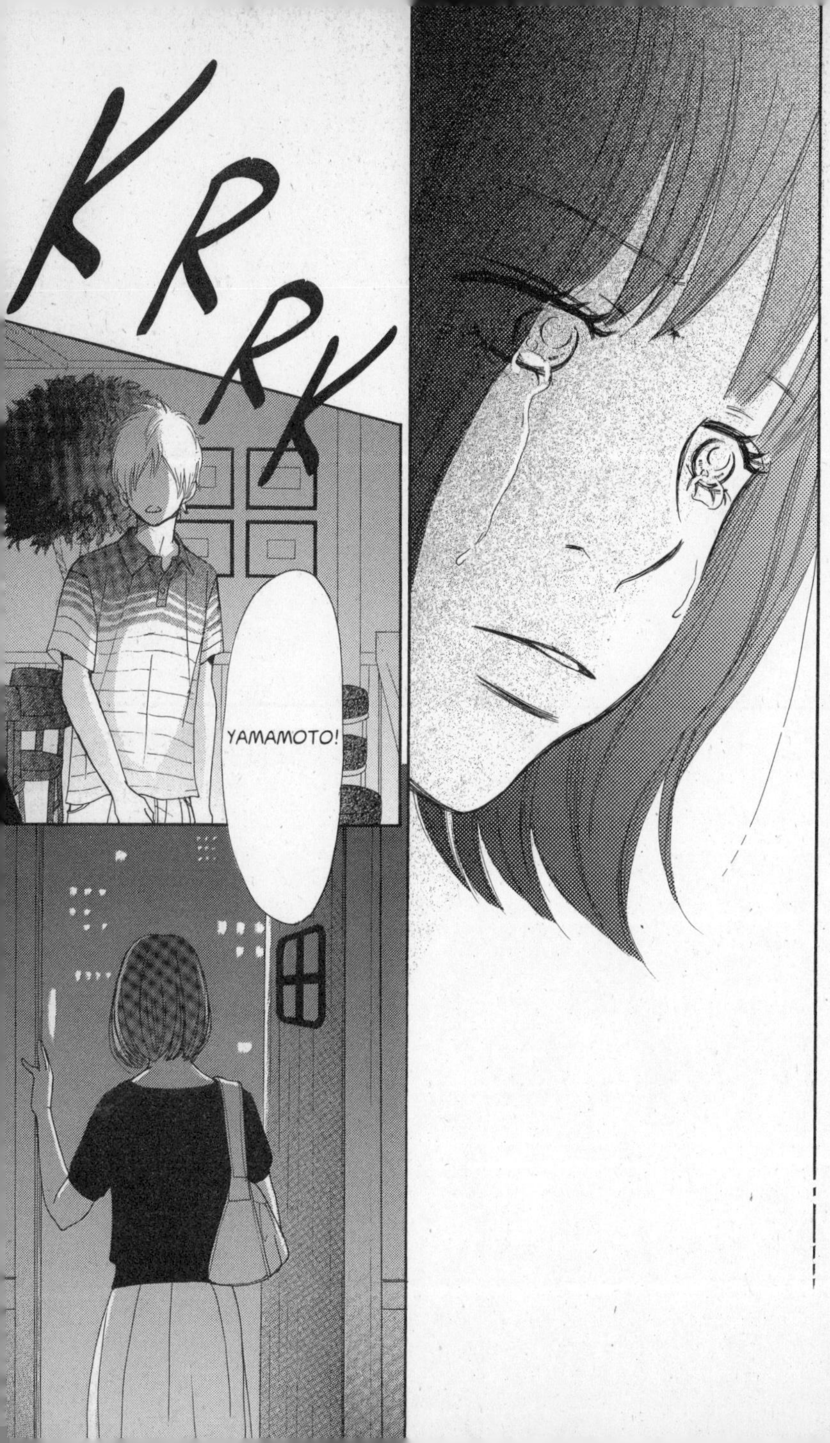
KRRK
YAMAMOTO!

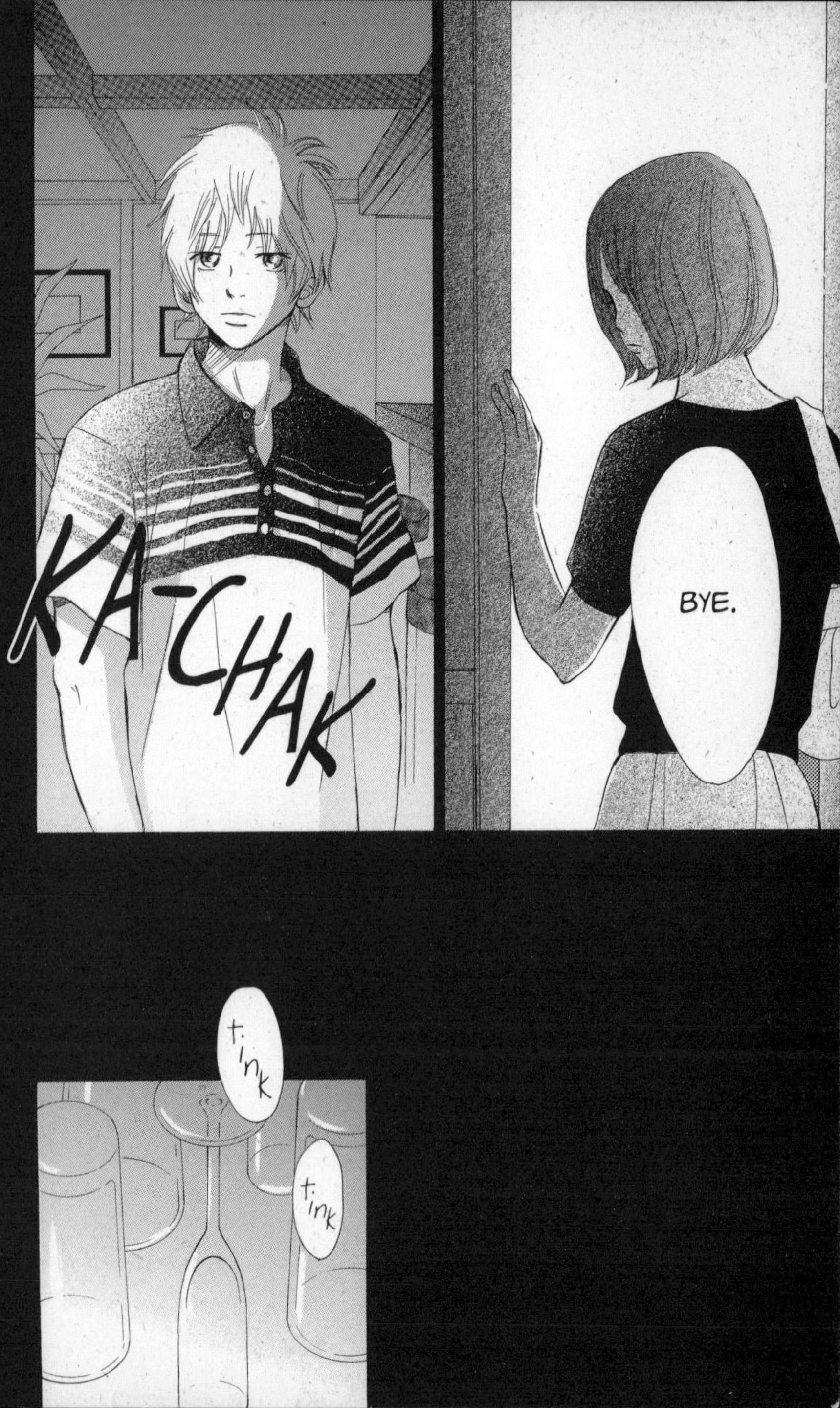
BYE.
KA-CHAK
tink
tink

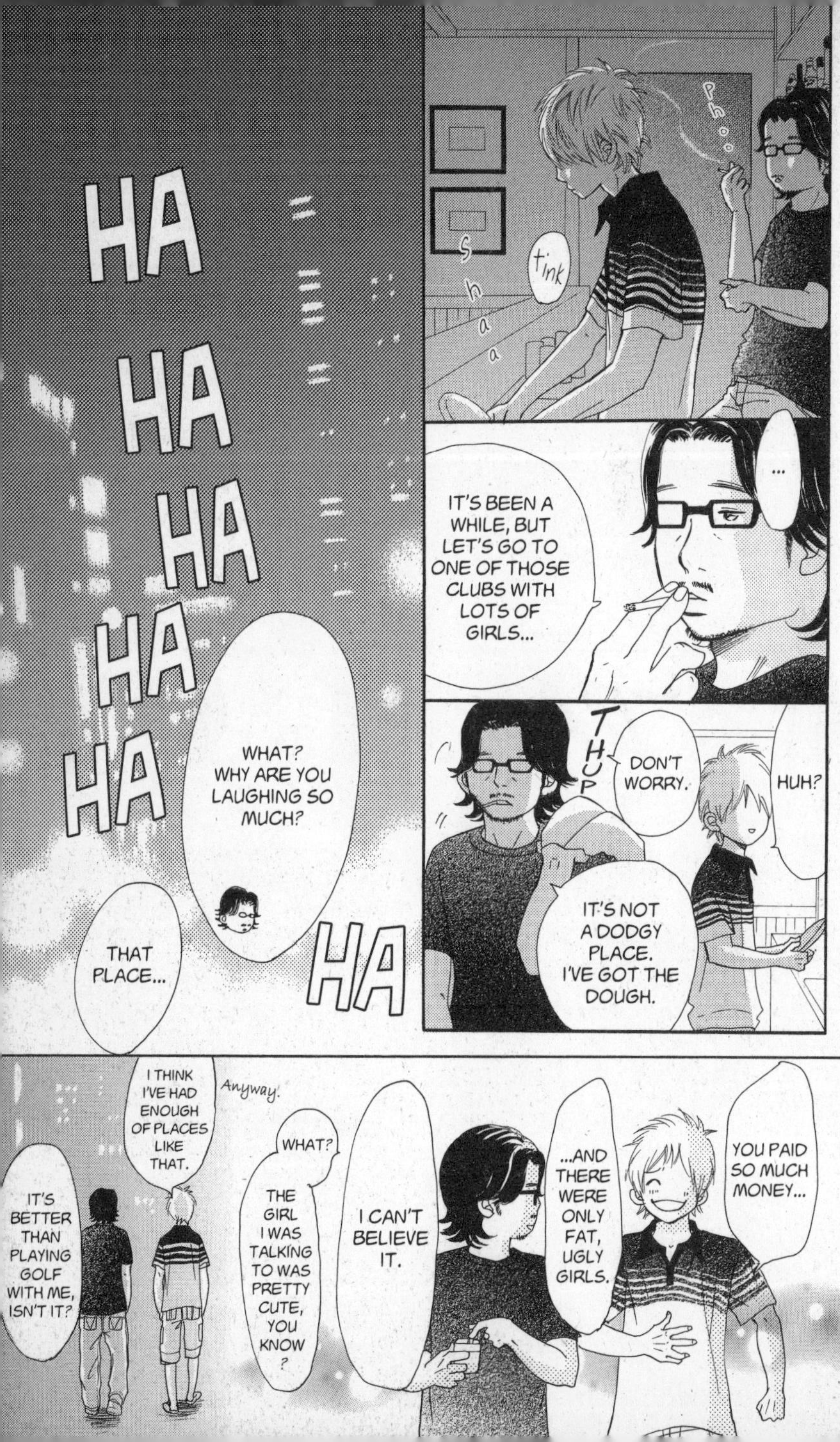
Phooo
tink
Shaaa
...
IT'S BEEN A WHILE, BUT LET'S GO TO ONE OF THOSE CLUBS WITH LOTS OF GIRLS...
HUH?
DON'T WORRY.
THUP
IT'S NOT A DODGY PLACE. I'VE GOT THE DOUGH.
HA
HA
HA
HA
HA
WHAT? WHY ARE YOU LAUGHING SO MUCH?
HA
THAT PLACE...
YOU PAID SO MUCH MONEY...
...AND THERE WERE ONLY FAT, UGLY GIRLS.
I CAN'T BELIEVE IT.
WHAT?
THE GIRL I WAS TALKING TO WAS PRETTY CUTE, YOU KNOW?
Anyway.
I THINK I'VE HAD ENOUGH OF PLACES LIKE THAT.
IT'S BETTER THAN PLAYING GOLF WITH ME, ISN'T IT?

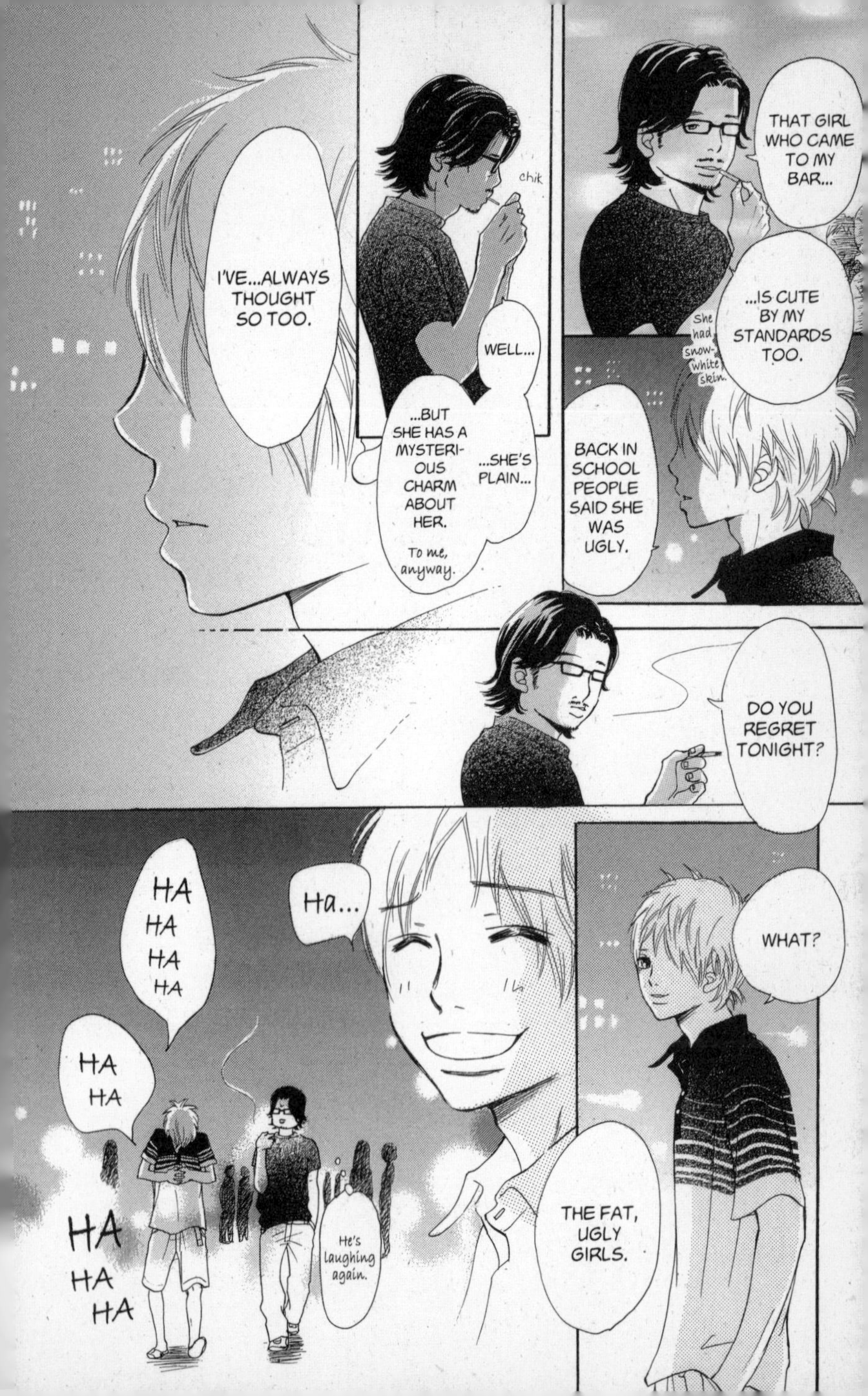
THAT GIRL WHO CAME TO MY BAR...
...IS CUTE BY MY STANDARDS TOO.
She had snow-white skin.
BACK IN SCHOOL PEOPLE SAID SHE WAS UGLY.
chik
WELL...
...SHE'S PLAIN...
...BUT SHE HAS A MYSTERIOUS CHARM ABOUT HER.
To me, anyway.
I'VE...ALWAYS THOUGHT SO TOO.
DO YOU REGRET TONIGHT?
WHAT?
THE FAT, UGLY GIRLS.
Ha...
HA HA HA HA
HA HA
He's laughing again.
HA HA HA

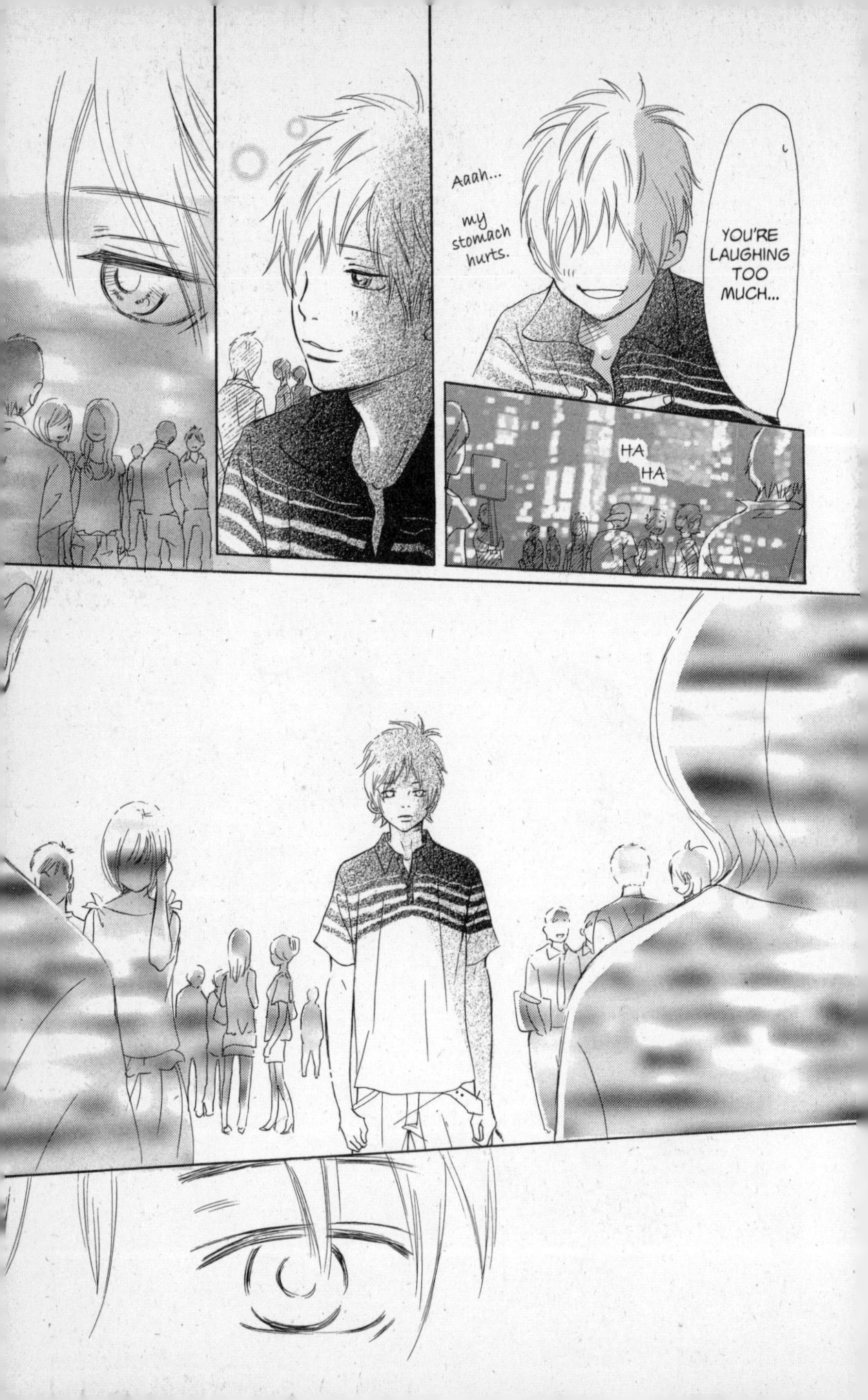
YOU'RE LAUGHING TOO MUCH...
Aaah...
my stomach hurts.
HA HA

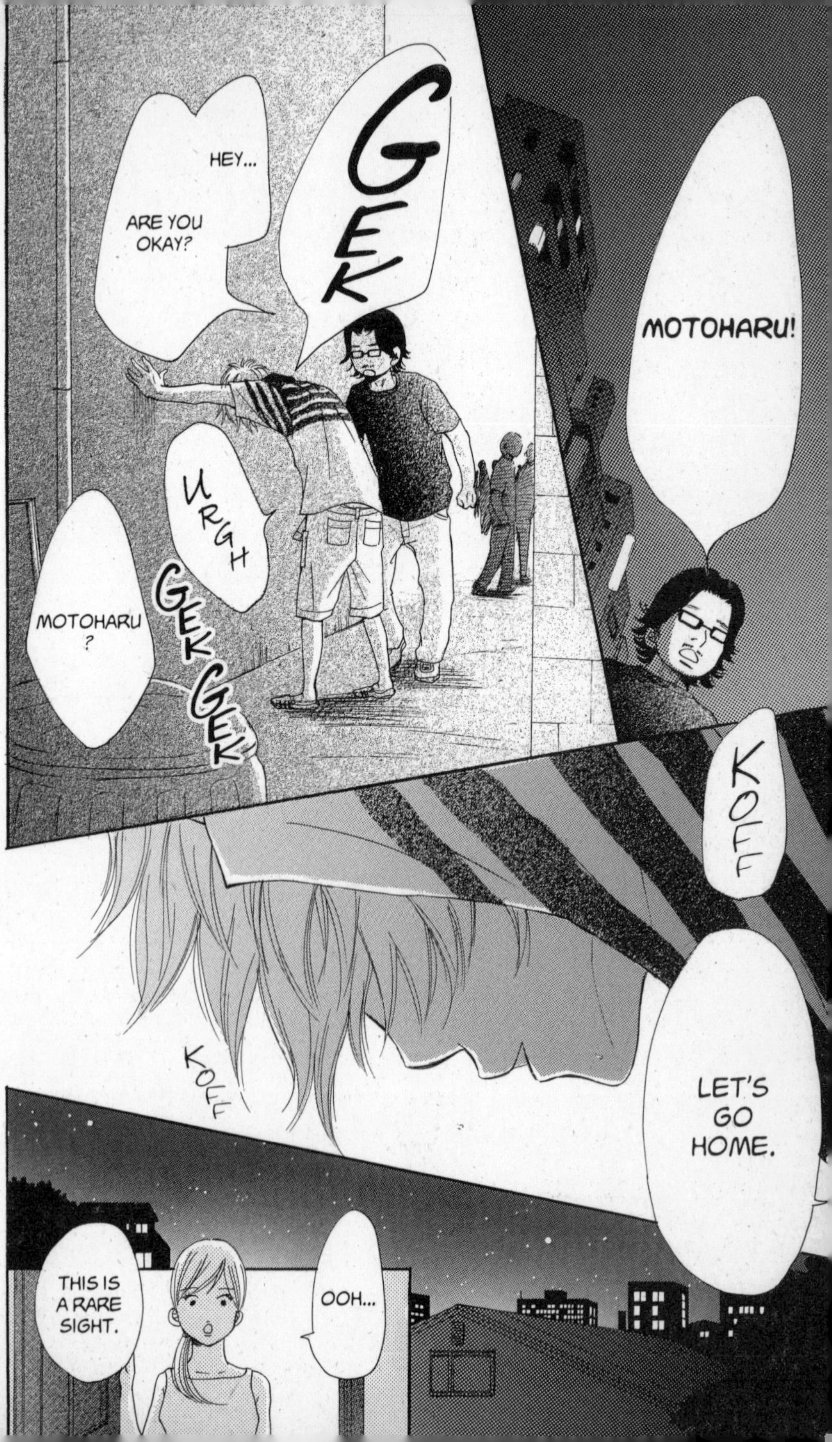
MOTOHARU!
GEK
HEY...
ARE YOU OKAY?
URGH
GEK GEK
MOTOHARU?
KOFF
LET'S GO HOME.
KOFF
OOH...
THIS IS A RARE SIGHT.

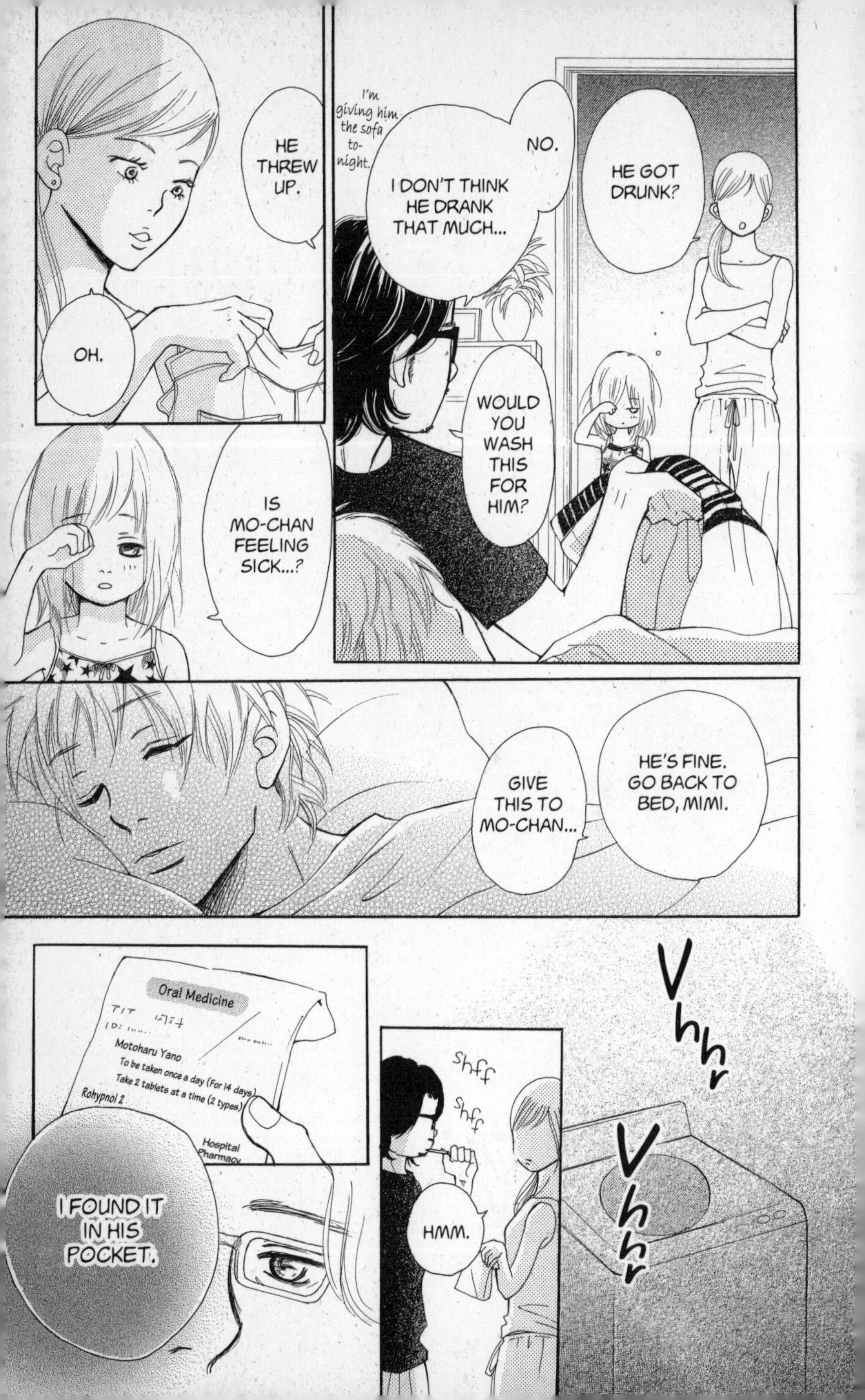
HE GOT DRUNK?
NO.
I'm giving him the sofa tonight.
I DON'T THINK HE DRANK THAT MUCH...
WOULD YOU WASH THIS FOR HIM?
HE THREW UP.
OH.
IS MO-CHAN FEELING SICK...?
HE'S FINE. GO BACK TO BED, MIMI.
GIVE THIS TO MO-CHAN...
Vhhr
Vhhr
shff
shff
HMM.
Oral Medicine
Motoharu Yano
To be taken once a day (For 14 days)
Take 2 tablets at a time (2 types)
Rohypnol 2
Hospital Pharmacy
I FOUND IT IN HIS POCKET.

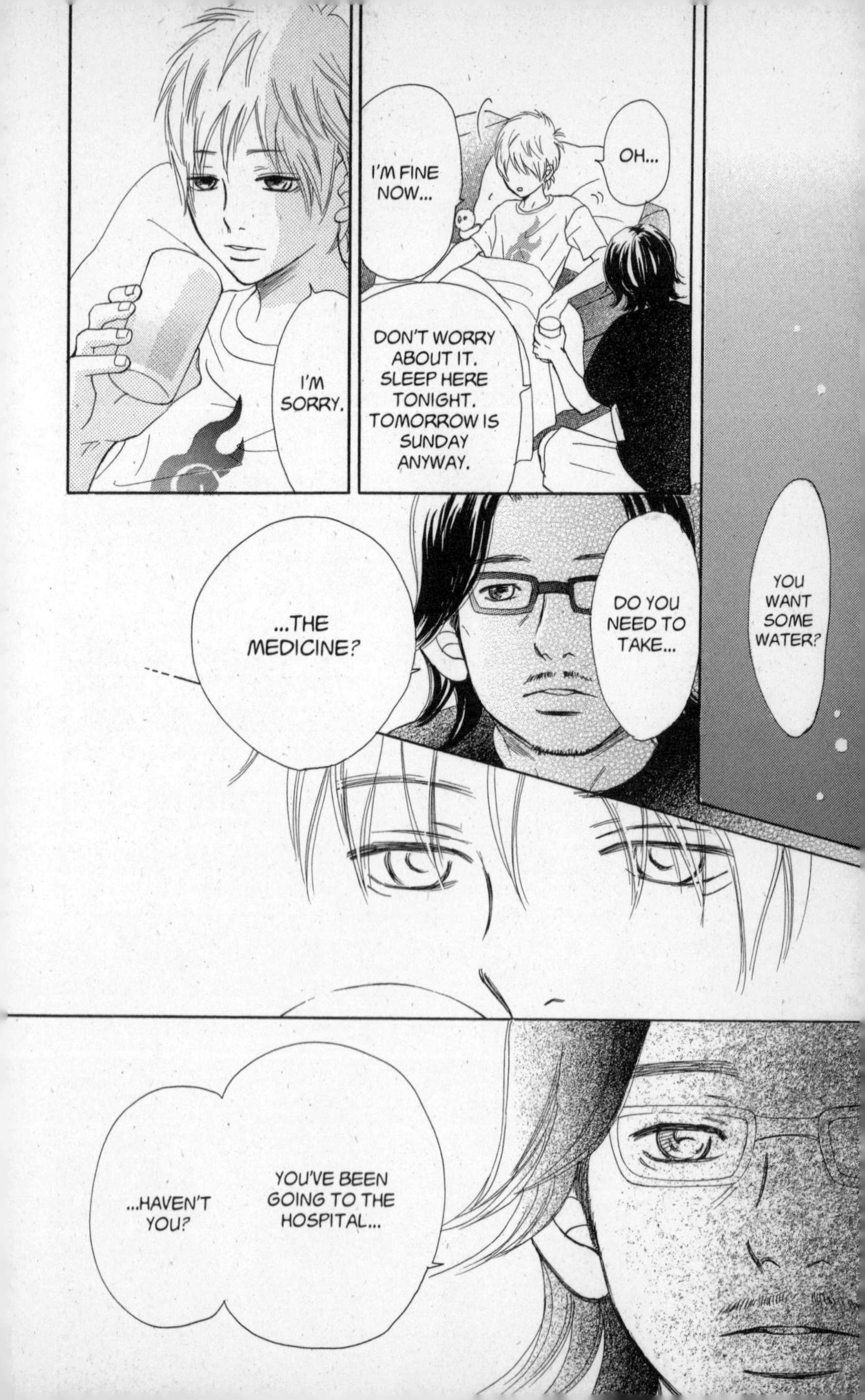
YOU WANT SOME WATER?
OH...
I'M FINE NOW...
DON'T WORRY ABOUT IT. SLEEP HERE TONIGHT. TOMORROW IS SUNDAY ANYWAY.
I'M SORRY.
DO YOU NEED TO TAKE...
...THE MEDICINE?
YOU'VE BEEN GOING TO THE HOSPITAL...
...HAVEN'T YOU?

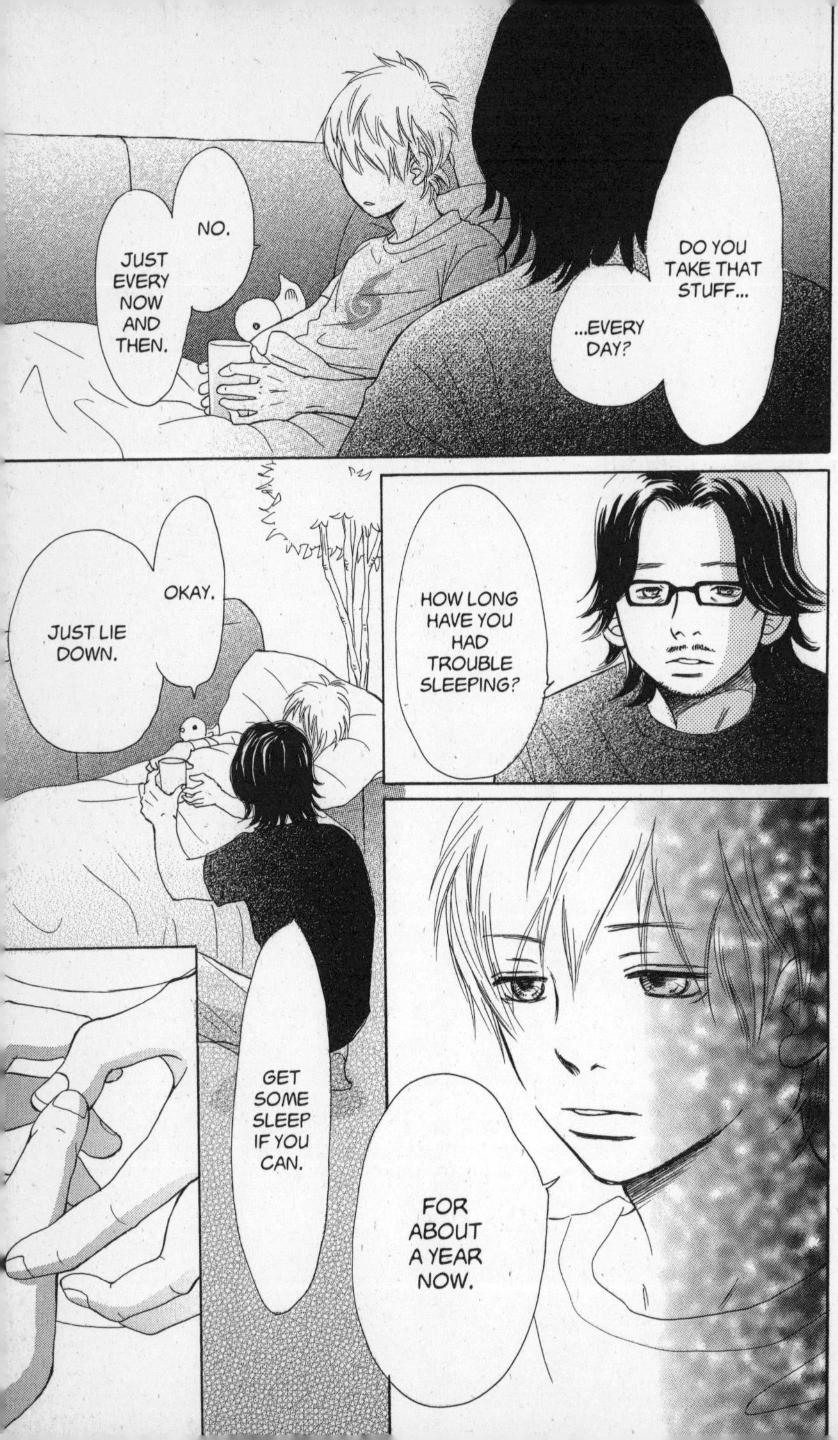
DO YOU TAKE THAT STUFF...
...EVERY DAY?
NO.
JUST EVERY NOW AND THEN.
HOW LONG HAVE YOU HAD TROUBLE SLEEPING?
FOR ABOUT A YEAR NOW.
OKAY.
JUST LIE DOWN.
GET SOME SLEEP IF YOU CAN.

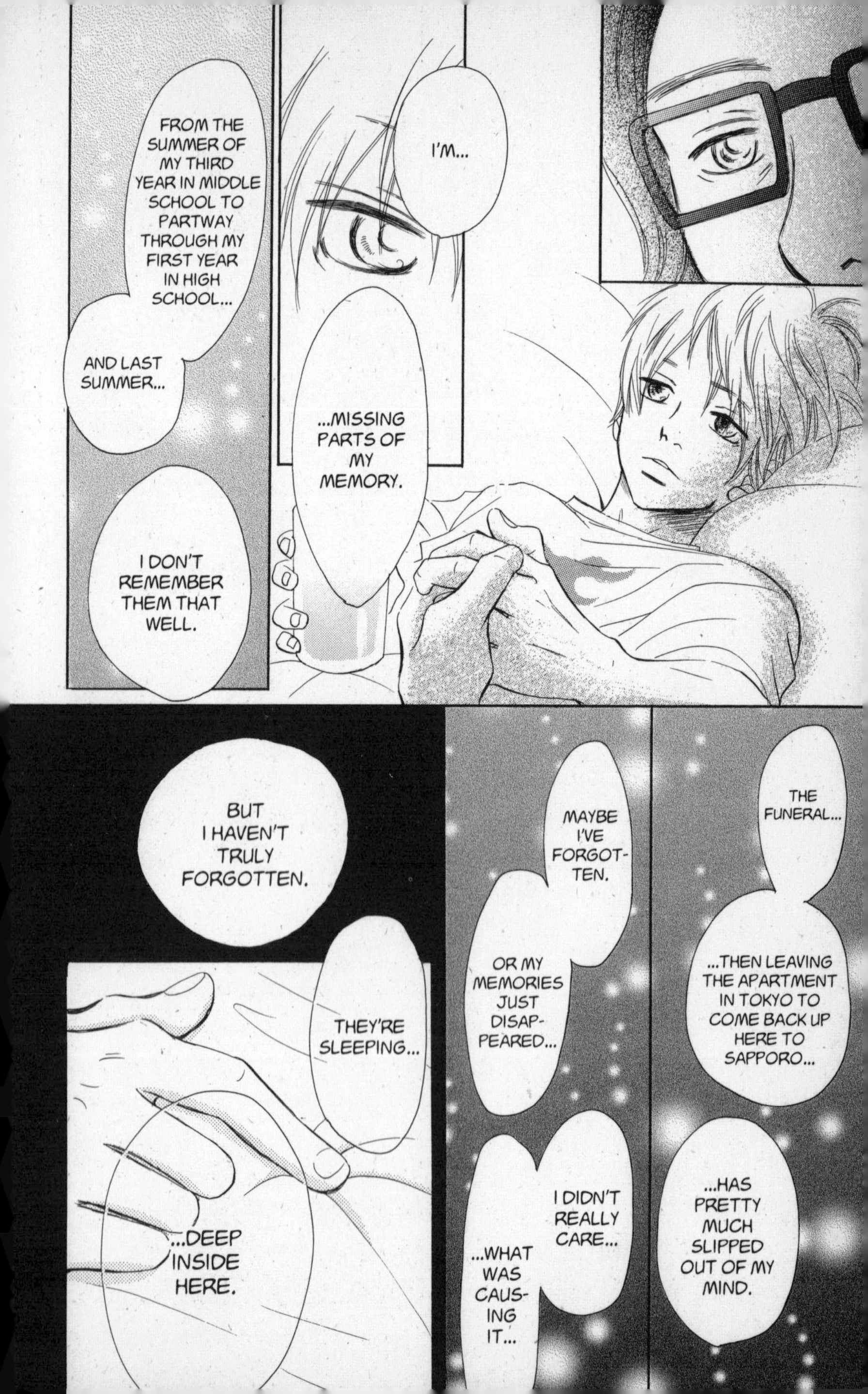
I'M...
...MISSING PARTS OF MY MEMORY.
FROM THE SUMMER OF MY THIRD YEAR IN MIDDLE SCHOOL TO PARTWAY THROUGH MY FIRST YEAR IN HIGH SCHOOL...
AND LAST SUMMER...
I DON'T REMEMBER THEM THAT WELL.
THE FUNERAL...
...THEN LEAVING THE APARTMENT IN TOKYO TO COME BACK UP HERE TO SAPPORO...
...HAS PRETTY MUCH SLIPPED OUT OF MY MIND.
MAYBE I'VE FORGOT-TEN.
OR MY MEMORIES JUST DISAP-PEARED...
I DIDN'T REALLY CARE...
...WHAT WAS CAUS-ING IT...
BUT I HAVEN'T TRULY FORGOTTEN.
THEY'RE SLEEPING...
...DEEP INSIDE HERE.

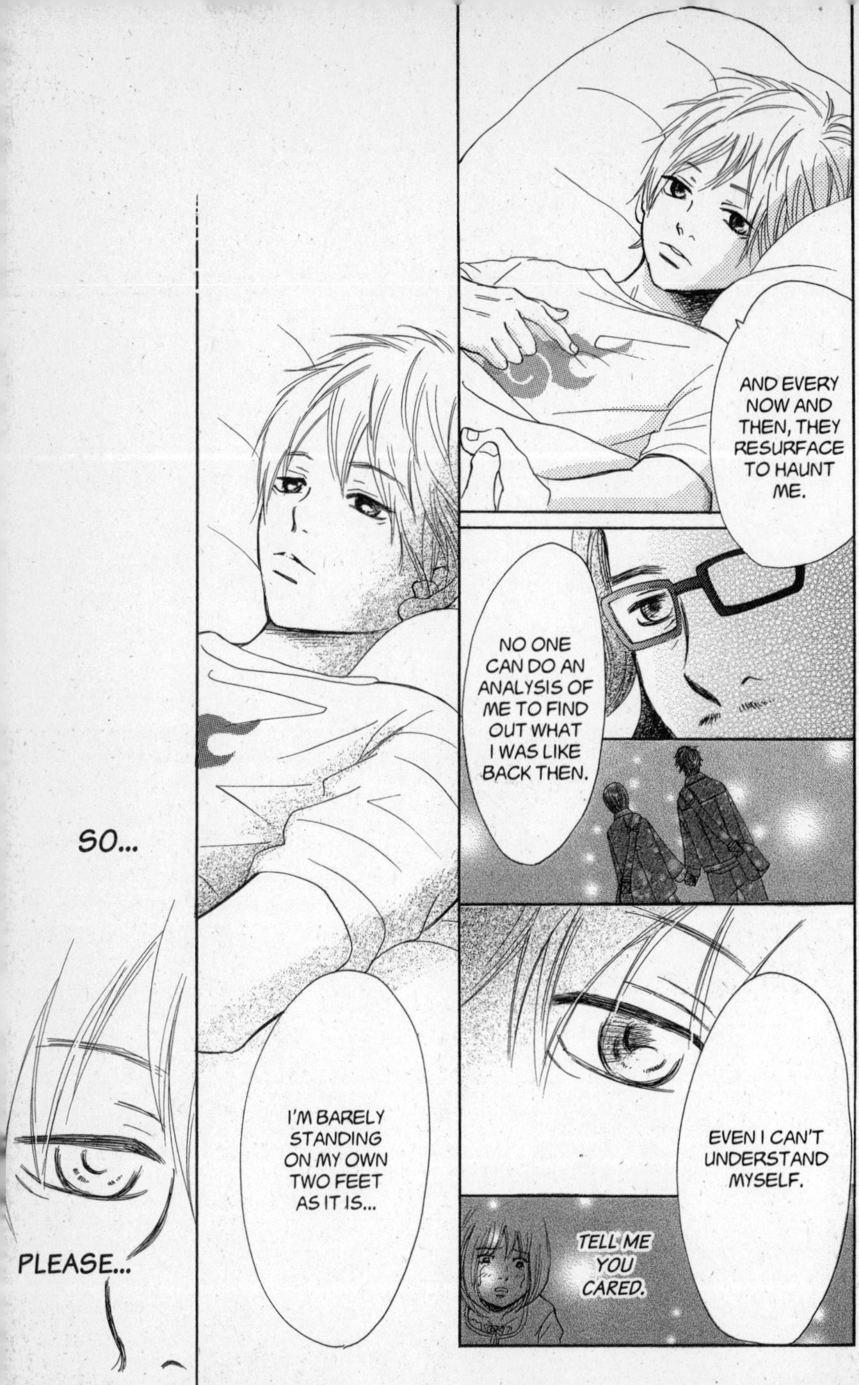
AND EVERY NOW AND THEN, THEY RESURFACE TO HAUNT ME.
NO ONE CAN DO AN ANALYSIS OF ME TO FIND OUT WHAT I WAS LIKE BACK THEN.
EVEN I CAN'T UNDERSTAND MYSELF.
TELL ME YOU CARED.
I'M BARELY STANDING ON MY OWN TWO FEET AS IT IS...
SO...
PLEASE...

...DON'T
ASK ME
TO
SAVE
YOU.

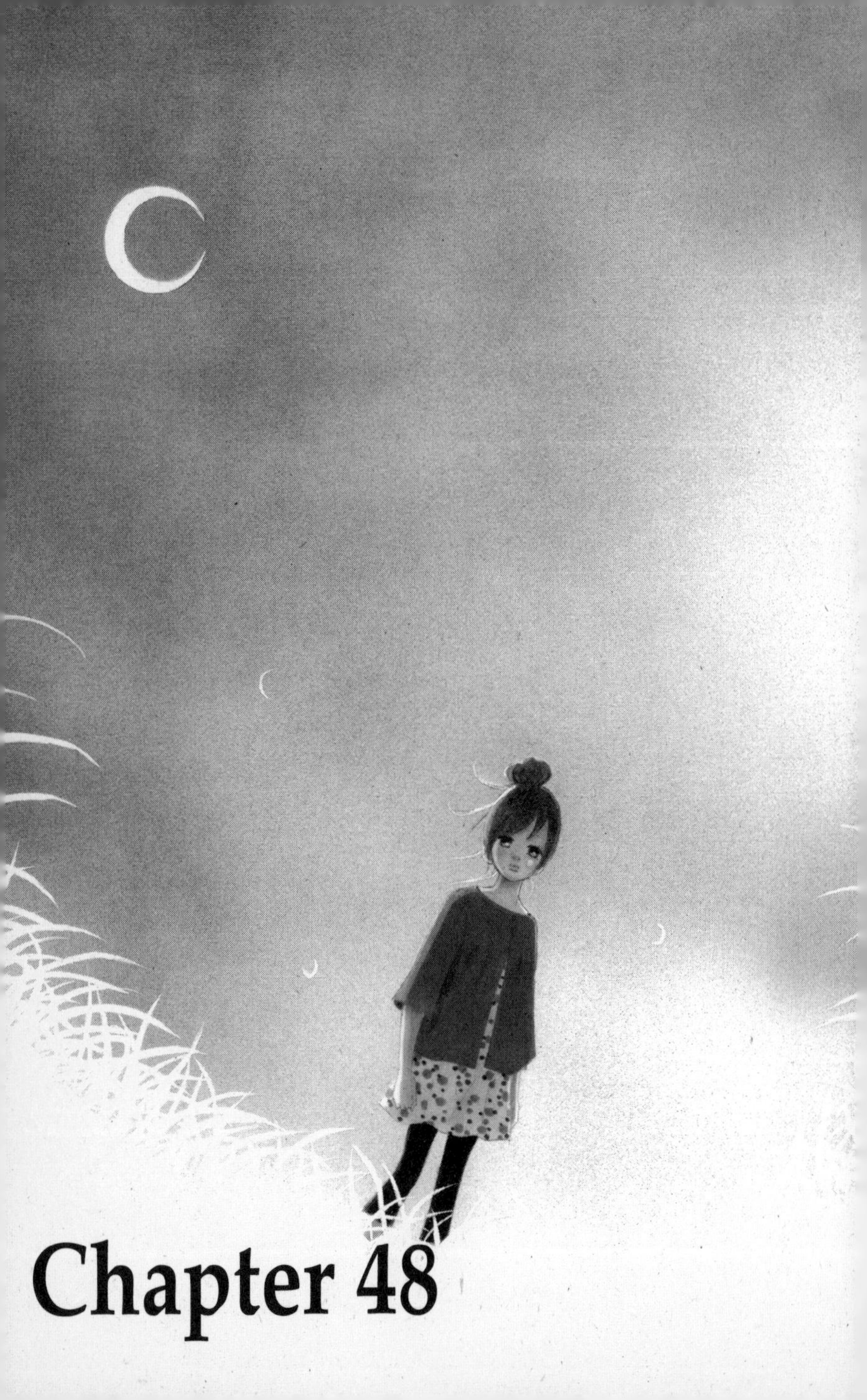

Chapter 48

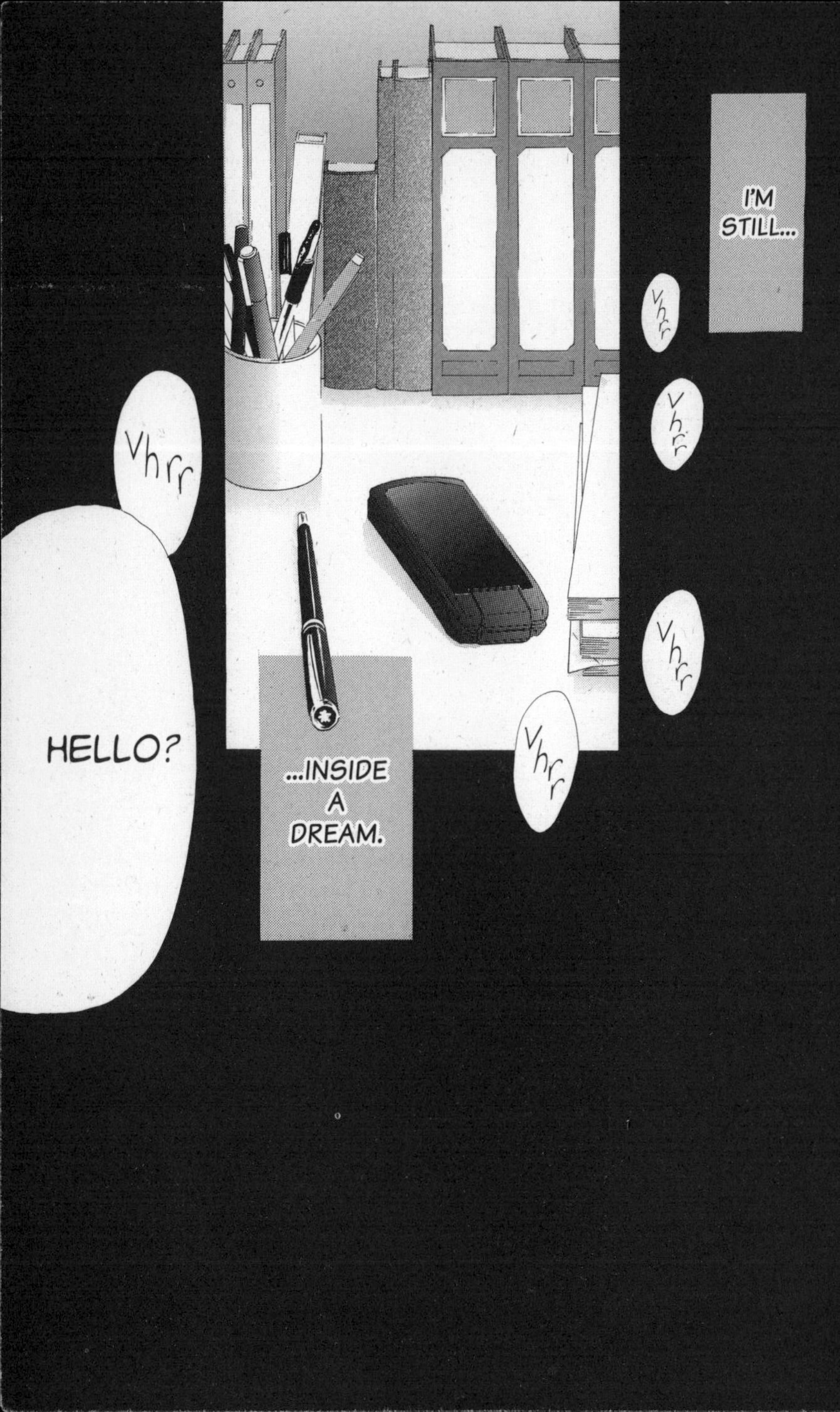
I'M STILL...
Vhrr
Vhrr
Vhrr
Vhrr
...INSIDE A DREAM.
Vhrr
HELLO?

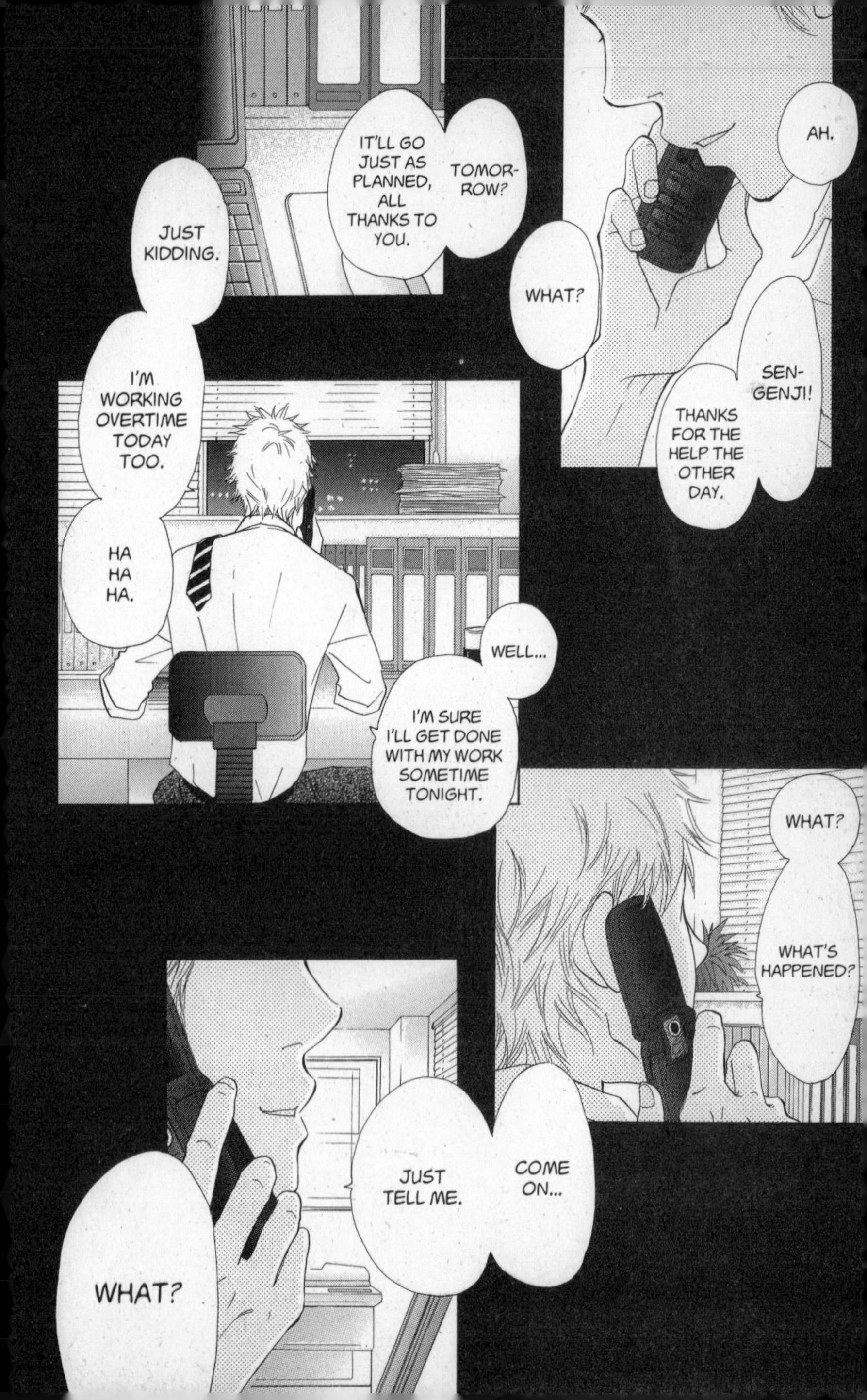
AH.
SEN-GENJI!
THANKS FOR THE HELP THE OTHER DAY.
WHAT?
TOMOR-ROW?
IT'LL GO JUST AS PLANNED, ALL THANKS TO YOU.
JUST KIDDING.
I'M WORKING OVERTIME TODAY TOO.
HA HA HA.
WELL...
I'M SURE I'LL GET DONE WITH MY WORK SOMETIME TONIGHT.
WHAT?
WHAT'S HAPPENED?
COME ON...
JUST TELL ME.
WHAT?

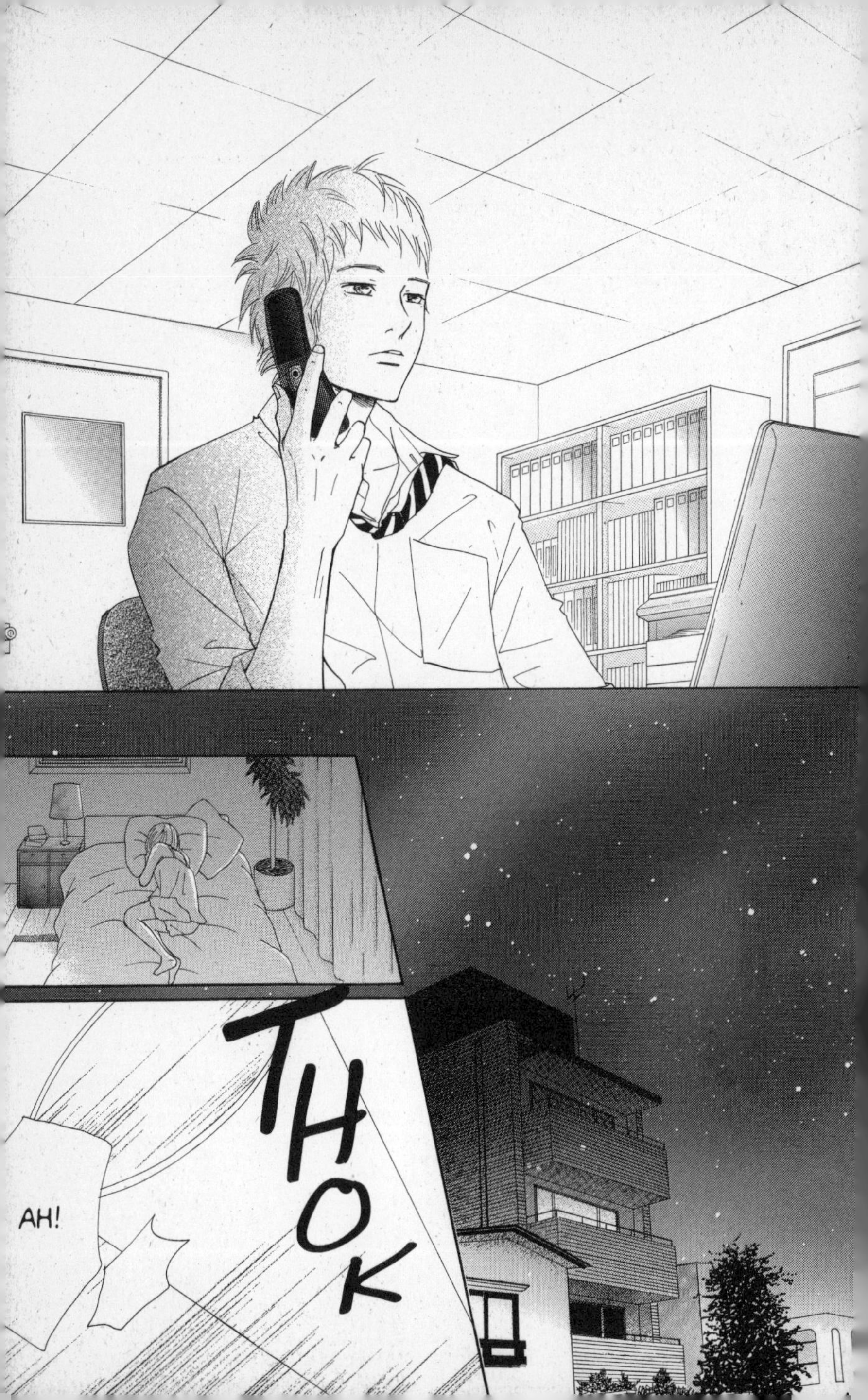
THOK
AH!

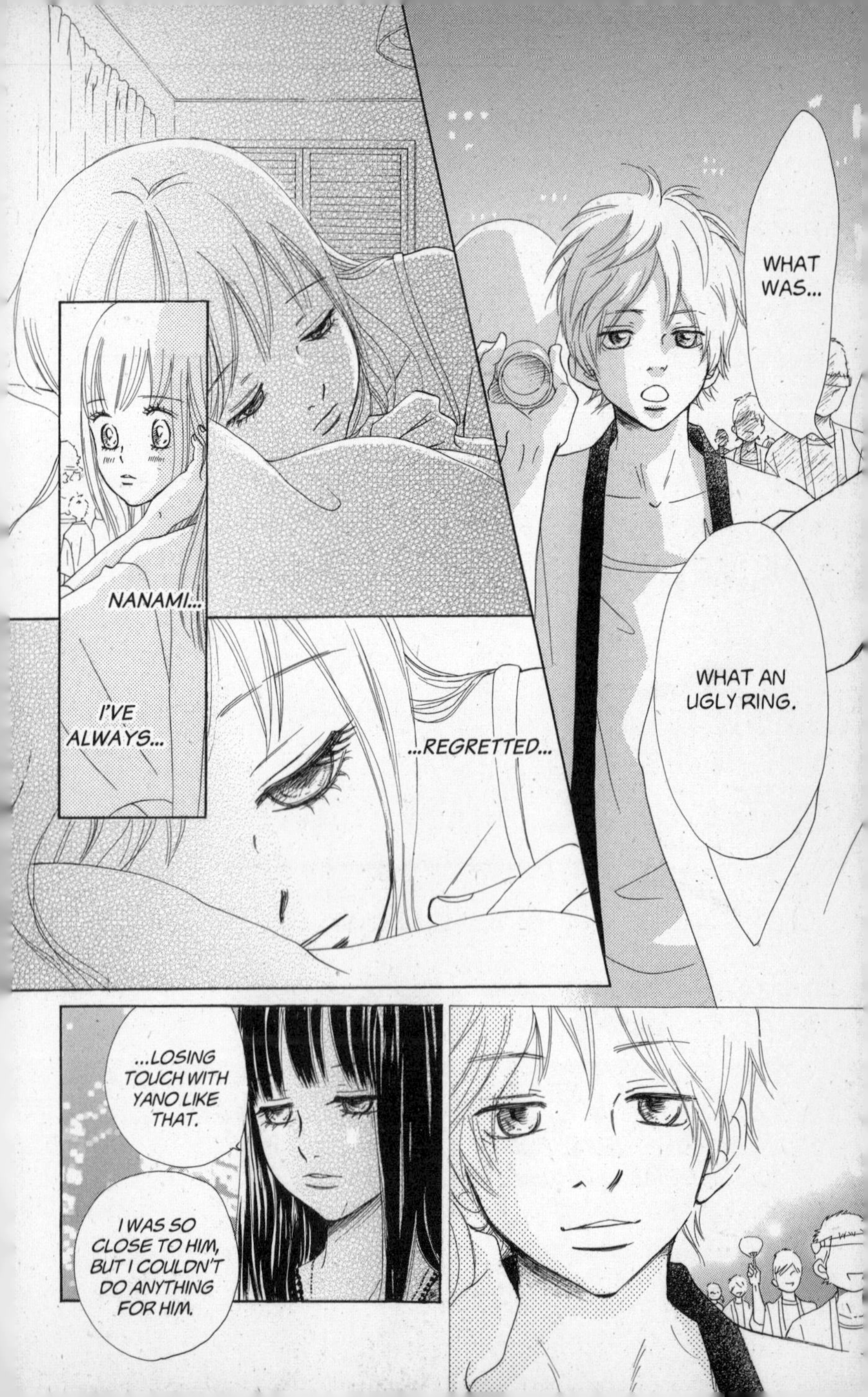
WHAT WAS...
WHAT AN UGLY RING.
NANAMI...
I'VE ALWAYS...
...REGRETTED...
...LOSING TOUCH WITH YANO LIKE THAT.
I WAS SO CLOSE TO HIM, BUT I COULDN'T DO ANYTHING FOR HIM.

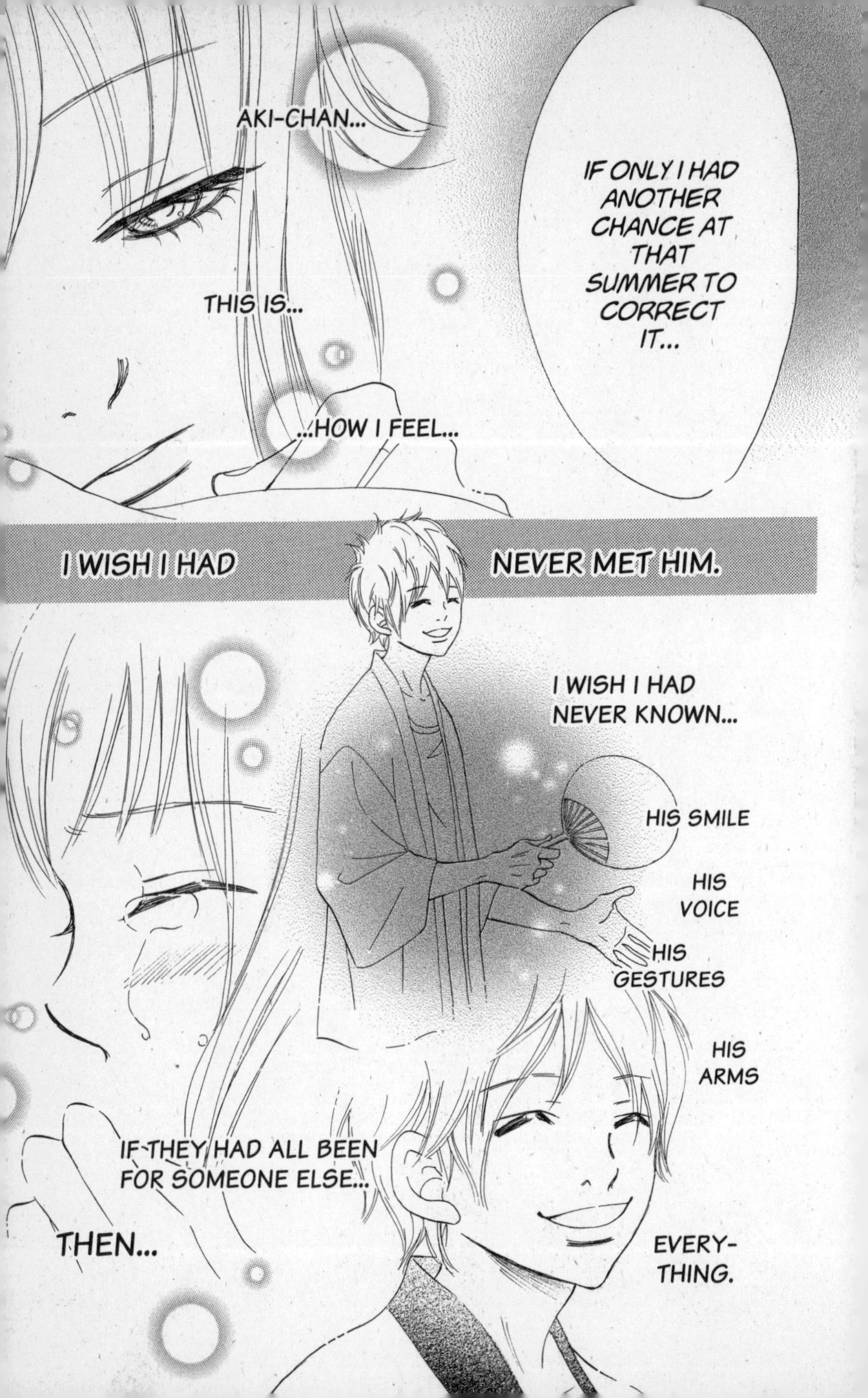
IF ONLY I HAD ANOTHER CHANCE AT THAT SUMMER TO CORRECT IT...
AKI-CHAN...
THIS IS...
...HOW I FEEL...
I WISH I HAD NEVER MET HIM.
I WISH I HAD NEVER KNOWN...
HIS SMILE
HIS VOICE
HIS GESTURES
HIS ARMS
EVERY-THING.
IF THEY HAD ALL BEEN FOR SOMEONE ELSE...
THEN...

AKI-CHAN.

I'M WEAK...

BUT I STILL...

...DREAM OF HIM...

I THOUGHT I HAD GIVEN UP ON HIM A YEAR AGO ON THAT DAY...

I THOUGHT MY TEARS HAD RUN DRY...

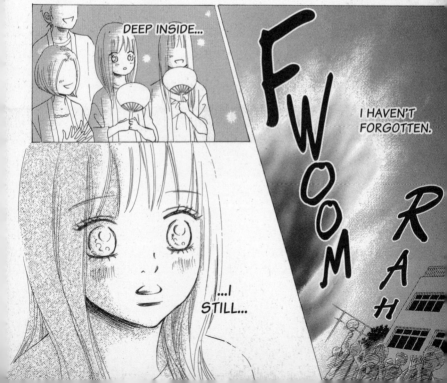

DEEP INSIDE...

I HAVEN'T FORGOTTEN.

...I STILL...

FWOOM

RAH

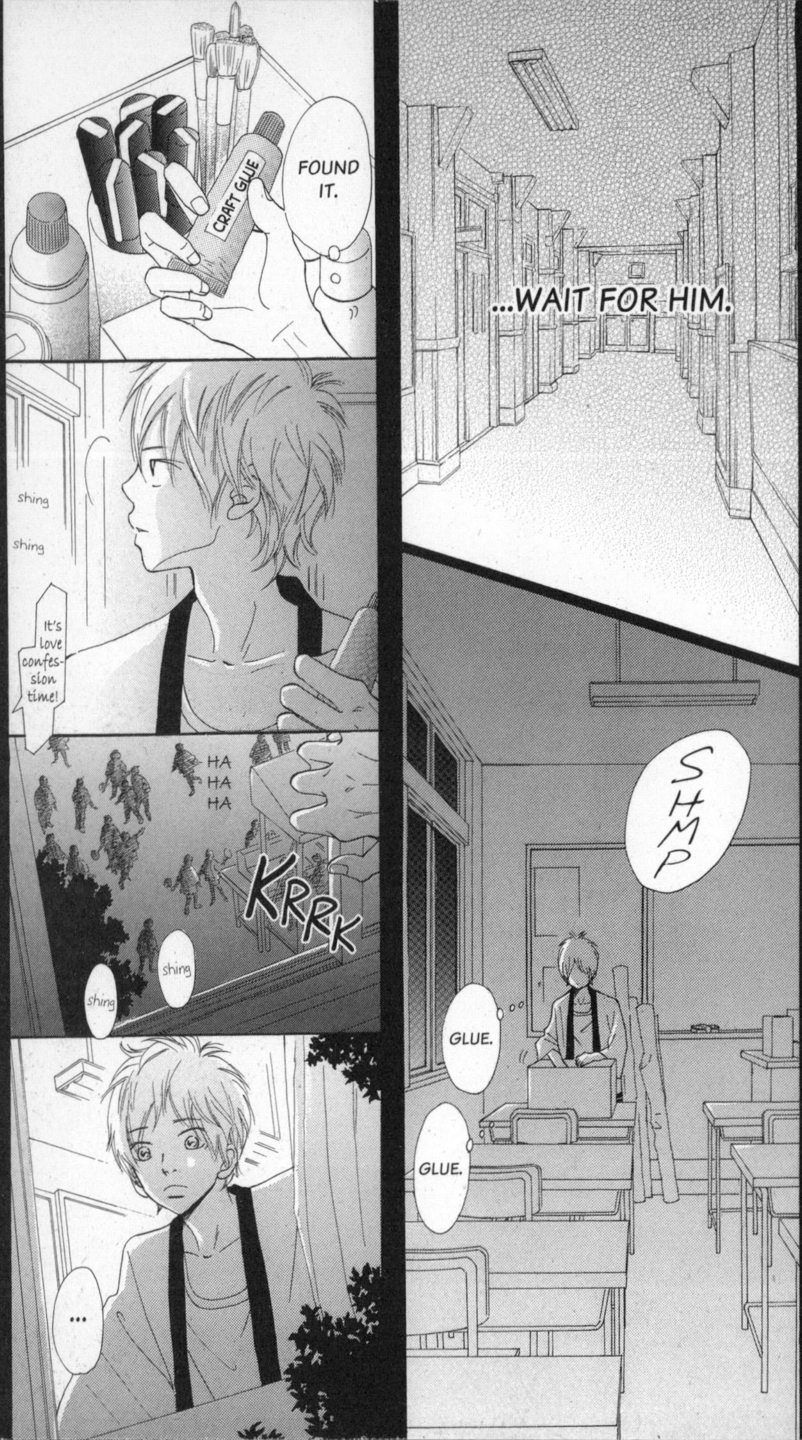
...WAIT FOR HIM.
SHMP
GLUE.
GLUE.
FOUND IT.
CRAFT GLUE
shing
shing
It's love confes-sion time!
HA HA HA
KRRK
shing
shing
...

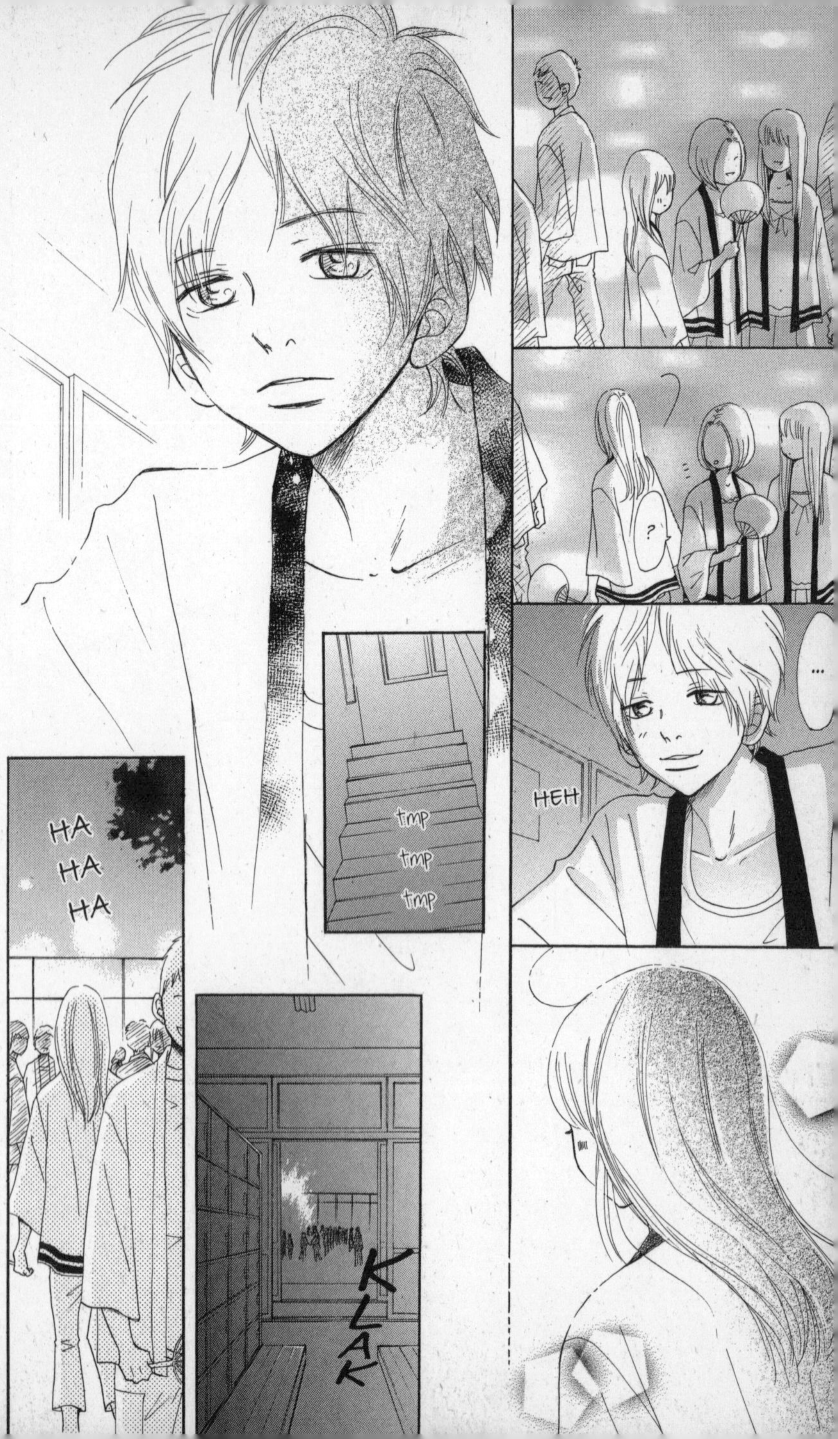
?
...
HEH
tmp
tmp
tmp
HA
HA
HA
KLAK

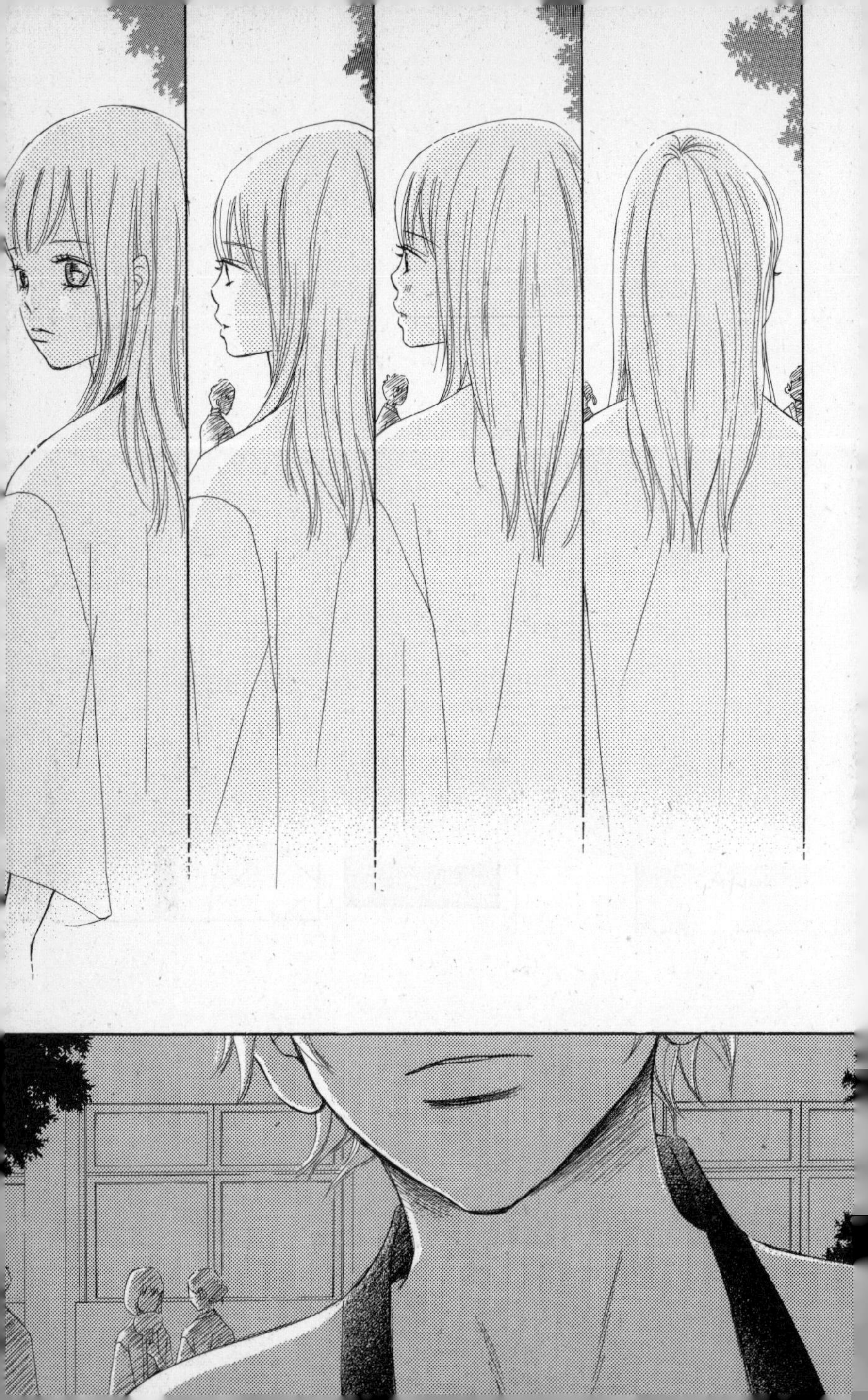

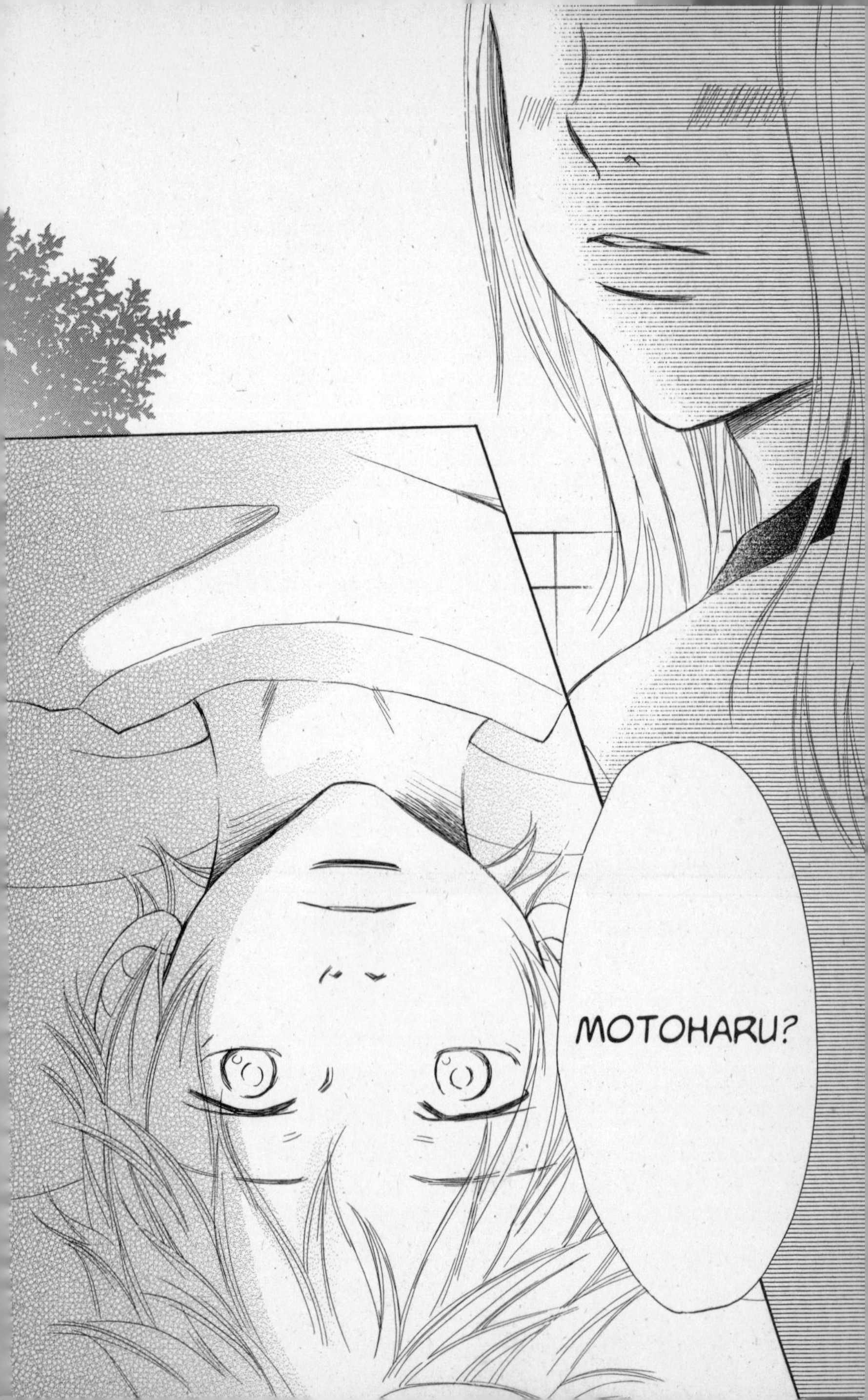
MOTOHARU?

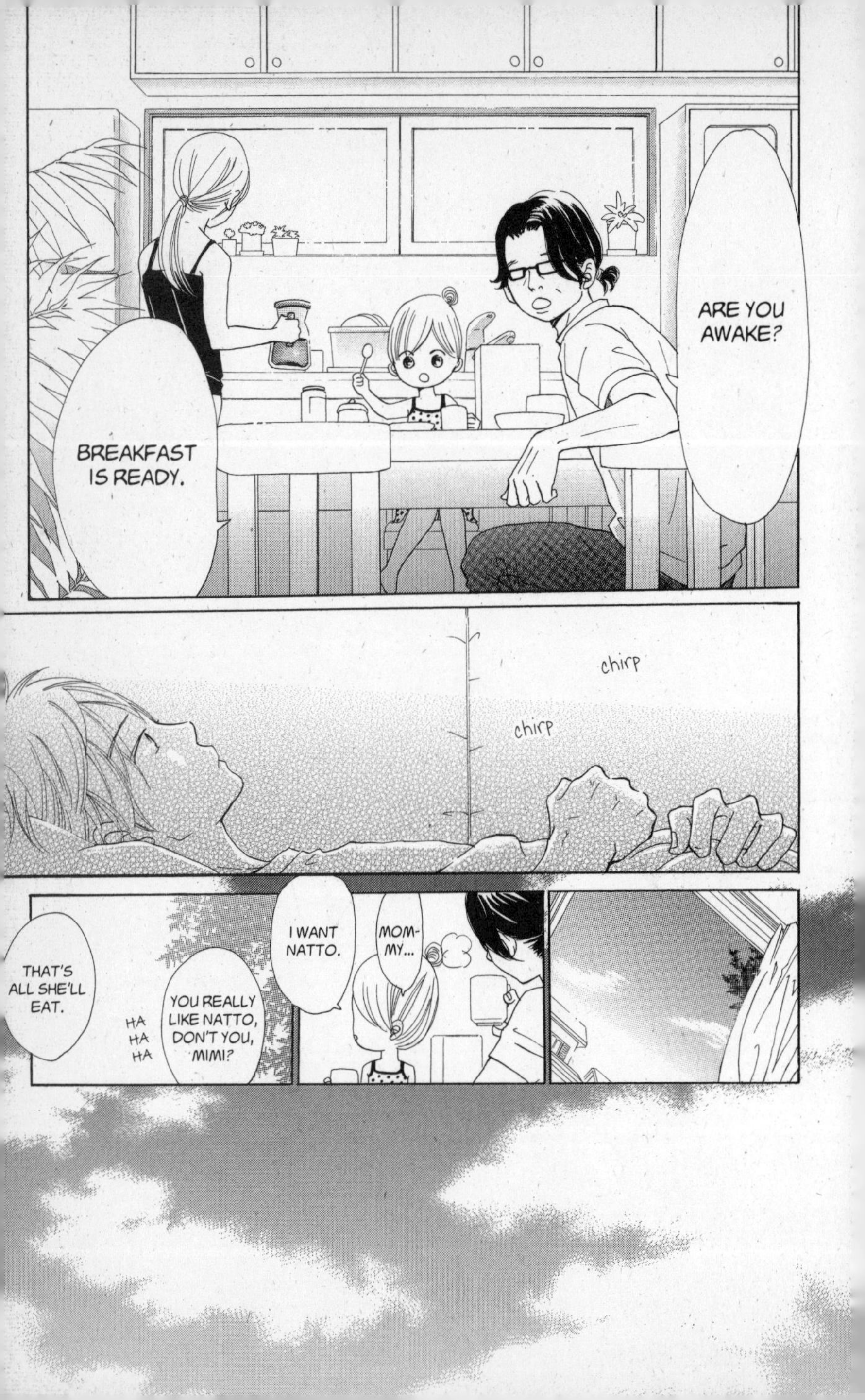
ARE YOU AWAKE?
BREAKFAST IS READY.
chirp
chirp
MOM-MY...
I WANT NATTO.
YOU REALLY LIKE NATTO, DON'T YOU, MIMI?
HA HA HA
THAT'S ALL SHE'LL EAT.

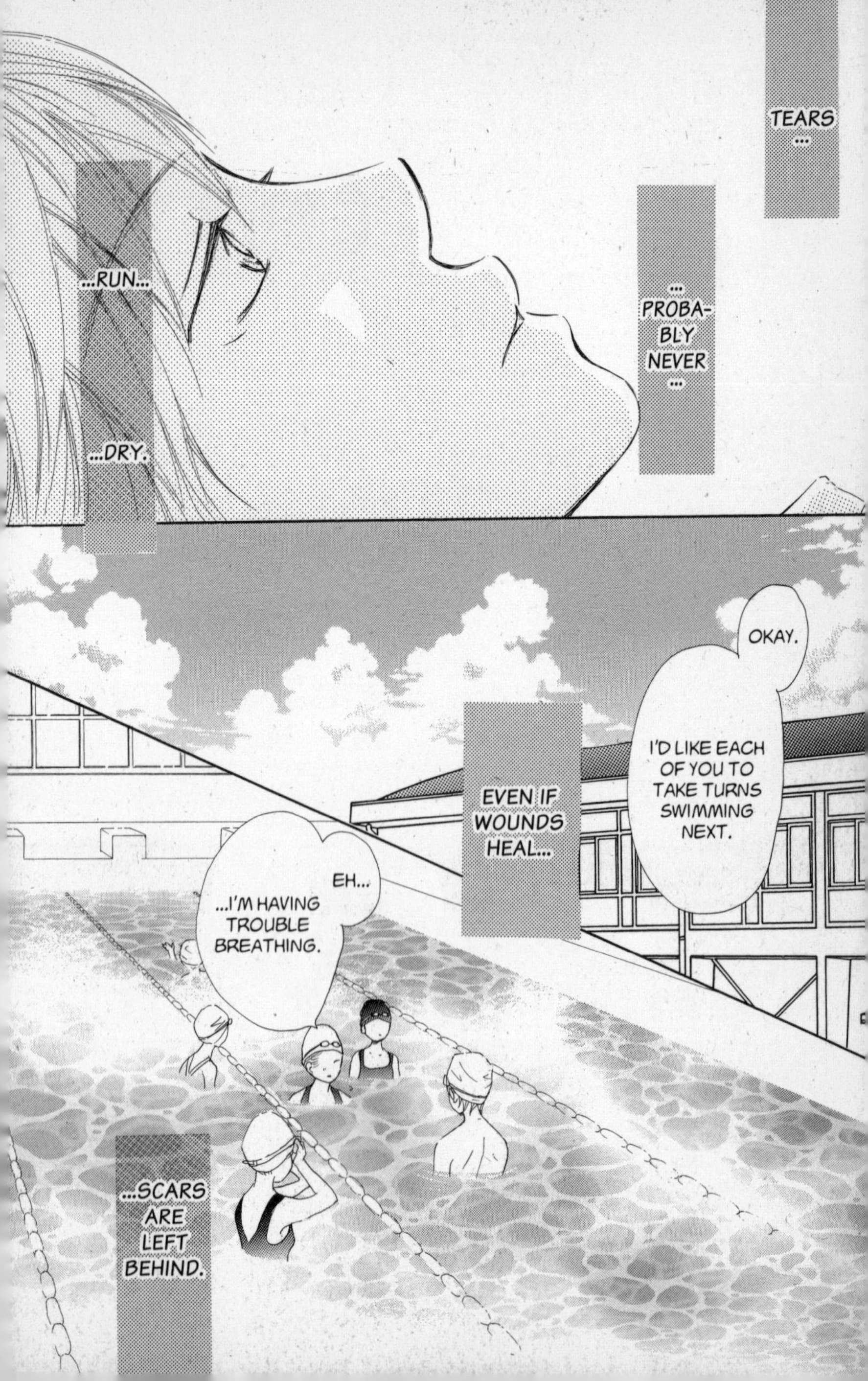
TEARS...
...PROBA-BLY NEVER...
...RUN...
...DRY.
OKAY.
I'D LIKE EACH OF YOU TO TAKE TURNS SWIMMING NEXT.
EVEN IF WOUNDS HEAL...
EH...
...I'M HAVING TROUBLE BREATHING.
...SCARS ARE LEFT BEHIND.

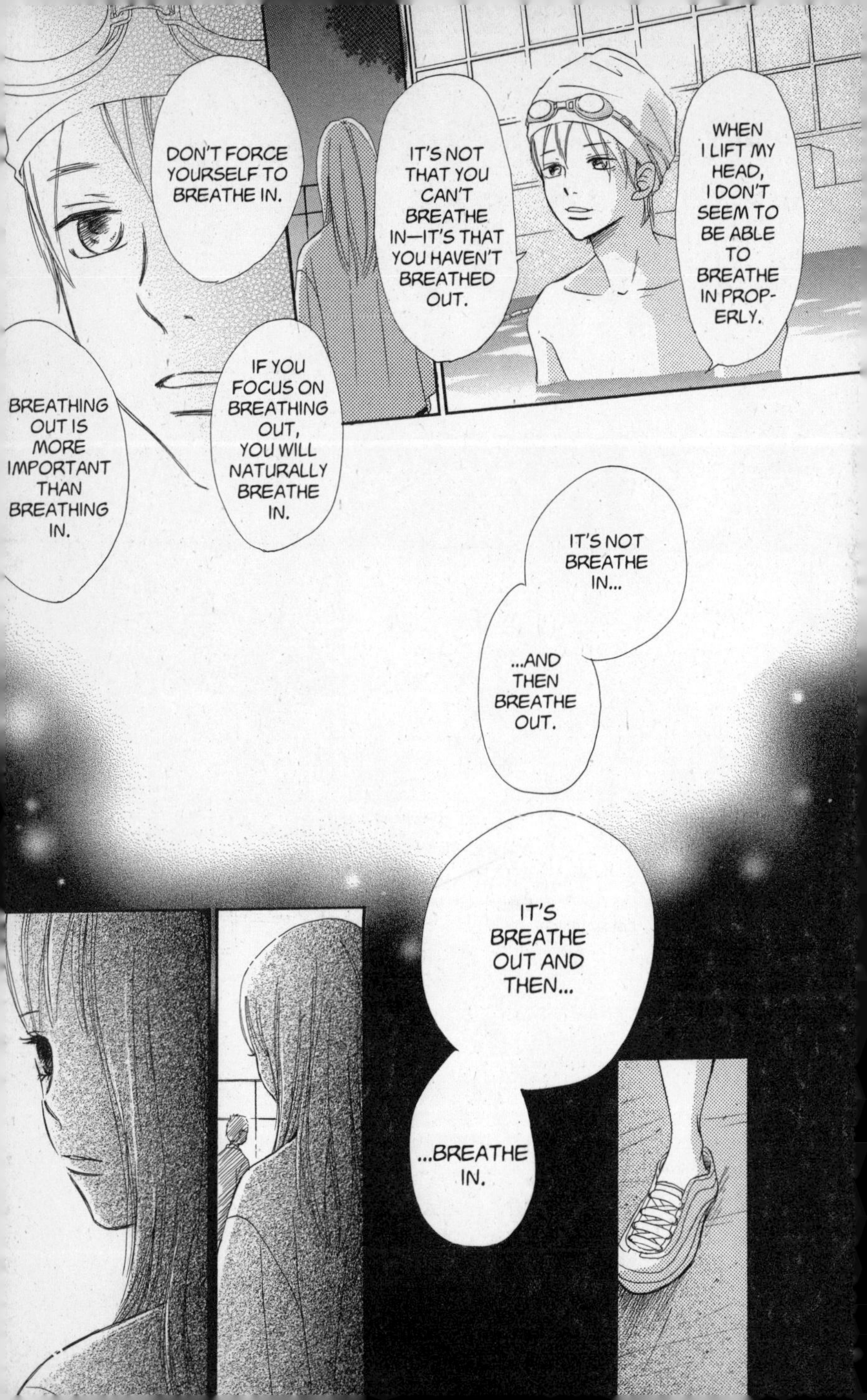
WHEN I LIFT MY HEAD, I DON'T SEEM TO BE ABLE TO BREATHE IN PROPERLY.
IT'S NOT THAT YOU CAN'T BREATHE IN—IT'S THAT YOU HAVEN'T BREATHED OUT.
DON'T FORCE YOURSELF TO BREATHE IN.
IF YOU FOCUS ON BREATHING OUT, YOU WILL NATURALLY BREATHE IN.
BREATHING OUT IS MORE IMPORTANT THAN BREATHING IN.
IT'S NOT BREATHE IN...
...AND THEN BREATHE OUT.
IT'S BREATHE OUT AND THEN...
...BREATHE IN.

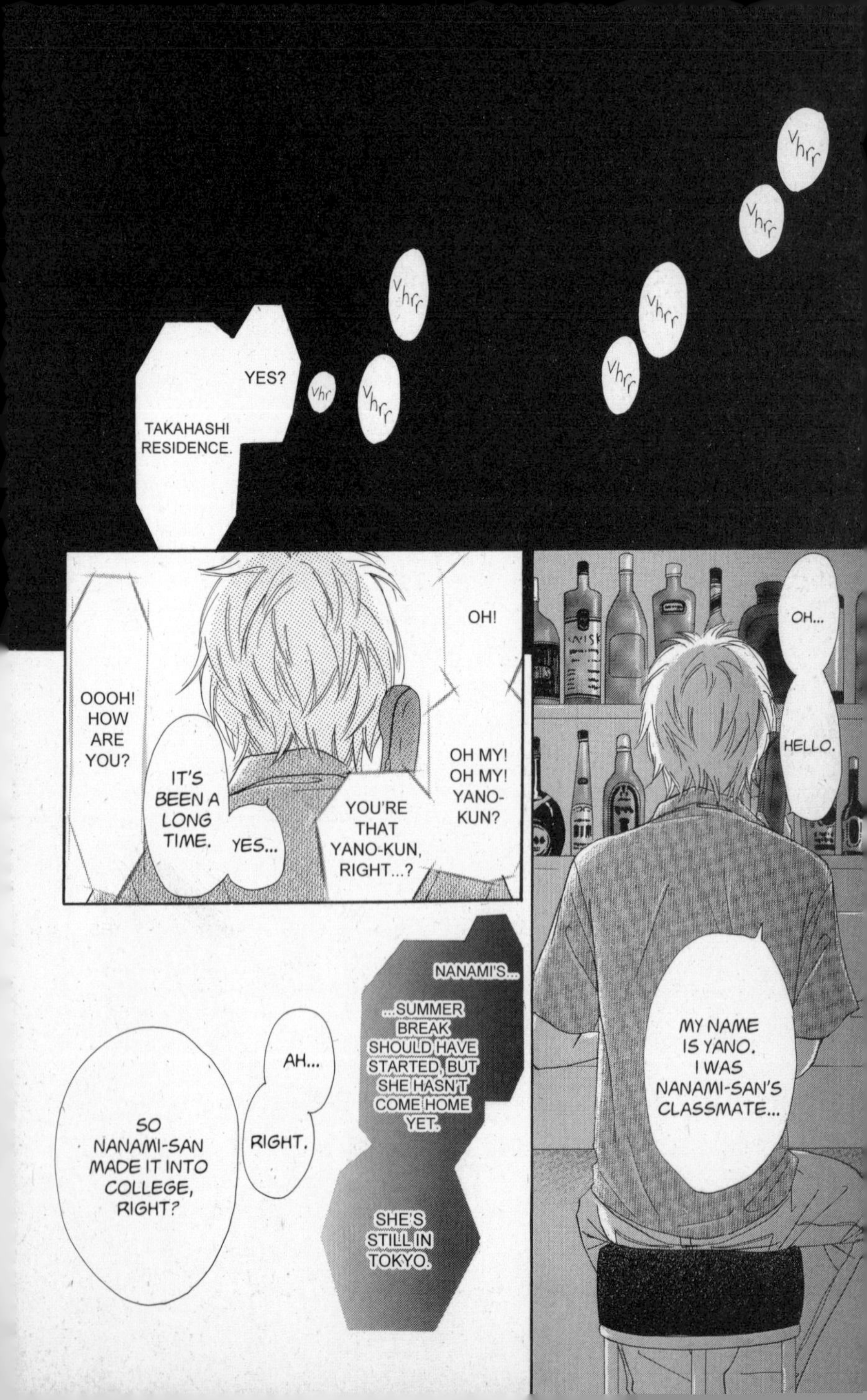
Vhrr
Vhrr
Vhrr
Vhrr
Vhrr
Vhrr
Vhr
YES?
TAKAHASHI RESIDENCE.
OH...
HELLO.
MY NAME IS YANO. I WAS NANAMI-SAN'S CLASSMATE...
OH!
OH MY! OH MY! YANO-KUN?
YOU'RE THAT YANO-KUN, RIGHT...?
YES...
IT'S BEEN A LONG TIME.
OOOH! HOW ARE YOU?
NANAMI'S...
...SUMMER BREAK SHOULD HAVE STARTED, BUT SHE HASN'T COME HOME YET.
SHE'S STILL IN TOKYO.
AH...
RIGHT.
SO NANAMI-SAN MADE IT INTO COLLEGE, RIGHT?

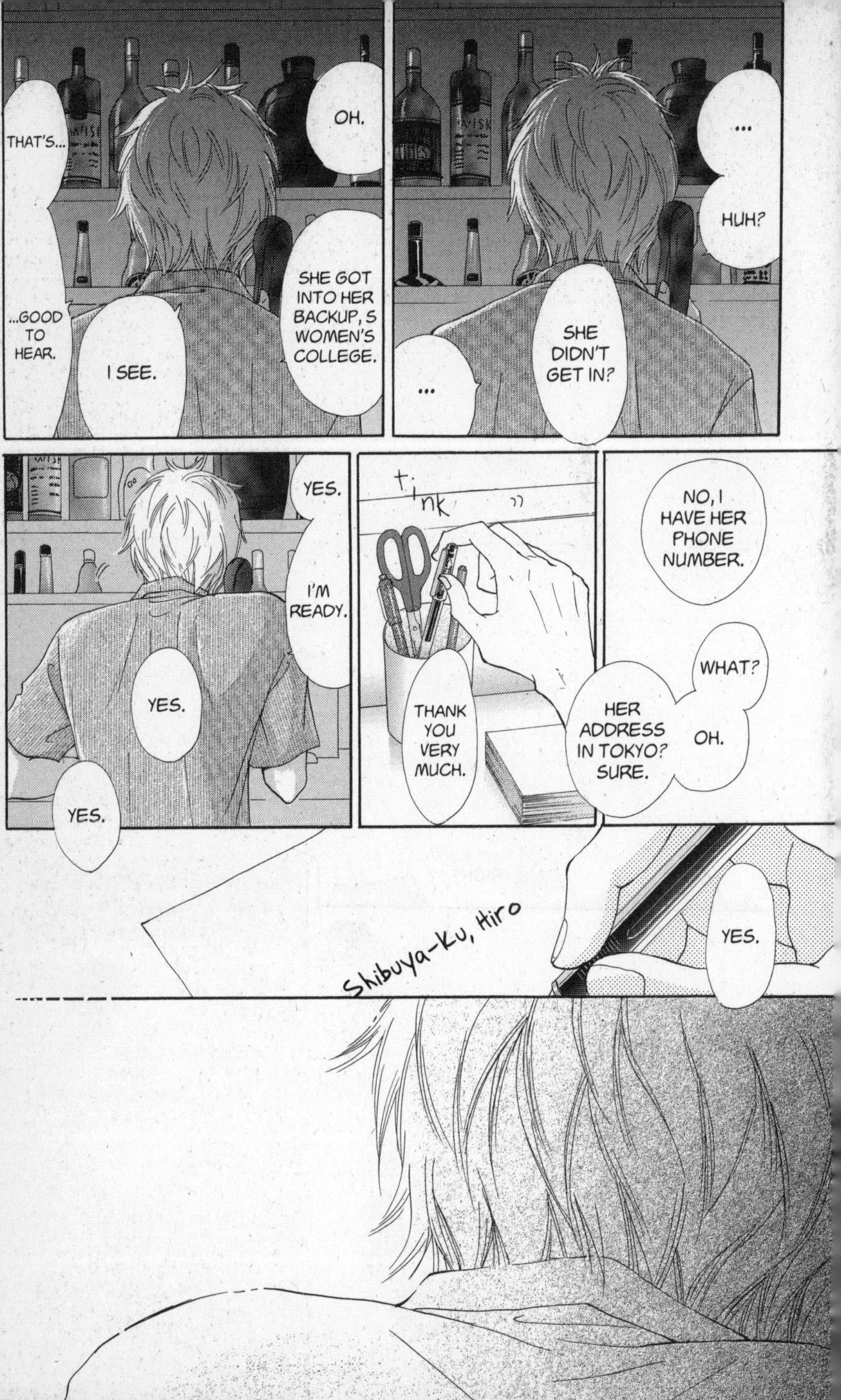
...
HUH?
SHE DIDN'T GET IN?
...
OH.
SHE GOT INTO HER BACKUP, S WOMEN'S COLLEGE.
THAT'S...
...GOOD TO HEAR.
I SEE.
NO, I HAVE HER PHONE NUMBER.
WHAT?
OH.
HER ADDRESS IN TOKYO? SURE.
tink
THANK YOU VERY MUCH.
YES.
I'M READY.
YES.
YES.
YES.
Shibuya-Ku, Hiro

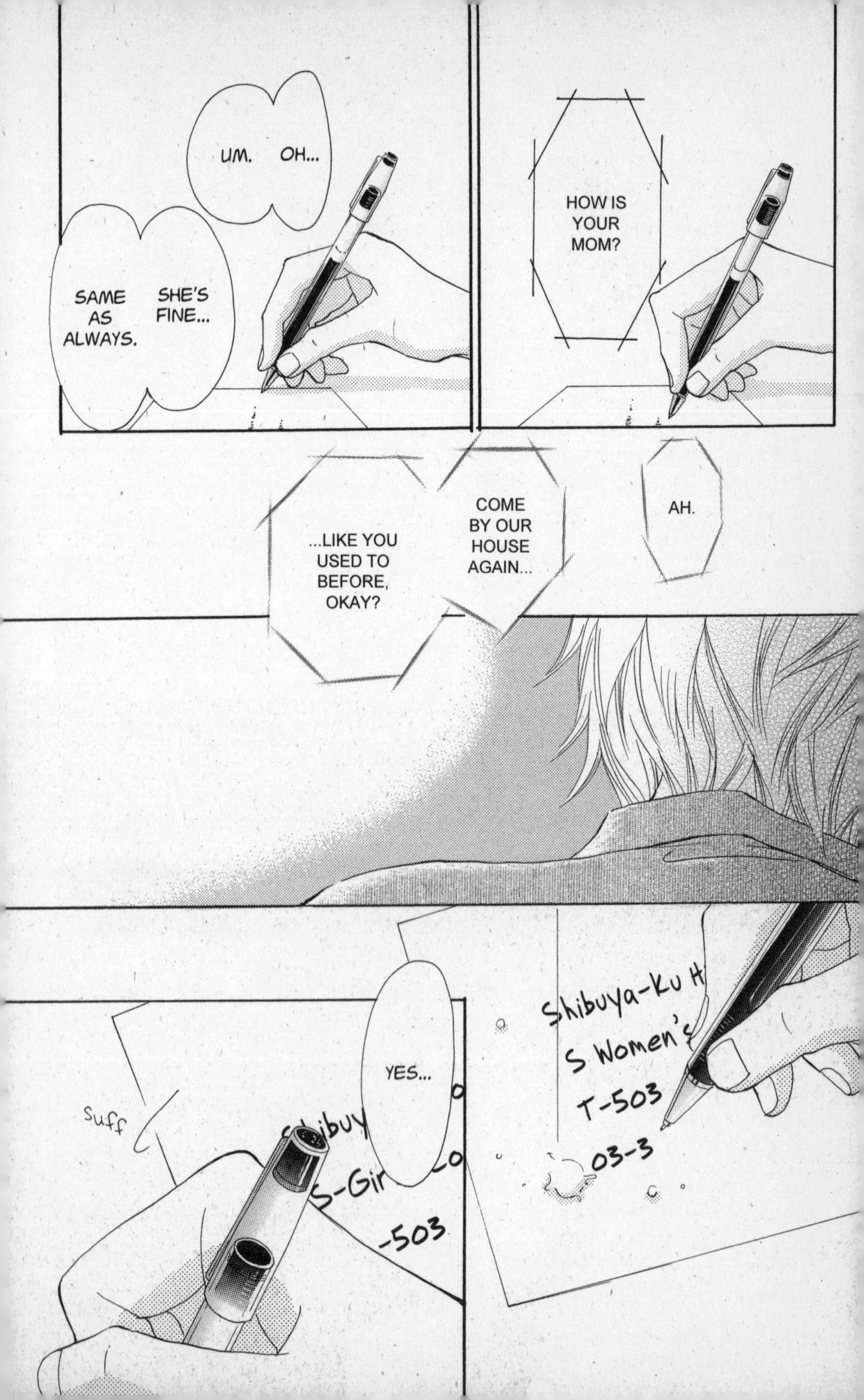
HOW IS YOUR MOM?
UM. OH...
SHE'S FINE... SAME AS ALWAYS.
AH.
COME BY OUR HOUSE AGAIN...
...LIKE YOU USED TO BEFORE, OKAY?
Shibuya-Ku H
S Women's
T-503
03-3
YES...
Suff
S-Gir
-503

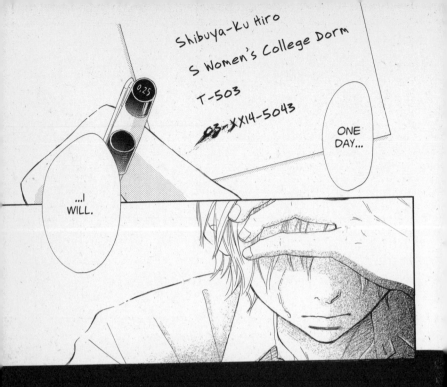

Shibuya-ku Hiro
S Women's College Dorm
T-503
03-XX14-5043

0.25

ONE DAY...

...I WILL.

...THE PAIN...

I CAN'T EXHALE...

...THE TEARS...

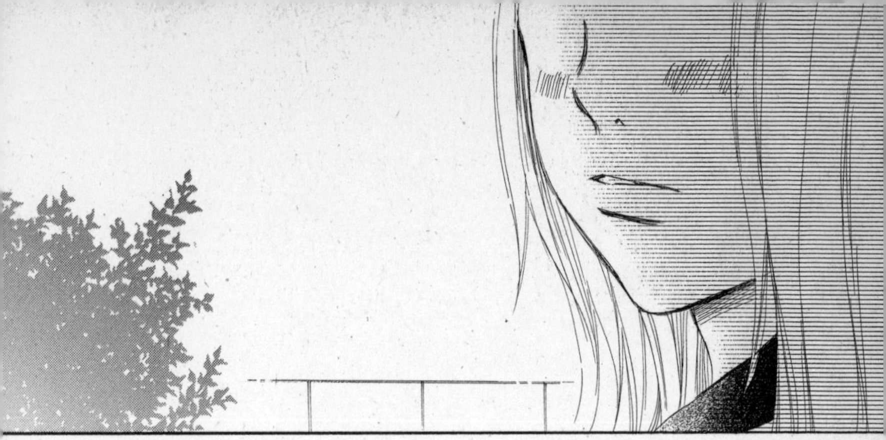

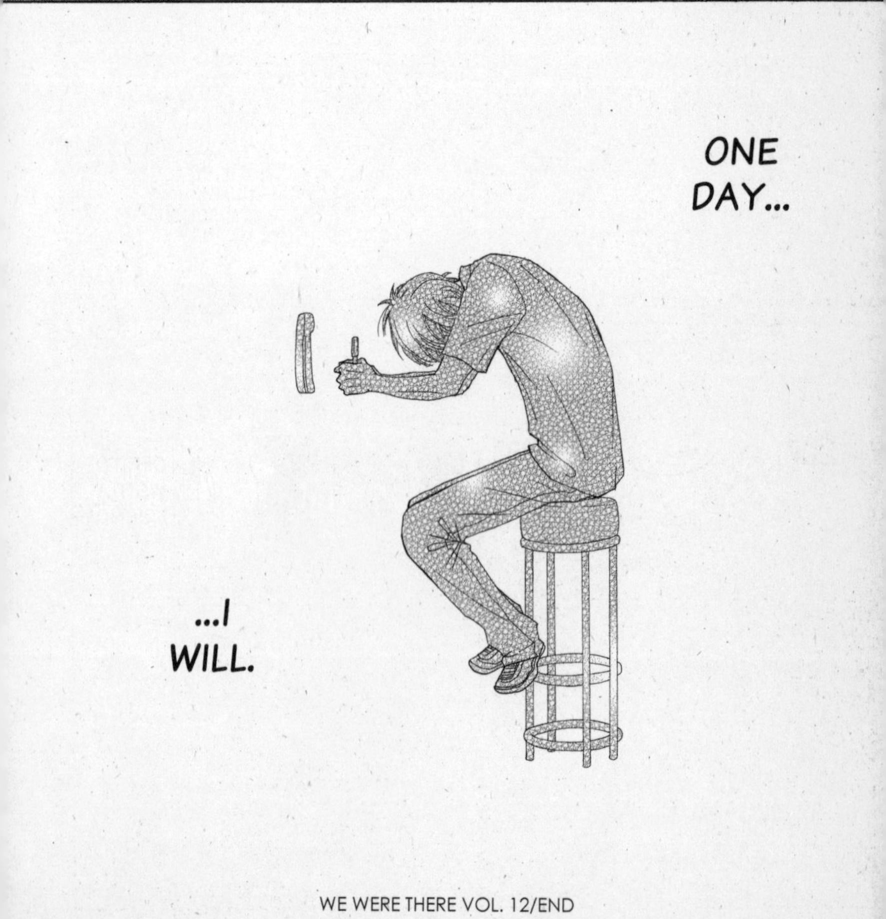
ONE DAY...
...I WILL.

WE WERE THERE VOL. 12/END

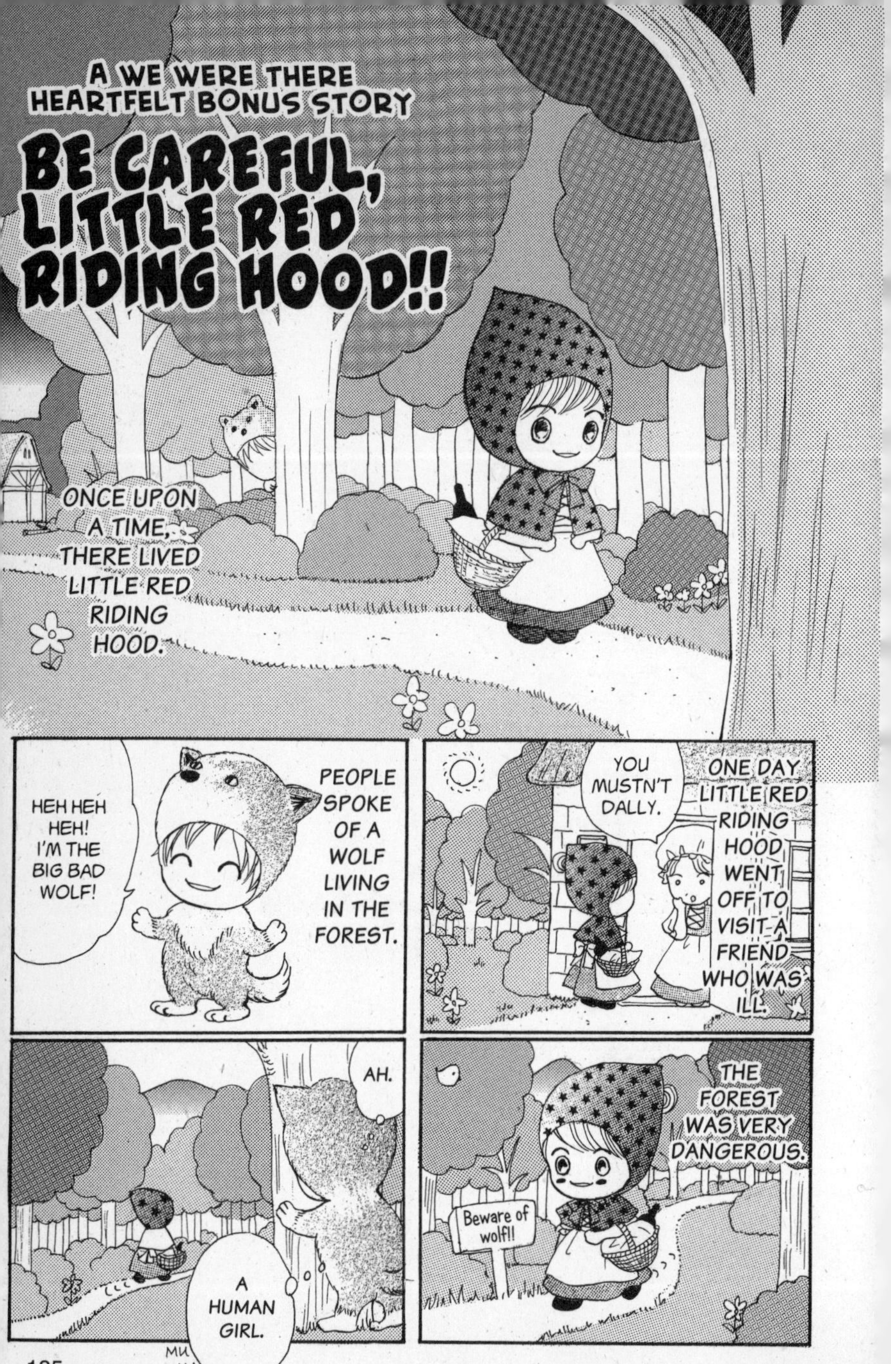
A WE WERE THERE HEARTFELT BONUS STORY
BE CAREFUL, LITTLE RED RIDING HOOD!!
ONCE UPON A TIME, THERE LIVED LITTLE RED RIDING HOOD.
ONE DAY LITTLE RED RIDING HOOD WENT OFF TO VISIT A FRIEND WHO WAS ILL.
YOU MUSTN'T DALLY.
PEOPLE SPOKE OF A WOLF LIVING IN THE FOREST.
HEH HEH HEH! I'M THE BIG BAD WOLF!
THE FOREST WAS VERY DANGEROUS.
Beware of wolf!!
AH.
A HUMAN GIRL.
MU HA HA

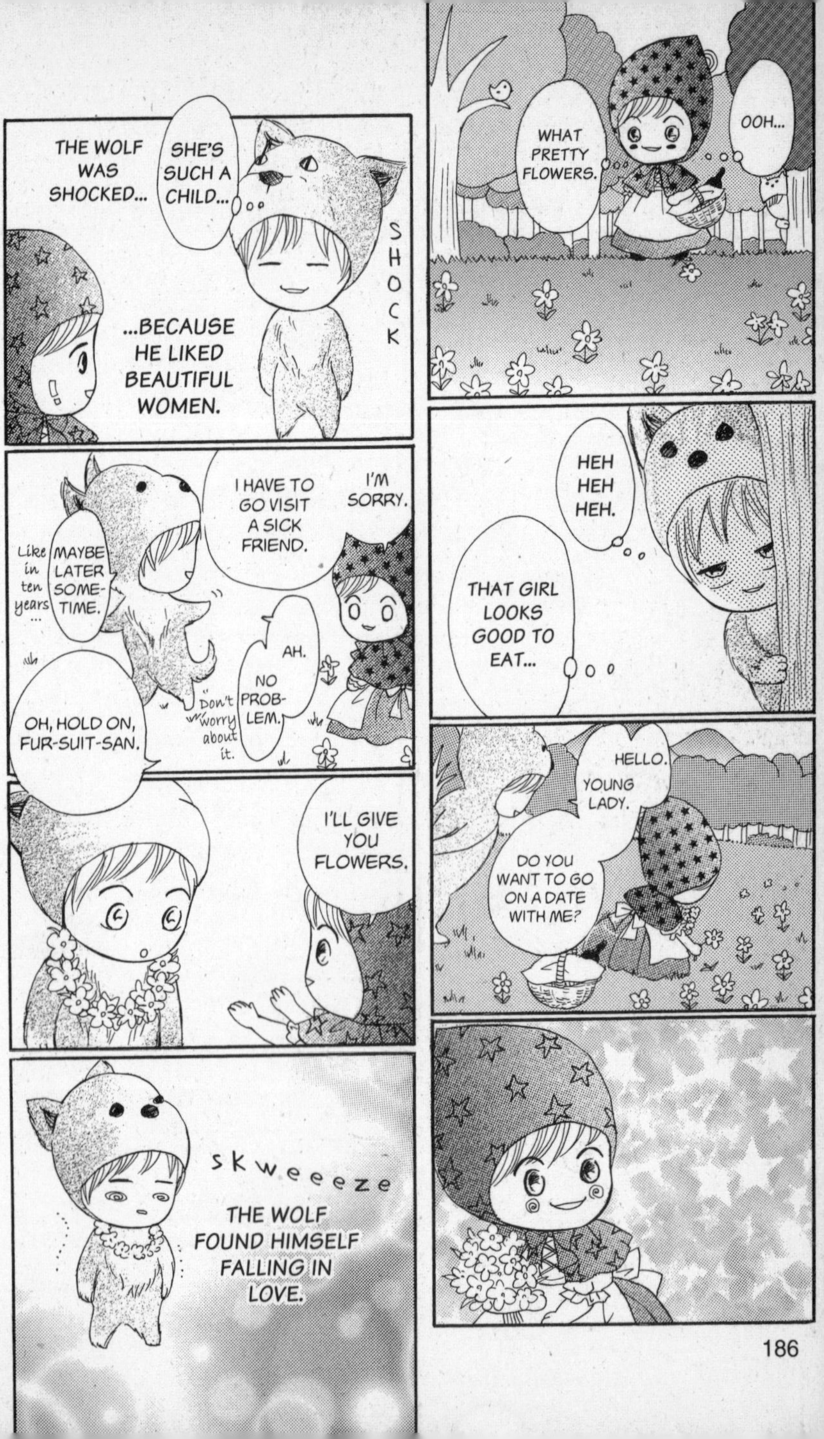
OOH...
WHAT PRETTY FLOWERS.
HEH HEH HEH.
THAT GIRL LOOKS GOOD TO EAT...
HELLO. YOUNG LADY.
DO YOU WANT TO GO ON A DATE WITH ME?
SHE'S SUCH A CHILD...
THE WOLF WAS SHOCKED...
SHOCK
...BECAUSE HE LIKED BEAUTIFUL WOMEN.
I'M SORRY.
I HAVE TO GO VISIT A SICK FRIEND.
MAYBE LATER SOMETIME.
Like in ten years...
AH.
NO PROBLEM.
Don't worry about it.
OH, HOLD ON, FUR-SUIT-SAN.
I'LL GIVE YOU FLOWERS.
skweeeze
THE WOLF FOUND HIMSELF FALLING IN LOVE.

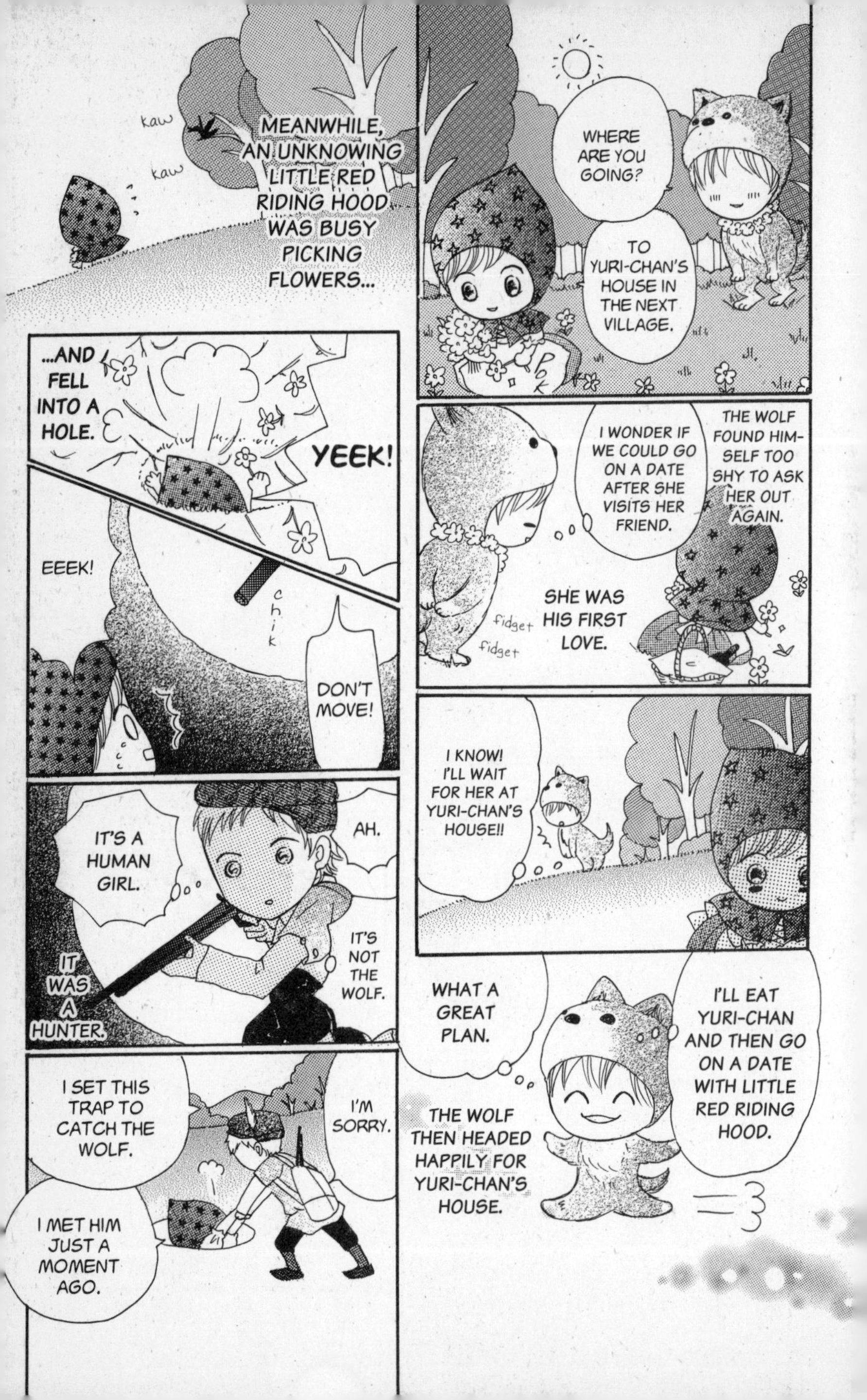
WHERE ARE YOU GOING?
TO YURI-CHAN'S HOUSE IN THE NEXT VILLAGE.
POK
THE WOLF FOUND HIMSELF TOO SHY TO ASK HER OUT AGAIN.
I WONDER IF WE COULD GO ON A DATE AFTER SHE VISITS HER FRIEND.
SHE WAS HIS FIRST LOVE.
fidget
fidget
I KNOW! I'LL WAIT FOR HER AT YURI-CHAN'S HOUSE!!
I'LL EAT YURI-CHAN AND THEN GO ON A DATE WITH LITTLE RED RIDING HOOD.
WHAT A GREAT PLAN.
THE WOLF THEN HEADED HAPPILY FOR YURI-CHAN'S HOUSE.
kaw
kaw
MEANWHILE, AN UNKNOWING LITTLE RED RIDING HOOD WAS BUSY PICKING FLOWERS...
...AND FELL INTO A HOLE.
YEEK!
DON'T MOVE!
chik
EEEK!
AH.
IT'S A HUMAN GIRL.
IT'S NOT THE WOLF.
IT WAS A HUNTER.
I'M SORRY.
I SET THIS TRAP TO CATCH THE WOLF.
I MET HIM JUST A MOMENT AGO.

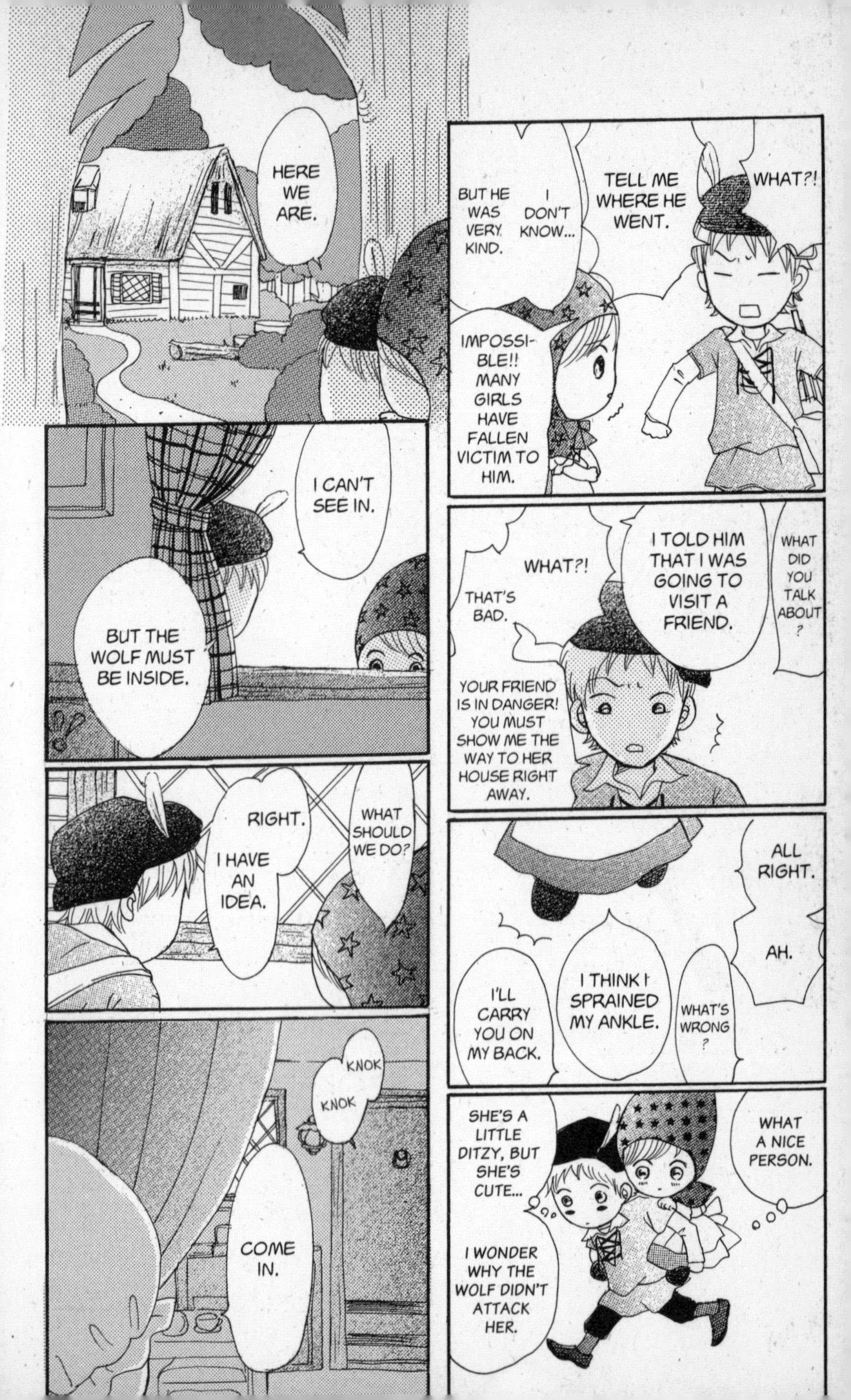
WHAT?!
TELL ME WHERE HE WENT.
I DON'T KNOW...
BUT HE WAS VERY KIND.
IMPOSSIBLE!! MANY GIRLS HAVE FALLEN VICTIM TO HIM.
WHAT DID YOU TALK ABOUT?
I TOLD HIM THAT I WAS GOING TO VISIT A FRIEND.
WHAT?!
THAT'S BAD.
YOUR FRIEND IS IN DANGER! YOU MUST SHOW ME THE WAY TO HER HOUSE RIGHT AWAY.
ALL RIGHT.
AH.
WHAT'S WRONG?
I THINK I SPRAINED MY ANKLE.
I'LL CARRY YOU ON MY BACK.
WHAT A NICE PERSON.
SHE'S A LITTLE DITZY, BUT SHE'S CUTE...
I WONDER WHY THE WOLF DIDN'T ATTACK HER.
HERE WE ARE.
I CAN'T SEE IN.
BUT THE WOLF MUST BE INSIDE.
WHAT SHOULD WE DO?
RIGHT.
I HAVE AN IDEA.
KNOK
KNOK
COME IN.

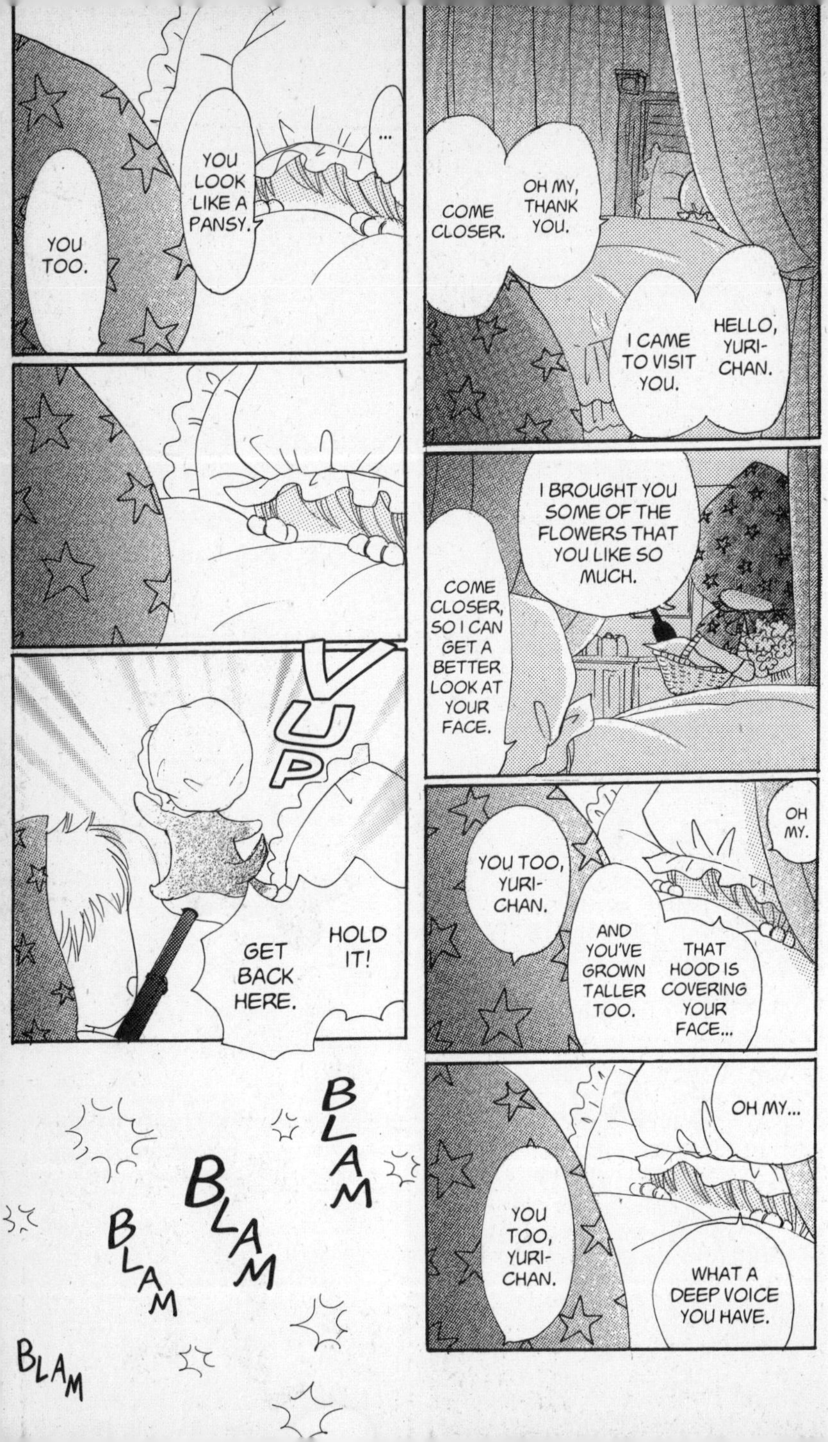
HELLO, YURI-CHAN.
I CAME TO VISIT YOU.
OH MY, THANK YOU.
COME CLOSER.
I BROUGHT YOU SOME OF THE FLOWERS THAT YOU LIKE SO MUCH.
COME CLOSER, SO I CAN GET A BETTER LOOK AT YOUR FACE.
OH MY.
THAT HOOD IS COVERING YOUR FACE...
AND YOU'VE GROWN TALLER TOO.
YOU TOO, YURI-CHAN.
OH MY...
WHAT A DEEP VOICE YOU HAVE.
YOU TOO, YURI-CHAN.
...
YOU LOOK LIKE A PANSY.
YOU TOO.
VUP
HOLD IT!
GET BACK HERE.
BLAM
BLAM
BLAM
BLAM

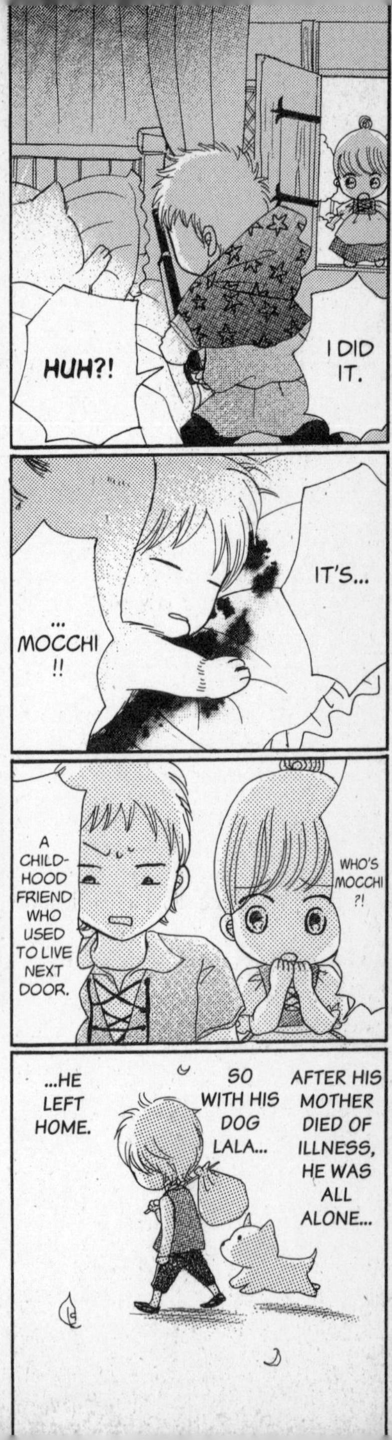
I DID IT.
HUH?!
IT'S...
...MOCCHI!!
WHO'S MOCCHI?!
A CHILDHOOD FRIEND WHO USED TO LIVE NEXT DOOR.
AFTER HIS MOTHER DIED OF ILLNESS, HE WAS ALL ALONE...
SO WITH HIS DOG LALA...
...HE LEFT HOME.

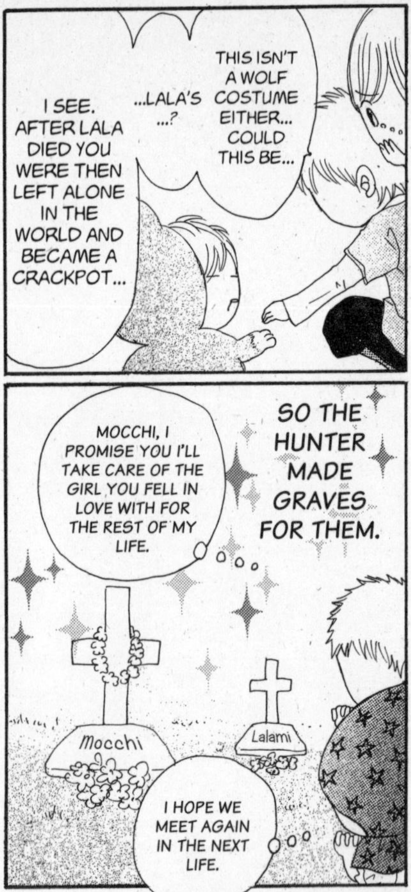
THIS ISN'T A WOLF COSTUME EITHER... COULD THIS BE...
...LALA'S ...?
I SEE. AFTER LALA DIED YOU WERE THEN LEFT ALONE IN THE WORLD AND BECAME A CRACKPOT...
SO THE HUNTER MADE GRAVES FOR THEM.
MOCCHI, I PROMISE YOU I'LL TAKE CARE OF THE GIRL YOU FELL IN LOVE WITH FOR THE REST OF MY LIFE.
Mocchi
Lalami
I HOPE WE MEET AGAIN IN THE NEXT LIFE.

END

Be Careful Little Red Riding Hood Heartfelt Bonus Story/End

From *Betsucomi* 2006 December Edition Special Furoku

Notes

Honorifics
In Japan, people are usually addressed by their name followed by a suffix.
The suffix shows familiarity or respect, depending on the relationship.
Male (familiar): first or last name + kun
Female (familiar): first or last name + chan
Adult (polite): last name + san
Upperclassman (polite): last name + senpai
Teacher or professional: last name + sensei
Close friends or lovers: first name only, no suffix

Nana-chan vs. Nana-san
Nanami's nickname is "Nana-chan." Yano's ex-girlfriend
was a year older, so she was known as "Nana-san."

Terms
In Japan, raising your pinkie finger is a gesture that indicates you're
speaking about a female lover.

Jingisukan is grilled mutton with vegetables. It is very popular
in Hokkaido.

"Mitsuo" is in reference to Mitsuo Aida, a famous Japanese poet.
His most famous collection of poetry is *Ningen Damono* (We're
Human After All). Each poem in the collection contains that phrase.

Rohypnol is a sleep-inducing drug used to treat extreme insomnia
in Japan.

This is the last volume... Just kidding.
But it has a cover that makes it
look like it's the last volume.
—Yuki Obata

Yuki Obata's birthday is January 9. Her debut manga, *Raindrops*, won
the Shogakukan Shinjin Comics Taisho Kasaku Award in 1998. Her
current series, *We Were There* (*Bokura ga Ita*), won the 50th Shogakukan
Manga Award and was adapted into an animated television series. She
likes sweets, coffee, drinking with friends, and scary stories. Her hobby
is browsing in bookshops.

WE WERE THERE
Vol. 12
Shojo Beat Edition

STORY & ART BY
YUUKI OBATA

© 2002 Yuuki OBATA/Shogakukan
All rights reserved.
Original Japanese edition "BOKURA GA ITA"
published by SHOGAKUKAN Inc.

Adaptation/Nancy Thistlethwaite
Translation/Tetsuichiro Miyaki
Touch-up Art & Lettering/Inori Fukuda Trant
Design/Courtney Utt
Editor/Nancy Thistlethwaite

Printed in Canada

Published by VIZ Media, LLC
P.O. Box 77010
San Francisco, CA 94107

10 9 8 7 6 5 4 3 2 1
First printing, May 2011

www.viz.com

www.shojobeat.com

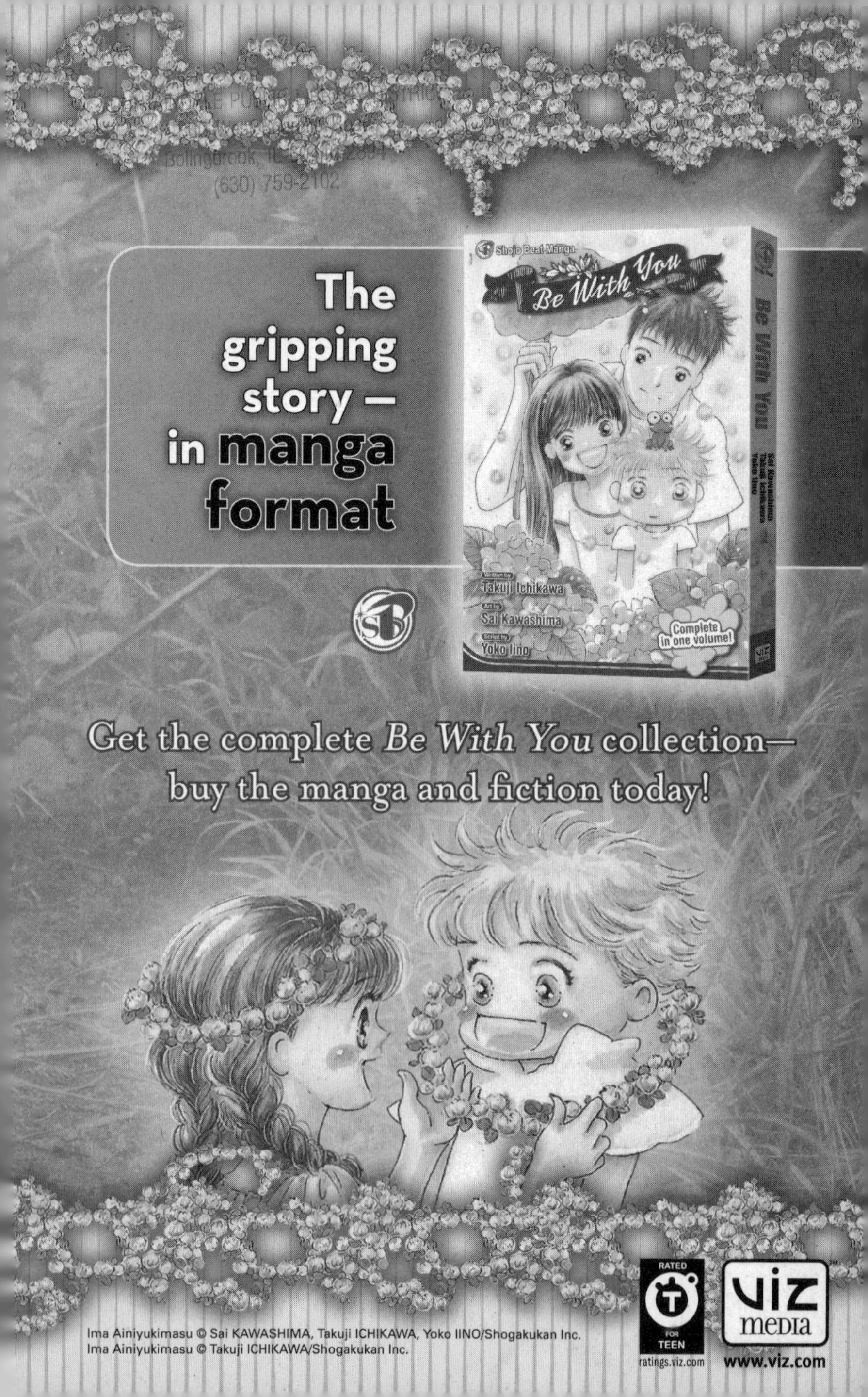
The gripping story – in manga format
Shojo Beat Manga
Be With You
Written by Takuji Ichikawa
Art by Sai Kawashima
Script by Yoko Iino
Complete in one volume!
Get the complete *Be With You* collection—buy the manga and fiction today!
Ima Ainiyukimasu © Sai KAWASHIMA, Takuji ICHIKAWA, Yoko IINO/Shogakukan Inc.
Ima Ainiyukimasu © Takuji ICHIKAWA/Shogakukan Inc.
RATED T FOR TEEN
ratings.viz.com
VIZ MEDIA
www.viz.com

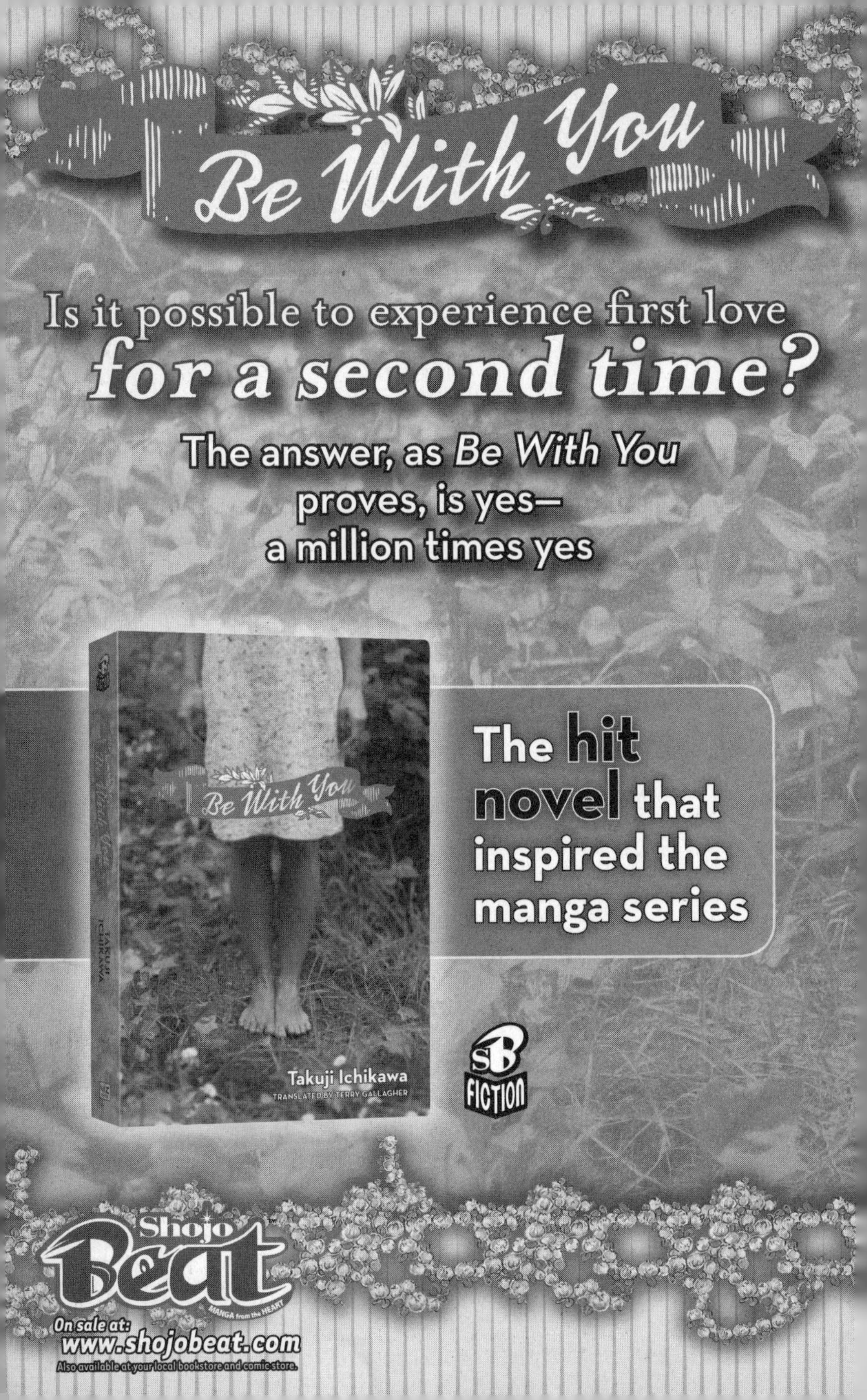
Be With You
Is it possible to experience first love
for a second time?
The answer, as Be With You
proves, is yes—
a million times yes
Be With You
Takuji Ichikawa
TRANSLATED BY TERRY GALLAGHER
The hit novel that inspired the manga series
SB FICTION
Shojo Beat
MANGA from the HEART
On sale at:
www.shojobeat.com
Also available at your local bookstore and comic store.

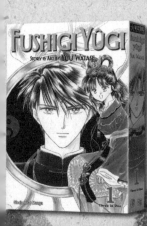

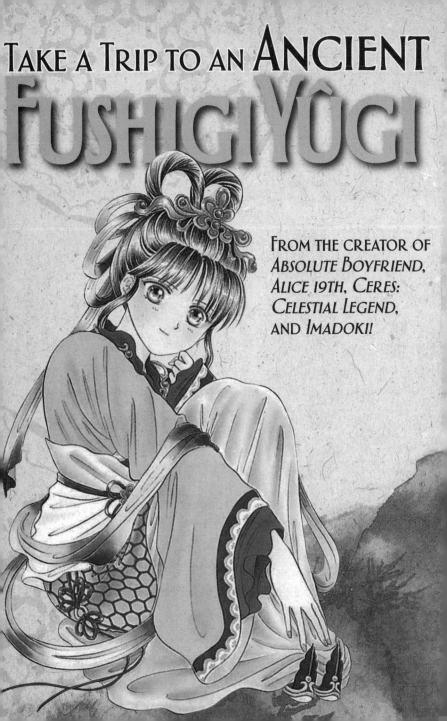